Language Variation – European Perspectives

Studies in Language Variation

The series aims to include empirical studies of linguistic variation as well as its description, explanation and interpretation in structural, social and cognitive terms. The series will cover any relevant subdiscipline: sociolinguistics, contact linguistics, dialectology, historical linguistics, anthropology/anthropological linguistics. The emphasis will be on linguistic aspects and on the interaction between linguistic and extralinguistic aspects — not on extralinguistic aspects (including language ideology, policy etc.) as such.

Editors

Peter Auer
Universität Freiburg

Frans Hinskens
Meertens Instituut &
Vrije Universiteit, Amsterdam

Paul Kerswill
Lancaster University

Editorial Board

Volume 1

Language Variation – European Perspectives
Selected papers from the Third International Conference on Language Variation
in Europe (ICLaVE 3), Amsterdam, June 2005
Edited by Frans Hinskens

Language Variation – European Perspectives

Selected papers from the Third International
Conference on Language Variation in Europe
(ICLaVE 3), Amsterdam, June 2005

Edited by

Frans Hinskens

Meertens Instituut & Vrije Universiteit, Amsterdam

John Benjamins Publishing Company

Amsterdam / Philadelphia

™ The paper used in this publication meets the minimum requirements of American National Standard for Information Sciences – Permanence of Paper for Printed Library Materials, ANSI z39.48-1984.

Library of Congress Cataloging-in-Publication Data

International Conference on Language Variation in Europe (3rd : 2005 : Amsterdam)
    Language variation-European perspectives : selected papers from the Third
    International Conference on Languagre Variation in Europe (ICLaVE 3),
    Amsterdam, June 2005 / edited by Frans Hinskens.
      p.   cm. (Studies in Language Variation, ISSN 1872-9592 ; v. 1)
    Includes bibliographical references and index.

       1. Language and languages--Variation--Congresses. 2. Europe--Languages--
    Variation--Congresses. I. Hinskens, Frans. II. Title.

    P120.V37I58   2006

417.2--dc22   2006051687
ISBN 90 272 3481 7 (Hb; alk. paper)

John Benjamins Publishing Co. · P.O. Box 36224 · 1020 ME Amsterdam · The Netherlands
John Benjamins North America · P.O. Box 27519 · Philadelphia PA 19118-0519 · USA

Table of Contents

Twenty-five authors on twelve languages, sixteen language varieties, and eighteen hundred and eighty-eight speakers

Frans Hinskens

Meertens Instituut (KNAW) and Vrije Universiteit, Amsterdam

1. Foreword: background

From June 23 until 25, 2005, the third edition of the International Conference on Language Variation in Europe (ICLaVE 3) took place in Amsterdam. Over 160 linguists from 25 different countries participated in this conference, which was sponsored by the *Royal Netherlands Academy of Arts and Sciences (KNAW)*, the *Netherlands Organisation for Scientific Research (NWO)*, the *Meertens Instituut*, the *Amsterdam Center for Language and Communication (ACLC)* of the *Universiteit van Amsterdam*, as well as the *Vrije Universiteit, Amsterdam*. The conference program featured 96 'regular talks', which had been selected on the basis of some 135 abstracts, 5 workshops with a total of 19 talks, and invited talks by Miklós Kontra (Budapest), Shana Poplack (Ottawa) and Johan Taeldeman (Ghent) — cf. the conference website www.iclave.org/2005/index.html, which still contains all the abstracts.

The texts of the three invited talks, as well as the texts of 40 'regular talks' and workshop presentations were subsequently submitted for publication. From the latter 40 texts, 13 have been selected for the present volume; the selection was based on the extensive evaluations by an international group of reviewers. Each paper was read, commented upon and evaluated by at least three reviewers; the reviewers were: *Sjef Barbiers, Hans Bennis, Ivo van Ginneken, Ton Goeman, Ben Hermans, Aniek IJbema, Mathilde Jansen, Willy Jongenburger, Olaf Koeneman, Wouter Kusters, Marika Lekakou, Alexandra Lenz, Marc van Oostendorp, Gertjan Postma, Maike Prehn, Marco-René Spruit* and the present author. The 13 selected papers as well as the texts of the contributions by the invited speakers, which were all edited and partly rewritten in the Spring and Summer of 2006, are presented in this volume.

The contributions by non-native speakers of English were corrected by *Jeroen van de Weijer. Aniek IJbema* was singlehandedly responsible for the technical realization of the book.

The remainder of this brief introduction is intended to provide a modest overview of the contributions, to point out a few aspects which make these contributions relevant to the overall issue of language variation in Europa at the beginning of the 21st century, as well as to tie together some of the aspects of the various studies.

2. An overview

Table 1 contains very brief (and, inevitably, superficial) sketches of four main aspects of the studies presented in the various contributions.

Table 1: *Four aspects of the studies presented in this volume*

author(s)	lg variety	lg component(s)	phenomenon/-a	method
Benincà & Poletto	Venetan Italian	syntax	2 classes of particle verbs	syntactic analysis; perception tests (n subj = 22)
Bergmann	Cologne German	intonation (phonetics, phonology)	nuclear rise-fall contours	conversation analysis; phonetic analyses of 350 utterances from 10 hrs of spont. dialogue (from 6 interviews & episodes of a reality TV show)
Campmany	north-east. Catalan	morpho-phonology, morphosyntax	variation in shape sg pron. and partitive clitics	dialect-geographical, phonological, syntactic and sociological analysis of spontaneous speech data from 2 corpora (n spks = 32)
Fraurud & Boyd	Sweden	n.a.	deconstruction of the concept of 'native speaker'	'linguistic profiling' (categorizing for 15 background variables relevant to nativeness) of 222 speakers
Ghimenton & Chevrot	Venetan, regional & standard Italian	n.a.	code choice and dialect acquisition	quantitative analysis of conversational child (2 sisters) and relatives' (n = 13) speech
Kehrein	regional West Middle German	phonology, phonetics	several types of characteristics of regional standard varieties	analyses of dialect features in and dialectality of a corpus (under construction) of emergency calls (n spks = 8)
Kontra	standard Hungarian	morpho-phonology, morphosyntax, syntax	awareness and (over-)application of prescriptive standard norms	production (oral sentence completion) and evaluation (grammaticality judgments; correction) tasks (n subj = 832
Moisl et al.	Tyneside English	phonetics	sociological classification of speakers	advanced exploratory statistical analyses of speech data for 63 speakers
Nardy & Barbu	standard French	late phonology and syntax	social differentiation in the acquisition of obligatory & variable liaison	statistical analyses of data for production and evalution of 188 native French 2-6 year olds
Pappas	Patras Greek	phonetics, phonology	variability in allophonic palatal /n/	statistical analyses of age & sex distribution of the variants (n spks = 21)

(handwritten note in left margin: "Alpha order by 1st author")

Table 1 continued

author(s)	lg variety	lg component(s)	phenomenon/-a	method
Poplack & Malvar	16th-20th century continental & Brazilian Portuguese	morphosyntax	diachronic developments in expression of future tense	quantitative sociolinguistic analyses of data from plays (16th -20th c) and conversational speech (20th century)
Rys & Bonte	Maldegem Flemish Dutch	phonology	internal factors affecting the acquisition of a 2nd dialect	statistical analyses of elicitation data from 164 speakers
Sloboda	Belarusian Russian	n.a.	folk linguistic classification of mixed & contact systems	interpretative sociological & ethnographic analyses of claims by 29 respondents about language use & ling. identity in the research area
Taeldeman	Flemish & Brabantine Dutch	phonology	geographical & linguistic continuity & abruptness	geographical & internal distribution of phonological dialect features & development of both compromise and polarized variants
Torgersen & Kerwill	native & ethnic London English	phonetics	variability in the realization of short vowels	formant measurement of data from several speech corpora from 1968 onward (n spks = 86)
Tsiplakou et al.	Cypriot Greek	phonetics, morpho-phonology, morphology, morpho-syntax, syntax, lexis	consequences of the demise of the separation between standard and Cypriot Greek	diasystemic analysis of data from intuitions, participant observation and "preliminary testing with appr. 200 native speakers"

3. Overlap and complementarity in focus, research questions and approach

The **languages** covered by the studies in this volume represent the three main European families: Germanic, Romance and Slavic, plus Greek and Hungarian. In the absence of Brazilian material from the 16th to 18th century, Poplack & Malvar had to base their diachronic analyses of the expression of future tense in Brazilian Portuguese during this period on European Portuguese data (which is common practice amongst Brazilian linguists). In their view, expressed in note 3, this is not problematic as until the beginning of the 19th century continental Portuguese was the generally recognized norm in Brazil.

As far as the types of **language varieties** are concerned, variation is studied
• in or across dialects or dialect groups (Benincà & Poletto; Bergmann; Campmany; Moisl et al.; Pappas; Taeldeman),

- in the standard variety (Kontra; Nardy),
- in an emerging regional variety of the standard (Ghimenton & Chevrot; Kehrein; Pappas — in particular a phonetic compromise between the dialectal palatal allophone of /n/ and standard Greek plain /n/ —; Sloboda; Tsiplakou et al.). Regional standard varieties constitute a relatively new type of language variety, which in general appears to have developed especially in urban and urbanized areas and which seems to gradually supplant the traditional dialects from the verbal repertoires. In most cases, the standard variety, however young it may be, is rooted either in a single traditional dialect or in a group of dialects (often a koiné). The differences between a geographically coherent group of traditional dialects on the one hand and the standard variety on the other are usually large enough to allow sufficient structural space for the development of recognisable regional varieties of the standard. In the Old World, the structural space between related language varieties is sometimes so deep that their relationship seems to be of a rather discontinuous or discrete nature, although in most cases they are merely the extreme ends of a continuum (Hinskens 1998: 176-7). For the Greek situation in Cyprus, this is exemplified by the *vareta xorkatika* ("heavily peasantly") and *kalamaristika* ("pen-pusher speech", i.e. standard modern Greek) versions of the sentences "I have not seen him" and "Where have you gone?", (5a), (6a) and (5e), (6e), respectively, in the contribution by Tsiplakou et al. This type of constellation typically results from historical dialect divergence, which in turn is a consequence of (compared to e.g. the Anglo-American situation) great time depth.

Poplack & Malvar and especially Kontra zoom in on areas of tension between language variation and standard norms, tensions which result from deep-rooted differences between normative and variationist views of language. While Poplack & Malvar focus on diachronic changes, Kontra concentrates on synchronic data in his discussion of social discrimination on the basis of language use.

Among the **linguistic components** covered by the studies in this volume are phonetics (Moisl et al.; Torgersen & Kerswill; Tsiplakou et al.), phonology (Bergmann; Nardy & Barbu; Kehrein; Pappas; Rys & Bonte; Taeldeman), morpho-phonology (Campmany; Kontra; Tsiplakou et al.), morpho-syntax (Campmany; Kontra; Poplack & Malvar; Tsiplakou et al.), syntax (Benincà & Poletto; Kontra; Tsiplakou et al.) and lexis (Tsiplakou et al.). Many instances of phonological variation deal with segmental phonology (Kehrein; Pappas; Rys & Bonte; Taeldeman).

In connection with the linguistic components, the contributions by Fraurud & Boyd, Ghimenton & Chevrot and Sloboda file under the category 'not applicable'. It is not the case that these studies are not focused, but they are just not confined to one or a few phenomena which can be easily categorised under the label of one or a few linguistic subcomponents.

Re **phenomena**: six studies focus on aspects of the variability of a specific (type of) element (Campmany; Pappas; Poplack & Malvar; Torgersen & Kerswill) or structure (Benincà & Poletto; Bergmann). Interestingly, in connection with clitic placement both Campmany (in the morpho-syntactic part of her analyses of the formal variability of certain clitics in dialects of north-east Catalan) and Tsiplakou ('clitic-second' phenomena in Cypriot Greek) refer to Tobler-Mussafia's Law, a Romance version of Wackernagel's Law.

Ten studies are not concerned with variability in specific areas of grammar, but with phenomena related to the behaviour vis-à-vis prescriptive standard norms (Kontra), regional standard varieties and regiolects (Kehrein; Tsiplakou et al.), problems of linguistic classification (from a folk linguistic (Sloboda) or dialect-geographical perspective (Taeldeman)) and the classification of speakers (Fraurud & Boyd; Moisl et al.). Finally, language acquisition plays a main role in the studies of Ghimenton & Chevrot, Nardy & Barbu and Rys & Bonte. Both Ghimenton & Chevrot and Rys & Bonte study dialect acquisition (Ghimenton & Chevrot as a mother tongue, Rys & Bonte as a 'second dialect' in teenagers), while Nardy & Barbu concentrate on the acquisition of an aspect of the phonology of the standard variety. Although language acquisition is not as such at issue in Fraurud & Boyd's study of speaker profiles, a given speaker's degree of 'nativeness', multilingualism as well as emerging ethnolectal varieties of the dominant language are very closely connected to questions regarding language acquisition. On the basis of the findings of their exploratory, yet many-sided study, Tsiplakou et al. hypothesize that, in the post-diglossic, 'diaglossic' (Bellmann 1998: 24) Cypriot situation, it may not necessarily take "natural acquisition of the H variety", i.e. of standard Greek, to correctly use its morpho-syntactic elements without effort.

Salience plays an explicit role in the studies by Ghimenton & Chevrot (who, in this connection, refer to recent work by Givón on pragmatics), Kehrein (who refers to Trudgill's operationalisation of the notion) as well as Taeldeman. For the structural and geographical distance of a fair number of dialect features typical of (Dutch) dialect areas in several parts of Belgium, Taeldeman proposes an extension of Schirmunski's (1930) much disputed distinction between primary and secondary dialect features.

No single contribution *explicitly* addresses the role of language contact, variation and change in linguistic theory. In a more implicit way, such considerations are made in the constributions by Benincà & Poletto (which contains hints at relevant areas within generative syntactic theory) and Pappas (whose account of the variability in the allophonic palatality of /n/ in Patras Greek[1] within the framework of Optimality Theory is part of a multifacetted description of the phenomenon). On the basis of their rich findings, Poplack &

---

[1] Which, in the same linguistic context, also displays variability in the realisation of the allophone of /l/. Cf. Papazachariou (2004).

Malvar critically discuss Kroch's (1989) Constant Rate Hypothesis, which is also relevant to the question of the position of the study of language variation within linguistic theory at large. The lack of explicit reflection on this issue — which may well be related to the limited space available to the authors — is counterbalanced by a wealth of interesting data and thorough analyses which often exceed the idiographic level.

The research questions addressed in three contributions are not linguistic *stricto sensu*; this applies to the studies by Fraurud & Boyd, Moisl et al., and Sloboda. Fraurud & Boyd demonstrate how problematic the concept of the native speaker is in modern West European multilingual urban environments such as Göteborg, Malmö and Stockholm. Moisl et al. give a new answer to the old question of how to derive sociological order from seemingly chaotic data on language variation. For the Belarusian-Russian and formerly Polish border region, an area with a long and turmoiled political, ethnic and religious history (cf. Woolhiser 2005), Sloboda presents findings from ethnolinguistic fieldwork regarding linguistic identity and the folk linguistic perception of, among other things, koinés, mixed and contact systems (in the sense of Preston's 2002 'folk theory of language').

The studies in this volume represent a wide variety of **methods**, including
- ethnographic and 'interpretative' sociological approaches (Sloboda);
- the analysis of the embedding of an utterance within the context of the larger conversation or interactional setting (Bergmann; Ghimenton & Chevrot);
- analysis of the internal and geographical distribution of specific dialect features, on the basis of databases and maps (Campmany; Taeldeman);
- classification and quantitative analyses of demographic and sociological speaker background data (Fraurud & Boyd);
- quantitative analyses of both diachronic (Poplack & Malvar) and synchronic language data (Kehrein; Kontra; Moisl et al.; Nardy & Barby; Pappas; Rys & Bonte);
- phonetic measurements (Bergman: F_0 contours — implicitly, through GToBI; Torgersen & Kerswill: F_1 and F_2 values; Pappas: F_1 and F_2 values for the sake of the validation of the phonetic transcriptions)
- perception, either in a quasi-experimental study (Benincà & Poletto), with evaluation experiments (Kontra; Nardy & Barbu), or in a linguistically more impressionistic, though ethnographically deeper study (Sloboda).

4. Concluding remarks

In all four respects, this collection is characterised by richness. Thus, it is a microcosmic reflection of the macrocosmos of the world-wide research of linguistic variability in originally European languages. It is to be hoped that the linguistic expression of cultural diversity will keep flourishing. May this volume be a further impulse to its investigation.

This is the first title in a new series founded (with the support of Benjamins' Ms Anke de Looper) and edited by Peter Auer, Paul Kerswill and the present author. We hope that many titles will follow, not only selections of contributions to future editions of ICLaVE and other collective volumes, but also monographs.

References

Bellmann, G. 1998. "Between base dialect and standard language". Dialect levelling and the standard varieties in Europe (= Folia Linguistica XXII/1-2) ed. by P. Auer, 23-34

Hinskens, F. 1998. "Variation studies in dialectology and three types of sound change". Linguistics of variation (= Sociolinguistica 12) ed. by U. Ammon, 155-193.

Kroch, A. 1989. "Reflexes of grammar in patterns of linguistic change". Language variation and change 1. 199-244

Papazachariou, D. 2004. "A quantitative study of the lateral variable /l/ in the dialect of Patras". Proceedings of the Second International Conference on Modern Greek Dialects and Linguistic Theory ed. by M. Janse, B. Josef & A. Ralli, 298-313. Mytiline: University of Patras Press.

Preston, D. 2002. "Language with an attitude." The handbook of language variation and change ed. by J. Chambers, P. Trudgill & N. Schilling-Estes, 40-66. Malden/Oxford: Blackwell.

Schirmunski, V. 1930. "Sprachgeschichte und Siedelungsmundarten". Germanisch-Romanische Monatschrift XVIII, 113-22 (Teil I), 171-188 (Teil II)

Woolhiser, C. 2005. "Political borders and dialect divergence/convergence in Europe". Dialect change. Convergence and divergence in European languages ed. by P. Auer, F. Hinskens & P. Kerswill, 236-262. Cambridge: CUP.

Phrasal Verbs in Venetan and Regional Italian

Paola Benincà & Cecilia Poletto
University of Padova & University of Venice and CNR-ISTC Padova

Abstract: In this contribution we investigate phrasal verbs in a group of Northern Italian dialects and provide evidence for two classes of constructs, which display distinct syntactic properties both in terms of constituency and with respect to the status of the preposition involved. We present the results from a test showing that the same constructs occur in the regional Italian variety spoken in the area and that they have the same properties in the dialect and in the regional standard. Moreover, a pilot study provides preliminary evidence for the idea that monolingual Italian speakers and bilingual Italian-dialectal speakers (contrasted with a control group of speakers of other regions) perceive the two classes of constructs in a different way and might play different roles in the development of this construction.

1. Introduction

In this article we intend to show that Veneto dialects have two types of phrasal verbs with distinct syntactic properties: transparent ones and non-transparent ones. In Sections 2 and 3, we will see that only non-transparent phrasal verbs display interesting connections with the thematic structure of the V, with the effect of modifying it, while transparent ones are neutral with respect to the thematic grid of the predicate.

On the basis of a small test, we will show in Section 4 that non-Venetan speakers only recognize and understand transparent phrasal verbs, thus providing further evidence for the division into two classes made on the basis of the syntactic behaviour. Here we use the adjective *Venetan*, first introduced by Mair Parry and Martin Maiden in their dialectological work (see Maiden & Parry 1997), to refer to speakers and varieties of the whole Veneto region, while the traditional English adjective *Venetian* is restricted to the speakers and language spoken in Venice.

As phrasal verbs also occur in regional Italian, we applied the test to bilingual (Venetan and Italian) and monolingual (only Italian) speakers and discovered that they perceive the two classes of phrasal verbs differently. On the basis of this split, we can postulate the hypothesis that monolingual and bilingual speakers have different roles in the spreading of the interference through the linguistic community. As far as we know, there is no work on phrasal verbs in the Veneto dialects (nor in Northern Italian dialects), while the bibliography on this topic in the Germanic languages is very large; we refer the reader to den Dikken (1995) and Dehe (2002) for a general overview. We do not take into consideration other dialects, although the phenomenon of phrasal verbs is widespread in the whole Northern Italian domain. In Central and Southern dialects and standard Italian the phenomenon is far less systematic, although, as we will see, Central and Southern speakers recognize transparent constructs, while non-transparent ones are very rare (*far fuori*, *gettar via* are examples of this otherwise rare phenomenon; see Masini 2005 on standard Italian cases).

2. The formal properties of phrasal verbs

2.1   Verbs and prepositions

Phrasal verbs (from now on PhVs) are usually considered a phenomenon typical of Germanic languages (see den Dikken 1995, in particular ch. 2, for a general account). Although they are rare in standard Italian, they are widely attested in Northern Italian dialects and in the regional varieties of colloquial Italian spoken in northern and central Italy. We will here examine Venetan dialects, where all verb types can enter into a PhV, so we find examples with transitives, unaccusatives, inergatives, statives, achievements, accomplishments, and activities, as the following sentences show:

(1)   a. Vago fora
          [I] go out
       b. I   ga   magnà   fora   tuto
          they have eaten   out   everything
          "they ate up everything"
       c. I   ghe   varda   drio
          They to him look   behind
          "they looked at him from behind (disapprovingly)"
       d. El ghe   sta   drio
          he to him/her stays behind
          "he goes after her (he courts her)"
       e. S-ciopa   fora   tuto
          [It] burst   out   everything
          "Everything is going to burst"

Capitalizing on Rizzi (1988), we assume that Romance languages have two types of prepositions, "lexical" and "functional" ones, with distinct syntactic properties. In Standard Italian only lexical prepositions, such as *fuori* and *sotto*, can be part of a PhV, i.e. prepositions that i) can occur without an object (cf. (2a)), ii) do not admit clustering with the article (as in (2b)), and iii) can (in some cases) select a PP — not directly a DP — headed by a functional P (cf. (2c)).

(2)   a. Gianni è andato fuori
          Gianni is gone   out
          "G. went out"

    b. *L'ho   messo   sottol   tavolo
       [I] it-have put   under-the table
       "I have put it under the table"
    c. Gianni è andato fuori di casa
       Gianni is gone   out of home
       "G. went out"

Functional prepositions, which do not have the properties (i, ii, iii) outlined above, are *di* "of", *a* "to", *da* "from", *in* "in", *con* "with", *per* "for, by", *tra/fra* "between": they never occur in a PhV. Lexical prepositions are *su* "up", *giù* "down", *sotto* "under", *sopra* "on, above", *dentro* "in", *dietro* "behind", *fuori* "out", *in mezzo* "between", *davanti* "in front": they can appear in a PhV.

    Su in fact has the properties both of a functional and a lexical preposition, as the following standard Italian examples show.

(3)   a. L'ho   portato su
         [I] it-have taken   up
         "I took it up / upstairs"
      b. L'ho   messo   sul   tavolo
         [I] it-have put   on-the table
         "I put it on the table"
      c. *L'ho   messo   su al   tavolo
         [I] it have put   on at-the table
         "I put it on at the table"

We hypothesize that this preposition belongs to both classes.

2.2   Transparent PhV constructions in Venetan

We define as transparent those PhVs in which the meaning of the compound is a function of the meaning of the two constituent elements, V and P. In other words, in transparent PhVs the preposition retains its original locational/directional status. This type of construct only occurs with verbs that imply a motion, such as the Venetan equivalents of 'go', 'come', 'pull', 'push', 'put', 'raise', 'lower', etc., even if they are not all unaccusative. In some cases transparent PhVs permit the expression of the location with respect to the speaker, while the corresponding synthetic forms of standard Italian do not: standard Italian *uscire* means both "go out" and "come out", while Venetan distinguishes *ndar fora* "go out" and *vegner fora* "come out". Venetan transparent PhVs can select a PP:

(4)   a. El   ze ndà su sul   tetto
         He   is gone up up-the roof
         "He went up on the roof"

    b. El   ze vegnuo fora in   giardin
       He   is come   out   in(to) the garden
       "He came out into the garden"
    c. El   ze vegnuo zo   par le scale
       He   is come   down for the stairs
       "He went down the stairs"

In transparent PhVs, the lexical P of the construct forms a constituent with the PP following it, as shown by the fact that they positively respond to the usual constituency tests: they can be moved together in topicalizations and cleft clauses, they can be used in isolation when answering a question (cf. (5)), and they cannot be split moving only the PP without the P (as shown by (6)).

(5) a. Su   sul   teto, el ze ndà
       Up   up-the roof, he is gone
       "Up on the roof, he went!"
    b. Dove zelo ndà?   Su   sul   teto
       Where is-he gone? Up   up-the roof
       "Where has he gone? Up on the roof"
    c. Ze   su sul   teto, che el ze ndà, no   in cantina
       [It] is up up-the roof, that he is gone, not   in the cellar
       "It's up on the roof that he has gone, not into the cellar"
(6) a. *Sul   teto, el ze ndà su
       Up-the roof, he is gone up
    b. *Dove zelo ndà su?
       Where   is-he gone up?
    c. * Ze sul   teto, che el ze ndà su
       [It]is up-the roof, that he is gone up

In a few cases the PP following the preposition can also be moved alone, stranding the lexical preposition:

(7) a. El   ze ndà fora par la finestra
       He   is gone out for   the window
       "He went out of the window (through it)"
    b. Dove ze-lo ndà el folio?
       Where is-it gone the sheet?
       "Where did the sheet get to?"
    c. Fora par la finestra,   el ze ndà
       Out for   the window, he is gone
       "Out of the window, it went"
    d. Par dove   ze-lo nda fora, Mario?
       For where is-he gone out, Mario?
       "Through where did Mario go out?"

e. Par   la finestra,   el ze nda   fora
   For   the window,   he is   gone   out
   "Through the window, he went out"

These cases need to be further examined and possibly attest another distinction internal to the class of transparent constructs, which we will not investigate in the present study.

When the preposition is not followed by a PP, it can occur in isolation as the answer to a question, or it can be coordinated, modified or focalized. This shows that it cannot be analyzed as a clitic head.

(8) a. Dove   zelo ndà?   Su
      Where   is-he gone?   Up
      "Where has he gone? Up(stairs)"
    b. El   ze ndà   su e   zo   par   do ore
      He   is gone   up and   down for   two hours
      "He went up and down for two hours"
    c. El   ze ndà   solo   su (e no zo)
      He   is gone   only   up (and not down)
      "He only went up (not down)"

These properties are not shared by non-transparent constructs.

2.3   Non-transparent constructs

Non-transparent PhVs have a 'lexical' character; since the meaning of the PhV is not a compositional function of the two components, the P does not retain its original 'locational / directional' meaning. The syntax of these constructs is also different, as the P never forms a constituent with the following object, which has to be moved alone in topicalization and cleft clauses:

(9) a. El   se   ga   magnà   FORA I SCHEI
      He   himself has   eaten   out the money
      "He spent / squandered all his money"
    b. *FORA I SCHEI   el se   ga   magnà
      Out the money   he himself has   eaten
    c. I SCHEI   el se   ga   magnà FORA
      The money he himself has   eaten   out
    d. Ze I SCHEI   che   el ga   magnà FORA
      [It]'s the money   that   he has   eaten   out
    e. *Ze   FORA I SCHEI   che   el se ga magnà
      [It]'s out   the money   that   he   has eaten

Moreover, the P cannot occur in isolation, nor can it be coordinated or modified, which testifies to its status as a head: in (10a) the only possible interpretation of the V+P is the transparent one (as indicated by the translation), not the non-transparent one.

(10) a. %Ilo   ga   tirà   su e   zo[1]
        They him have pull up and down
        "They pulled him up and down"
        "*They alternatively cheered him up and made him sad"
     b. Come   li   ga-lo   magnai? *Fora
        How   them has-he   eaten?   Out
        "How did they eat it? Out".
     c. *I lo   ga   magnà solo fora
        they it have   eaten only out
        "They ate it only out"

Contrary to transparent PhVs, in these cases the verb is not necessarily a motion verb. Moreover, the preposition does not seem to keep its original meaning: this is also shown by the fact that different dialects use different prepositions for the same semantics: *broar su/zo* (lit. wash up/down) "wash the dishes" *buttar fora/tirar su* (lit. throw out, pull up) "throw up". In non-transparent constructs, the preposition acquires an aspectual value and can change the thematic grid of the verb. Contrary to transparent PhVs, which are identical in the whole Northern Italian area, aspectual ones differ from one dialect to the other (as noted for the case of *broar zu/zo*, wash up/down "wash the dishes", which has the same meaning and a different preposition in two dialects).

3. The aspectual use of two Ps, *fora* "out" and *su* "up".

3.1   Terminative aspect and the preposition *fora* "out"

The Venetan preposition *fora* conveys terminative aspect, but not all verbs that can in principle have terminative aspect can occur with the preposition *fora*. Here are some examples: *magnar fora*, literally eat out, "use up", *brusar fora*, burn out, "burn up", *dir fora*, speak out, "spill the beans", *sbrigar fora*, "tidy up", *parar fora*, pull out, "conclude, complete", *vendar fora*, "sell out", *bevar fora*, "drink up", *darghene fora,* give out of it, "work out", *ndarghene fora*, go out of it, "id.", *spacar fora*, break out, "break open", *robar fora,* rob out, "rip off", *marsarse fora,* ´rot out", *netar fora*, clean out, "clean up" *verzarse fora*, open out, "clear up", *cavarse fora*, pull oneself out, "to get oneself out of trouble" or else "grow up well after a difficult start", *ciamarse fora*, call oneself out, "withdraw". All the verbs that can be construed with the P *fora* require a direct, indirect or reflexive object (a deep object in the case of unaccusatives, as in (11d)).

---

[1] The symbol % indicates that the sentence is only possible in the non-relevant interpretation (described in the text) of a transparent construct. In the relevant reading of a non-transparent construct, the sentence is ungrammatical.

(11) a. El   se   ga   magnà fora tuto
         He   himself has   eaten up   everything
         "He has eaten up everything"
    b. El   ga   parà   fora el lavoro
        He   has   pushed out   the work
        "He finished his work"
    c. El   ghe ne da   fora
        He   of-it   gets   out
        "He works it out"
    d. El tempo   el se ga verto   fora
        The weather   it   is cleared up
        "The weather cleared up"

No intransitives are found in these constructions. Moreover, no detransitivisation process can apply to a transitive verb with the P, even if the bare verb has an intransitive version:

(12) a. El   magna
         He   eats
    b. %El magna fora
        "He eats up"

In (12a) the verb 'to eat' is detransitivized, but if the P *fora* is added, only a transparent construct is possible ("he has eaten outdoors"), and the interpretation "eat up" is blocked.

Interestingly, the speakers who were interviewed for this study tend to realize 'everything' as the object of the terminative construct, and the object in all cases is understood as either destroyed or removed. Hence, the presence of *fora* as a terminative marker requires a special affected object.[2]

3.2   Aspectual usages of the preposition *su* "up"

In Venetan the P *su* "up" can also convey a terminative meaning, as in the case of *serar su* "close up":

---

[2] There are also other constructions which are sensitive to the specific thematic role of the object: the auxiliary of passive *andare* 'to go' can only be used with verbs that imply this type of affected object (Benincà & Poletto 1994):
(i) a. I   documenti   sono   andati bruciati /perduti   /distrutti
     The   documents   are   gone   burnt   /lost   /destroyed
   b. *I   documenti   sono   andati letti   /archiviati /firmati
     The   documents   are   gone   read   /filed   /signed

(13) a. El   ga   serà   su tuto   da note
          He   has   closed   up all   for night
          "He shut up everything for the night"
      b. El   se   ga   serà   su
          He   himself has   closed   up
          "He shut himself up"

In some cases the PhV is similar to its English counterpart: *taser su*, in the dialect of Fossalta di Piave, corresponds literally and semantically to *shut up*. Some cases that are apparently intermediate between a transparent and a non-transparent interpretation look like metaphors, in which on the one hand the preposition retains part of its original meaning, and while the form also displays the behaviour of non-transparent cases; see for example *tirar su* pull up "bring up, give an education":

(14) a. *SU I FIOI   el ga   tirà   da solo   (no   su i nevodi)
          UP THE KIDS, he has   pulled   by himself (not   up the nephews)
          "UP THE KIDS, he brought by himself"
      b. I FIOI,   el ga   tirà   su da solo (no   i nevodi)
          THE KIDS,   he has   pulled   up by himself (not   the nephews)
          "THE KIDS, he brought up by himself"

For the moment we do not investigate these cases.

It may be hard to see why the same dialect should have two Ps that seem to express the same aspectual value, while more complex forms are used for other aspectual usages such as the durative, as illustrated below:

(15) El.   ze che   el lavora   come un mato
          He   is that   he works   like   a mad[man]
          "he is working madly, a lot"

Notice, however, that there is a basic difference between the two Ps, as *fora* requires an affected object, while *su* does not (as shown by cases like (13)). Hence, the thematic structure of the verb is crucial in selecting the P. Moreover, in some dialects *su* also has a different aspectual value, viz. of 'prospective' (i.e. 'not completely') with verbs like the following: *inbroiar su* "cheat up", *far su* lit. do up, "fold", *intrigar su* "mix up", *imbastir su* "draft up", *giustar su,* fix up, "mend", *incalcar su* "press up", *pacagnar su* "glue up", *petar su* "stick up", *ingrumar su* "gather up". In most cases the verb also contributes to the meaning of incompleteness, but at least in the case of *giustar su* "remedy up" it does not. Notice that when the P has a prospective value, it also requires the presence of an affected object.

3.3 Changes in the argumental structure

As seen above, while Venetan *fora* requires a special affected object when expressing terminative aspect, *su* does not require any special thematic role if it expresses terminative aspect, but it does when it expresses prospective aspect. More generally, the presence of the P can also change the type of argument selected by the verb:

(16)   Co le so barzelete i   ga   tirà   su Giani
        With their jokes   they have pulled up Gianni
        "With their jokes, they brought up G."

In (16) the type of thematic role of the object is necessarily animate, while the corresponding basic verb does not impose such a requirement. The same is true with *fora* in the case of *saltar fora* literally "jump up" meaning "crop up", which can have an inanimate subject, while usually the verb *saltar* "jump" has an animate subject.

Furthermore, in some cases *su* induces the presence of a dative:

(17) a. El   me   ze saltà   su
        He   to-me   is jumped up
        "He answered back rudely"
     b. Me   go   messo su le braghe
        [I] to-me have put   up the trousers
        "I put my trousers on"

In other cases the presence of *su* seems to further enlarge the thematic grid from an intransitive to a ditransitive:

(18) a. I   ghe   la ga petà   su
        They to-him it have sticked up
        "they made him/her have it"
     b. Sta teccia la peta
        This pan   it sticks
        "This pan is sticky"

In yet other cases *su* seems to absorb the thematic role of the object leaving only the dative object, e.g. *dir* "say" is a ditransitive verb, while *dir su* "tell off" only has a dative and the object is normally implicit (in some cases an 'internal object' of the type "dream a dream"):

(19) a. El   me   ga   dito su (parole/de tuto)
        He   to-me has   told up (words/everything)
        "He scolded me"

b. *El   me   ga   dito su complimenti / questo / che el va via
   He   to-me has   told up compliments / this   / that he goes away

We can conclude that aspectual Ps influence the thematic grid of the verb in different ways: they impose semantic restrictions on arguments that are already present in the thematic grid of the verb, but they can also add an argument or render it implicit.

4. The distribution of phrasal verbs in the linguistic spectrum

In Veneto the linguistic competence of a native speaker normally comprises four levels, with the most informal level taken up by the dialect, the highest level by standard Italian, and two intermediate levels, the regional dialect and the regional variety of Italian (cf. Pellegrini 1974, Lepschy & Lepschy 1977: 13 ff.). Phrasal verbs are a good test for examining how interference phenomena spread through the community, as they are originally dialectal constructs, which have, however, become extremely common in regional spoken Italian. So the PhV's examined above occur in the local dialect, in the regional dialect and in the regional variety of Italian — but not in standard Italian.

4.1   The perception test

We conducted a pilot test with three classes of speakers: a) seven bilingual speakers (of Venetan and Italian), b) five monolingual Italian speakers brought up in Veneto, c) 10 non-Venetan speakers from other regions, as a control group (3 from Sicily, 1 from Tuscany, 2 from Puglia, 2 from Campania, where the systematic PhVs constructions seen above are not found, and 2 from northwestern regions, where only transparent constructs are the same). The age span ranges from 28 to 40 and includes both female and male subjects. All informants have a university degree.

The test consists of 13 Italian sentences each containing a phrasal verb of either the transparent or the non-transparent (aspectual) type. Informants were asked to judge the sentences as "normal colloquial Italian" or as "dialectal Italian". Although the scale suggested was either 0 (for normal Italian) or 1 (for dialectal Italian), a few speakers spontaneously used a more detailed scale when providing their judgments.

4.2   The results

Some generalizations clearly emerge from this first pilot test, others need further testing and more refined hypotheses. We summarize here only the data from the pilot test, which include transparent constructions and non-transparent constructions with *fuori* "out" and *su* "up".

Table 1: *The results of the pilot test*

Construction	Type of speaker		
	Bilingual Italian/Veneto class (a)	Monolingual in Veneto class (b)	Control group class (c)
Transparent	100% colloquial Italian	100% colloquial Italian	87% colloquial Italian 13% dialectal
Non-transp. *fuori*	12% colloquial Italian 88% dialectal	100% dialectal	5% colloquial Italian 95% dialectal
Non-transp. *su*	8% colloquial Italian 92% dialectal	100% colloquial Italian	23% colloquial Italian 77% dialectal

Non-Venetan speakers (the control group) recognize transparent phrasal verbs as colloquial Italian in the majority of the cases (as the table indicates, they do so in the 87% of the cases). Among the non-transparent ones, some are incomprehensible to them or, if interpreted, are mainly felt as dialectal variants from another region. No difference was found in the judgments according to age (span from 28 to 40) or sex (3 men and 6 women). All informants have a university degree.

Among the monolingual Italian speakers brought up in Veneto (group b) only the non-transparent phrasal verbs with *fuori* "out" are perceived as dialectal, while all constructs with *su* "up" are accepted as colloquial Italian, as well as all transparent constructs. The polarization between the two prepositions seems interesting, as it might suggest that *su* has already grammaticalized as an aspectual affix while *fuori* has not.

Bilingual speakers (group a), on the other hand, considered the majority of the cases of non-transparent constructs as dialectal, while accepting as colloquial Italian the transparent ones, thus reproducing essentially the judgments of class (c) speakers.

4.3   Interpreting the results

It seems as if transparent PhVs are interpreted by non-Venetan speakers using a general compositional device, which adds the meaning of the P to the meaning of the verb. Therefore, these cases are perceived as possible, although the speaker might not use them in his/her own variety of Italian. Non-compositional constructs (like aspectual ones) cannot be subject to the same interpretive compositional procedure, thereby confirming that it is correct to distinguish the two types of constructs on the basis of their meaning. Interestingly, no speaker added as a note that he/she did not understand the sentence in the case of transparent constructs, while this was often the case with non-transparent ones. As we pointed out above, the semantic distinction is matched by syntactic differences between the two classes of phrasal verbs, because the P of non-transparent constructs forms a constituent with the verb and affects the thematic grid.

As for the difference between monolingual and bilingual speakers living in Veneto (types (b) and (a), respectively), it is clear that bilingual speakers perceive most non-transparent constructs as dialectal because of their dialectal competence. In other words, they can compare the two languages, and consider as dialectal also those cases that are commonly used by non-dialectal speakers. On the basis of this difference, we propose as a first working hypothesis that monolingual and bilingual speakers have different 'roles' in the spreading of the interference across the linguistic community: bilingual speakers would be those originally producing the interference between Venetan and colloquial Italian, hence the source of the change, but, given the fact that they have competence in both languages and can compare them, they recognize it immediately as dialectal when asked, and will probably also refrain from using the forms judged as dialectal in more formal contexts, i.e. when speaking standard Italian. In this perspective, monolingual speakers, who do not have competence in the dialect, would acquire the forms circulating in the community, but, as they cannot compare them with the dialect of their competence, they would not recognize them as an interference with Venetan and would possibly use them (only those with *su*, though) also in more formal registers. Moreover, only one of the two Ps examined here (namely *su*) is already interpreted as colloquial Italian by monolingual speakers, the other (namely *fuori*) is still judged as a dialectal construct in 100% of the cases.

Summing up: bilingual speakers would seem to be the source, but probably not the transmitter, of the change; monolingual speakers act like 'pivots' in extending the form to more formal contexts.

4.4   A second test

One further interesting field of investigation concerns the formal properties of PhVs. We have seen that the two classes of transparent and non-transparent constructs have different syntactic properties. When these forms are extended to colloquial Italian, do they maintain their original syntactic properties?

A further test was conducted only with the same monolingual speakers brought up in Veneto (type (b)), and specifically the speakers who did not identify aspectual constructs with *su* or transparent constructs as non-standard. They were asked to judge the same sentences presented for Venetan speakers in Section 2 and 3, which show that transparent and non-transparent constructs behave differently with respect to constituency tests. In contrast to our examples above, the test sentences were in Italian, rather than in Venetan, as shown below. The subjects provided exactly the same judgments as bilingual speakers:

(5') a. Su   sul tetto,   è andato
         Up   up-the roof,   is gone
         "Up on the roof, he went"
      b. Dove   è andato? Su   sul   tetto
         Where   is gone?   Up   up-the   roof
         "Where did he go? Up on the roof"

c. E'   su sul   tetto,   che   è   andato, non   in   cantina
[It] is up up-the   roof,   that   [s/he] is gone, not   into   the cellar
"It's up on the roof that s/he went, not into the cellar"

(6') a. ??Sul   tetto,   è   andato   su
Up-the   roof,   is   gone   up
"On the roof he went up"

b. ??Dove è andato   su?
Where   is gone   up?
"Where did he go up?"

c. ??E'   sul   tetto che   è   andato   su
Is   up-the   roof that is   gone   up
"It's on the roof that he went up"

(8') b. * Lo   ha   messo   su per   tre ore
It   has   put   up for   three hours
"He put it on (= cooked) for three hours"

(9') b. *Fuori   i soldi   si   è   mangiato
Out   the money himself is   eaten
"He spent / squandered his money"

c. I soldi   si   è   mangiato   fuori
The money himself is   eaten   up
"The money himself is eaten up"

Hence, the formal properties of the PhV constructs do not vary when they are borrowed from Venetan into colloquial Italian.

5. Conclusion

In this article we have postulated the hypothesis that phrasal verbs in Venetan fall into two classes with distinct semantic and syntactic properties. When they are borrowed from colloquial regional Italian those properties remain constant. Moreover, we have hypothesized that monolingual speakers of standard Italian and bilingual speakers of Venetan and Italian have different roles in the speech community: bilingual speakers would be the first to transfer these constructs from one language to the other, while monolingual speakers would be those that extend it to more formal contexts. This hypothesis obviously needs further scrutiny in the domain under investigation and outside it.

References

Dehé, N. 2002. "Particle verbs in English: Syntax, information structure, and intonation". Linguistik Aktuell/Linguistics Today 59. Amsterdam/Philadelphia: John Benjamins .

den Dikken, M. 1995. Particles: on the syntax of verb-particles, triadic, and causative constructions. Oxford and New York: Oxford University Press

Lepschy, G. & A. L. Lepschy. 1977. The Italian language today. London: Hutchinson.

Maiden, M. & M. Parry. 1997. The dialects of Italy. Cambridge: Cambridge University Press.

Masini, F. 2005. "Multiword expressions between the syntax and the lexicon: the case of Italian verb-particle constructions". Journal of Linguistics 18. 145-173.

Pellegrini, G. B. 1974. "Dal dialetto alla lingua (esperienze di un veneto settentrionale)". Atti del IX convegno per gli studi dialettali italiani, Pacini, Pisa. 175-194.

Interesting enough; perception aspect is useful

Regional variation in intonation
Nuclear rising-falling contours in Cologne German

Pia Bergmann
University of Freiburg

Abstract: Previous research on regional variation in intonation has shown that varieties may differ with respect to their tonal inventory and details of phonetic realisation as well as with respect to the functions or 'meanings' of specific intonation contours. The present study deals with the nuclear rising-falling intonation contour in the regional variety of Cologne. A sample of 350 utterances with a nuclear rise-fall was chosen from naturally occurring dialogue and was then submitted to formal and functional analysis within the frameworks of autosegmental metrical theory and interactional linguistics, respectively. In the present study, the Colognian rise-fall will be compared to rise-falls in other varieties of German. Four different types of rise-falls will be presented, according to their tune-text association. The functional analysis strongly relies on the participant perspective. By analysing the co-occurrence of the contour with turn-holding devices on other linguistic levels and by taking into account the way the participants themselves react to it in ongoing interaction, it will be demonstrated that the Colognian rise-fall serves as a turn-holding device.

1. Introduction[*]

This study reports on the form and functions of the nuclear rising-falling intonation contour in the regional variety of Cologne. The variety of Cologne is part of the Central Franconian dialect area, located in the north-western part of the West Middle German dialect area (Newton 1990). One of its specific suprasegmental characteristics is the existence of lexical tone contrasts, which it shares with the dialects of the Central Franconian region and some dialects of the southern Low Franconian region.[1] As has been shown by Peters (2004), Gilles (2005), Gussenhoven & Peters (2004) and others, the lexical tones may interfere with sentence intonation on the phonetic level: Tone accent 1 leads to a rapid rise or fall on the accented syllable, while tone accent 2 leads to a lengthened accented syllable with level intonation.

Since the primary concern of the present study is with the nuclear intonation movement as a whole and not with the details of its phonetic realisation, tone accents will not be considered here.[2] The nuclear rise-fall has been described not

---

[*] For comments on an earlier draft of this paper I thank Frank Kügler, Frans Hinskens, and two anonymous reviewers.

[1] Gussenhoven (2000), Gussenhoven & Aarts (1999), Gussenhoven & Peters (2004), Gussenhoven & van der Vliet (1999), Heike (1964), Peters (2004), Schmidt (1986, 2002).

[2] It should be mentioned that the problem at hand is in fact a little bit more complex: According to Peters (2004), who himself refers to a study of Künzel & Schmidt (2001), the final fall of the

only for the variety of Cologne, but for other regional varieties of German too (Barker 2005, Fitzpatrick-Cole 1999, Gilles 2005, Kügler 2003, 2004, 2005, Peters 2004). Furthermore, some, though not all descriptions of Standard German include the rise-fall in the intonational inventory of the Standard variety (Féry 1993, Grice & Baumann 2002, Pheby 1975, Uhmann 1991).

Nevertheless, one should be cautious about concluding that the mere existence of a nuclear rise-fall in different varieties can already be interpreted as the existence of the "same" contour in these varieties. Firstly, intonation contours can have the same shape, but differ in their functions. Secondly, although rising-falling contours might have the same overall shape, they can differ with respect to the status of the tonal targets forming the shape. Within the framework of autosegmental metrical theory[3] on which the present study is based, this means that the high or low tonal targets of a contour might not be associated with the same element in the segmental string of an utterance, i.e. they might have a different tune-text association. A rising movement, for example, may be due to a combination of a low leading tone[4] followed by a high accent tone (L+H*), where the high tone is associated with a stressed syllable (indicated by the *), or it may be due to a combination of a low accent tone followed by a high trailing tone (L*+H), where it is the low tone which is associated with the stressed syllable. Thirdly, the "same" contour can additionally vary with respect to phonetic detail, e.g. the steepness of a rise or fall. Following Gilles (2005), these three dimensions of variation should be considered for a comprehensive comparison of intonational contours in different varieties. They are termed the 'phonetic', the 'tonological', and the 'phonological' dimension. While functional differences of a contour are captured on the phonological level, differences in tune-text association are referred to on the tonological level. The phonetic level is concerned with gradual variations in the realisation of a contour.

The question of the functions of intonation contours can be approached from different directions. Many studies have successfully demonstrated the contribution of intonation to the organisation of information structure (new vs. given information, narrow vs. broad focus, etc.) (e.g. Uhmann 1991, Féry 1993), and others have concentrated on the structuring of discourse. Still others view intonation as a resource which the participants can make use of to organize an ongoing interaction.[5] This approach, couched in the framework of Interactional Linguistics (Couper-Kuhlen & Selting 1996), forms the background of the present study. Here, intonation is viewed as co-occurring with devices on other linguistic levels to solve certain conversational tasks like turn-taking. An intonation contour

---

rising-falling movement is due to a so-called "epitone", which is supposed to occur in connection with tone accents (see Section 2 for a short comment on this fact).

[3] For an introduction to autosegmental metrical theory, see Ladd (1996).

[4] Since lexical tones are not dealt with in the present study, the notion "tone" refers to the tonal targets of an intonation contour.

[5] For a survey of different functional approaches to intonation, see Couper-Kuhlen (1986).

has no fixed meaning that is valid across all contexts of occurrence, but receives it in its actual, contextually bound implementation.[6]

The present study aims to characterise the Colognian rise-fall with respect to its tonology as well as its conversational functions. Phonetic variation will not be considered (but see Bergmann in prep., Gilles 2005, and Peters 2004 for details). It will be shown that the Colognian rise-fall differs from the Standard German rise-fall with respect to tonological as well as functional aspects. Furthermore, while being a central feature of the intonational inventory of Cologne, the rise-fall is only marginal in Standard German.[7] The next section will present the tonology of the rise-fall in different varieties of German. Section 3 outlines the materials and methods of the study, and Section 4 describes the conversational functions of the rise-fall in Cologne, concentrating on its function for the organisation of turn-taking. Finally, Section 5 compares the use of the rise-fall in Standard German to its use in the variety of Cologne.

2. Tonology of the nuclear rise-fall

Except for the dialect of Cologne, the nuclear rise-fall occurs in the regional varieties of Tyrol (Barker 2005), Bern Swiss German (Fitzpatrick-Cole 1999), Swabian (Kügler 2004, 2005), Upper Saxony (Kügler 2003), and in the varieties of Freiburg, Mannheim and Duisburg (Gilles 2005, Peters 2004). For Standard German, it has been mentioned by Pheby (1975), Uhmann (1991), Féry (1993), and it is included in the GToBI inventory of nuclear contours (Grice & Baumann 2002). The GToBI system (German Tone and Break Index) has been developed for the transcription of German intonation patterns. Like all other ToBI systems[8] it is based on autosegmental metrical theory, labelling high and low tonal targets which occur at accented syllables or the edges of prosodic constituents, and which are combined by interpolation.

The varieties can be grouped roughly into four tonological types, which are presented in the following schematic figures. The figures illustrate the association of tonal targets with tone bearing units (i.e., syllables) in the segmental string of an utterance. (The dark shaded boxes indicate the position of the main stressed syllable, the lighter shade of grey indicates the position of a secondarily stressed syllable. The rising-falling intonation contour is shown by the black line, whereas the letters beneath the boxes give the notation of the tonal targets in GToBI-style (Grice & Baumann 2002). Here, alignment with a main stressed syllable is indicated by the '*', alignment with a secondarily stressed syllable by a '-'. The % stands for alignment of the tone with the boundary of the intonation phrase, the +h

---

[6] This view has more far reaching consequences, since it argues against approaches in the framework of 'intonational morphology' (see e.g. Gussenhoven 1984, Kügler 2005), where formal and functional interpretations of a contour are conflated into one level of description. For a detailed discussion, see Bergmann (in prep.).

[7] Féry (1993: 94) comments on this fact by saying that the rise-fall "has relatively few possible usages".

[8] For a collection of accounts of different intonation systems in ToBI-style, see Jun (2005).

characterises the H-tone as a trailing tone, which is located near the low accent tone. In contrast to GToBI, small letters are chosen to underline the fact that the tonological level of description does not make any presumptions with respect to the meanings or functions of the contour.)

Type 1[9]

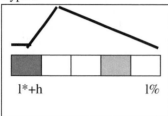

This tonological type can be found in the varieties of Swabian and Upper Saxony. The nuclear syllable is low, followed by a rise to a high peak. The final fall is aligned with the end of the intonation phrase.

Type 2

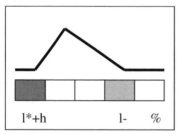

In type 2, the rise to high starts immediately after the low nucleus syllable. If there is a secondarily stressed syllable, the intonation then falls there and stays low until the end of the intonation phrase. This rise-fall occurs in the varieties of Tyrol, Swabian, and Standard German (according to GToBI).

Type 3

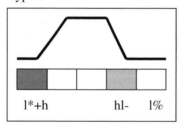

The third tonological type shows a high plateau after the rise to the high intonation level. There is a steep fall to a low level on a secondarily stressed syllable, after which the intonation stays low until the end of the phrase, as in type 2. This variant of the rise-fall is typical for the varieties of Bern Swiss German and Freiburg.

---

[9] This description is valid for Kügler (2003) with respect to interrogatives in Upper Saxonian. The Upper Saxonian rise-fall discussed in Kügler (2005), however, refers to a different contour, consisting of a falling accent tone H*L with L-prefixation.

Type 4

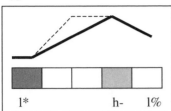

In contrast to all other types, the rising movement of type 4 does not follow immediately after the low accent tone, but is systematically aligned with a secondarily stressed syllable in the nuclear stretch. The intonation then falls to medium height until the end of the intonation phrase. The dotted line indicates that in rare cases the rise-fall can occur with a high plateau.

Contrary to type 3, however, the rise of the type 4 plateau is not systematically aligned immediately after the low accent tone.[10] Furthermore, the fall to low does not occur in the secondarily stressed syllable. Type 4 is the typical rise-fall in the varieties of Mannheim, Cologne, and Duisburg. The analysis of the Colognian rise-fall has shown that 59 out of the 350 utterances with a rise-fall analysed are realised with a high plateau. While the right edge of the plateau is systematically aligned with a secondarily stressed syllable, for the left edge, i.e. the beginning of the plateau, no fixed distance or segmental anchoring point could be detected. Furthermore, whether a plateau is realised or not does not depend on the length of the stretch between the low accent tone and the edge of the intonation phrase. It is not the case that longer stretches necessarily lead to a high plateau while shorter stretches never do. Since the functional analysis did not yield any explanation for the realisation of the high plateau as compared to the single high peak either, the internal variation of the type 4 rise-fall may be considered as 'free variation' (Bergmann, in prep.).

Map 1 gives a rough impression of the spatial distribution of the four tonological types in the German speaking area. The type 1 rise-fall occurs in the East Middle German area as well as in the western part of the Upper German area. Type 2 is reported for south-eastern and western parts of the Upper German area. Type 3 and type 4, on the other hand, occur exclusively in the western German varieties, type 3 being typical for the Upper German area, type 4 for the West Middle German area. Quite remarkably, large parts of this type 4 area coincide with the dialect area having lexical tone contrasts (see Section 1). Indeed, Peters (2004) ascribes the final fall of this type's rising-falling movement to a so-called "epitone", a concept he adopts from Künzel & Schmidt (2001). The epitone is supposed to occur with lexical tone. While Künzel & Schmidt describe the occurrence of the epitone in a rather restricted environment (in interrogatives with a stressed tone accent 1 word in IP-final position), Peters generalises its occurrence to all environments with an IP-final H tone. According to Peters, whether the final fall is realised or not depends on several factors like speech rate

---

[10] This presentation is not in agreement with the analysis of Peters (2004). In his systemic account of the varieties of Cologne, Mannheim, and Duisburg, he establishes bitonal as well as monotonal accent tones for all of the varieties in question. For a critical discussion, see Bergmann (in prep.).

and segmental material available for the fall. That is, the final fall may be truncated, if time or material is not sufficient.[11]

Map 1: *Distribution of the tonological types of the rise-fall in the German speaking area (map taken from Barbour & Stevenson 1990: 76)*

After this background on the tonological structure of the rise-fall and its distribution, I now turn to a more detailed discussion of the rise-fall in Cologne, including its conversational functions. First, some comments on the data and methods of the study are in order.

3. Data and methods

The present study is based on about 10 hours of spontaneous dialogue of dialect speakers from Cologne. The data comprise 6 interviews with elderly male and female speakers, 8 episodes of a half-documentary serial about a working-class

---

[11] Consequently, in Peters' (2004) account of the Colognian tonal inventory, no difference is made between nuclear rising and rising-falling movements. See Bergmann (in prep.) for a critical discussion of this view.

family (*Die Fußbroichs*), and some episodes of the reality-tv show *Big Brother*. The tv serials were broadcast in the 1980s and 1990s, the interviews were recorded in the year 2001.

Out of this corpus, 350 tokens of the nuclear rise-fall were selected auditorily and then subjected to acoustic analysis with Praat (Boersma & Weenink 2006). The tonal analysis is, as mentioned above, based on autosegmental metrical theory, with GToBI serving as the basic notation system.

The functional analysis draws on the insights of Interactional Linguistics (Couper-Kuhlen & Selting 1996). This approach assumes that conversational functions of intonation can be reconstructed by looking at the way specific contours are embedded and reacted to by the participants. Therefore, it is essential to take naturally occurring data as the starting point of the analysis. One prominent, often stated conversational function of intonation is its contribution to the organisation of turn-taking. Turn-taking, i.e. the change of speaker, has to be coordinated by the participants of a conversation in order not to produce longer stretches of overlap or silence. This is done by projecting a 'transition relevant place' (TRP), i.e. a point in time when an utterance is possibly complete and another speaker may take over. In addition to intonation, the projection of a TRP is based on different linguistic devices, notably lexico-semantics, syntax, and semanto-pragmatics (see Gilles 2005). As has been shown by Ford & Thompson (1996) for English, the more complex the signal for completion is, i.e. the more linguistic levels 'work together' in signalling the possible end of a unit, the more often a speaker change takes place.

With this in mind, two questions guided the research of the impact of the rise-fall on turn-taking: First, how is the contour embedded by the current speaker, i.e. does the contour co-occur with other linguistic devices which signal the turn-holding or turn-yielding intention of the speaker? And second, how does the recipient react to the rising-falling utterance? Does a speaker change take place or not? These questions were investigated quantitatively on the basis of 307 out of the 350 utterances. (The remaining 43 utterances are interrogatives, which — as a first part of an adjacency pair — make a speaker change highly expectable and were therefore excluded from the quantitative analysis). First, all rising-falling utterances were categorized with respect to their possible completeness on the lexico-semantic, syntactic, and semanto-pragmatic level. This step resulted in a co-occurrence pattern for the utterances with a rising-falling contour. Then, the speaker uptake after the utterances was recorded. Finally, the co-occurrence pattern was correlated with the occurrence of speaker change, in order to see whether the complexity of the turn-yielding or turn-holding signal has an impact on the speaker reactions.

Next, the results of the analysis of co-occurrence will be reported. After that the occurrence of speaker change will be discussed.

4. Conversational functions of the Colognian nuclear rise-fall

4.1   Co-occurrence

The co-occurrence pattern of the rising-falling contour can indicate how the speakers themselves embed the contour with respect to other linguistic devices that have a specific impact on the organisation of turn-taking. The analysis yielded the result that the rise-fall co-occurs with turn-holding devices in 60.3% of all cases.[12]

Turn-holding devices include words like *first* (German *erstmal*) on the lexico-semantic level, incomplete utterances or initial subordinate clauses, e.g. initial if-clauses (*if you go there/wenn du da hingehst*) on the syntactic level, and utterances which are part of story-telling or some other 'big package' on the semanto-pragmatic level. The following extract from an interview gives an example of co-occurring turn-holding devices on the lexico-semantic and semanto-pragmatic level, together with the rising-falling intonation contour. The speaker explains the route of a bicycle tour she undertook several years ago.

(1)   Co-occurrence of lexico-semantic and semanto-pragmatic turn-holding devices

L*   H- L%

⇨843   **k07: Erst mit der kleenen SIESCHfähre**
          [ʔeɐst mɪt dɛ kleːnən ziːʃfeːʁə]
          ("first you take the small sieg(river)ferry")

844   und dann mit der rhEInfähr=auf die ander SEIte,
          [ʔʊn dan mɪt dɛ ʁaɪnfeː ʔaʊf diː ʔandɐ zaɪtə]
          ("and then the rhineferry to the other side")
          (k07-a-1382)

In this example, the utterance in question is the first utterance (line 843), bearing the rising-falling intonation contour. The word *erst* "first" projects that there is more to come on the lexico-semantic level. On the semanto-pragmatic level, too, the turn is judged to be incomplete, since the utterance is part of an extended explanation of a larger route. The utterance therefore is categorized as turn-holding on the semanto-pragmatic and the lexico-semantic level, i.e. its turn-holding signal is complex. As expected, no speaker change occurs after the rise-fall, and the speaker continues with the description of the route (line 844).

The high overall percentage of co-occurrence of the rise-fall with turn-holding devices suggests that the contour is used by the participants as one resource to contextualize their wish to continue talking.[13] Still, of course, there are roughly

---

[12] For detailed results, see Bergmann (in prep.).

[13] A comparison with the co-occurrence patterns of 50 rising and 50 falling utterances showed a resemblance of the rise-fall with the final rise, but not with the final fall, which is generally considered to be turn-yielding (see Selting 1995).

40% of the rising-falling utterances that do not co-occur with turn-holding devices on other levels. Are these utterances turn-holding or turn-yielding? In other words, does the rise-fall by itself work as a turn-holding device, or is it crucially dependent on the co-occurrence with turn-holding devices on other linguistic levels? The best indicator for the impact of the nuclear rise-fall on turn-taking is of course the actual uptake by the speakers. Equivalent to the findings of Ford & Thompson (1996) concerning turn completion, it may be hypothesised that the more complex the turn-holding signal is, the fewer speaker changes take place. Nevertheless, if the rise-fall on its own is to be judged as turn-holding, it should evoke fewer speaker changes than a simple falling contour in comparable contexts.

The next section demonstrates the results of the occurrence of speaker change in general and in correlation with the complexity of the turn-holding signal. The impact of the rise-fall will be compared to the impact of a simple falling intonation contour.

4.2   Speaker change

Only 9.1% of all declaratives with a rising-falling contour are followed by a speaker change (28 out of 307 utterances). That is, more than 90% of all utterances are marked by turn continuation. This clearly suggests the turn-holding effect of the contour bearing utterances. The results will show that the rising-falling utterances are indeed followed by a speaker change to a significantly lesser degree than comparable utterances with a simple falling contour. It will be shown, too, that the more turn-holding devices co-occur at one time, the more often we encounter turn continuation after the utterances with a rise-fall. Thus, as hypothesised, the complexity of the turn-holding signal correlates with the speaker uptake.

This can be seen in the following diagram (Figure 1). It shows how the total of 28 speaker changes is distributed over the utterances of differing turn-holding complexity. The first category consists of utterances with lexico-semantic and semanto-pragmatic turn-holding devices (LS+SP), the second category of utterances with syntactic and semanto-pragmatic turn-holding devices (S+SP). In both categories the turn-holding signal is therefore complex. The third category comprises utterances with turn-holding devices on only one linguistic level (SP, i.e. semanto-pragmatic), whereas in the last category no turn-holding devices occur ((-LS)+(-S)+(-SP)).

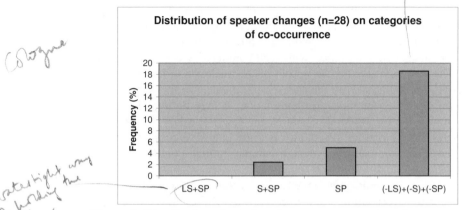

Figure 1: *Distribution of speaker changes on categories of co-occurrence*

On the whole, an increase in speaker changes with decreasing turn-holding complexity can be perceived: In the first group (LS+SP), no speaker change could be observed. 2.4% of the utterances in the second group (S+SP) are followed by a speaker change. The third group comprising turn-holding devices on only one linguistic level (SP) is characterised by 5% speaker changes. Finally, in the group without any turn-holding devices ((-LS)+(-S)+(-SP)), 18.6% of all utterances are followed by a speaker change. This means that 75% of all speaker changes occur in the group of rising-falling utterances with no turn-holding devices (21 out of 28 speaker changes). This clearly shows that intonation alone is the weakest predictor for turn continuation.

On the other hand, the comparison of rising-falling utterances without any turn-holding devices with a reference group of rising (n=50) and falling utterances (n=50) without any turn-holding devices yielded the following results: 18.6% speaker changes after rising-falling utterances are opposed to 44% speaker changes after falling utterances. That is, the rate of speaker change after the simple fall is significantly higher than after the rise-fall. Similarly to utterances with a rise-fall, rising utterances are followed by a speaker change in 17.7% of all cases. This is demonstrated by the following diagram (fig. 2). The low percentage of speaker changes after utterances with a nuclear rise-fall indicates that the rise-fall does in fact contribute to turn-holding, since — everything else being equal — the difference in speaker reactions can only be attributed to intonation.

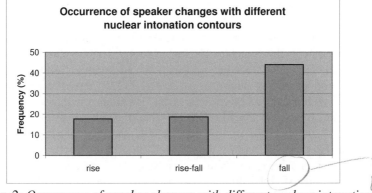

Figure 2: *Occurrence of speaker changes with different nuclear intonation contours*

To sum up, the co-occurrence pattern as well as the speaker reactions demonstrate that one of the conversational functions of the rising-falling contour in the regional variety of Cologne is to contextualize the turn-holding intentions of the speaker. This confirms the results of Gilles (2005) and Peters (2004), who also describe the rise-fall contour as turn-holding.

Furthermore, the results of speaker reactions in correlation with the complexity of the turn-holding signal demonstrate that complex signalling leads to turn continuation more unambigously. These findings are equivalent to the results of Ford & Thompson (1996) on turn completion.

5. Comparison with the nuclear rise-fall in Standard German

Due to the divergent approaches to the functions of intonation, it is sometimes difficult or even impossible to compare the 'semantics' of specific intonation contours established by different researchers. With respect to the rise-fall, all studies referred to are based on autosegmental metrical theory concerning the formal description,[14] but concerning the functional description the studies diverge widely. Only two studies discuss conversational functions in a comparable way to the present study. In these studies, the type 4-rise-fall of Mannheim, Cologne, and Duisburg is described as turn-holding, whereas the type 3-rise-fall of Freiburg, on the other hand, is described as turn-yielding (Gilles 2005, Peters 2004). The type 3-rise-fall of Bern Swiss German is said to occur with neutral declaratives (Fitzpatrick-Cole 1999), which is also true for the type 2-rise-fall of Tyrolian (Barker 2005), and the type 1-rise-fall of Swabian (Kügler 2005). Furthermore, the type 1-rise-fall of Swabian contrasts with its type 2-rise-fall, with the former being associated with broad focus, and the latter with narrow focus (Kügler 2005). Finally, the type 1-rise-fall of Upper Saxonian is reported for a specific type of

---

[14] An exception is Pheby (1975), who chooses a tonemic approach.

interrogatives, where the speaker already has a certain expectation concerning the answer (Kügler 2003).

To illustrate just one rise-fall in more detail, the following section is dedicated to the rise-fall in the Standard German variety. Tonologically it belongs to the type 2-rise-fall.[15] Its 'meaning' or functions are mainly formulated in terms of introspection or ad-hoc impressions. Pheby (1975) describes its meaning as a statement with a tad of self-consciousness or defiance, e.g. on the utterance *Das WEISS ich schon* ("I already KNOW that"). Uhmann (1991) recurs on one instance of the rise-fall in her data. There, the rise-fall is associated with a question. Féry (1993) reports the rise-fall on address forms in certain criminal series, when the inspector addresses a suspicious person, and in this context describes it as slightly threatening. Moreover she ascribes to the rise-fall a meaning of "of course". The most recent account of the rise-fall is given by Grice & Baumann (2002), where it is viewed as self-evident, respectively engaged or sarcastic statement. The utterance *Der Blick ist ja FAbelhaft* ("The view is GORgeous") is given as an example. Uttered with a nuclear rise-fall (beginning on the syllable 'FA'), the statement has a sarcastic meaning, saying that the view is not gorgeous at all.

With the exception of Uhmann, all descriptions of the rise-fall associate the contour with a declarative. Nothing is said on its conversational embedding with respect to turn-position, so that for a comparison with the Colognian rise-fall, we can only guess at its conversational function. The mostly hypothetical examples of typical occurrences of the rise-fall, however, strongly suggest that the Standard German rise-falls are not intended to be turn-holding. Neither do they co-occur with turn-holding devices on other linguistic levels, which has been proved to be a typical characteristic of the Colognian rise-fall. Nor do the outlined contexts and 'extra' meanings make a continuation by the same speaker plausible. Concerning the mentioned 'extra' meanings of sarcasm, threatening, self-evidence, and so on, no equivalence can be found in the Colognian data. Recalling the extract of a Colognian interview in (1), which gives a good impression of a typical rise-fall in Cologne, no negative or aggressive connotation can be attributed to the rising-falling utterance. Thus, a 'semantic' comparison of the Standard German rise-fall with the rise-fall in the variety of Cologne yields no similarities. The tonological dissimilarity is thus mirrored by disparate functions. (That this is not necessarily the case is demonstrated by the existence of comparable functions of the type 1-, type 2- and type 3-rise-fall in different varieties.) Additionally, the rise-fall can be viewed as a very marginal contour in the Standard variety. The very specific connotations attributed to the rise-fall underline this assumption, and it is further supported by the fact that there are some accounts which do not integrate the rise-

---

[15] This judgement relies mainly on the GToBI account, where the final fall is explicitly aligned with a secondarily stressed syllable. The examples given by Uhmann (1991) and Féry (1993) are not suited to decide on the tonal status of the final low tone, since they comprise maximally three syllables, and therefore do not leave enough space for a 'free decision' of the low tone which syllable to align with.

fall into the intonational inventory of Standard German at all (e.g. Wunderlich 1988, Grabe 1998). In Cologne, on the contrary, the rise-fall is a very central contour, fulfilling basic functions for the organisation of interaction.

6. Summary and conclusions

The present study gave an overview of nuclear rising-falling intonation contours in different varieties of German, including the Standard variety. The varieties were differentiated on formal as well as on functional grounds. Dimensions of regional variation of intonation were introduced, drawing on the analysis of Gilles (2005).

It was demonstrated that, despite the superficial similarity of the nuclear rising-falling contour, crucial differences concerning tonology and functions of the rise-fall characterise the varieties. The variety of Cologne and the Standard variety were discussed in more detail. Tonologically, in these varieties the rise-fall belongs to different variants. Functionally, too, fundamental differences arise: whereas the Standard rise-fall seems to occur turn-finally and is reported to have a threatening or sarcastic connotation, none of this is true for the rise-fall in Cologne. Here, it serves as a turn-holding device without any aggressive connotations. While being a marginal contour in Standard German, it can be viewed as a central contour in Cologne and, most importantly, as *the* salient dialect feature of its intonation system.

References

Barbour, S. & P. Stevenson. 1990.   Variation in German. A critical approach to German sociolinguistics. Cambridge: CUP.
Barker, G. 2005. Intonation patterns in Tyrolian German: an autosegmental-metrical analysis. Berlin: Lang.
Bergmann, P. (in prep.). Regionalspezifische Intonationsverläufe im Kölnischen. Formale und funktionale Analysen steigend-fallender Konturen. PhD diss., Freiburg University.
Boersma, P. & D. Weenink. 2006. Praat: Doing phonetics by computer.
   <http://www.fon.hum.uva.nl/praat/> (April 2006).
Couper-Kuhlen, E. 1986. An introduction to English prosody. Tübingen: Max Niemeyer Verlag.
Couper-Kuhlen, E. & M. Selting. 1996. "Towards an interactional perspective on prosody and a prosodic perspective on interaction". Prosody in conversation ed. by E. Couper-Kuhlen & M. Selting, 11-56. Cambridge: CUP.
Féry, C. 1993. German intonational patterns. Tübingen: Max Niemeyer Verlag.
Fitzpatrick-Cole, J. 1999. "The Alpine intonation of Bern Swiss German". Proceedings of the 14th International Congress of Phonetic Sciences (ICPhS). San Francisco.
Ford, C.E. & S.A. Thompson. 1996. "Interactional units in conversation: syntactic, intonational, and pragmatic resources for the management of turns". Interaction and grammar ed. by E. Ochs & E. Schegloff, 134-184. Cambridge: CUP.
Gilles, P. 2005. Die Intonation von Abschluss und Weiterweisung in deutschen Regionalvarietäten. Funktionale und phonetische Analysen. Berlin: De Gruyter.
Grabe, E. 1998. Comparative intonational phonology: English and German. Wageningen: Ponsen and Looijen.
Grice, M. & S. Baumann. 2002. "Deutsche Intonation und GToBI". Linguistische Berichte 191. 267-298.

Gussenhoven, C. 1984. On the grammar and semantics of sentence accents. PhD diss., Nijmegen University. Dordrecht: Foris.

Gussenhoven, C. 2000. "The lexical tone contrast in Roermond Dutch in Optimality Theory". Prosody: Theory and experiment ed. by M. Horne, 129-167. Dordrecht: Kluwer.

Gussenhoven, C. & F. Aarts. 1999. "The dialect of Maastricht". Journal of the International Phonetic Association 29. 155-166.

Gussenhoven, C. & J. Peters. 2004. "A tonal analysis of Cologne Schärfung". Phonology 21. 251-285.

Gussenhoven, C. & P. van der Vliet. 1999. "The phonology of tone and intonation in the Dutch dialect of Venlo". Journal of Linguistics 35. 99-135.

Heike, G. 1964. Zur Phonologie der Stadtkölner Mundart. Marburg: N.G. Elwert Verlag.

Jun, S.-A. (ed.). 2005. Prosodic typology. The phonology of intonation and phrasing. Oxford: Oxford University Press.

Kügler, F. 2003. "Do we know the answer? - Variation in yes-no-question intonation". Linguistics in Potsdam 21. 9-29.

Kügler, F. 2004. "The phonology and phonetics of nuclear rises in Swabian German". Regional variation in intonation ed. by P. Gilles & J. Peter, 75-98. Tübingen: Niemeyer.

Kügler, F. 2005. Swabian and Upper Saxon intonational patterns. PhD. diss., Potsdam University.

Künzel, H.J. & J.E. Schmidt. 2001. "Phonetische Probleme bei Tonakzent 1. Eine Pilotstudie". Beitäge zu Linguistik und Phonetik. Festschrift für Joachim Göschel zum 70. Geburtstag ed. by A. Braun, 421-439. Stuttgart: Franz Steiner Verlag.

Ladd, R. 1996. Intonational phonology. Cambridge: CUP.

Newton, G. 1990. "Central Franconian". The dialects of modern German. A linguistic survey ed. by C.V.J. Rus, 136-209. London: Routledge.

Pheby, J. 1975. Intonation und Grammatik im Deutschen. Berlin: Akademie-Verlag.

Peters, J. 2004. Intonatorische Variation im Deutschen. Studien zu ausgewählten Regionalsprachen. Habilitation, Potsdam University.

Schmidt, J.E. 1986. Die mittelfränkischen Tonakzente (Rheinische Akzentuierung). Wiesbaden: Franz Steiner Verlag.

Schmidt, J.E. 2002. "Die sprachhistorische Genese der mittelfränkischen Tonakzente". Silbenschnitt und Tonakzente ed. by P. Auer, P. Gilles & H. Spiekermann, 201-233. Tübingen: Niemeyer.

Selting, M. 1995. Prosodie im Gespräch. Tübingen: Niemeyer.

Uhmann, S. 1991. Fokusphonologie. Tübingen: Niemeyer.

Wunderlich, D. 1988. "Der Ton macht die Melodie - zur Phonologie der Intonation im Deutschen". Intonationsforschungen ed. by H. Altmann. Tübingen: Niemeyer.

uses GToBI only - instrumental measurements by way of backing up qualitative observations would have been desirable!

Internal and external factors for clitic-shape variation in North-Eastern Catalan

Elisenda Campmany

Universitat de Barcelona

Abstract: Traditional studies of Catalan dialectology have always included the variety spoken in the north-eastern area within the group of dialects that have CV pronominal clitics instead of the innovative VC standard forms. It is now well accepted that there is variation between CV and VC clitics, the latter being considered the result of the increasing influence of the Standard variety. The aim of this study is to check the extent of this variation and determine which internal and external factors favour the shift (i.e. change) to VC forms. Unlike previous studies, the description is not based on data from questionnaires but on data from spontaneous speech recorded in two corpora, compiled in the 1960s and in the 1990s, respectively. Unexpectedly, the data show that although there is a tendency towards the loss of CV clitics over time, all speakers, including the oldest ones, use more VC than CV forms, which cannot be entirely attributed to the influence of the Standard variety. It is concluded that VC clitics have a deep-rooted presence in this area and are favoured by certain syntactic contexts.

1. Introduction[*]

The aim of this paper is to present the results of a comprehensive study about clitic-shape variation in North-Eastern (mainland) Catalan (Campmany 2004).[1] The paper provides both a description and an analysis of the distribution of four pronominal clitics: first person singular (1st), second person singular (2nd), third person reflexive (3rd) and the partitive (part.) clitic. In Catalan, each of these clitics appears with different realizations (1), depending mostly on the phonological context in which they occur. In (2) these realizations are illustrated for the Standard Catalan variety.

(1)	1st	[m], [əm], [mə]	3rd	[s], [əs], [sə]
	2nd	[t], [ət], [tə]	Part.	[n], [ən], [nə]

[*] I am especially grateful to Maria-Rosa Lloret for her valuable ideas and insights on this paper. I would also like to express my thanks to Maria Pilar Perea, who has provided me with extra information about the *Corpus Oral Dialectal* (COD), and to Òscar Bladas for his suggestions on syntactic and pragmatic matters. Finally, the paper has also benefited from the reviewers' comments. This work was supported by a grant from the Departament d'Universitats, Recerca i Societat de la Informació of the Generalitat de Catalunya (2003 FI 00481, 2004 XT 00078, 2005 SGR-01046) and by the project ECOD (HUM2004 – 01504/FILO) of the Ministerio de Ciencia y Tecnología and the FEDER.
[1] See the map in the Appendix for the location of the north-eastern Catalan area within Catalonia.

proclitics

(2) a. ell [əm] castiga   castigant [mə]   *enclitics* — *only after infinitive / imperative / gerund*
        "he punishes me"   "punishing me"
        ell [ət] castiga   castigant [tə]
        "he punishes you"   "punishing you"
        ell [əs] castiga   castigant [sə]
        "he punishes himself"   "punishing himself"
        ell [ən] castiga   castigant [nə]
        "he punishes some"   "punishing some"
    b. ell [m] indica   indica [m]
        "he shows me"   "show me!"
        ell [t] indica   indica [t]
        "he shows you"   "show yourself!"
        ell [s] indica   indiqui [s]
        "he shows himself"   "show (polite) yourself!"
        ell [n] indica   indica [n]
        "he shows some"   "show some!"

proclitics only this paper

All these sequences show that each clitic surfaces with a fixed consonant. Before or after this consonant a schwa may appear, which in most cases is considered an epenthetic vowel. As can be observed in (2a), this vowel is required when the verb to which the clitic attaches starts or ends with a consonant. In this context, if the epenthetic vowel was not inserted, the sequence of clitic + verb or verb + clitic would not be properly syllabifiable. In contrast, epenthesis is not necessary in (2b) because the verb starts or ends with a vowel and, consequently, no problems of syllabification arise.

Note that the examples in (2) show both proclitics (first column) and enclitics (second column). In Catalan, enclitics only appear after an imperative, an infinitive or a gerund. In this paper only proclitics will be analysed, particularly those that appear before a consonant-initial verb. Although in Standard Catalan these proclitics have a VC shape, there are many other Catalan dialects that have retained the old, traditional CV forms before a consonant-initial verb. Traditional studies of Catalan dialectology have always included the variety spoken in the north-eastern area within the group of dialects that have CV pronominal clitics instead of the innovative VC standard forms (e.g., *me castiga* instead of *em castiga* "s/he punishes me"). Although there is no comprehensive study on this topic, some authors have nevertheless pointed out that in North-eastern Catalan pronominal clitics are subject to variation, mainly due to the increasing influence of the Standard variety (DeCesaris 1987, Lloret 2001 [2002]). It has also been suggested that not all clitics have the same distribution. In this regard, Lloret & Viaplana (1996) showed that the partitive clitic has a VC shape in North-eastern Catalan, while 1st, 2nd and 3rd person clitics usually display a CV shape. The distribution of these clitics is illustrated in (3). Examples of enclitics are also given in order to make clear the different behaviour of the partitive.

(3) Clitics (CL) in North-eastern Catalan (data from Lloret & Viaplana 1996: 274-275)

1st	CL (m) # V-	[m] estima	"(s/he) loves me"
2nd	CL (t) # V-	[t] estima	"(s/he) loves you"
3rd	CL (s) # V-	[s] estima	"(s/he) loves her/himself"
Part.	CL (n) # V-	[n] estima	"(s/he) loves some"
1st	CL (m) # C-	[mə] canta	"(s/he) sings (to) me"
2nd	CL (t) # C-	[tə] canta	"(s/he) sings (to) you"
3rd	CL (s) # C-	[sə] compra	"(s/he) buys (for) her/himself"
Part.	CL (n) # C-	[əŋ] canta	"(s/he) sings some"
1st	-V # CL (m)	canta [mə]	"sing (to) me!"
2nd	-V # CL (t)	canta [tə]	"sing (to) yourself!"
3rd	-V # CL (s)[2]	_____	
Part.	-V # CL (n)	canta [n]	"sing some!"
1st	-G # CL (m)	canteu [mə]	"sing (pl.) (to) me!"
2nd	-G # CL (t)	mou [tə]	"move yourself!"
3rd	-G # CL (s)	_____	
Part.	-G # CL (n)	canteu [ən]	"sing (pl.) some!"

However, these studies have not provided enough data to check the exact extent of clitic-shape variation or to establish whether there are internal factors, such as phonetic context or syntactic cohesion, which favour the shift to VC forms. In this paper, new data have been used in order to check, first, if CV clitics are still generally found in North-eastern Catalan and, secondly, if partitive clitics are the only ones with a VC shape or if there is more variation than stated in previous literature. The paper also explores different factors that may cause clitic-shape variation. These factors range from linguistic constraints about the position of unstressed material (Wackernagel's Law) to different external factors (e.g., level of formality during the elicitation).

The paper is organized as follows: Section 2 provides a brief description of the data sources. Section 3 summarizes the methodology followed in order to obtain relevant results. Section 4 contains the distribution of CV and VC clitics in North-eastern Catalan. Section 5 is devoted to data analysis: internal and external factors that affect clitic-shape variation are explored. Finally, the conclusions are drawn in Section 6.

---

[2] In this dialect the 3rd person reflexive pronoun is not used in the enclitic position.

2. Data sources

In contrast to previous studies, the present research did not use data from questionnaires but rather from spontaneous conversations recorded in the *Corpus Oral Dialectal* (COD) of the University of Barcelona (cf. Lloret & Perea 2002, Viaplana & Perea 2003). The COD compiles data from the main dialects of Catalan and includes both a large questionnaire and samples of spontaneous speech elicited by the same informants. Data from this corpus were compiled between 1994 and 1996. The age of the informants chosen ranged from 30 to 45 years old, and they lived (and had been born) in county towns. The spontaneous conversations selected for this research belong to eight towns, which correspond to the eight counties where North-eastern Catalan is spoken. The Appendix provides a map of Catalonia where the area under study has been highlighted and the different county towns have been represented by numbers. The varieties spoken in these county towns are identified as variety 1, variety 2, variety 3, and so on.

In order to complete the data from these samples and, at the same time, provide evidence with respect to the diachronic development of clitics, data from the *Atles lingüístic del domini català. Etnotextos del català oriental* (ALDC; Veny & Pons 1998) were used. This corpus also includes spontaneous conversations, but the informants are much older than those of the COD. The data were compiled between 1965 and 1975. The informants were 60-85 years old and lived in small villages. Recordings from all the small villages of the corpus that belong to the north-eastern area were analysed. Throughout the paper these villages will be identified as variety *a*, variety *b*, and so on (see the map in the Appendix).

The comparison between the data from the ALDC and those from the COD caused a number of methodological problems. First, the number of speakers is not the same: in the COD three speakers were interviewed in every town, whereas in the ALDC only one informant was interviewed in every village. Therefore, the overall number of tokens with clitics is not the same in the two corpora. Second, texts have different characteristics: in the ALDC speakers used to talk about different aspects of rural life without being interrupted. As a result, the texts contain a low proportion of 1st and 2nd person singular clitics. In contrast, these clitics are strongly represented in the COD, where there is a constant exchange of information between the interviewer and the informant.

3. Methodology

The research on clitic-shape variation in North-eastern Catalan was carried out in four basic steps. Firstly, all the VC and CV clitics that appear in the samples of spontaneous speech were counted to get a general idea of the distribution of proclitics in this dialect. Secondly, traditional dialectal characteristics that are considered to be typical of the North-eastern Catalan area were listed. The goal was to check whether people whose speech has many of these characteristics are more likely to use the old, traditional CV forms.

Thirdly, the whole sentences containing singular proclitics were transcribed in order to classify them according to their phonetic and syntactic contexts and check if these are factors that may affect their shape. As far as the phonetic context is concerned, all the different kinds of segments (both consonants and vowels) that may precede or follow clitics were considered. The goal here was to check if the language tends to avoid some consonant clusters or sequences of identical consonants through the appearance of the schwa in the clitics. As for the syntactic context, clitics were classified according to their morphological category and the syntactic function of the word that preceded them.

Finally, the analysis also considered external factors that may cause clitic-shape variation, such as age, gender or level of formality in the elicitation. It should again be noted that clitics have a VC shape in Standard and Barceloní Catalan; hence, these clitics may be considered more prestigious or more formal, especially by younger speakers who have a higher educational background. Information about level of formality comes from the clitic database included in the phonetic and morphological questionnaire of the COD, which represents a more formal type of speech compared to that of the spontaneous conversations.

4. Distribution of VC and CV clitics

According to the findings reported in previous studies, it was expected that the majority of clitics would have a CV shape in the two corpora. Furthermore, it was considered likely that these clitics would be less common in the COD because of the increasing influence of the Standard variety, which nowadays is very widespread (especially because of the influence of mass media). However, the data did not corroborate these hypotheses. None of the speakers in the COD uses only CV clitics. In fact, all speakers use more VC than CV clitics. There is variation, but VC clitics are clearly predominant. And, more surprisingly, this predominance is already present in the ALDC.

Table 1 shows the different degrees of clitic-shape variation obtained from the COD data. The first column refers to informants who use CV and VC forms in a similar way, whereas the last one refers to informants who only use VC forms. The greyed cells indicate that the situation described in the first row, that is, the heading of each column, is satisfied. Thus, the different columns — from left to right — show a progressive loss of CV clitics in favour of VC clitics.

It can be seen that only two of the 24 speakers use a similar number of VC and CV clitics. But, in general, CV clitics have low proportions. For example, there are four informants who only use between one and five CV forms (column 3), and four informants use a single CV form (column 5). The last column shows that there are up to eight speakers who only use VC clitics. It is interesting to note that varieties 6, 7 and 8 only have VC clitics. As will be seen later, these varieties represent a transitional area between North-eastern and Central Catalan.

Table 1: *Different degrees of clitic-shape variation (COD)*

		Similar number of CV and VC forms	More VC than CV forms (minimum of 5 CV forms)	More VC than CV forms (between 1 and 5 CV forms)	VC forms + a single CV form and some *se* + [sibilant][3]	VC forms + a single CV form	VC forms + a single *se* + [sibilant][3]	Only VC forms
Variety 1[4]	MB[5]		■					
	LFA[6]						■	
	JPO					■		
Variety 2	CBF	■						
	PGG					■		
	JST							■
Variety 3	JSPU			■				
	JBV			■				
	NTA					■		
Variety 4	DFM			■				
	MPB			■				
	AMC	■						
Variety 5	AMQ			■				
	LRM				■			
	PPC							■
Variety 6	SPM						■	
	AMM						■	
	PVN						■	
Variety 7	NCC							■
	OGP							■
	REF						■	
Variety 8	JOIG							■
	JCOP							■
	BCC							■

Table 2 shows the number of tokens of the different clitics. It only contains information for the speakers who show variation between VC and CV clitics. The table illustrates that the VC form of the reflexive clitic (*es*) is the most common pattern (62 tokens). In fact, VC forms are predominant in all cases; the exception is the 2nd person clitic, which shows more CV than VC forms, although the difference is very small (27 compared with 25 tokens). What is more interesting is

---

[3] This sequence (3rd person reflexive clitic + sibilant) is specified because it favours the shift to CV forms due to a general OCP-sibilant effect shown by Catalan (cf. Bonet & Lloret 2002).

[4] The numbers correspond to different county towns (see the Appendix).

[5] Upper case letters identify the speakers in the corpora.

[6] The informants that appear in non-italics are the ones not taken into account in Table 1, either because they show no variation or only few instances.

that there is no CV form of the partitive clitic, which is consistent with the findings reported by Lloret & Viaplana (1996).

Table 2: *Tokens of the different clitic variants (COD)*

		EM 1st p. sing.	ET 2nd p. sing.	ES 3rd p. refl.	EN part.	ME 1st p. sing.	TE 2nd p. sing.	SE[7] 3rd p. refl.	NE part.
Variety 1	MB	13	4	12	3	1	4	1	
Variety 2	CBF	1		12			9	1 (+sib.)	
Variety 3	JSPU	3	2	4	2	1	1	1 +1 (+sib.)	
	JBV	9	11	6	3	3			
Variety 4	MPB	3	1		4	1		1 +1 (+sib.)	
	AMC	4	5	10	5	6	13		
Variety 5	AMQ		2	6					2
	LRM	2		12	7			1 +4 (+sib.)	
		35	25	62	24	12	27	6 +7 (+sib.)	

It is difficult to compare these data with those of the ALDC because the latter contains fewer clitics. However, it is easy to see once again the predominance of VC clitics, which is illustrated in Tables 3 and 4. Table 3 shows that none of the speakers in the ALDC uses a similar number of VC and CV clitics: there are always more VC clitics. The last column shows that two speakers only use VC forms.

Table 3: *Different degrees of clitic-shape variation (ALDC)*

		Similar number of CV and VC forms	More VC than CV forms	Minimal presence of CV forms	Only VC forms
Variety a[8]	BP		■		
Variety b	JCR		■		
Variety c	AMP[9]				■
Variety d	JCSM			■	
Variety e[10]	ASP		■		
	JCS		■		
	JCV		■		
Variety f	PMG		■		
Variety g	MCA			■	
Variety h	JDC		■		
Variety i	JCOT				■
Variety j	FPT		■		

---

[7] 3rd person reflexive clitics that are followed by a sibilant are separated from the rest because this context favours the shift to CV forms (see note 3).
[8] These letters identify the different small villages where data from the ALDC were collected (see the Appendix).
[9] See note 6, here with respect to Table 4.
[10] In this variety three speakers were interviewed.

Table 4 shows the number of tokens of the different clitics.

Table 4: *Tokens of the different clitic variants (ALDC)*

[handwritten margin note: would be in Table 3? collapsed with Table]

		EM 1st p. sing.	ET 2nd p. sing.	ES 3rd p. refl.	EN part.	ME 1st p. sing.	TE 2nd p. sing.	SE[11] 3rd p. refl.	NE part.
Variety a	BP			3	11			2	3
Variety b	JCR			6	1			3	
Variety d	JCSM			17	1			2	
Variety e	ASP		2	2	1			1	
	JCS			1	2			1 (+sib)	1
	JCV			8	1			5	
Variety f	PMG			3	1				1
Variety g	MCA	11	2	2		1			
Variety h	JDC		2	3	2			1	
Variety j	FPT			7	3			2	
		11	6	52	23	1		16+1(+sib)	5

Tables 2 and 4 show that only two clitics can be compared in the two corpora: only 3rd person reflexive and partitive clitics display a similar number of tokens. Unfortunately, 1st and 2nd person singular clitics are rarely present in the ALDC: to be precise, there are only 18 tokens, whereas the COD contains approximately 100 tokens of these pronouns. These figures cannot be compared. Table 5 compares the number of tokens of 3rd person reflexive and partitive clitics in the two corpora. Although in both cases VC forms are by far the most predominant, the ALDC contains more CV clitics than the COD. Hence, considering only these two pronouns, there seems to be a tendency towards the loss of CV clitics over time. Old speakers interviewed in the 1960s and 1970s could still use the form *ne*, which has now disappeared. The use of *se* has also dramatically decreased in recent years. This evolution may be due to the prestige and increasing influence of the Standard variety, but there must be other factors that favour the shift to VC clitics in North-eastern Catalan, because these forms were already predominant among old speakers who lived in small and isolated villages in the 60s and 70s. These speakers did not have a high educational background and had no contact at all with the Standard variety, but nevertheless show a strong preference for the VC shape.

---

[11] See notes 3 and 7.

Table 5: *Partitive and reflexive clitics in the ALDC and the COD*

	PARTITIVE CLITIC		REFLEXIVE CLITIC	
	EN	NE	ES	SE
ALDC	22	5	52	16
COD	24	0	62	6

One of this paper's initial hypotheses was that a major presence of traditional dialectal characteristics would lead to a major presence of CV clitics (= old forms). The data have not completely corroborated this point either. It is easy to find informants who regularly use VC clitics but also preserve plenty of traditional dialectal characteristics. Therefore, less standardized conversations do not necessarily entail more CV clitics, although the reverse is usually true: whenever CV clitics appear in a conversation, other dialectal characteristics do so as well. In other words, informants whose speech is nearly standardized do not use CV clitics. Hence, there is some type of interaction between the presence of dialectal characteristics and clitic distribution, but only in one direction. This finding corroborates the idea that the presence of VC clitics cannot only be explained by the influence of the Standard variety.

By listing the dialectal characteristics of each informant it was possible to establish the boundaries of the North-eastern Catalan dialect. The main characteristics found in this area are shown in (4).

(4) North-eastern dialectal characteristics (cf. Veny 1982, Colomina 1999, Adam, 2002).
   a. Variation in the quality of *e* and *o*. Ex. *fl[ó]r* instead of *fl[ɔ́]r* "flower".
   b. Categorical deletion of plural *-s* in prenominal position. Ex. *el nens* instead of *els nens* "the children", *poc nens* instead of *pocs nens* "few children", *tot dos* instead of *tots dos* "all two".
   c. Changes in the gender of nouns. Ex. *la fred* (fem.) instead of *el fred* (masc.) "the cold".
   d. Use of the masculine possessive with feminine nouns. Ex. *la meu mare* instead of *la meva mare* "my mother".[12]
   e. Special forms within the paradigm of the verb *ser* "to be". Ex. *soms, sous*… instead of *som, sou*… "we are", "you (pl.) are"…
   f. Use of other peculiar verbal forms. Ex. *iré* instead of *aniré* "I will go".

According to the data, North-eastern Catalan includes varieties 1, 2, 3, 4 and 5, which show some of the dialectal characteristics presented in (4). In contrast, these characteristics are rarely present in varieties 6, 7 and 8. Recall that these are also the varieties in which clitics always surface with a VC shape. Therefore, they can be considered a transitional area between North-eastern and Central Catalan (see the map in the Appendix).

---

[12] The gender of the speaker does not have any influence on the possessive form.

5. Data analysis

This section analyses both internal and external factors that may have favoured the shift to VC forms: on the one hand, phonetic and syntactic contexts; on the other, age, gender and level of formality. It will be seen that the conclusions drawn from the analysis of the syntactic context are the most relevant.

As far as the phonetic context is concerned, all that can be noted is the well-known tendency to avoid sequences of sibilants in Catalan. Example (5) shows some instances of this OCP effect (cf. Bonet & Lloret 2002). Note that if a reflexive clitic is followed by a verb starting with a sibilant, it shows the CV shape. In contrast, if the clitic is preceded by a word ending with a sibilant, it shows the VC shape. The schwa vowel always appears between the sibilants. Apart from this example, there is no other tendency to avoid clusters or sequences of identical consonants through the appearance of the clitic vowel. Therefore, except for sibilant avoidance, the position of the vowel does not depend on the characteristics of the adjacent segments.

(5) ALDC:
– ...sə ˈsɛmbrə...	se sembra	"it is sowed"
– ...əmˈprez̺ əs̺ ˈpasə...	emprés es passa	"afterwards s.th. happens"

COD:
– ...sə sirkuˈlaβə...	se circulava	"it was driving"
– ...ɛn̪trə ˈɛjz̺ əs̺ ˈparlən	entre ells es parlen	"they talk among themselves"

In contrast, the analysis of the syntactic context where clitics appear has shown that VC clitics systematically occur in some particular contexts, which are very frequent in spoken discourse. In both the ALDC and the COD, clitics have a VC shape when preceded by a series of monosyllabic particles such as the complementizer *que* "that", the negative adverb *no* "not", and the conjunctions *i* "and" and *si* "if", among others. These elements can also be considered clitics because they are unstressed particles that are phonologically dependent on an adjacent word (cf. Mascaró 2002). The hypothesis now is that the grammatical similarity between these elements and pronominal clitics causes an attraction between both kinds of particles. For example, the sentences in (6) show how such monosyllabic particles seem to be tied to the consonant of the pronouns, which appears in the same syllable. If pronouns had a CV shape the two particles would not appear in the same syllable.

(6) a. Ella sap   que's   troba millor
       She knows   that.**she** feels better
       "She knows that she feels better..."
    b. La senyora que   ve   i'**m**   diu
       The lady who comes   and.**me** says
       "The lady who comes and says to me..."

c. No'**m**   sembla   tan   bé
   Not.**me**   think   that right
   "I don't think it's so right."
d. Si'**t**   posessis a comptar
   If.**you**   started to count
   "If you started to count…"

These pronominal clitics can be interpreted as being phonologically enclitic to the monosyllabic particles rather than being proclitic to the verb.[13] This finding matches the basic postulates of Wackernagel's Law (1892), according to which clitics cannot stand in the clause-initial position, but preferentially appear in the second position, due to their status as phonologically enclitic elements (cited in Fischer 2002: 26-27). Many studies of Old Romance clitics have 'adopted' a Romance version of Wackernagel's Law, namely the Tobler-Mussafia Law (Tobler 1875, Mussafia 1888), to explain why clitics used to follow the verb in matrix clauses but never in embedded clauses. Examples are given which illustrate the Tobler-Mussafia effect in Old Italian (7) and Old Portuguese (8).[14]

(7)   Offerse-**gliene**   due   marchi di guadagno
      Offered-**him.it**   two   marks   of interest
      "He offered him two marks of interest…"
(8)   e   pedio   a Nosso   Ssenhor que**lhe**   desse fruyto
      and   asked   to Our   Senhor that**him** let please
      "… and asked Our Lord   that pleased him…"

In both sentences pronominal clitics need a host to their left to attach to. Nevertheless, it has been argued that Old Catalan pronominal clitics differ from other Old Romance clitic elements in that they can precede or follow the verb in matrix clauses as well as in embedded clauses, irrespective of whether the verb is preceded by a constituent or not (Fischer 2003: 260). The following examples show some of the possibilities of clitic attachment in Old Catalan:[15]

(9)   e   Déus donava-**ls**   manera
      and   God gave-**them** way
      "… and God showed them how to…"
(10) Ambdós **se**   concordaren   e.**s**   pacifficaren[16]
      Both   **ref** agreed   and.**ref** pacified
      "They both agreed and made peace…"

---

[13] In these examples and in the following discussion, the terms enclitic *vs.* proclitic are not being used to define the position with respect to the verb, but rather to define the direction of phonological cliticization (cf. Fischer 2003: 262).
[14] Examples of Old Romance clitic elements come from Fischer (2002).
[15] These examples also come from Fischer (2002).
[16] It has been argued that the conjunction *e* was unable to host other Old Romance object clitics in the medieval period (Fischer 2003: 262).

(11) L'alberque   e   la   viny   que possehia, **l'**embargave
      The refuge   and the vineyard   that possessed, **him'**hindered
      "The refuge and the vineyard he possessed hindered him..."
(12) e   diu que lo   primer respòs-**li**   hòrreament
      and said that the first   answered.**him** horrified
      "...and he said that the first answered him horrified..."
(13) El rey   **se**   perdé, que no.l   trobà   hom
      The king **ref**   lost,   that not.**him** found   man
      "The king got lost, nobody found him."

According to Fischer (2002, 2003), syntax — not phonology — is responsible for clitic distribution in Old Catalan. Phonological cliticization takes place only after the order of the constituents has been linearized. Thus, Old Catalan clitics can phonologically attach either to the left or to the right, depending mostly on where there is a vowel to lean on (Fischer 2002: 183-193). In fact, the examples that appear in Fischer's book show that although the distribution of Old Catalan clitics differs in some ways from that of other Old Romance clitics, the direction of phonological cliticization is usually the same: most Old Catalan clitics are phonologically enclitic elements.[17] The constituents they lean on are verbs and adverbs, but also relative pronouns, negators and conjunctions, which are the particles that attract VC clitics in the data analysed in this study.[18]

The attraction between a series of monosyllabic particles and clitics has also been analysed from the point of view of language universals. According to research on person clitics carried out by Cysouw (2004), there are many languages that show a series of contexts in which person marking does not cliticize on the verb but on other elements. Cysouw calls them "cross-linguistic common person marking attractors", because they attract the clitics away from the verb. According to this author, in most languages this attraction is a relic of an older stage in which verbs did not function as hosts for the clitics. What is more interesting is that these "person marking attractors" include conditional and copulative conjunctions, complementizers and negative adverbs, that is, the same particles that attract VC clitics in the Catalan data. Therefore, the spreading of VC clitics in North-eastern Catalan is favoured by their systematic appearance in some particular — and frequent — syntactic contexts.

Finally, external factors do not seem to have a systematic influence on clitic-shape variation.[19] It can only be noted that older speakers tend to use more CV clitics, which seems to indicate a progressive loss of these variants in future generations. Additionally, some of the speakers who use more CV clitics are

---

[17] Obviously, exceptions can also be found. See, for example, number (11).

[18] Pronominal clitics in Old Spanish also used to be enclitic to relative pronouns, adverbs, prepositions and conjunctions, often with loss of their final vowel: _Que·s viesse_ "That (he) could see him", _No·l cogieron_ "(They) did not catch him", _Siempre·t maldizré_ "I will always curse you", etc. (Menéndez Pidal 1958: 254).

[19] However, our results are not completely representative. A larger amount of data would be necessary to obtain more reliable conclusions.

women, and this shows that women's speech is not always closer to Standard varieties than men's speech, as some sociolinguistic studies about Catalan have asserted (Boix & Vila 1998). As far as the level of formality is concerned, VC clitics tend to be more frequent in formal speech. However, there are no strong differences in clitic distribution between formal and informal speech: the same basic regularities are found.

6. Conclusions

This paper has reported the results of a study that challenges one of the most common statements made in traditional studies of Catalan dialectology: namely, the classification of North-eastern Catalan within the group of dialects that have CV pronominal clitics. The paper has illustrated that in this variety clitics are subject to a high degree of variation, although VC forms are clearly predominant. CV forms have been reduced to 1st and 2nd person singular clitics, and nowadys the partitive clitic always surfaces with a VC form. However, the predominance of VC clitics is not only due to the influence of the Standard variety. These clitics have a deep-rooted presence in this area and are favoured by syntactic contexts that are well determined by diachronic evidence and language universals. These contexts involve a series of monosyllabic particles such as conjunctions, complementizers and adverbs.

References

Adam, M. 2002. El català septentrional de transició: nova visió des de la morfologia. Unpublished PhD diss., Universitat de Barcelona.
Boix, E. & F. Xavier Vila. 1998. Sociolingüística de la llengua catalana. Barcelona: Ariel.
Bonet, E. & M.-R. Lloret. 2002. "OCP effects in Catalan cliticization". Catalan Journal of Linguistics 1. 7-27.
Campmany, E. 2004. Els clítics pronominals en posició proclítica al català central septentrional. Unpublished MA Thesis, Universitat de Barcelona.
Colomina, J. 1999. Dialectologia catalana. Introducció i guia bibliogràfica. Alacant: Universitat d'Alacant.
Cysouw, M. 2004. "The rise of person inflection with special reference to the Munda languages". Paper presented at the 11th International Morphology Meeting 2004, Vienna.
DeCesaris, J.A. 1987. "Epenthesis in Catalan". Studies in Romance languages ed. by C. Neidle et al. Dordrecht: Foris. (= Publications in Language Sciences, 25. 79-92).
Fischer, S. 2002. The Catalan clitic system: A diachronic perspective on its syntax and phonology. Berlin & New York: Mouton de Gruyter.
Fischer, S. 2003. "Rethinking the Tobler-Mussafia Law: Data from Old Catalan". Diachronica 20:2. 259-287.
Lloret, M.-R. 2001 [2002]. "Canvi lingüístic i variació fònica". Les claus del canvi lingüístic ed. by M. Antònia Cano et al., 331-363. Alacant: Institut Interuniversitari de Filologia Valenciana.
Lloret, M.-R. & M. Pilar Perea. 2002. "A report on the Corpus Oral Dialectal del Català Actual". Dialectologia et Geolinguistica 10. 59-76.
Lloret, M.-R. & J. Viaplana. 1996. "Els clítics pronominals singulars del català oriental: una aproximació interdialectal". Estudis de llengua i literatura catalanes, XXXII. Miscel·lània Germà Colón vol. 5. 273-309. Barcelona: Publicacions de l'Abadia de Montserrat.
Mascaró, J. 2002. "Morfologia: aspectes generals". Gramàtica del català contemporani ed. by Joan Solà et al., 465-482. Vol 1. Barcelona: Empúries.

Menéndez Pidal, R. 1958. Manual de gramática histórica española. Madrid: Espasa-Calpe.

Mussafia, A. 1888. "Enclisi o proclisi del pronome personale atono quale oggeto". Romania 27. 145-146.

Tobler, A. 1875. "Besprechung von J. Le Coultre, De l'ordre des mots dans Chrétien de Troyes". Vermischte Beiträge zur französischen Grammatik 5. 395-414.

Veny, J. 1982. Els parlars catalans: Síntesi de dialectologia. Palma: Moll.

Veny, J. & L. Pons. 1998. Atles lingüístic del domini català. Etnotextos del català oriental. Barcelona: Institut d'Estudis Catalans.

Viaplana, J. & M. Pilar Perea (ed.). 2003. Textos orals dialectals del català sincronitzats. Una selecció. Barcelona: Universitat de Barcelona.

Wackernagel, J. 1892. "Über ein Gesetz der Indogermanischen Wortstellung". Indogermanische Forschungen 1. 333-436.

Interesting that findings conform expected pattern

Appendix

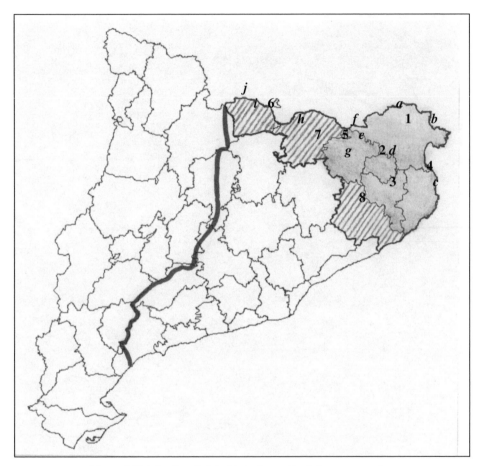

Map of Catalonia, divided into 'counties' (*comarques*).

Central Catalan corresponds to the area located on the right side of the thick line.

- *COD* (1994-1996): varieties 1 (Figueres), 2 (Banyoles), 3 (Girona), 4 (la Bisbal d'Empordà), 5 (Olot), 6 (Puigcerdà), 7 (Ripoll) and 8 (Sta. Coloma de Farners).
- *ALDC* (1965-1975): varieties *a* (Maçanet de Cabrenys), *b* (Roses), *c* (Begur), *d* (Banyoles), *e* (Oix), *f* (Bassegoda), *g* (St. Privat d'en Bas), *h* (Planoles), *i* (Alp) and *j* (Meranges).

The native / non-native speaker distinction and the diversity of linguistic profiles of young people in Swedish multilingual urban contexts

Kari Fraurud & Sally Boyd
Stockholm University & Göteborg University

Abstract: The notion of 'native speaker' (NS) has played a central role in all areas of linguistics, but it is also perennially questioned. This paper aims to contribute to the discussion of the usefulness of the binary distinction between native and non-native speakers (NNS) by exploring a relatively large body of empirical data collected in a study of language and language use among young people in contemporary multilingual urban settings in Sweden. Data about linguistic background and practices from 222 informants were analyzed by means of so called 'linguistic profiling', here involving a number of variables reflecting various nativeness criteria. The resulting complex and varied linguistic profiles display the great diversity among informants. This diversity is presumably not unique to these 222 young people, but can also be expected to be found in other similar contexts. The application of a binary NS/NNS distinction in such contexts will either — if a single criterion is used — result in a categorization of informants into two widely heterogeneous groups, or — if multiple criteria are combined and only clear cases considered — result in the exclusion of a considerable number of language users from the object of study. These observations should also have implications for the study of language variation and change in multilingual contexts more generally.

1. Introduction

Language contact in many contexts around the globe has led to a revival of the perennial discussion of concepts such as 'native / non-native speaker' and 'first / second language'.[1] In this paper, we would like to contribute to this discussion by contrasting the first of these binary distinctions with a 'linguistic profile' analysis of data from 222 young people living in multilingual settings in Sweden's three largest cities. While our conclusions relate to this particular group of informants, we believe that several of the observations made in this paper are also applicable in studies of young people in other contemporary European multilingual settings[2] and, more generally, in any study of language variation and change involving multilingualism.

---

[1] E.g., Firth & Wagner (1997) and other contributions in The Modern Language Journal 81:3; 82:1; Kramsch (1997/2003), Leung et al. (1997), Singh (1998), Cook (2002), Block (2003), Davies (2003).

[2] Cf. Rampton (1995), Quist (2000), Doran (2002, 2004), Kallmeyer & Keim (2003), Appel & Schoonen (2005), and Kerswill & Torgersen (2005).

Our main point is that it is not only the case that the native/non-native speaker distinction turns out to be difficult to apply in some, more or less exceptional, individual cases. Rather, the distinction appears to be fundamentally unsuited to capture the linguistic background, practices and proficiencies of an important number of young people today. In our study, an overwhelming majority of the 222 informants did not fit neatly into any of the categories 'native' or 'non-native' as defined in the literature. There is still a need for characterizing and generalizing over informants, however, and as an answer to this need we have developed a method of analysis that we call 'linguistic profiling', further described below.

The data we use has been collected and analyzed within the project 'Language and language use among young people in multilingual urban settings'.[3] The overarching goal of the project is to describe, analyze and compare the everyday language and language use of young people in multilingual areas of Göteborg, Malmö and Stockholm. The project is being carried out by a team of senior researchers and graduate students, who are studying various phonological, grammatical and pragmatic features of the varieties used by young people with different linguistic backgrounds in these settings. The first step in the fieldwork was a series of interviews with 222 young people (age 16-21, median 17) in our target informant group.[4]

In an earlier paper, we looked at the concept of 'second language' and 'second language speaker' (Boyd & Fraurud 2004) in relation to this informant group; in this paper, we examine critically the related concept of 'native speaker' (NS) to assess its usefulness in studies such as ours. We begin by briefly looking at this concept in various branches of linguistics in order to see which criteria are normally used to identify native speakers. Then, using these criteria as a point of departure, we look at the diversity of backgrounds represented in our informant group, and propose, rather than using one or two of the suggested criteria, combining several criteria to produce a multitude of 'linguistic profiles'. In the final part of the paper, we suggest ways in which a linguistic profile analysis can give a more accurate and detailed picture of the diversity of linguistic backgrounds in settings such as the one we have studied.

2. Definitions and uses of 'native speaker' (NS) within linguistics

In an anthology from the early 1980's, *A Festschrift for Native Speaker*, which examined the concept of native speaker, the editor Florian Coulmas (1981:1) calls

---

[3] Cf. http://hum.gu.se/institutioner/svenska-spraket/isa/verk/projekt/pag/sprakbruk_eng/.
We would like to acknowledge the practical assistance and helpful comments of our colleagues on the project, as well as those of our colleagues at our respective departments. We are also grateful for the financial support of The Bank of Sweden Tercentenary Foundation, which has financed the research project as a whole.

[4] The informant group is not a random sample of young people living in these areas. Rather, schools and classes in these schools were selected in order to fulfill various criteria of representativity and comparability among the three cities. All the students in the chosen classes were invited to participate in the study, and all but a few accepted.

this concept "a common reference point for all branches of linguistics" [...] "of fundamental importance to the field." Despite the centrality of the concept however, it turns out, not surprisingly, that the concept is conceived of and used somewhat differently by different linguists. There is, on the one hand, the idealized native speaker as a theoretical construct in, e.g., generative grammar. Chomsky's view is that (1963: 3): "Linguistic theory is concerned primarily with the ideal speaker-listener, in a completely homogeneous speech community, who knows its language perfectly". On the other hand, more empirically oriented linguists (some of whom may actually also need an idealized native speaker for their theories) are faced with methodological problems regarding whom they should choose as their source of empirical data about a particular language. Others are in need of a native speaker as a norm (a control group) against which to measure non-native speakers of the language. Our paper is oriented toward the question of the usefulness of the concept of NS in empirical work, i.e. the second conceptualization, in particular in studies of language and language use in contemporary multilingual contexts.

In his introduction to the *Festschrift*, Coulmas (1981) makes a conceptual analysis which takes up several of the central criteria for a native speaker of a certain language. The criterion he considers to be most necessary and common to all conceptualizations of NS is that of language acquisition in early infancy, in conjunction with primary socialization (Coulmas 1981: 4). This criterion is closely related to most meanings of the term 'native' in the collocation 'native speaker'.

In the same volume, Thomas Ballmer (1981) presents a typology of native speakers, where he enumerates a number of additional criteria. In the passage quoted below, he summarizes the practical problems of finding a suitable native speaker for typologically oriented or other studies within the broad field of descriptive linguistics. He draws the conclusion (1981: 57) that a good candidate can actually be difficult to find:

> "A native speaker is old enough to know the language and not so old as to have forgotten it. He is healthy in every relevant respect, thus especially neither blind, deaf, handicapped, paralysed, nor does he lisp, stutter or have a cleft palate. He is monolingual, he lives in his birthplace, his family, especially his mother, speaks natively his natural language L, the place where he lives is strictly monolingual: there is no standard speech/dialect split and there are not other competing languages. [...] The native speaker is educated enough to enter the experiment, but not so educated as to call into question its outcome".

Taking Coulmas (1981) and Ballmer (1981) as points of departure, we can say that these sources bring forward several important criteria for NSs, primarily thought of as adequate representatives for a community of speakers of a language.

Also within sociolinguistics, the concept of native speaker has been needed for practical reasons, as a necessary criterion for informants. In his dissertation, Labov (1966) describes how he selected informants for his New York City study, based on an earlier random sample carried out on the Lower East Side. However,

Labov excluded almost half of the persons selected for the earlier study because they were born abroad, had not come to the neighborhood until after the age of eight, or had "marked foreign characteristics" in their English (1966: 175). Of the original sample of 553 individuals, Labov's sample comprised only 312, or 56%. His criteria for selecting informants thus included birthplace, monolingualism and sedentaryness, while age of (dialect) acquisition is operationalized in terms of age of arrival in New York City.

Moving on to the area of second language acquisition (SLA) research, the concept of native speaker here builds to a high degree on the Chomskyan conception that universal grammar and the language acquisition device (LAD) is not available to (at least late) second language learners.[5] The definition of the field is in fact dependent on a conception of second language learning or acquisition as different from first language acquisition. Usually, the distinction is conceived of in terms of age of acquisition or age of onset. In addition, native speakers are often selected to act as standards of comparisons to persons learning a second language; they are conceived of both as necessary sources of input and as targets for the second language learning process. This role accentuates native speaker proficiency as an important further criterion. Proficiency is either implicitly assumed to be entailed by other criteria, or explicitly specified (as in Davies 2003, 2004) to include intuitions about one's own idiolect and its relation to standard grammar, one's fluency, communicative competence in production and comprehension, creative writing ability, etc.

In a paper outlining future directions for research in the field, Michael Long (1993: 205) wrote about experimental studies comparing non-native speakers and native speakers:

> "NS subjects clearly need to be more comparable to NNS comparison groups than has sometimes been the case in the SLA literature in the past. The most crucial requirement [is] that NSs speak the L2 variety or second dialect that was the acquisition target for the NNSs [...] In addition NS controls should be comparable in age, sex, education and social class [...] Ideally, they should also be monolinguals, since there is increasing experimental and anecdotal evidence that learning additional languages can sometimes affect first language abilities in as yet poorly understood ways, [...]".

Here, then, we see some similarities to Ballmer's conception, quoted above, in that Long considers the native speakers' age, sex and education to have a potential effect on their native speaker competence. Crucially, they should also be monolinguals, because multilingualism can have an effect on first language abilities (see e.g. Jaspaert et al. 1986, Cook 2003).

Also in foreign language research and teaching, the concept of native speaker has routinely been taken for granted as a norm for students in the classroom. In response to arguments against the feasibility of such a norm for all learners (e.g.

---

[5] As evidenced in, e.g., the vast literature on ultimate attainment, opinions differ widely as regards at what age this happens (cf. Hyltenstam & Abrahamsson 2003).

Kramsch 1997/2003), several researchers defend the need for the native speaker norm in foreign language classrooms (e.g. Koike & Liskin-Gasparro 2003: 263):

> "[I]f the native speaker is not to be considered the model for learners to emulate, then who should provide that linguistic model? [...] [Without the native speaker,] the teachers and learners of foreign language are left (1) without a target language norm, and (2) with an unrealizable dream of becoming native-like speakers. These two notions render any efforts in the FL classroom unproductive".

In this passage, the authors bring out another proposed quality of the native speaker, that of *identity*. For many, the native speaker should identify her/himself and be identifiable (or at least able to pass, cf. Piller 2002) as a full-fledged member of the speech community by other native speakers.

Drawing on these and other sources, we summarize our brief survey with the following list of common criteria for the concept of native speaker. The first criterion, the essential one according to most definitions, is that of early exposure during primary socialization, the 'age of onset' criterion. Other criteria vary in importance in the various sources or are assumed to be entailed by age of onset. They include continued *use* of the language throughout the lifespan; a particular (usually high) level of *proficiency* in the language; an adequate, but not too high level of *education* (or, similarly, *class*); *monolingualism* (albeit to different degrees); and a number of criteria that can be subsumed under the heading of *context* and that assume a homogeneous environment without influences from other varieties or languages (see further below). A final criterion is having an *identity* as a native speaker.

Like many others, we perceive a number of ideological, theoretical and methodological problems associated with the use of the binary NS/NNS distinction, and with the NS criteria and their operationalization. In this paper, however, we will confine our discussion to some issues raised by our empirical material.

3. Applying the concept of native speaker in a contemporary multilingual context

No one acquainted with current multilingual settings can have failed to meet individuals whose linguistic background and practices challenge the binary NS/NNS distinction (for a particularly insightful analysis, see Leung et al. 1997). It is still common, however, both in research and in popular discourse, to talk and act as if such individuals would be more or less exceptional; the majority of speakers in a community or group is thought of as being either NS or NNS. Behind such a 'dichotomy-with-exceptions view' lies an underlying assumption of homogeneity, implying a strong association between the various nativeness criteria mentioned above. In this study we therefore wanted to explore the NS/NNS distinction in relation to a larger database, built up within the project mentioned above.

Background data about the 222 young people participating in the project was collected through a questionnaire filled out by the researchers during individual audio-recorded interviews. The questionnaire comprised 80 items, consisting of both multiple choice questions with follow-ups and open questions, generating a high degree of detail and heterogeneity in the replies. In addition to the pre-processing required in encoding data into SPSS, the profiling procedure illustrated in this paper involves making the database more manageable by further grouping values and merging variables at different levels of detail. It should be remembered that, while each such step increases comparability and generalizability, it is at the cost of loss of (possibly important) information. We will return to this below.

3.1   Operationalizing NS criteria

A large number of background variables in the database are potentially relevant to an assessment of our informants' nativeness according to the criteria reviewed above, including also such variables as, for example, writing practices and media consumption preferences. For the present discussion, however, we have selected some variables that more immediately relate to the NS criteria. These are listed in Table 1 with brief descriptions.

Table 1: *Native speaker criteria and some related background variables in the database, all reported data. (SS=Swedish/Sweden only, SO=Swedish/Sweden and other, OO=Other only. Values within parentheses are theoretically possible but non-occurring values.)*

Criteria	*Some related background variables in the database*	*Values*	*Code*
Age of onset	age of onset of Swedish	early/late	AGEON
	age of arrival to Sweden	early/late	AGEARR
	where Swedish first spoken	home/other	SWFIRST
	first learned language	SS/SO/OO	FIRSTLG
Proficiency	best language(s)	SS/SO/OO	LFPROF
	proficiency in mother tongue, mother tongue 2 & Swedish, respectively: speak/understand/write/read		
	& understand	1-5	[several]
Use	preferred language(s)	SS/SO/OO	LGPREF
	language(s) used with parents	SS/SO/OO	LGPAR
	language(s) used with siblings	SS/SO/OO	LGSIB
	language(s) used with close friends	SS/SO/(OO)	LGFRIEN
Context	born in Sweden / abroad	SS/OO	BORN
	parents born in Sweden / abroad	SS/SO/OO	PARBORN
	mother tongues of close friends	SS/SO/(OO)	FRIENLG
Mono-/bilingualism	several, including languages spoken, language practices in relation to various contexts, media etc.	[open]	[several]
Education & social class	several, including education and occupation of parents/step parents in Sweden & country of origin, living area and type of housing, etc.	[open]	[several]

For several of the relevant variables in our database it makes sense to divide responses into three main categories: *Swedish/Sweden only (SS), Swedish/Sweden and other (language/country) (SO),* and *Other (language/country) only (OO),* as shown under *Values* in Table 1. For reported age of onset and age of arrival, in the present illustration of the profiles we use a binary division of responses into *early* (before three years of age) and *late.* Just as in the case of selection of specific variables, this is but one of several possible options. Responses to the open question as to where Swedish was first spoken were divided into *home,* contrasted to all *other* settings, such as at pre-school or school, or with friends. The values *Swedish/Sweden only (SS), early,* and *home* will collectively be referred to as 'NS-values', as opposed to all other, 'NNS values'. Almost all variables involve a number of theoretical and methodological problems, of which we can only briefly mention a few here.

Determining an individual's *age of onset* (AO) is far from trivial, at least for individuals who were not born into families and communities where only one language is used. Somewhat surprisingly, the notion and its operationalizations are rarely problematized in the literature. Theoretically, it is not clear what conditions should be fulfilled for an individual's contact with a language or language development to be counted as an onset of language acquisition. It is possible to imagine a broad continuum from active interaction to mere exposure to the language, which may be infrequent, only receptive, limited in mode (e.g. only television), etc. Methodologically, determining AO is problematic since in most cases one must rely on reported data, which may have low reliability due to respondents' insufficient memory of details on language use early in life and their different interpretations of 'onset' (or 'when you start to speak/learn the language' or whatever wording is used in the question). Operationalizing onset by replacing it with (probably more reliable) reports of age of arrival at a specific place may reduce the validity of the data; arriving in a country does not necessarily imply starting to acquire the majority language in any other sense than that of minimal exposure. In our background database we are of course faced with the same reliability and validity problems, and we here try out the possibility of combining and comparing several onset-related variables. In addition to reported AGEON and AGEARR, we include the variables FIRSTLG, reported first learned language(s), and SWFIRST, whether Swedish was introduced within or outside the family, which in many cases indirectly indicates age of acquisition

Language proficiency as assessed by analyses of oral and written production and various tests is clearly relevant in descriptions of linguistic profiles insofar as the tests are valid and relevant to the research questions. It should be noted, however, that such tests/analyses inevitably involve problems with the choice of norm against which to measure. This is something which is especially pertinent in our context, where the presence of alternative language models due to the emergence of new multiethnic youth varieties complicates the analysis of non-standard features (cf. Kotsinas 1988, 1992; Bodén 2004; Fraurud & Bijvoet 2004). Since our database does not include test data, we here only consider self-reported data, in particular the responses to the question "Which language or languages do you think you know best?".

With regard to *language use*, we include the responses to one general question, "Which language or languages do you prefer to use?", and three questions of habitual use: language(s) used with parents (and step parents), siblings and friends. Even these questions tend to hide important quantitative as well as qualitative variation. The code 'Swedish and other' for language use with parents can e.g. include instances of code-switching, varying language choice in different situations, speaking one language to one parent and one to another, parents' speaking one language and children speaking another (in a single conversation) and many other variants.

Context is in Table 1 represented by but a few of several possible variables. Country of origin (of parents and child) is often referred to in studies of bilingualism and SLA in Sweden, partly due to the fact that it — together with citizenship — is the only resource in official Swedish statistics for conjectures about ethnic or linguistic affiliation (cf. de Geer 2004). As elsewhere, people who were born abroad or have parents born abroad are often grouped together under the label 'first and second generation immigrants',[6] subsequently used for generalizing about this 'group' as opposed to '(native) Swedes'. Obviously, the birthplace of an individual or of his/her parents does not necessarily imply anything about his/her mono-/multilingualism. Still BORN and PARBORN are included in Table 1 under 'Context', as two of several variables that indicate the potential presence of languages other than Swedish in an individual's earlier and current environment. The variables AGEARR and SWFIRST, listed under *Age of onset*, can, or perhaps should, also be seen as context variables. Another possible source of linguistic influence, especially for this group of young people, is the mono-/multilingualism of friends, here reflected in the question: 'What are the mother tongues of the friends you see most?' (FRIENDLG).

Mono- and multilingualism (to different degrees) can in our database be traced in responses to several different questions, including one open question of currently spoken languages (see below). It is also reflected in the proficiency, use and preference variables that we described above, and which we will use here.

Education and *social class*, finally, are reflected in our database with answers to some open questions about parents' education and earlier and current occupation etc. They are highly complex variables, especially in settings like ours, where migration sometimes involves dramatic changes in the socio-economic status both within and between generations, while information about education in countries of origin is difficult to assess. Furthermore, the linguistic literature using the native speaker concept gives different signals about which social class or level of education is ideal for a native speaker. The criteria of education and class is not included in our present analysis.

---

[6] Recent statistics, however, use the term 'foreign background', applied *either* to persons born abroad and/or with both parents born abroad, *or* only to those born abroad and/or with a foreign citizenship.

3.2   Distribution with regard to nine 'NS variables'

Let us consider the distribution of some putative nativeness variables (hereafter 'NS variables') over the 222 young people participating in our project. According to the simplistic 'dichotomy-with-exceptions view' described above, our informants would split into two main groups, clear native and clear non-native speakers — leaving a small number of unclear or mixed cases in between. In our database, there is one variable that produces this kind of distribution, viz. reported first learned language(s) (FIRSTLG, cf. Figure 1).

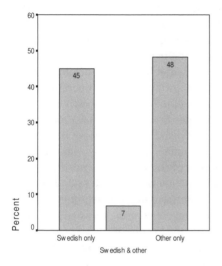

Figure 1: *Reported first learned language(s).*

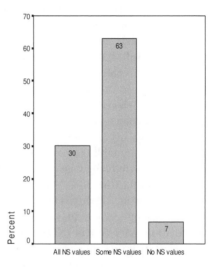

Figure 2: *Nativeness/non-nativeness calculated on nine variables: AGEON, AGEARR, SWFIRST, FIRSTLG, LGPROF, LGPREF, LGPAR, LGSIB, LGFRIEN.*

It is illuminating to evaluate the responses to questions about FIRSTLG and the other onset-related variables, AGEON, AGEARR, and SWFIRST, compared with each other. The separate frequencies for NS values on all four onset related variables are: AGEARR=early (73%), AGEON=early (58%); SWFIRST=home (45%), FIRSTLG=SS (45%). Pair-wise comparisons show that the overlap between these variables (including the two latter) in our data is only partial, and — more importantly — that there is no absolute implicational relationship among them. Thus, an 'early' age of arrival does not imply an 'early' age of onset. In our dataset there are 35 exceptions to this assumption, with a difference of up to seven years, while an 'early' age of onset does not imply learning Swedish at home. In this instance, there are 30 exceptions. Furthermore, the reliability and validity problems connected with AO, discussed above, may be even more serious for responses to the question of which language was learned first. For example, nine informants claimed Swedish (only) to be their first language *and* to have started to speak Swedish outside the family, two of them also saying that this was after three years of age. This and other observations suggest that the questions of which language(s) one learnt first and when are open to different interpretations and are difficult to answer.[7] It may be easier to remember *where* one started to speak/learn a language than *when*, hence the variable SWFIRST in an important way complements the other age related variables.

As may be expected in a group comprising many young people with immigrant parents or grandparents the distribution of FIRSTLG and other onset-related variables contrasts sharply with those of current best language (LGPROF) and preferred language (LGPREF). A large majority of young people consider Swedish to be the language they know best and a large (but not identical) majority prefers to speak Swedish. For the group as a whole, then, this may suggest a general trend of language shift, but, as we will show below, the picture is in fact more complex.

Translating central nativeness criteria to variables in our database, the NS group among our informants could, as a first approximation, be operationalized to include those who (i) have acquired Swedish in the family at an early age, as their only first language, and in Sweden, (ii) consider Swedish their best and preferred language, and (iii) are monolingual in the restricted sense of using only Swedish with parents, siblings or friends (besides possessing no additional first/best/preferred language). Nearly one third of the informants fulfill all of these nine NS criteria (the 30% 'All NS values' in Figure 2). Very few, 7%, did not have an NS value on any one of the nine criteria. An overwhelming majority of the 222 young people in our study, therefore, falls 'in between' — with a combination of NS and NNS values. The exclusion of this large group of informants from the object of study is of course no option if we want to study language and language use in current multilingual settings. Hence we need to develop tools for capturing possible general patterns among our informants without imposing new unwarranted categories or assumptions.

3.3   Multilingual profiles of 222 Swedish adolescents

As we have already pointed out, our initial analyses of the data indicated that there is no single nativeness criterion which produces a neat division of our informant group into two homogeneous groups. Instead, we need a method that allows us to explore and systematize the variation in our informant group prior to further both statistical and qualitative analysis. For our needs it is essential to be able to group informants according to linguistic background and practices (i) at different levels of detail and (ii) without losing track of either the individuals within groups or the different variables and possible combinations of values. What we call *linguistic profiling* analysis provides such a characterization of groups and individuals through combinations of (a variable number of) values of (a variable number of) variables hypothesized to be relevant for the particular study at issue.

---

[7] Some of these problems could, of course, be partially overcome by more extensive fieldwork, such as detailed interviews with informants, care-takers and other members of the families.

In the present application of this method, we wanted to explore common nativeness criteria against empirical data. We have here used eight of the nine variables in Figure 2 above:[8] three with two, four with tree, and one with four[9] possible values. It should again be emphasized that this particular choice of variables and values is one of several possible alternatives for illustrating the complexity of the data with regard to nativeness criteria by means of the profiling procedure.

Altogether, 88 combinations of values were represented among the 222 informants (see Table 2). In order to save space, only 26 of the profiles are included in the table: all profiles shared by three or more informants plus a few others with only one or two members, illustrating different points in the discussion.

In Table 2, each row represents a unique combination of values on eight NS variables, a *linguistic profile*. For each profile, column one contains a reference number and column two the number of informants sharing the profile. The variables are ordered from left to right according to (*non-absolute*) implicational relationships established by means of pair-wise cross-tabulations comparing the probabilities that one NS-value predicts another NS-value. The profiles are then ordered from top to bottom by sorting the contents of the columns according to highest NS-value, starting from the left-most column.

The young people sharing profiles 1 and (without siblings) 2,[10] are those 67 forming the 30% with 'All NS values' in Figure 2 above. That is, they have the values *early* for AGEARR and AGEON, *home* for SWFIRST, and *Swedish only* for LGPAR, LGSIB (if not missing), LGFRIEND, LGPREF and LFPROF. Depending on how strictly the monolingualism criterion is applied, however, some or all of these informants' nativeness could also be questioned. The earlier mentioned context variables, PARBORN, BORN and FRIENDLG, reflect some potential sources for multilingual influence not revealed in the eight NS variables included in the profiles presented in Table 2. Twelve of the 67 'all NS' young people have one or more parents born abroad and one is himself born abroad. More than half of them have close friends with mother tongues other than Swedish. If these context variables were included among the NS variables, the 'NS group' would be reduced to 12% of all the young people. Perhaps more importantly, all the young people (including this 12%) are multilingual in various degrees due to other factors than parents: school, of course, but also mass media and friends. When asked about which languages they speak, all 222 informants except one[11] report that they in addition to Swedish speak at least one (often English), or more commonly, two or up to six other languages.

---

[8] The variable FIRSTLG has here been excluded for reasons discussed above.

[9] LGSIB: SS, SO, OO, and 'no sibling'.

[10] In Table 2, however, missing values due to no siblings are not replaced.

[11] This response is probably due to a narrower interpretation of 'speaking a language'.

Table 2. *Multilingual profiles on (only) eight variables. (SS=Swedish only, SO=Swedish and other, OO=Other only.)*

Profile no.	N inf.'s	Age of onset			Language use				Proficiency
		AGE ARR	AGE ONS	SW FIRST	LG PAR	LG SIB	LG FRIEN	LG PREF	LG PROF
1	65	early	early	home	SS	SS	SS	SS	SS
2	2	early	early	home	SS	no sibling	SS	SS	SS
3	3	early	early	home	SS	no sibling	SO	SS	SS
4	1	early	early	home	SS	SS	SO	SS	SS
5	2	early	early	home	SS	SS	SS	OO	SS
6	10	early	early	home	SO	SS	SS	SS	SS
7	3	early	early	home	SO	SS	SO	SS	SS
8	6	early	early	other	SO	SS	SS	SS	SS
9	3	early	early	other	SO	SO	SS	SS	SS
10	1	early	early	other	SO	SO	SO	SS	SS
11	1	early	early	other	SO	SO	SO	SO	SO
12	3	early	early	other	OO	SO	SS	SS	SS
13	1	early	late	home	SO	SS	SO	OO	SS
14	5	early	late	other	SO	SS	SS	SS	SS
15	3	early	late	other	SO	SS	SO	SS	SS
16	5	early	late	other	SO	SO	SO	SS	SS
17	3	early	late	other	SO	SO	SS	SS	SS
18	1	late	late	other	SS	SS	SS	SS	SS
19	5	late	late	other	SO	SS	SS	SS	SS
20	8	late	late	other	SO	SO	SO	SS	SS
21	5	late	late	other	SO	SO	SS	SS	SS
22	3	late	late	other	SO	SO	SS	SO	SS
23	3	late	late	other	SO	SO	SS	OO	SS
24	4	late	late	other	OO	SO	SO	SS	SS
25	4	late	late	other	OO	SO	SO	OO	OO
26	1	late	late	other	OO	OO	SO	OO	OO
Subtotal:	*152*								
27-88	70	(70 informants distributed over 62 different profiles not represented in the table)							
Total: 88	222								

The informants who do not have NS values for all eight variables are distributed over 86 different profiles. For a few young people, 'non-heritage' multilingualism turns up in the use of both Swedish and another language with friends (profiles 3-4) or as a preference for speaking another language (profile 5). Several young people report that they learn languages through friends, resulting in degrees of competence ranging from merely a familiarity (understanding words in many languages or when friends speak a particular language, picking up words and everyday phrases) to a more active command. Similar phenomena has also been observed in, e.g., Switzerland (Franceschini 1999) and Germany (Auer & Dirim 2003, Dirim & Auer 2004). An example in our data is Emmy[12] (profile 3), who,

---

[12] All names are pseudomyms.

when asked which languages her friends have as mother tongues, reports that they can be 'everything you can think of'. Then she specifies that most have Arabic or Farsi and describes her language use with them like this:

> Emmy: "I mostly speak Swedish with them, but, you can say a little of this and that in Farsi and like that".

She also claims later in the interview that she writes SMS in different languages (including Arabic) and can understand some of what her boyfriend and his mother say when they speak Farsi with each other. In another study which is part of this project (Bodén & Grosse forthcoming), Emmy's speech in another speech situation is judged by young local listeners to be a good example of 'Gårdstenska', a label which is associated with language use in multilingual areas of Göteborg. Although she has 'NS values' on all other variables, language use with friends seems to have made an impact on how she speaks Swedish.

A majority of all informants are more or less multilingual in Swedish and one or more (other) heritage language(s). Many of them acquired Swedish in early childhood, report it to be their best and preferred language (e.g. profiles 6-10 and 12) and often also consider it their first language, either alone or in addition to another language. An important group of early learners (N=30) have started to acquire Swedish outside the family, usually at nursery school (in Table 2 represented by 14 informants in profiles 8-12). One example is Semra (profile 10), who is born in Sweden and started speaking Swedish at the age of one at nursery school. She regards Swedish as one of her first languages, along with Turkish. She uses Swedish and Turkish with parents, one older sibling and friends, but has a preference for and thinks she is best at Swedish. Conversely, there are late learners of Swedish who started learning Swedish at home; Maria (profile 13), who is also born in Sweden, started to speak Swedish by the age of three and a half, presumably with her parents and elder siblings.

As regards heritage languages other than Swedish, different patterns of language shift and maintenance are represented among the young people, from the radical shift of Julli (profile 18) to various degrees of maintenance. Heritage language(s) may be retained with parents only (e.g. profile 6), or in the entire family domain (e.g. profile 9), or also with friends — as in the case of Xavier (profile 11), from whom we know that it is Spanish, one of his first languages, that he sometimes uses with friends. He also says he is equally good at both Swedish and Spanish, and has no preference for one language over the other.

As mentioned above, most of the informants regard Swedish as their best language. The exceptions are naturally found among very late learners, such as Data (profile 26), who arrived and started to learn Swedish at school at 18 years of age. But there are also a few informants (not represented in the table) with an early age of onset of Swedish who prefer and/or think they are best at another language. And conversely, there are several with an age of onset up to ten who now favor Swedish.

4. Concluding discussion

Our presentation of the linguistic profiles which emerge from an analysis of data on our 222 informants shows, we believe, that binary distinctions such as native/non-native are not very useful in studies of language and language use in multilingual environments such as the ones in our study. When binary distinctions are used by themselves, different nativeness criteria lead to different categorizations of an informant group, while, within categories, important variation remains hidden. On the one hand, we have suggested that heterogeneity within the group of 'good candidates' for native speakership in Swedish can have significant consequences for studies of language variation in multilingual contexts such as ours. On the other, we have noted that there is enormous diversity among the young people in our informant group who do *not* qualify as 'good candidates' for native speakership in Swedish. In fact, significant numbers within our informant group don't seem to qualify to be native speakers of any language. Considering them to be non-native speakers of all their languages seems like a very unsatisfactory solution, both theoretically and methodologically. Finally, we have shown that there is no absolute implicational relationship among 'nativeness' criteria, which would make the use of one or a small number of variables adequate to divide our informants into a small number of categories. We would now like to draw some methodological and theoretical conclusions of our analysis.

When working with a fairly large and diverse informant group in a multilingual setting, such as the one in our study, we suggest that the only defensible way of proceeding is to treat the informant group initially as a single group, defined by whatever geographical, age or other criteria that have been used to delineate the object of study. Rather than dividing the group into two or three a priori categories based on one or two background variables, we have found it rewarding to learn more about our informant group by carrying out a linguistic profile analysis using combinations of a larger number of variables.[13]

Another important aspect of working with a multitude of linguistic profiles instead of a few gross categories, is the way it inspires and facilitates going back into the individual data, taking into account further variables or the same variables at a higher level of detail, or a return to the original recordings, for example to try to find explanations when apparent anomalies arise in the profile analysis. The risk if one doesn't do this is that assumptions about the relationships between background variables (e.g. age of onset and age of arrival) never actually get tested. It also allows the researcher to see the relevance of variables (e.g. in our study: mother tongues of good friends) that normally are not used as a basis for categorizing informants in terms of nativeness. In this way, less biased research can be carried out at both a macro and a micro level alternately. By moving between macro and micro, we both reduce the risk that interesting relationships and explanations are 'swept under the rug' in order to manage the data, and at the

---

[13] As noted in footnote 4, our informant group included all students of eight selected high-school classes who were willing to participate.

best chapter so far.

same time allow ourselves to make generalizations above the level of individual cases.

In this paper, linguistic profiling has been used to explore the usefulness of the binary NS/NNS distinction and various native speaker criteria in the light of data from 222 young people in multilingual urban settings in Sweden. In the near future, we plan to apply profiling to analyses of linguistic variation in the same informant group.

In conclusion, we do not exclude the possibility that a binary NS/NNS distinction may be usefully operationalized, for example, in experimental studies focusing on one particular factor in language acquisition, where subjects are chosen according to this factor and other factors carefully controlled for. But we do not believe that this distinction is useful in studies of language use, variation and change in contemporary multilingual contexts for at least two reasons. One is that no single or small number of nativeness criteria can categorize informants into (in relevant respects) homogeneous groups. The other is that there is no implicational relationship between the criteria, which would allow one criterion (e.g. age of onset) to stand for many. We find it likely that the diversity of linguistic profiles illustrated in this paper is not unique to the 222 young people in our project, but is also to be found in other similar settings. The application of a binary NS/NNS distinction in such contexts will either — if a single criterion is used — result in a categorization of informants into two widely heterogeneous groups, or — if multiple criteria are combined and only clear cases considered — result in an exclusion of a considerable number, possibly a majority, of language users from the object of study.

References

Appel, R. & R. Schoonen. 2005. "Street Language: A multilingual youth register in the Netherlands." Journal of Multilingual and Multicultural Development 26: 2. 85-117.
Auer, P. & İ. Dirim. 2003. "Socio-cultural orientation, urban youth styles and the spontaneous acquisition of Turkish by non-Turkish adolescents in Germany." Discourse constructions of youth identities, ed. by J.K. Androutsopoulos & A. Georgakopoulou, 223-246. Amsterdam: Benjamins.
Ballmer, T. 1981. "A typology of native speaker". A Festschrift for Native Speaker ed. by F. Coulmas, 51-68. The Hague: Mouton.
Block, D. 2003. The social turn in second language acquisition. Edinburgh: Edinbugh University Press.
Bodén, P. 2004. "A new variety of Swedish?" Proceedings of the Tenth Australian International Conference on Speech Science and Technology (Macquarie University, Sydney, December 8-10, 2004), 475-480. Sydney, Australia: Australian Speech Science and Technology Association Inc.
Bodén, P. & J. Grosse (forthc.) "Accent and youth language in multilingual Göteborg". Proceedings of FONETIK 2006. Lund: Department of Linguistics and Phonetics, Lund University.
Boyd, S. & K. Fraurud. 2004. "Who is an L2 speaker? Some observations based on interviews with 222 young people living in multilingual urban environments in Sweden." Presentation at Societas Linguistica Europaea 37th International Meeting (Kristiansand, Norway, July 29-August 1, 2004).
Chomsky, N. 1963. Aspects of a theory of syntax. Cambridge, MA: MIT Press.

Cook, V. J. (ed.) 2002. Portraits of the L2 User. Clevedon: Multilingual Matters.

Cook, V. J. 2003. Effects of the second language on the first. Clevedon, Buffalo: Multilingual Matters.

Coulmas, F. 1981. "Introduction: The concept of native speaker". A Festschrift for Native Speaker ed. by F. Coulmas, 1-25. The Hague: Mouton.

Davies, A. 2003. The native speaker: Myth and reality. Clevedon: Multilingual Matters.

Davies, A. 2004. "The native speaker in applied linguistics". The Handbook of Applied Linguistics ed. by A. Davies & C. Elder. Oxford: Blackwell.

de Geer, E. 2004. "Where do we find the speakers of the new minority languages in the Nordic countries?". Multilingualism in global and local perspectives ed. by K. Fraurud & K. Hyltenstam, 221-240. Selected papers from the 8th Nordic conference on Bilingualism (Stockholm: Centre for Research on Bilingualism & Rinkeby Institute of Multilingual Research, November 1-3).

Dirim, I. & P. Auer. 2004. Türkisch sprechen nicht nur die Türken. Über die Unschärfebeziehung zwischen Sprache und Ethnie in Deutschland. Berlin: Walter de Gruyter.

Doran, M. 2002. A sociolinguistic study of youth language in the Parisian suburbs: Verlan and minority identity in contemporary France. PhD diss., UMI, Ann Arbor, MI.

Doran, M. 2004. "Negotiating between bourge and racaille: Verlan as youth identity practice in suburban Paris". Negotiation of Identities in Multilingual Contexts ed. by A. Pavlenko & A. Blackledge. Clevedon: Multilingual Matters.

Firth, A. & J. Wagner. 1997. "On discourse, communication and some fundamental concepts in SLA research". Modern Language Journal 81:3. 286-300.

Franceschini, R. 1999. "Sprachadoption: der Einfluss von Minderheitssprachen auf die Mehrheit, oder: Welche Kompetenzen der Minderheitensprachen haben Mehrheitssprecher." Bulletin suisse de linguistique appliquée 69:2. 137-53.

Fraurud, K. & E. Bijvoet. 2004. "Multietniska ungdomsspråk och andra varieteter av svenska i flerspråkiga miljöer [Multiethnic youth language and other varieties of Swedish in multilingual settings]". Svenska som andraspråk ed. by K. Hyltenstam & I. Lindberg, 377-405. Lund: Studentlitteratur.

Hyltenstam, K. & N. Abrahamsson. 2003. "Maturational constraints in SLA". Handbook of Second Language Acquisition ed. by C. Doughty & M.H. Long, 539-588. Oxford: Blackwell.

Jaspaert, K., S. Kroon & R. van Hout. 1986. "Points of reference in first-language loss research". Language attrition in progress ed. by B. Weltens, K. de Bot & T. van Els, 37-52. Dordrecht: Foris Publications.

Kallmeyer, W. & I. Keim. 2003. "Linguistic variation and the construction of social identity in a German-Turkish Setting. A case study of an immigrant youth group in Mannheim, Germany". Discourse constructions of youth identities ed. by J.K. Androutsopoulos & A. Georgakopoulou, 29-46. Amsterdam: Benjamins.

Kerswill, P. & E. Torgersen (this volume). "Ethnicity as a source of changes in the London vowel system".

Koike, D. A. & J. Lispin-Gasparro. 2003. "The privilege of the non-native speaker meets the practical needs of the language teacher". The Sociolinguistics of Modern Language Classrooms: Contributions of the Native, the Near-native and the Non-native speaker ed. by C. Blyth, 263-266. Boston: Thomson Heinle.

Kotsinas, U-B. 1988. "Immigrant childrens' Swedish – a new variety?". Journal of Multilingual and Multicultural Development, Special Issue 1988:1/2. 129-140.

Kotsinas, U-B. 1992. "Immigrant adolescents' Swedish in multicultural areas". Ethnicity in Youth Culture ed. by C. Palmgren, K. Löfgren & G. Bolin, 43-62. Stockholm: Youth Culture at Stockholm University.

Kramsch. C. 1997/2003. "The privilege of the non-native speaker". Orig. in Publications of the Modern Language Association 112. 359-369. Reprinted in The sociolinguistics of modern language classrooms: Contributions of the native, the near-native and the non-native speaker ed. by C. Blyth, 251-263. Boston: Thomson Heinle.

Labov, W. 1966. The social stratification of English in New York City. Washington, D.C.: Center for Applied Linguistics.

Leung, C., R. Harris. & B. Rampton. 1997. "The idealised native speaker, reified ethnicities, and classroom realities". TESOL Quarterly 31:3. 543-576.

Long, M. 1993. "Second language acquisition as a function of age: Research findings and methodological issues". Progression and regression in language. Sociocultural, neuropsychological, & linguistic perspectives ed. by K. Hyltenstam & Å. Viberg, 196-221. Cambridge: CUP.

Piller, I. 2002. "Passing for a native speaker: Identity and success in second language learning". Journal of Sociolinguistics 6:2. 179-206.

Quist, P. 2000. "Ny københavns 'multietnolekt'. Om sprogbrug blandt unge i sprogligt og kulturelt heterogene miljøer [New Copenhagen 'multiethnolect'. About language use among young people in linguistically and culturally heterogeneous settings]". Danske talesprog bind 1. 143-211.

Rampton, B. 1995. Crossing: language and ethnicity among adolescents. London: Longman.

Singh, R. ed. 1998. The native speaker: Multilingual perspectives. London: Sage.

Language acquisition in a multilingual society
A case study in Veneto, Italy

Anna Ghimenton & Jean-Pierre Chevrot
Laboratoire LIDILEM, Grenoble

Abstract: Language construction in a multilingual environment requires using socially acceptable code, in the appropriate context. This pilot study investigates how multilingual caregivers' interactions provide children with cues for the construction and usage of the languages, within their socialisation framework. The study involves the multilingual acquisition of two sisters living in Veneto, Italy, where Italian and dialect form the extremes of a linguistic continuum. The interactions of the two siblings, aged 9 and 5, with thirteen other members of their family network were recorded. The results show that the use and the grammar of the dialect are acquired even if it is less frequently utilised in child input and output. Moreover, after a mixed utterance is addressed to the children, the children augment their dialect production. This suggests that children employ dialect as it appears more salient to them. As paradoxical as it may seem, if a given language is less frequently used as input to children in a multilingual society, this may attract their attention to it.

1. Introduction

Numerous sociolinguistic studies have been conducted in Italy, mainly due to its multilingual repertoire, given the presence of the regional dialects still spoken to this day.[1] As far as psycholinguistic research is concerned, the acquisition of Italian has been the primary focus of a number of studies.[2] The cross-fertilisation between language acquisition and language socialisation research would shed new light on both socio- and psycholinguistics, which are complementary disciplines, because language is acquired within a social network. An interdisciplinary approach, combining first language acquisition and language socialisation is a new research direction, especially as far as multilingual acquisition is concerned. The challenge in dealing with language acquisition in such a research field lies in the fact that the origin of variation, as Roberts (2002) points out, may be either developmental or societal in nature. In the case of the Italian sociolinguistic context, we shall see that both are intertwined.

The present pilot study was conducted in Veneto, one of Italy's north-eastern regions, where the acquisition of the Veneto dialect by two siblings was

---

[1] Banfi & Sobrero (1992), Berruto (2004), D'Achille (2003), De Mauro (1963), Grassi, Sobrero & Telmon (1997), Job & Vigolo (1980), Marcato (1980), Sobrero (1993).
[2] Bates, Burani, D'Amico & Barca (2001), D'Amico & Devescovi (2003), Pizzuto & Caselli (1994).

investigated. Before presenting the study and the results obtained, a brief historical and sociolinguistic outline of the Veneto region within the Italian linguistic context shall be presented. First of all, what today is considered to be standard Italian was in fact originally the dialect of Tuscany, which in the fourteenth century was chosen to be the language of culture and prestige (De Mauro 1963). The fact that there was a choice implies that numerous other languages were spoken in the area concerned. The Veneto dialect is one of these languages and it enjoyed a special status, for it was the official language of the Republic of the Serenissima, which was a powerful political force at that time (Cortelazzo 2002). Hence dialect was, and in part still is, associated with a prestigious historical-political background (Lepschy & Lepschy 1981).

Today numerous varieties are spoken in the Veneto region, depending on the locality or area. Moreover, Veneto is renowned for its dialect koiné (Grassi, Sobrero & Telmon 1997), meaning that despite the differences in, for example, the lexical or phonological aspects distinguishing one variety from another, there remains a cohesive communicative context with regard to the comprehension between speakers of different varieties. In fact, the existence of a dialect koiné implies the mutual adjustment of speakers of divergent varieties in order to find a common linguistic ground functioning as an efficient carrier of their communicative intentions (Grassi, Sobrero & Telmon 1997).

We have presented a very rough sketch of the sociolinguistic background of the region. Yet, we should point out that variation is an intrinsic part of the linguistic reality of the inhabitants of Veneto, where the language environment is prone to variation from two viewpoints. Firstly, from a local viewpoint, variation is a result of the daily contact between speakers of different varieties, given the existing koiné. Secondly, from a global viewpoint, variation is a result of the daily contact between standard and dialect. The Veneto dialects and Italian are situated on a linguistic continuum (Berruto 2004) for their use in close proximity promotes a kind of osmotic linguistic environment where languages become interwoven with one another. Language use in a multilingual society consists of the sharing of multiple codes. Within the exchanges between members of the Veneto speaking community, there is a large amount of code-switching (Grassi, Sobrero & Telmon 1997), illustrating the porous nature of languages.

Veneto's multilingual repertoire, as described so far, has led us to investigate the manner in which a child living in such an environment builds up her language repertoire. Language construction in a multilingual environment entails using a socially acceptable code in the appropriate context for the successful transmission of one's communicative intentions. One could presume that through their code use, caregivers transmit the appropriate contexts in which the respective languages may appear, providing cues for children to integrate their language socialisation and language construction.

2. The pilot study

Our pilot study was carried out in the town of Castelfranco Veneto, in the province of Treviso. We observed the repertoires of two sisters, the oldest being nine and the youngest five years old. Their mother is a secretary and their father is a truck driver and travels frequently throughout Europe. We focused on the children's language use within their family network by selecting four typical situations, indicative of their weekly routine. Table 1 below presents the details of the thirteen participants interacting with the two children and gives their family connection to the children, followed by their respective ages and places of residence, an estimate of the frequency of their contact with the children, and finally the answer to the question in which of the four situations they participated.

Table 1: *Summary table of participants*

Participant	Age	Residence	Frequency of Contact	Situation
1. Mother	35	Castelfranco	Daily	All 4
2. Father	33	Castelfranco	Twice a week (due to his occupation)	3 and 4
3. Grandmother	60	Castelfranco	Daily	3 and 4
4. Great-grandmother	88	Castelfranco	Daily	3 and 4
5. Aunt (father's sister)	35	Castelfranco	Regularly	3 and 4
6. Uncle (father's brother)	38	Castelfranco	Twice a week	3 and 4
7. Aunt	40	Castelfranco	Twice a week	3 and 4
8. Cousin	3	Castelfranco	Twice a week	3 and 4
9. Great-uncle	50	Verona	Once a month	4
10. Great-aunt	44	Verona	Once a month	4
11. Cousin C	12	Verona	Once a month	4
12. Cousin	5	Verona	Once a month	4
13. Cousin/Investigator	24	Grenoble	School holidays	1

The first situation took place at the two siblings' home, in which their mother as well as one of the investigators participated. It should be noted that the investigator's presence, as a member of the extended family, did not create any particular uneasiness since that both children are accustomed to regular family visits. The second situation took place in the children's home, where the mother was the only addressee of the siblings. It was divided into two sessions: the first at breakfast time and the second during a play session with the two sisters. In the latter, the mother did not actively participate: she only intervened to settle disputes. The third and fourth interactions took place at the grandmother's home, where the paternal extended family usually gathers to have Sunday lunch. In these two multiparty interactions, the thirteen participants present belong to four generations.

A total of six hours was recorded, comprising 2608 speech turns. The data collected were orthographically transcribed. In order to observe the code usage of each participant as well as potential age-related language choice tendencies, all exchanges were transcribed, considering them to be part of the children's daily language input. The mere analysis of each child's language output would entail detaching their language use from its social environment and thus would be counterproductive to the principal focus of our research.

Language use in a multilingual society implies the use and the mixing of multiple codes. In our case, we were confronted with utterances ranging from Italian to the Veneto varieties. The utterances collected were coded in the following categories: Italian, dialect (in all its varieties) and mixed (utterances containing both Italian and dialect words and morphemes). To justify our word classification, dialect and Italian handbooks were used (Marcato & Ursini 1998 and Dardano & Trifone 2003, respectively). The resulting criteria were mainly based on phonological cues. Ambiguous cases were not taken into consideration (for further details, see Ghimenton 2004).

Once the data were coded, we proceeded to the four analyses. Firstly, we focus on the code-switching observed in the children's input and output. As a first approach to our data, all four situations were taken into consideration: we wanted a rough sketch of the speakers' manipulation of the various languages, thus leading to more fine-tuned analyses. Secondly, taking into account the fact that the children spent most of their time with their mother, we focused on the way in which she speaks to her children, comparing it to the way she speaks to adults present in the multiparty exchanges (situations 3 and 4). Thirdly, we focused on the second situation, because given the limited number of speakers, each participant had more opportunities to produce utterances. For this analysis we first observed the children's code choice as a function of their interlocutors and then we proceeded to analyse both children's language choices in relation to the language choice in the speech turn preceding their own. Our final analysis aimed at the children's grammatical development in each language, by looking at the number of words produced per utterance in each category by each child, comparing it to the quantity produced by their mother.

3. Findings

In Sections 3.1 to 3.4 below we present the results of the four analyses of our data sketched above.

3.1   The codes in the children's input and output

In the first analysis, we extracted the minimum and maximum values for language production in Italian, the dialect or a mix of both, taking *all* four situations recorded into consideration. To illustrate, the results in Tables 2 and 3 show the production (output) and reception (input) ranges in each coded category for each child. For example, looking at the oldest child's *output* column, we can see that, out of all four situations recorded, her Italian production ranges from 72.4% to 85.3%.

Table 2: *Children's production range - mean for four situations*

	CODE	OLDEST		YOUNGEST	
		Min	Max	Min	Max
OUTPUT	Italian	72.4%	85.3%	65.2%	77.9%
	mixed	9.7%	21.6%	18.6%	31.8%
	dialect	4.6%	10.3%	1.8%	4.7%

Table 3: *Children's reception range - mean for four situations*

	CODE	OLDEST		YOUNGEST	
		Min	Max	Min	Max
INPUT	Italian	68.4%	83.1%	79.0%	87.1%
	mixed	6.8%	19.4%	8.9%	14.1%
	dialect	8.9%	12.1%	3.8%	9.8%

From this first analysis, one general trend stands out for both children in their input and output (Tables 2 and 3): the most frequently employed variety is Italian (from 65.2% to 87.1%), in second place is the mixed variety (from 6.8% to 31.8%) which is followed by dialect in third place (from 1.8% to 12.1%). Focusing on the dialect category, we notice that each child systematically receives more dialect than she produces (the input values 8.9, 12.1, 3.8, 9.8 are larger than the output values 4.6, 10.3, 1.8, 4.7, respectively). Furthermore, we can observe that the oldest receives (input value range: 8.9-12.1) and produces (output value range: 4.6-10.3) more dialect than the youngest (input value range: 3.8-9.8; output value range: 1.8-4.7).

Since age-related factors seem to impinge on the proportion of use of the respective languages, our second analysis observes how the mother addresses her children and the adult participants jointly.

3.2   Mother's code distribution in relation to her respective interlocutors

The mother's language use in all four situations is shown in Table 4 below. In situations 1 and 2, in which there were fewer participants, the mother had more opportunities to speak and consequently produced more utterances, as opposed to situations 3 and 4, which were multiparty interactions. The percentages were calculated only for situations 1 and 2, where a substantial number of utterances per cell was produced by the mother.

Table 4: *Mother's code distribution in relation to her respective addressees*

	MOTHER'S ADDRESSEE	ITALIAN	MIXED	DIALECT
Situation 1	Youngest	88.5% (31/35)	5.7% (2/35)	5.7% (2/35)
	Oldest	73.6% (28/38)	5.2% (2/38)	21.0% (8/38)
	Cousin/investigator	10.8 % (4/37)	21.6% (8/37)	67.5% (25/37)
Situation 2	Youngest	89.1% 148/166)	8.4% (14/166)	2.4% (4/166)
	Oldest	64.2% 113/176)	18.7% (33/176)	17% (30/176)
Situation 3	Youngest	9/10	1/10	0/10
	Oldest	2/2	0/2	0/2
	Aunt	0/4	2/4	2/4
	Grandmother	0/5	0/5	5/5
	Group	0/7	0/7	7/7
Situation 4	Youngest	8/12	4/12	0/12
	Oldest	3/5	0/5	2/5
	Cousin C	6/8	0/8	2/8
	Father	0/2	0/2	2/2
	Aunt	0/3	0/3	3/3

Summarising the tendencies observed from all four situations, three trends emerge. Firstly, in all situations where there were adult participants, the mother uses dialect when speaking to them. In the first situation, the mother uses 67.5% dialect when she addresses the cousin/investigator. All the utterances directed to the grand-mother (5/5) and the group of adults (7/7) are entirely in dialect. The same is true in Situation 4, where the mother addresses only dialect utterances to the father (2/2) and the aunt (3/3). Secondly, the mother prefers to use Italian when she speaks to a child. In situations 1 and 2, where it was possible to calculate the percentages, the mother's Italian production towards her children ranges from 64.2% to 89.1%. In the other situations, the values point at the same tendencies. Thirdly, the amount of dialect used by the mother when talking to a child varies according to the age of the child: the youngest child's dialect reception percentages range from 2.4% to 5.7% whereas the elder's ranges from 17% to 21%. Hence, the younger the child, the less dialect she receives. Interestingly then, there are children in Veneto who grow up in an environment where on the one hand, adults speak to them in Italian, limiting the use of dialect, although dialect is the most frequently used code in inter-adult speech.

3.3   Children's code choices as a function of the environment

This section presents a two-staged analysis of situation 2, where there were only three participants: the two children and their mother. For the first part of our analysis, we focused on the children's code choice as a function of the interlocutor, while here we look at their code choice as a function of the environment.

Table 5: *Language convergence between pairs of speakers*

	SPEAKER PAIRS	ITALIAN	MIXED	DIALECT
1.	Younger → Elder	72.0% (147/204)	20.0% (41/204)	7.8% (16/204)
	Elder → Younger	72.0% (175/243)	18.1% (44/243)	9.8% (24/243)
2.	Younger → Mother	79.2% (92/116)	18.9% (22/116)	1.7% (2/116)
	Mother → Younger	89.1% (148/166)	8.4% (14/166)	2.4% (4/166)
3.	Elder → Mother	78.8% (93/118)	11.0% (13/118)	10.1% (12/118)
	Mother → Elder	64.2% (113/176)	18.7% (33/176)	17.0% (30/176)

In Table 5, focusing on the dialect usage of the youngest towards her mother, we can see that the child produces merely 1.7% of dialect. The mother also uses very little dialect when speaking to her youngest daughter (2.4%). Yet, when speaking to her elder sister, the youngest increases the quantity of dialect, producing 7.8%. She converges toward the 9.8% that the oldest produces in the direction of her younger sister. The mother too augments her dialect production when speaking to the oldest child, producing 17% in that category. The elder sister's production of dialect, however, remains relatively stable with her respective interlocutors (9.8% and 10.1%).

To sum up, the mother's uneven code distribution appears to influence the youngest child's dialect production: with her older sister, she augments her dialect production whereas she decreases her use of dialect when speaking to her mother. This may be due to the pressure exerted by the mother's distinct language preference when she talks to the youngest child. Sensitive to the mother's limited amount of dialect produced, the youngest also limits its use when speaking to her. In the case of the elder daughter, there would seem to be less pressure exerted on her code choice by her mother. This may explain why her dialect production does not alter considerably according to her respective interlocutors.

In the second stage of the analysis, we examined the language environment's potential impact on the speakers' language choice (in this case the mother and the two children). We wanted to observe if the speaker's code choice varied according to the code selected in the previous speech turn. For each speaker, we established a contingency table linking her code choice in the current turn to the previous speaker's one. The significant results emerging from the table are those concerning the mother and the elder child's production, whose language choices depend upon the code selected in the speech turn preceding their own (χ^2=28,2, df=4, p<.0001). However, as for the youngest, the results indicate a tendency (χ^2=8,5, df=4, p< .10).

For a more precise idea of the influence of the previous turn, we calculated positive or negative deviations for each code's usage rate in the current turn. Each speaker's deviations were obtained by taking the total production rate of use of a given code in the whole situation recorded, and subtracting it from the rate of use of the same code after an Italian, dialect or mixed utterance found in the previous speech turn. For instance, in Table 6, in the first cell of the first column, it is shown that 13.5% of the mother's utterances produced in the entire corpus of situation 2 recordings are mixed utterances. The 16.6% refers to the mother's rate of mixed utterances she produces following a dialect utterance. In the second column, we noted the difference between the two values (16.6 – 13.5 = 3.1). Thus after a dialect utterance, the mother's mixed category rate increases by 3.1%. In Table 6, for each speaker, we list each code's deviations after a dialect utterance and after a mixed utterance.

Table 6: *Language choice probabilities after dialect and mixed utterances in situation 2*

SPEAKER	DEVIATIONS AFTER *DIALECT*		DEVIATIONS AFTER *MIXED*	
	Frequency after dialect utterance – Frequency in corpus		Frequency after mixed utterance – Frequency in corpus	
Mother	**m** 16.6% - 13.5%	+3.1%	9.6% - 13.5%	-3.9%
	d 29.1% - 9.9%	+19.2%	8.0% - 9.9%	-1.9%
	I 54.1% - 76.5%	-22.4%	82.2% -76.5%	+5.7%
Youngest	**m** 30.4% - 20.2%	+10.2%	23.9% - 20.2%	+3.7%
	d 6.5% - 4.7%	+1.8%	8.4% - 4.7%	+3.7%
	I 63.0% - 74.9%	-11.9%	67.6% - 74.9%	-7.3%
Oldest	**m** 18.0% - 15.1%	-6.3%	18.0% - 15.1%	+2.9%
	d 32.3% - 10.3%	+22.0%	13.8% - 10.3%	+3.5%
	I 58.8% - 74.4%	-15.6%	68.0% - 74.4%	-6.4%

Starting with the dialect column, we notice that a dialect utterance has a similar impact on both the mother's and the younger child's code choice. Although quantitatively different, they are qualitatively similar. Dialect in the preceding utterance favours the production of both dialect and mixed utterances, compared to the total amount of mixed and dialect speech produced in the second situation, reducing the chances of finding further Italian. For the oldest, dialect in the preceding utterance also presents the most favourable dialect production scenario, although it decreases the quantity of mixing. Generally speaking, for all 3 speakers, a dialect utterance favours the production of further dialect in the following utterance. This is the only constant observable fact common to all the speakers.

As for the code choice after a mixed utterance, the mother displays a different trend than her children. In her case, a mixed utterance increases her Italian production rate, whereas for her children, a mixed utterance favours the further production of both mixing and dialect.

Since children do modulate their language choice in function of their addressee (the youngest child) and of the preceding speech turn (the oldest child), we can deduce that they are probably in the process of acquiring the communicative use of dialect.

3.4   Number of words per utterance produced in each category

So far we have seen that the older the child is, the more dialect she uses. Yet, this does not necessarily imply progress in the construction of dialect grammar. This augmentation of dialect usage may be due to the fact that older children receive more dialect input and thus they feel allowed to use it.

In the previous analysis, we focused on the children's language usage. In our final analysis, we investigate the children's language construction. This analysis allowed us to obtain a general idea on the developmental level in each language for each child, by using the Mean Length of Utterance, which is an index of grammatical development as well as a simple way of making one child's data comparable with another's (Brown 1973). We kept the focus on the second situation. Figure 1 shows the mean quantity of words per utterance in each category produced by each child, as well as the mother's mean, allowing for comparison.

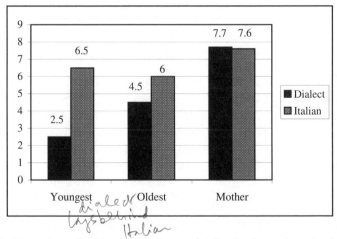

Figure 1: *Mean Length of Utterance (n words) for the 3 speakers in situation 2*

The values of the children's means per Italian utterance are close to their mother's (youngest: 6.5; oldest: 6; mother: 7.6). However, the dialect means are considerably different. The mother produces the longest dialect utterances, with

7.7 words per dialect utterance. In second place is the oldest, who produces 4.5 dialect words per utterance. The youngest produces the shortest utterances in the category, having a mean of 2.5 dialect words per utterance, which is half the number of dialect words the oldest sister produces. Whilst the children's Italian level is close to the adult's, dialect acquisition would appear to be in progress.

4. Discussion

The two children in our case study are growing up in an environment where dialect is used profusely in inter-adult speech, but it is scarcely present in child-directed speech. All our results suggest that despite this fact, the two siblings in our study are acquiring the dialect grammar and the pragmatics of dialect use. As seen in analysis 1, besides receiving more dialect, older children seem to use more of it than younger children. Thus, even if dialect is used less frequently in both the input and output of the children, its use increases with age.

Despite the fact that Italian is used very frequently in the children's input and output, the infrequent use of dialect by adults when interacting with children seems to provide cues for its appropriate communicative use. Evidence of such communicative skill was found in the first stage of analysis 3, where the youngest girl modulates her language choice in function of her addressee (in this case, the mother and the oldest daughter). Similarly, the two children tune into the language selected in the previous speech turn, as seen in the second stage of the same analysis.

Moreover, the prolific use of dialect in inter-adult speech appears to provide cues for the way the grammar functions. Indeed, in analysis 4, the elder child's mean length of utterances for dialect (4.5 words) is larger than her younger sibling's (2.5 words). Since the Mean Length of Utterance is an indication for grammatical development, this result suggests that the children are in the process of acquiring dialect.

Finally, we have evidence that the children are sensitive to dialect. We have seen this in the second stage of the third analysis, in which it appeared that the children favour dialect after a mixed speech turn, whereas the mother favours Italian. Because a mixed utterance contains both Italian and dialect, the presence of a mixed utterance in the previous speech turn provides a good indication of the saliency of each language for the respective speakers. 'Saliency' is a notion in pragmatics whereby a form stands out in the context in which it appears (Givón 2005). In our case, dialect in the preceding mixed utterance appears more salient than Italian for both siblings. A possible interpretation of the saliency of the dialect may lie in its rarity in child-directed speech: it is precisely its rarity that could attract children's attention to it. Due to its contrastive nature in child-directed speech, the dialect becomes the child's object of attention, favouring its acquisition. As noted in Givón (1995), it would appear that with time, even the less frequent marked form becomes the perceptually more salient one. So, the fact that dialect is less frequently utilised in adult-to-child speech does not necessarily imply that its early transmission is not possible or even delayed. As paradoxical as it may seem, the fact that a given language is infrequently used in input to children in a multilingual society may indeed increase its saliency, attracting their attention and enhancing their acquisition.

References

Banfi, E. & A.A. Sobrero. 1992. Il linguaggio giovanile degli anni novanta. Roma, Bari: Laterza.

Bates, E., C. Burani, S. D'Amico & L. Barca. 2001. "Word reading and picture naming in Italian". Memory and cognition 29:7. 986-999.

Berruto, G. 2004. Prima lezione di sociolinguistica. Roma/Bari: Laterza.

Brown, R. 1973. A first language: The early stages. Cambridge, Massachusetts: Harvard University Press.

Cortelazzo, M. 2002. Noi Veneti: Viaggi nella storia e nella cultura veneta. Verona: Cierre Edizioni.

D'Achille, P. 2003. L'italiano contemporaneo. Bologna: Il Mulino.

D'Amico, S. & A. Devescovi. 2003. Comunicazione e linguaggio nei bambini. Roma: Carocci.

Dardano, M. & P. Trifone. 2003. Grammatica italiana: Con nozioni di linguistica (3rd ed.). Bologna: Zanichelli.

De Mauro, T. 1963. Storia linguistica dell'Italia unità. Bari: Laterza.

Ghimenton, A. 2004. "Acquisitions langagières en situation de plurilinguisme: Etude exploratoire en Vénétie". Mémoire de DEA de Sciences du Langage, Grenoble 3.

Grassi, C., A.A. Sobrero & T. Telmon. 1997. Fondamenti di dialettologia italiana. Roma/Bari: Laterza.

Givón, T. 1995. Functionalism and grammar. Amsterdam & Philadelphia: John Benjamins.

Givón, T. 2005. Context as other minds: The pragmatics of sociality, cognition and communication. Amsterdam/Philadelphia: John Benjamins.

Job, R. & M.T. Vigolo. 1980. "Dialetto e lingua: L'aspetto psicolinguistico". Guida ai dialetti veneti II ed. by M. Cortelazzo, 149-167. Padova: Cleup.

Lepschy, A.L. & G. Lepschy. 1981. La lingua italiana : Storia e varietà dell'uso della grammatica. Milano: Bompiani.

Marcato, G. 1980. "Il significato dell'attuale recupero del dialetto nel panorama culturale veneto". Guida ai dialetti veneti II ed. by M. Cortelazzo, 9-25. Padova: Cleup.

Marcato, G. 1998. "Dialetto, storia e oralità". Dialetti Veneti: Grammatica e storia ed. by G. Marcato & F. Ursini, 5-43. Padova: Unipress.

Pizzuto, E. & C. Caselli. 1994. "The acquisition of Italian verb morphology in crosslinguistic perspective". Other children, other languages ed. by Y. Levy, 137-188. Mahwah, New Jersey: Erlbaum.

Roberts, J. 2002. "Child language variation". The handbook of language variation and change ed. by J.K. Chambers, P. Trudgill & N. Schilling-Estes, 501-525. Malden, Oxford: Blackwell Publishers.

Sobrero, A.A. 1993. Introduzione all'italiano contemporaneo. La variazione e gli usi. Bari: Laterza.

Regional accent in the German language area
How dialectally do German police answer emergency calls?

Roland Kehrein
Universität Marburg

[handwritten annotations: "op, comuns/ forensic lx."]

Abstract: The current situation of the overall language system of German — i.e., local dialects, the standard language, and intermediate varieties or styles — is very complex. This is a result of the historical development of those varieties. In this paper a case study will be presented in which the two major questions emerging from this situation are addressed: First, what do near-standard styles observable in comparable situations 'look like' in different dialect areas? Emergency call data from four locations will be studied here. It will be shown that the degree of dialectality of the speakers' styles used in the emergency calls is very similar in all cases. Second, for any one single location, how is the variation space between standard German and the local dialect shaped? The results for this issue are in line with results of existing studies dealing with the variation space in the West Middle German area, showing that speakers' competences are limited to one of three possible varieties: the regiolect.

1. Introduction[*]

This paper presents a pilot study from a comprehensive project[1] exploring the horizontal and vertical dimensions of language variation in the German language area. After introducing the project's point of departure and its principal goals and research questions, the methods and results of the pilot study will be described. The main research objectives of the project are, first, to give an exhaustive account across the entire German language area of the near-standard styles of a defined social group, i.e., policemen (the horizontal component), and, second, to describe for the same social group the variation space encompassing between standard German and the local dialects (the vertical component). The data obtained for this social group will later be complemented by comparable data from a second group for each location; so-called NORMs (i.e., "non-mobile, old, rural, male" speakers, the typical informants in traditional dialectology studies (cf.

[*] The collection of the 'emergency calls' data is funded by the German Federal Criminal Police Office (*Bundeskriminalamt*) who, in a joint project with the Research Institute for German Language "Deutscher Sprachatlas", will use parts of the data to construct a forensic database of German regional language.

[1] The project I refer to — its title is "Regionalsprache.de (REDE)" — is currently confined to the national boundaries of Germany. It is a joint project of the Research Institute for German Language "Deutscher Sprachatlas" (Marburg) and the Institute for German Language (Mannheim). Additionally, there is already a cooperative project for the German speaking parts of Switzerland being run by Helen Christen (University of Fribourg, Switzerland) using our method. Another cooperative project for Austria is currently being planned.

Chambers & Trudgill 1998: 29)). In the study presented in this paper only policemen were taken into consideration. Data of NORMs have not been collected yet.

2. Point of departure

To date, in comparison to other parts of the dynamic and variable system of the German language, only little is known about these phenomena. What is well known are the following facts. For spoken language at least, the dialects into which the German language area could be historically divided are very well described, if not the best described worldwide. This is the result of, first, the work of Georg Wenker and his collaborators, who collected data on the German dialects from almost 50,000 locations at the end of the 19th century. On the basis of these data they produced the *Sprachatlas des Deutschen Reichs* ("Linguistic Atlas of the German Empire"). It contains 570 huge, hand-drawn multi-coloured maps; over the last four years the complete atlas has been published for the first time as *Digitaler Wenker-Atlas (DiWA)* ("Digital Wenker Atlas"). Second, our comprehensive knowledge of the German dialects comes from numerous post-1960 atlas-projects which set out to collect and map the dialects of particular regions within the language area, especially central and southern regions. Comparing the older dialect data with the more recent material shows that many dialect features have remained stable for almost a century. However, and not just since the number of dialect speaking individuals seems to be constantly decreasing, dialects have nearly vanished from everyday communication in many regions. To put it in another way: in most situations, language use is oriented towards the norms of standard German. Many reasons for this state of affairs can be postulated — above all the spread of Standard German pronunciation norms as a result of by national broadcasts since the 1920s, which led to a re-evaluation of the styles previously regarded as standard German (for an exhaustive discussion of these issues, see Schmidt 2005), or the misperception of dialect-speaking individuals as having a restricted linguistic competence or a general lack of education — but these are not the topics of this paper. However, although standard-oriented styles are employed in most contexts, the regional origin of a speaker can usually still be recognised — this speech style we call the 'regional accent' (German: *Regionalakzent*).[2] It has never been studied systematically for the whole German language area (i.e., the horizontal dimension).[3] This is one of the issues about which only little is known.

Another is the question of how the variation space between dialects and standard German is structured in the different dialectal areas of the German language area (i.e., the vertical dimension — How many varieties are there in

---

[2] In this respect the term 'regional accent' is used in a manner similar to Chambers & Trudgill (1998: 4) who mostly base it on the phonetic and phonological level.
[3] There is only one atlas mapping reading styles (König 1989) plus atlases dealing with the so-called *Umgangssprache* "colloquial speech" at a lexical level (Eichhoff 1977-2000, Friebertshäuser & Dingeldein 1988, Protze 1997).

different regions?). To date, the only studies that have looked at styles pitched between standard language and dialects were focused on single locations or confined areas (cf. Macha 1991, Kreymann 1994, Lausberg 1993, Steiner 1994, Lenz 2003). Furthermore, these studies are not compatible with one another, since they use different methods of data collection and description (cf. König 1997, or Schmidt 1998).

Why are these such important and interesting issues for the overall linguistic system of German? A short glance at the development of German as a (spoken) standard language will answer this question.[4] For medieval times, the horizontal coexistence of two disparate systems — Low German in the north and High German in the middle and south of the area — can be presumed. Historically, the predominant form of oral communication in the German language area was the rural dialect, which differed from village to village. Several written vernacular traditions existed within both the Low and the High German areas. The emergence of a written German standard language is still a contentious issue. However, when people started to pronounce the new written norm — beginning in the 16th century (cf. Mattheier 2003: 229) — the speakers in the northern part of the language area had to learn this new system as if it were a second, foreign language (cf. König 1992: 110, Menke 2004: 112; see also Besch 1987). The pronunciation of this written standard in this region was therefore strongly oriented to the way it was spelled (cf. Mattheier 2003), while in the other areas the pronunciation was still strongly influenced by the local dialects and thus regionally marked (speakers could only draw on the inventory of their individual phonetic/phonological competence when pronouncing the new, written variety). Because of its close agreement between spelling and pronunciation, the northern way of pronouncing the standard language became regarded as the best way of speaking German (cf. Mattheier 2003, or Auer 2005) and thus found its way into pronunciation dictionaries, which — in the beginning — were essentially training resources for actors (e.g. Siebs 1898). This way of pronouncing the written standard language could only spread over the whole language area in the wake of the launch of a national broadcast programme in the 1920s, thus establishing the new, regionally non-marked pronunciation norm (cf. Schmidt 2005).

This means, firstly, that the relation between the old dialects and the new pronunciation norms differs in the various German dialect areas, and secondly, that the spread of the regionally non-marked pronunciation norm is only recent. Varying processes of vertical accommodation in the individual regions of the language area must therefore be expected to show up in the near-standard styles and in the variation space between the local dialects and the pronunciation norm of standard German. These, however, can only be described and analysed on the basis of comparable data from across the whole language area.

---

[4] The following statements are radically summarized and not without controversy. For an extensive discussion see already Besch (1967) and (1987), and, more recently, concerning the development of a spoken standard, Mattheier (2000), Mattheier (2003), Menke (2004), or Schmidt (2005).

What do recent studies dealing with individual locations or confined areas tell us about these related issues? I will choose two studies that are exemplary in their points of departure, construction, and methods of analyses. For the horizontal component (i.e., the near-standard styles throughout the language area) Lameli (2004a, 2004b) was able to show that city councillors in their public meetings (i.e., in a very formal situation) use a style which is close to the standard pronunciation norm but which still retains regional phonetic variants, the regional accent. Furthermore, Lameli's study suggests that, by the end of the 20th century, this style was practically the same[5] in two distinct dialectal areas (the West Middle German and Lower German areas). Only for some of the speakers who were analysed, listeners stated that they used standard German. The comparison of the results of these perception tests and the phonetic measurement of the degree of dialectality results in the claim that there might be a threshold of about 0.2 regional phonetic features per word for the perception of a sample as standard German — which means that if a sample exhibits higher values, listeners perceive it as non-standard and vice versa (cf. Lameli 2004b: 242).[6] The question now arises as to which degree of dialectality speakers from other German dialect areas display in comparable contexts and which variants constitute this linguistic style.

The second study which is of interest here was conducted by Lenz (2003). By analysing the frequency of 23 dialectal/regional variants (compared to the frequency of standard German variants) in the city of Wittlich and surrounding villages, she was able to show that the relevant variation space (vertical dimension) is occupied by three so-called 'full varieties'. According to Schmidt and Herrgen, at the individual/ cognitive level, full varieties are particular segments of linguistic knowledge (i.e., individual competences / cognitive subsystems) that are determined by independent prosodic/phonological and morphosyntactic structures and are associated with different types of social contexts (cf. Schmidt 2005). Without going into details, what is important for the project outlined in this paper is that the boundaries between the individual varieties are claimed to represent thresholds in the speakers' individual competences, as evidenced by the production of hypercorrections and dialectal hyperforms. Since Lenz's findings are hardly comparable to the few other available studies of the structure of the variation space between standard German and the base dialect of a particular location it is not yet possible to draw a complete picture for the whole German language area.

3. The 'Regional accent in the German language area' project

Our project thus addresses these two desiderata: it sets out to describe and analyse both the regional accent and the variation space between the standard language and the dialects across the entire language area. The reason for the lack of

---

[5] In terms of the degree of dialectality, not in terms of specific (chiefly consonantal) features.
[6] For details about the method used to measure dialectality and to display the phonetic differences of a sample from the pronunciation norm of standard German, see below, and Lameli (2004b).

knowledge about these subjects is in the first place a methodological one. As mentioned above, the regional accent is a style in which the speaker aims to produce standard German, but it still gives sufficient clues about his/her regional origin. This level of language in use cannot be deliberately produced. Rather, it involves a style of everyday language conditioned by extralinguistic factors, e.g. formal situation, or interlocutors who do not know each other. While people can be asked to try to speak their deepest dialect or their best standard German, it does not work when they are asked to try to speak their everyday language in front of a microphone. William Labov referred to the problems related to this as the observers' paradox: "... the aim of linguistic research in the community must be to find out how people talk when they are not being systematically observed; yet we can only obtain these data by systematic observation." (Labov 1972: 209). These problems are exacerbated in our study, in that the project aims to collect data from the whole language area. This means that a way of collecting data from a comparable context and set of speakers has to be found. The solution for these problems is not easy to find. In order to overcome the observers' paradox, we will observe the everyday language of a defined social group in a stable context using speech recordings which have not been made for linguistic analysis and in which the recorder is not visible to the speakers: we observe policemen when they answer emergency calls. Only the policemen are analysed in our studies, because only data of their social background can be obtained (they have to be born and raised in the locations or regions of interest).[7] This context displays the following characteristics:

- communication with people not known to the speaker;
- communication at a distance;
- communication in a (more or less) formal situation;
- conversations which are always recorded for forensic reasons (thus, the policemen do not feel disturbed by the recorder);
- conversations which take place in a comparable (macro-)context; the micro-contextual variation is accounted for by analysing only those emergency calls in which callers employ the standard language or can be identified as belonging to another dialectal region;
- the speakers belong to a relatively uniform social group; and
- emergency call centres are distributed across the entire language area.

The involvement of the German Federal Criminal Police Office (*Bundeskriminalamt*) in the joint project was one of the reasons we were allowed to obtain these sensitive data for our analyses. Secondly, we have coordinated principles with a data protection officer — these principles including the anonymisation of callers, the depersonification of the police staff, and secure storage of all sensitive information about criminal prosecution techniques and strategies. I will not go into further details here. All sixteen German states support our project.

---

[7] The idea of observing this social group in this particular context was developed together with Jürgen Erich Schmidt and Hermann J. Künzel.

How are the locations distributed and what is the language material like? In the project described, we will choose 150 locations evenly spread across the language area, of over 600 potential locations that are currently available. In each location linguistic data taken from two policemen and one NORM will be analysed. The emergency call recordings are of variable technical quality. This depends on the type of recorder used in the police stations. Where only inferior quality recordings are available, we will be deploying additional recorders to enhance the registration system.[8] The acoustic quality is that of a phone call, which means we will be able to analyse frequencies of between 300 and 3,400 Hertz. This has to be taken into consideration in any acoustic analysis. Regarding the content of the recordings, there are both longer passages of 'free speech' and frequently recurring sentences. This means that we have directly comparable speech material from an everyday communicative context from right across the language area.

The emergency call-answering data corpus will be supplemented by additional speech samples taken from four different contexts. Two of these investigate the individual competence in both the local dialect and standard German by asking all informants (i.e., the policemen and NORMs) to 'translate' standard sentences into their deepest dialect or their best standard German, respectively.[9] The other two represent somewhat 'natural' communicative contexts: first, an interview, i.e., a conversation with an unknown person of high social rank (a postdoctoral university employee); and second, a conversation with one or more acquaintances from the informant's home village selected by the informant. All four contexts have been empirically demonstrated to induce a particular style (located between standard German and near-dialectal styles) appropriate to the respective conversational context (vertical dimension).

4. Pilot study: How dialectally do German police answer emergency calls?

The map in Figure 1 shows the four locations chosen for the pilot study in their dialectal environments. In the following paragraphs, then, we will have a closer look at the cities of Wittlich from the Moselle-Franconian dialect grouping, Gießen in the Central Hessian dialect area, Mainz as an example of the Rhenish-Franconian dialects, and, finally, we will investigate speakers from the city of Berlin, representing the Berlinerisch dialect area. The first three all belong to the larger area of West Middle German, the latter forms a High-German linguistic enclave within the Low German territory.

The study looks at the following questions. First, what degree of dialectality can be found in the emergency call data from speakers in the four locations? This entails looking at how dialectal or regional phonetic features are distributed in the

---

[8] Namely, Marantz digital CF-recorders (PMD-670), which connect directly to the telephone, are voice controlled (i.e., the recording starts when there is a phone call and stops again as soon as the call is over), and are able to record in PCM quality.

[9] The 40 sentences developed by Georg Wenker in 1876 have been chosen as the basis for these investigations, in order to achieve comparability with the historical description of the German dialects in Wenker's *Sprachatlas des Deutschen Reichs* (see above).

speech samples. Second, for one location (Wittlich), which dialectal or regional variants of fixed variables occur in the emergency calls? Are the qualities of the variants found comparable to those Lenz detected in the styles displaying the regional accent in her study? Third, for Gießen, in what respects do speech samples taken from several of the communicative contexts described above differ from one another? How many non-standard phonetic features and which regional variants can be found in the different samples and what do the findings tell us about the speakers' individual competences (in terms of the number of handled varieties)? Our investigation is therefore quantitative as well as qualitative.

Figure 1: *Locations chosen for the pilot study*

4.1   The dialectality of emergency calls

The degree of dialectality is measured using a method developed by Herrgen and Schmidt in 1989 and improved by Lameli (2004b). It measures dialectality as, coarticulatory phenomena aside, the phonetic divergence of a sample from the codified standard pronunciation (as represented in pronunciation dictionaries).[10] The degree of dialectality of a sample is expressed as a D-value displaying the number of phonetic differences per word for a sample of at least 100 to 150 types. This method is purposefully confined to the level of segmental phonetics. Regional characteristics on other linguistic levels (morphosyntax, lexicon, or prosody) will be dealt with in subsequent analyses. The method was selected because it has been successfully tested for German dialects as well as near-standard styles, and thus allows making comparisons to existing studies.[11] In the

---

[10] For further details of the procedure see Lameli (2004a, 2004b, in press).

[11] Those are for example Lameli (2004b), Steiner (1994), Schmitt (1992), MRhSA, Hilgert (1995), Ottersbach (2002). For an exhaustive discussion of alternative methods to measure phonetic distances, see Herrgen & Schmidt (1989), or Heeringa (2004).

study described here, the measurement for each informant is based on more than 300 tokens. Although the codified standard pronunciation is a hypothetical reference point, it was empirically verified by Lameli (2004b) via measurements of the language use of speech-trained television newsreaders who produced a dialectality score of about 0.025 (cf. Lameli 2004b: 87), i.e., one phonetic segment in every 40th word differs from the pronunciation norm in just one phonetic feature, e.g. rounded vs. spread, or voiced vs. voiceless. However, in studies in which speech samples of NORMs have been measured, D-values of between 2.3 and 3.5 dialectal phonetic features per word can be observed (cf. MRhSA 1994-2002, Schmitt 1992, Hilgert 1995).

Table 1: *Degrees of dialectality in emergency calls and comparable studies*

Location	Informant	Emergency calls		City council meetings (Lameli 2004b)	Interviews (Ottersbach 2002)
		D-value	number of tokens	D-value	D-value
Gießen	GI1	0.55	328		
	GI2	0.46	340		
Wittlich	WIT1	0.48	331		mean: 0.41
	WIT5	0.42	319		
Mainz	MZ4	0.48	309	mean: 0.34	
	MZ7	0.55	311		
Berlin	B1	0.58	335		
	B2	0.54	363		

Table 1 shows the results of the measurement of dialectality in the answering of emergency calls. The values are obviously quite constant from speaker to speaker and thus from location to location. This should be ascertained statistically, but the test has not been implemented yet. The D-value of about 0.5 means that in every second word there is a phonetic segment which differs from the pronunciation norm in one feature that can clearly be classified as dialectal or regional. Secondly, on the basis of existing studies employing the same method, the D-values imply that the style employed in emergency calls is comparable to styles used in other quite formal situations (city council meetings, interviews) and, like the latter, ranges from directly below standard German within the variation space of interest (cf. Steiner 1994, Ottersbach 2002, Lameli 2004b). The phonetic segments which display regionally marked features predominantly belong to the consonantal system, as was also found by Lameli (2004b) in his study. In addition, in Berlin we find many regional deviations that are bound to certain lexemes (e.g. [dat] vs. [das], "that", [vat] vs. [vas], "what", [ik] vs. [iç], "I"). All in all, these findings imply that — at least for the four locations studied — we have empirical verification that a near-standard style which can be called regional accent can be observed in the communicative context of 'answering emergency calls'. Furthermore, the fact that the regionally marked features are primarily consonantal suggests that such features are rather inadvertently used by the speakers, given that these are less salient than vocalic features.[12]

premature

4.2   The characteristics of the regional features

As mentioned, Lenz (2003) showed for the varieties and styles within the variation space of interest in Wittlich that regional features in the near-standard styles do not necessarily originate from the historical local dialect recorded in *innovations* Georg Wenker's *Sprachatlas des Deutschen Reichs*. Rather, some of these features reflect more recent characteristics of larger areas. This prompted the control of two aspects for two different locations. First, do the regional features in the Wittlich emergency calls correspond to those with which Lenz characterised the regional accent of this location? Second, which of the features employed when translating sentences into their best local dialect are also found in the emergency call samples (from Gießen) — and why?

Let us turn to Wittlich first. Primarily via the analysis of the frequency of 23 selected variables in four different communicative contexts, Lenz performed an exhaustive study of the variation space (vertical dimension) in Wittlich. Each context forced the speakers to use a different style ranging between dialect and standard German.[13] These styles each correspond to particular dialectal or regional phonetic variants. The alignment of the linguistic variation space and the corresponding variants are depicted in Table 2 (cf. Lenz 2003: 188 and 395).

Table 2: *Linguistic variation space and corresponding variants in Wittlich*

Full Varieties	Styles	Variables occurring as regional variants (Lenz 2003)	Variables occurring as regional variants (Emergency calls)
Standard German			
Regiolect	Regional Accent	$V\text{-}g_{(x)}$; V-ch; $V\text{-}nicht_{(nisch)}$; $V\text{-}ig$; $V\text{-}pf_{(f)}$	$V\text{-}g_{(x)}$; V-ch
	Upper Regiolect	V-s; $V\text{-}nicht_{(nit)}$	V-s; $V\text{-}nicht_{(nit)}$
	Lower Regiolect	$V\text{-}auf_{(uf)}$; $V\text{-}g_{(ch, etc.)}$; V-auch	$V\text{-}auf_{(uf)}$; $V\text{-}g_{(ch, etc.)}$; V-auch
Dialect	Regional Dialect	V-a; V-oi; V-ö; V-ü; V-au; V-ā; V-ai; $V\text{-}pf_{(p)}$; V-heute; V-b	[not observed]
	Local Dialect	V-i; $V\text{-}auf_{(up)}$; V-haben	[not observed]

this is hard to interpret

A comparison of the regional phonetic features examined in Lenz's study (third column of Table 2) with the variants found in the emergency calls (right-hand column) shows that those variants which distinguish the near-standard styles in

---

[12] 'Salience' in this context means 'more or less apparent to speakers and listeners' (see also Trudgill 1986: 11). This has to be affirmed by perception experiments.
[13] Earlier studies which made use of the method of context-induced styles or language use include Macha (1991), Lausberg (1993), Kreymann (1994), Steiner (1994), Hilgert (1995).

Lenz's study occur in the latter. Some of these cannot be related to the historical dialect of Wittlich. In the other direction, those variants which only show up in dialectal communication in Lenz's study are completely absent from the emergency calls. Hence, in addition to the results of the quantitative analysis (D-values), the emergency call data can also be qualitatively classified as exhibiting the regional accent style.

The second question regarding the characteristics of the regional variants has been studied using data from Gießen. For this pilot study, policemen in Gießen were interviewed and also asked to translate Wenker's sentences into the local dialect.[14] In the interview contexts, the speakers essentially used the same style as in their emergency calls, an observation based on both the degree of dialectality and the qualities of the regional variants detected. So what does a comparison of these near-standard style contexts with the same informants' translation tasks show?

Table 3: *Degrees of dialectality in emergency calls and dialect translations in Gießen*

Location	Informant	Emergency calls		Dialect translations	
		D-value	number of tokens	D-value	number of types
Gießen	GI1	0.55	328	1.34	137
	GI2	0.46	340	1.80	147

As can be seen in Table 3, the degree of dialectality is clearly higher in the translations than in the emergency-call situation. The D-values of 1.34 and 1.8 are in line with other recent studies in which dialectal competence of non-NORMs was studied.[15] A closer view at the bandwidth between the individual D-values appearing in the two contexts reveals a considerable difference between the two speakers: While the D-values in the emergency calls are almost the same,[16] those of the translations clearly diverge. This could be due to differing degrees of dialect consciousness, where the speaker with a higher dialect consciousness (GI2) supresses his dialect features in certain contexts. The question which has to be answered now concerns the nature of the dialectal or regional variants found in the policemen's translation samples.[17] The following points can be made. The emergency call data contains regional variants which can be related to the historical local dialect. As in both Lameli's Mainz study and my own investigations in Mainz and Wittlich, most of these are consonantal features. This style also contains regional variants which most probably should be classified as

---

[14] The sentences were read out to them by myself in standard German.

[15] Cf. Steiner (1994) (mean D-value: 1.79), Ottersbach (2002) (mean D-value: 1.56).

[16] Remember that for both policemen only those emergency calls were analysed in which the caller used standard German or clearly showed regional or dialectal features from other dialect areas. The difference of 0.09 between the speakers will probably not be perceptually relevant.

[17] A frequency analysis of the regional or dialectal variants for each communicative context still needs to be performed using larger samples (of at least 1,000 tokens).

features of different larger areas, e.g. the shift of both [ç] and [ʃ] towards the intermediate [ɕ]. Detecting the current extents of those areas is one of the project's objectives. Finally, forms appear in the emergency call data which suggest that speakers are trying to suppress a presumably regionally marked form, giving rise to hypercorrections. The term 'hypercorrection' is not used in the Labovian sense here (cf. Labov 1972: 126), but is rather meant to express that these speakers unsuccessfully try to produce standard German forms; an example is the complete shift of [ʃ] to [ç]. In the translations, on the other hand, all the regional variants from the emergency calls — but not the hypercorrections — can be observed, along with additional features originating from the historical local dialect. In this case, however, most of the latter are variants in the vowel system. The translations also contain variants from dialects of both the immediate and more distant neighbourhood of the informants' places of birth. Finally, and this is especially interesting, the speakers employ variants which do not belong to any dialectal system in the area. We will call these variants dialectal hyperforms.

4.3   Discussion

How can these findings concerning the frequency and character (i.e., quantity and quality) of the regional or dialectal variants be interpreted? Speakers who in the interviews describe themselves as not competent in dialect nevertheless display a higher D-value in the translation tasks than in the emergency calls. However, the variants which occur in these translation tasks seem for the most part to be 'remembered', highly salient vocalic variants. There are three pieces of evidence for this lack of 'real' dialectal competence: First, it can be observed that the appropriate variants do not show up regularly but rather by accident. Second, the speakers use variants which occur only in neighbouring dialects. And third, the speakers produce dialectal hyperforms, i.e., variants which cannot be assigned to any dialect within the nearer or wider environments, but which merely sound dialectal to the speakers. All in all, this means that these speakers manage their communicative life using only one full variety — in Schmidt's and Herrgen's sense the so-called regiolect — within which they can shift between different styles, dependent on the communicative context. Every attempt to switch to another variety, however, whether the standard language or the local dialect, fails. The hypercorrections and dialectal hyperforms must be regarded as 'surface evidence' for cognitive barriers between individual competence segments which these speakers are unable to overcome completely.

  It can thus be concluded that, at least for the West Middle German area, speakers answering emergency calls (and probably in other contexts requiring remote communication with strangers) use a style that is explicitly oriented towards the pronunciation norm of standard German but still regionally marked — what we have been calling the regional accent style. This means, firstly, that the described method for observing this style in an everyday situation has been successfully tested for this dialect area. The analysis of the variation space between standard German and the local dialect performed so far validates an assumption raised by Bellmann as early as 1983:

> "Die praktische Kommunikation der überwiegenden Mehrheit der Individuen findet heute inventarmäßig in dem breiten Spektrum des mittleren Bereiches statt, meidet womöglich überhaupt den Dialekt und erreicht nicht völlig [...] die kodifizierte Norm der Standardsprechsprache" [With regard to the linguistic inventory, the practical communication of the vast majority of individuals today takes place within the broad spectrum of the middle zone, completely avoiding the dialect wherever possible, and not completely reaching the codified norm of the standard language] (Bellmann 1983, 117).

In this case, *mittlerer Bereich* "middle zone" is equivalent to what I referred to as regiolect, i.e. a transitional space between dialect and standard language, in which several styles can be differentiated. The question of how many styles can be differentiated within the regiolect still has to be answered by analysing additional speech samples taken from other communicative contexts. On the basis of the data analysed in the pilot study, at least two styles — it is not clear of how many, yet, — which the speakers use in different communicative contexts can be posited (see Figure 2): a regional accent for formal situations and a style which is comparable to Lenz's lower regiolect, if those speakers are asked to produce their deepest dialect.

Full Varieties	Styles
Standard German	
Regiolect	**Regional Accent**
	intermediate style?
	intermediate style?
	Lower Regiolect
Dialect	

Figure 2: *Possible linguistic variation space of policemen in Gießen*

5. Prospects

Measurement of the dialectality of emergency call and interview data from a policeman from Waldshut-Tiengen (High Alemannic language area) results in D-values of 1.2 and 1.1 (remember that the D-values for the emergency call data of the speakers from Gießen were 0.55 and 0.46). There are three competing interpretations for this preliminary result that shows a higher degree of dialectality in the same context of communication. 1) Either it means that dialectal or regional features are still playing a more important role — even with people not known to the speaker, or from different linguistic regions — in everyday communication in this area, compared to the West Middle German area analysed in the pilot study, or 2) that the individual analysed for the High Alemannic area represents a different type of speaker, whose competence spans a lower, near-dialectal segment of the variation space. Perhaps this speaker's field of competence even includes 'real' competence in the dialect variety. 3) Finally, it is possible that the variation space between standard German and the local dialects is shaped differently in this region, and does not show a relatively broad regiolect but instead consists of a dialect variety known to most speakers plus near-standard styles which are still strongly regionally marked.[18] The analyses, within the framework of the project sketched above, of, first, more speakers from this area, and second, speakers from the other German dialect areas will supply answers to questions like these.

References

Ammon, U. 2003. "Dialektschwund, Dialekt-Standard-Kontinuum, Diglossie: Drei Typen des Verhältnisses Dialekt – Standardvarietät im deutschen Sprachgebiet". Standardfragen. Soziolinguistische Perspektiven auf Sprachgeschichte, Sprachkontakt und Sprachvariation ed. by J.K. Androutsopoulos & E. Ziegler, 163-171. Frankfurt am Main: Peter Lang.
Auer, P. 2005. "Europe's sociolinguistic unity, or: A typology of European dialect/standard constellations". Perspectives on variation. Sociolinguistic, historical, comparative ed. by N. Delbecque et al., 7-42. Berlin/New York: Mouton de Gruyter.
Bellmann, G. 1983. "Probleme des Substandards im Deutschen". Aspekte der Dialekttheorie ed. by K.J. Mattheier, 105-130. Tübingen: Niemeyer.
Besch, W. 1967. Sprachlandschaften und Sprachausgleich im 15. Jahrhundert. Studien zur Erforschung der spätmittelhochdeutschen Schreibdialekte und zur Entstehung der neuhochdeutschen Schriftsprache. München: Francke.
Besch, W. 1987. Die Entstehung der deutschen Schriftsprache. Bisherige Erklärungsmodelle - neuester Forschungsstand. Opladen: Westdeutscher Verlag.
Chambers, J.K. & P. Trudgill. 1998. Dialectology. Second edition. Cambridge: CUP.
Digitaler Wenker-Atlas (DiWA) 2001-2003. Hrsg. von J.E. Schmidt und J. Herrgen. Bearbeitet von A. Lameli, A. Lenz, J. Nickel und R. Kehrein, K.-H. Müller, S. Rabanus. Erste vollständige Ausgabe von Georg Wenkers "Sprachatlas des Deutschen Reichs". 1888 - 1923 handgezeichnet von Emil Maurmann, Georg Wenker und Ferdinand Wrede. Marburg: Forschungsinstitut für deutsche Sprache "Deutscher Sprachatlas". <www.diwa.info> (23 July 2006).
Eichhoff, J. 1977-2000. Wortatlas der Deutschen Umgangssprachen. Bern etc.: Saur.
Friebertshäuser, H. & H.J. Dingeldein 1988. Wortgeographie der städtischen Alltagssprache in Hessen. Tübingen: Francke.
Heeringa, W. 2004. Measuring dialect pronunciation differences using Levenshtein distance. PhD diss., University of Groningen.
Herrgen, J. & J.E. Schmidt 1989. "Dialektalitätsareale und Dialektabbau". Dialektgeographie und Dialektologie. Günter Bellmann zum 60. Geburtstag von seinen Schülern und Freunden ed. by W. Putschke et al., 304-346. Marburg: Elwert.
Hilgert, P. 1995. Reliktdialektalität und Sprachvariation. Untersuchungen zur variativen Kompetenz/Performanz in Neurath/Westeifel. Ms., Mainz.

---

[18] For a description of different dialect/standard constellations, cf. Schmidt (1998), Ammon (2003), and Auer (2005).

König, W. 1989. Atlas zur Aussprache des Schriftdeutschen in der Bundesrepublik Deutschland. 2 volumes. Ismaning: Hueber.

König, W. 1992. dtv-Atlas zur deutschen Sprache. Tafeln und Texte. München: Deutscher Taschenbuch Verlag.

König, W. 1997. "Phonetisch-phonologische Regionalismen in der deutschen Standardsprache. Konsequenzen für den Unterricht 'Deutsch als Fremdsprache'?". Varietäten des Deutschen. Regional- und Umgangssprachen ed. by G. Stickel, 246-270. Berlin/New York: De Gruyter.

Kreymann, M. 1994. Aktueller Sprachwandel im Rheinland. Empirische Studie im Rahmen des Erp-Projektes. Köln [etc.]: Böhlau.

Labov, W. 1972. Sociolinguistic patterns. Philadelphia: University of Pennsylvania Press.

Lameli, A. 2004a. "Hierarchies of dialect features in a diachronic view - implicational scaling of real time data". Language variation in Europe. Papers from the Second International Conference on Language Variation in Europe (ICLaVE 2), Uppsala-University, Sweden, June 12-14, 2003 ed. by B.-L. Gunnarsson et al., 253-266. Uppsala: University Press.

Lameli, A. 2004b. Standard und Substandard. Regionalismen im diachronen Längsschnitt (ZDL-Beiheft 128). Stuttgart: Steiner.

Lameli, A. (in press). "Phonetic measurement and metalinguistic judgment". Canadian Journal of Linguistics 49:2/3. 1001-1034.

Lausberg, H. 1993. Situative und individuelle Sprachvariation im Rheinland. Köln [etc.]: Böhlau.

Lenz, A. 2003. Struktur und Dynamik des Substandards. Eine Studie zum Westmitteldeutschen (Wittlich/Eifel). (ZDL-Beiheft 125). Stuttgart: Steiner.

Macha, J. 1991. Der flexible Sprecher. Untersuchungen zu Sprache und Sprachbewußtsein rheinischer Handwerksmeister. Köln [etc.]: Böhlau.

Mattheier, K.J. 2000. "German". Germanic Standardizations. Past to Present ed. by A. Deumert & W. Vandenbussche, 211-244. Amsterdam/Philadelphia: Benjamins.

Mattheier, K.J. 2003. "Die Durchsetzung der deutschen Hochsprache im 19. und beginnenden 20. Jahrhundert: sprachgeographisch, sprachsoziologisch". Sprachgeschichte. Ein Handbuch zur Geschichte der deutschen Sprache und ihrer Erfoschung. 2. Teilband. 2. vollst. neu bearb. u. erw. Auflage, (HSK 2.2) ed. by W. Besch et al., 1951-1967. Berlin/New York: De Gruyter

Menke, H. 2004. "Niederdeutsch als Geber, Nehmer- oder Mittlersprache". Deutsch im Kontakt mit germanischen Sprachen ed. by H. Munske, 99-118. Tübingen: Niemeyer.

Mihm, A. 2004. Zur Geschichte der Auslautverhärtung und ihrer Erforschung. Sprachwissenschaft. 133-206.

Mittelrheinischer Sprachatlas (MRhSA) 1994-2002 ed. by G. Bellmann, J. Herrgen & J.E. Schmidt. 5 volumes. Tübingen: Niemeyer.

Ottersbach, L. 2002. Verdichtungsbereiche im Wittlicher Substandard. Zum Zusammenhang von Variablenanalyse und Dialektalitätsmessung. Ms., Marburg.

Protze, H. 1997. Wortatlas der städtischen Umgangssprache. Zur territorialen Differenzierung der Sprache in Mecklenburg-Vorpommern, Brandenburg, Berlin, Sachsen-Anhalt, Sachsen und Thüringen. Köln [etc.]: Böhlau.

Schmidt, J.E. 1998. "Moderne Dialektologie und regionale Sprachgeschichte". Zeitschrift für Deutsche Philologie 117. Sonderheft: Regionale Sprachgeschichte ed. by W. Besch und H.J. Solms, 163-179.

Schmidt, J.E. 2005. "Die deutsche Standardsprache: eine Varietät - drei Oralisierungsnormen". Standardvariation - Wie viel Variation verträgt die deutsche Sprache? ed. by L.M. Eichinger & W. Kallmeyer, 278-305. Berlin/New York: De Gruyter.

Schmitt, E.H. 1992. Interdialektale Verstehbarkeit. Eine Untersuchung in Rhein- und Moselfränkischen. Stuttgart: Steiner.

Siebs, T. 1898. Deutsche Bühnenaussprache. Ergebnisse der Beratungen zur ausgleichenden Regelung der deutschen Bühnenaussprache. Berlin [etc.]: Ahn.

Steiner, C. 1994. Sprachvariation in Mainz. Quantitative und qualitative Analysen. Stuttgart: Steiner.

Trudgill, P. 1986. Dialects in contact. Oxford: Blackwell.

Sustainable Linguicism

Miklós Kontra

University of Szeged and Hungarian Academy of Sciences, Budapest

[handwritten marginalia: like "racism", "sexism"]

Abstract: This paper concerns intralingual social discrimination between groups of people defined on the basis of language, or what Skutnabb-Kangas (1988) terms linguicism, Lippi-Green (1997) calls language subordination, and Cameron (1995) verbal hygiene. Dramatic social consequences of standard language ideology are demonstrated, drawing on the Hungarian National Sociolinguistic Survey and Myhill's (2004) concept of 'correctness'. Issues of learnability, second-dialect acquisition and the effects of educational mobility are discussed. It is shown that intralingual discrimination works best when prescriptive correctness and prestige-based correctness support each other, and the linguistic variants at issue are hard or impossible to learn in school or later in life. For language mavens, the most lucrative prescriptive rules are those that will always be violated. For linguicist societies such as most European societies, such prescriptive rules ensure sustainable linguicism. For sociolinguists and school teachers, the challenge is to make linguicism unsustainable.

[handwritten marginalia: great quote]

1. On linguicism and standard language ideology in Hungary[*]

This paper deals with social discrimination between groups of people defined on the basis of language, or, to use Tove Skutnabb-Kangas' term, it is about linguicism. The term was coined by Skutnabb-Kangas by analogy with racism, classism, sexism, and ageism. The original definition was conceived to deal with interlingual rather than intralingual discrimination:

> Linguicism can be defined as ideologies and structures which are used to legitimate, effectuate and reproduce an unequal division of power and resources (both material and non-material) between groups which are defined on the basis of language (on the basis of their mother tongues). (Skutnabb-Kangas 1988: 13)

If we delete the second parenthetical phrase, the definition also covers intralingual discrimination, i.e. the language subordination (Lippi-Green 1997) or verbal hygiene (Cameron 1995) that speakers of standard English, standard Hungarian,

---

[*] I would like to thank Jack Chambers, László Cseresnyési, Patricia Cukor-Avila, Anna Fenyvesi, Frans Hinskens, John Myhill, Dennis Preston, Peter Trudgill, and Tamás Váradi for their extremely helpful comments on an earlier draft of this paper. My gratitude is also extended to those members of the audience at the oral presentation in Amsterdam who asked questions or made critical remarks. Of course, the standard disclaimer applies.

or almost any standard variety in Europe impose on their nonstandard speaking compatriots.

In what follows, various aspects of intralingual discrimination will be addressed. The empirical foundation of much of the paper is derived from the work of Hungarian sociolinguists, much of which is published in English (see, for instance, Kontra & Pléh 1995, Kontra 2000, and Fenyvesi 2005). As a realist, I will not assume that readers are familiar with all things Hungarian and linguistic, and therefore I begin the exposition with a brief socio-historical and ideological background to the main story: language-based social discrimination of Hungarians by Hungarians.

For centuries, issues of national independence and the ('proper') use of Hungarian have been intimately tied together (see, e.g., Sherwood 1996). In 1825 the Hungarian Academy of Arts and Sciences was founded with the primary aim of enriching and cultivating the Hungarian language. The propagators of language cultivation (*nyelvművelés* in Hungarian) have had various institutional means for influencing language use. The Academy has several committees on spelling, lexicography, etc., which act sometimes as lawmakers, at other times as advisers. For instance, the official rules of Hungarian spelling issued by a committee of the Academy are held in extremely high esteem by everybody except a handful of non-linguists (what Dennis Preston refers to as "normal" people) and an even smaller handful of linguists. In spite of this high regard, at least one of these rules of spelling is violated by 98% of all Hungarians in Hungary.[1] In short, Hungarians live in what James Milroy (1999: 18) has called a "standard language culture" in which "the awareness of a superordinate standard variety is kept alive in the public mind by various channels (including the writing system and education in literacy) that tend to inculcate and maintain this knowledge – not always in a very clear or accurate form – in speakers' minds."

The linguistic profession in Hungary is split between prescriptivists, who are held in high esteem by almost everybody, including the highest-ranking academicians of the country,[2] and descriptivists, who are oftentimes regarded as traitors to the nation (see, for instance, Kontra 1997). Practitioners of linguistic science and the average Hungarian's views concerning language matters are in the same relationship as the proverbial American driver who overhears a radio

---

[1] There is a lot of variation of short u [u] and long ú [uː] in Hungarian speech, and pronunciation and spelling often disagree. For a VARBRUL study on this, see Pintzuk et al (1995). The Academy rules require the spelling *útitárs* "fellow traveler" in contrast to the normal pronunciation of the word with a short vowel. In a written correction task 97.6% of the respondents of the Hungarian National Sociolinguistic Survey (N=832) left the "incorrect" spelling *utitárs* (with short u) uncorrected (Kontra 2003a: 84 and 166). These results can safely be generalized to the entire adult population of Hungary at the fall of communism.

[2] They can be historians, brain scientists, or any other academics. My trivial point, well known from other cultures as well (see, e.g., Laforest 1999: 278, Johnson 2001: 595), is that whereas physicists or geneticists will never listen to a linguist's opinion concerning physics or genetics, they somehow feel entitled to pontificate on linguistic matters, no matter how ignorant they are. Hopefully, the reason for this is that linguists, so far, have been unable to show physicists and geneticists how ignorant they are when it comes to language matters.

conversation about some idiot who is driving down a highway in the wrong direction. "One?", he asks angrily, "Hundreds! Hundreds!"

Hungarian language cultivators or language mavens are a politically and socially powerful lobby, with extreme influence in the media and in public education. However, recently there have been a few unequivocal signs of doubt concerning their usefulness to the nation; see, for instance, Sándor (2001a), Lanstyák (2003–2004), Cseresnyési (2004), and Kálmán (2005), who have criticized language cultivators for disseminating language myths and maintaining and recreating language-based discrimination among Hungarians. Doubts concerning the social responsibility of linguists (read: language cultivators) are sometimes expressed in cartoons like the one published in the national daily Népszabadság on May 7, 2005:

Nyelvészfüllel

- Milyen jólesik ilyen régi, szép szavakat hallani, mint például ez a „cemende".!

With a linguist's ear
"My, isn't it gratifying to hear beautiful old language like
'You strumpet!'?"

Figure 1: *With a linguist's ear*

As can be seen from my translation into English, a scruffy man is brutalizing a woman in a park while two elegant linguists walk by, one of them saying: "My, isn't it gratifying to hear beautiful old language like 'You strumpet!'?"

Standard language ideology is extremely strong among Hungarians. The success of the indoctrination of teachers is well illustrated by Sándor (2001b), who asked 100 pre-service teachers of Hungarian whether there is a need for language cultivation in Hungary. Ninety-five students answered "yes", two said "no", and three admitted they did not know. The reasons given fall into four broad categories: (a) people make many mistakes, and language cultivators provide regularity to Hungarian, (b) Hungarian is intimately connected to national identity and its purity must be preserved, (c) language cultivation helps people to express themselves clearly by showing them the common and socially valid variety of the language, and (d) it is needed because it is important. This last reason, devoid of any logical argument, was the second most frequently given.

The strength of standard language ideology is also shown by the numbers of Hungarians who listen to language cultivation programs on radio or watch such programs on television. A representative survey we conducted in 1988 (cf. Kontra, ed., 2003) revealed that 33% of the adult population of Hungary watched language cultivation programs on TV frequently, and 41% watched them occasionally. Radio programs of the same kind were listened to frequently by 27%, and occasionally by 45%.

Linguistic insecurity is nevertheless rampant. For instance, cross tabulations of grammaticality judgments by respondents' rating of the importance of correct speech in "how successful one will be in life" show that the proportion of those who judge nonstandard sentences as "correct" is significantly greater among those who believe correct speech is important than among those who think it is not important (see Kontra, 2003b: 226–228). Close to half of the adult population of Hungary think that correct speech is important for success in life, but they do not exactly know what is and what is not correct.

Most Hungarian school teachers teach their subjects, whether biology, mother tongue or anything else, in a way that might cause psychological damage to pupils. When pupils use a linguistic variant that is not part of Codified Standard Hungarian (henceforth CSH), teachers will often correct them by saying "That's not Hungarian", "Hungarians don't speak that way", or "True Hungarians don't say such things". Such verbal humiliation often causes long-lasting psychological injuries in pupils because they translate the teachers' abuse as excluding their close relatives from "true Hungarians", for the simple reason that they learned the "incorrect", "non-Hungarian" forms from their mothers, fathers, siblings, grandparents, etc. The moral evaluation of such behavior was expressed in unequivocal terms by Halliday et al (1964: 105) over four decades ago:

> "A speaker who is made ashamed of his own language habits suffers a basic injury as a human being: to make anyone, especially a child, feel so ashamed is as indefensible as to make him feel ashamed of the colour of his skin."

Decades before Halliday et al, the Hungarian linguist Papp (1935) described in great detail how Hungarian school teachers stigmatized their pupils' vernacular, causing them to alienate from their families and to hypercorrect the stigmatized linguistic forms. With these unorthodox views of his, Papp always belonged to an insignificant minority among Hungarian linguists.

2. The Hungarian National Sociolinguistic Survey (HNSS)

In May 1988 we conducted a country-wide sociolinguistic survey, without having the slightest suspicion that communism would soon come to an end.[3] A random stratified sample was used (N=832; in 1990 there were 10.3 million inhabitants in Hungary, 7,474,000 of whom were 20 years of age or older), which represents the adult Hungarian population in terms of age, sex, education and residence (Budapest, cities, and villages). Ours was a truly random sample "of the type used in opinion polls, marketing research, and other social surveys" (Chambers 2003: 45). The HNSS sample had been thoroughly researched by our sociologist-collaborators, who had obtained over 1000 pieces of data from each respondent, with particular reference to their network relations (see Angelusz & Tardos 1995). Simply put, our sample allows us to generalize the findings of the HNSS to the entire adult population of Hungary at the eleventh hour of communism.

Four types of linguistic data were gathered: (1) grammaticality judgments, (2) oral sentence-completion data, (3) spotting and correcting mistakes in a written passage, and (4) choosing the correct variant of alternative forms provided in a written passage. Each respondent contributed a total of 68 tokens to the entire data set. In the judgment task, following a trial phase, respondents had to judge whether each of 34 sentences given to them on index cards was "grammatically correct." In the 16 oral sentence-completion tasks, respondents had to insert the appropriate form of a word (whose citation form was printed in the margin of the index card) into a blank in a sentence, and say the entire sentence out loud. In what follows I will only refer to the first three kinds of data: judgments, oral completions, and written corrections.[4]

There are two features of the HNSS which distinguish it from most western sociolinguistic investigations. First, we used grammaticality judgments and oral sentence-completion data, rather than tape-recorded speech. Thus, while in most western research statements like "women use more higher-prestige variants" describe the findings, in the HNSS statements like "more women used the higher-prestige variant" are appropriate. Second, most western research has been conducted in fairly well defined speech communities such as Lower Manhattan, Norwich (England), Copenhagen, etc. However, the HNSS is a country-wide study conducted in 100 localities across Hungary. This allows generalizations only for two speech communities: (1) the capital city of Budapest, which provided one-fifth of the respondents, and (2) Hungary as a country. As Mendoza-Denton (2002: 478) reminds us, "trading in one methodology for another [...] does not allow the object of investigation to remain constant". Because the HNSS is quite unique in sampling and unusual in methodology, any comparisons of its findings

---

[3] The survey was jointly administered by the Linguistics Institute of the Hungarian Academy of Sciences and the now defunct *Tömegkommunikációs Kutatóközpont* (Mass Media Research Institute) of Hungarian Radio and Television. The questionnaire was compiled by Csaba Pléh, Tamás Terestyéni and myself. For an English review of the major HNSS publication (Kontra, ed., 2003), see Cseresnyési (2005).

[4] For further details of sampling and data collection, see Kontra, ed., (2003).

to other published findings should be performed with utmost care. One could also say that of the three types of factors influencing variation with different strengths (Preston 2001: 280), the HNSS has much to say about the effect of social factors but (much) less about linguistic factors and stylistic factors.[5]

3. The linguistic variables in this study

Of the 16 linguistic variables studied in the HNSS, nine will be used in this paper. Their description below is somewhat simplified.[6] The variables will be numbered 1 through 9 in the following way: 1-(bVn) indicates variable 1 or the (bVn) variable, 2-(bV) indicates variable 2 or the (bV) variable and so on. The variants of a variable will also be numbered in the same way, for instance, 1-[bVn] is the standard variant and 1-[bV] the nonstandard variant of 1-(bVn).

1-(bVn) or the inessive case ending of nouns as in *ház-ban* "within (a) house" or *víz-ben* "within (the) water" depending on vowel harmony. (bVn) has two variants: CSH 1-[bVn] and nonstandard 1-[bV].

2-(bV) or the illative case ending of nouns as in *ház-ba* "into (a) house" or *víz-be* "into (the) water". The two variants are: 2-[bV] and hypercorrect 2-[bVn] (which coincides with the standard variant of the 1-(bVn) variable).

3-(m) or the 1Sg ending in the indefinite conjugation of verbs with the *-ik* formative (in the 3Sg present indicative some Hungarian verbs end in *-ik*, as in *esz-ik* "s/he eats" while others end in zero, as in *néz-0* "s/he looks". In the past, *-ik* and non-*ik* verbs formally differed in the indefinite conjugation, as in *eszem egy almát* "I eat an apple" vs. *nézek egy almát* "I look at an apple". In the definite conjugation there was no such formal difference: *eszem az almát* "I eat the apple" vs. *nézem az almát* "I look at the apple". Since about the 17th century, this formal difference has been breaking down and today there is variation between the original and more prestigious *eszem egy almát* and the often stigmatized *eszek egy almát*, both meaning "I eat an apple". The 3-(m) variable has a codified standard and high-prestige variant 3-[m] and a somewhat stigmatized and low-prestige variant 3-[k].

4-(nVk) or the 1Sg present conditional ending of verbs in the indefinite conjugation as in standard *lép-nék* "I would step" and *alud-nék* "I would sleep". The latter form violates vowel harmony, in contrast with the nonstandard form

---

[5] Nor does the design of the study allow us to say much about the effect of geographical factors, although some statistically significant differences can be found. For example, two-thirds of the respondents in the western Hungarian dialect area judged the nonstandard 1Sg present conditional verbal ending *-nák* correct, but only one-third of the respondents in the north-eastern dialect area did so.

[6] For more thorough structural descriptions, readers may consult Kenesei, Vago & Fenyvesi (1998) or Siptár & Törkenczy (2000).

alud-nák, which observes it. The variants are standard 4-[nék] and nonstandard 4-[nák].

5-(t-final verbs in the indicative). Speakers of standard Hungarian maintain a formal distinction between some of the indicative and imperative forms of verbs ending in -t or -szt, e.g. *látjuk* [laːt^{y}ːuk] "we see (it), definite conjugation" and *választjuk* [vaːlɔst^{y}uk] "we choose (it), definite conjugation" vs. *lássuk* [laːšːuk] "let us see (it)" and *válasszuk* [vaːlɔsːuk] "let us choose (it)".[7] Nonstandard speakers use the latter forms as both indicative and imperative. The two variants of this variable can be formalized as 5-[indicative ≠ imperative] and 5-[indicative = imperative]. The first is the standard variant, the second is nonstandard and badly stigmatized.

6-(t-final verbs in the imperative/subjunctive). In standard Hungarian an indirect command such as *Dénes azt mondta, hogy válasszuk ki a legjobb könyvet* "Dennis told us to choose the best book" has an imperative verb. Subjunctive clauses, which are complements to a distinct class of verbs and adjectives, have verbs formally identical to imperatives, e.g. *Nem szükséges, hogy kiválasszuk a legjobb könyvet* "It is not necessary that we should choose the best book" (note that in the indirect command the prefix *ki* "out" follows the verb but in the subjunctive the prefix obligatorily precedes it). Speakers who are stigmatized for using the nonstandard [indicative = imperative] conjugation of the previous variable will often avoid the imperative/subjunctive forms of t-final verbs in cases when standard speakers use them, which results in hypercorrection as in *Dénes azt mondta, hogy választjuk ki a legjobb könyvet* or *Nem szükséges, hogy kiválasztjuk a legjobb könyvet*. The two variants of this variable can be formalized as 6-[standard imperative/subjunctive forms] and 6-[standard indicative forms]. Use of the latter variant is hypercorrect.

7-(adjective+that-clause). CSH has structures like *Természetes, hogy beteg* "It is natural that s/he is ill" and *Természetesen beteg* "Naturally, s/he is ill". There is a vigorous ongoing syntactic change which appears to result from a contamination of the two standard structures, yielding *Természetesen, hogy beteg*, with the sentence adverb *természetesen* followed by a *hogy*-clause. The new structure is

---

[7] The phonology is actually more complicated than shown here. There are three subclasses of verbs ending in t: verbs ending in a vowel+t (Vt) such as *lát* "see", those ending in a sonorant+t (Rt) such as *márt* "soak, dip", and those ending in an obstruent+t (Ot) such as *választ* "choose". For a detailed discussion of t-final verbs in the HNSS, see Váradi & Kontra (1995) where it is shown that Hungarians fall into three groups: (a) standard speakers, who maintain the indicative vs. imperative distinction with all t-final verbs, (b) semistandard speakers, who maintain the distinction with verbs ending in Vt but not with verbs ending in Ot, and (c) nonstandard speakers, who never maintain the distinction. The nonstandard use of t-final verbs is differentially stigmatized: nonstandard Vt verbs are much more stigmatized than nonstandard Ot verbs. (Unfortunately, we did not include Rt-stems in the HNSS questionnaire, and therefore we cannot say anything about a possible sociolinguistic difference regarding Vt- vs. Rt-stem verbs.)

proscribed by language cultivators. It translates into English as ungrammatical "Naturally that s/he is ill". This variable has three variants: 7-[adjective+that-clause], 7-[adverb+clause] and 7-[adverb+that-clause]. The first two variants are standard, the third is nonstandard.

8-(e) or the question clitic *-e* "whether", which in CSH has to be cliticized onto the verb in imbedded yes-no questions, e.g. *Kérdezte, nem esik-e a hó* "S/he asked whether it was snowing" (where *esik* is the verb meaning "(it) falls"). In nonstandard Hungarian the question clitic can be attached to a preverbal focused constituent or to a preverbal negative particle as in (1):

(1)   Kérdez-te,   nem-e   es-ik   a hó.
       ask-PAST.3SG   not-particle fall-3SG the snow
       "S/he asked whether it was snowing."

For our purposes here the two variants are: standard 8-[verb+-e] and stigmatized 8-[nem+-e].

9-(*a miatt*). In CSH the demonstrative "that" has two allomorphs: *a* must precede words beginning with a consonant, e.g. *a miatt* "because of that", and *az* must precede words beginning with a vowel, e.g. *az alatt* "below that". In what is termed careless and nonstandard Hungarian by language cultivators, phrases like *az miatt* are fairly frequently used. This variable has two variants: standard 9-[a miatt] and nonstandard 9-[az miatt].

4. The independent social variables

In addition to sex, the following independent variables have been used:

- Educational achievement, or education for short, has four levels in the study: those who completed fewer than 8 grades, those completing 8 grades, then high-school graduates with 12 years of schooling, and finally college or university degree holders.[8]
- Residence has four levels: respondents in the capital city of Budapest, those living in cities (Hungarian *városok*) in the provinces, then those living in villages with more than 5000 inhabitants, and those in villages with fewer than 5000 residents.
- Age has 7 levels, sometimes collapsed into three (18–30-year-olds, 31–60-year-olds, and people 61 or older).

Apart from these stratifying variables also mentioned in Section 2 above, data were also collected for the following five social variables:

---

[8] When the HNSS was conducted, college (Hungarian *főiskolai*) degrees were awarded after four years of study while university (Hungarian *egyetemi*) degrees were awarded after 5 or 6 years.

– Occupation was used instead of social class, with four levels: (a) upper-level managers and college/university-trained intellectuals, (b) other white-collar workers, (c) skilled workers, and (d) unskilled workers.
– Commuters and non-commuters are the two levels defined for the factor of commuting.
– Ethnicity splits into those whom the fieldworkers judged to be Gypsies and those not so judged.
– Educational mobility has two levels: upwardly mobiles vs. immobiles together with downwardly mobiles. This variable captures mobility by comparing a respondent's educational level to that of his/her father.
– "Consumption of language cultivation" subsumes three variables: those constructed from the answers to the question (a) "(How often) do you listen to language cultivation programs on the radio?", then (b) "(How often) do you read articles on language cultivation in newspapers or books?", and (c) "(How often) do you watch language cultivation programs on TV?".

5. Standard Hungarian ideology and its targets

Standard language ideology in Hungary is hegemonic, in the sense in which Wiley (1996: 113) defines it:

> "Linguistic hegemony is achieved when dominant groups create a consensus by convincing others to accept their language norms and usage as standard or paradigmatic. Hegemony is ensured when they can convince those who fail to meet those standards to view their failure as being the result of the inadequacy of their own language […]. Schools have been the principal instruments in promoting a consensus regarding the alleged superiority of standardized languages."

What I will do now is look closely at the "others" who accept "the norms", and the norms themselves, one by one. At first blush, Wiley's description of linguistic hegemony fits all Hungarians in Hungary.[9] In reality, however, we see a lot of interesting variation. In a review, Miller (1999: 121) cogently states that "Tame standard codes can be laid down, but taming millions of exuberant users is quite a different task." The HNSS offers a dramatic demonstration of the differences between CSH and the judgments and oral completions of native speakers across Hungary.

The question we ask is as follows: What percentage of the entire adult population of Hungary is 'targeted' by language cultivators if, by definition, those who speak the codified standard variety are not targeted? To answer this, let us set up a 'Hungarian linguistic hurdle race' in which each hurdle is a linguistic variable, and respondents who opt for a nonstandard variant are eliminated from

---

[9] This restriction is necessary because Hungarians belong to 8 political nations. 10 million Hungarians live in the Republic of Hungary, and about 2.4 million in the neighboring countries (Austria, Slovakia, Ukraine, Romania, Serbia, Croatia, and Slovenia). Research has shown many linguistic similarities between Hungarians across the borders, but also important differences, see Kontra (2001, 2003c), and the studies in Fenyvesi (2005).

the race. Figure 1 shows the respondents who judged 1, 2, 3, … 10 sentences in accordance with CSH.

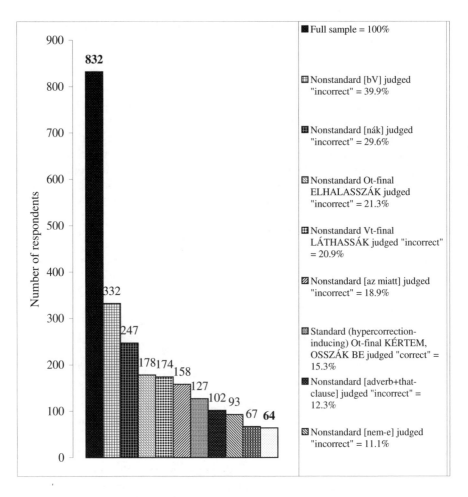

Figure 1: *Respondents who judged 1, 2, 3, … 10 sentences*
in accordance with CSH

We begin with the entire sample (N=832), and eliminate those who judged a nonstandard 1-[bV] "correct" (or keep those who judged it "grammatically incorrect"). 500 respondents are eliminated after the first hurdle. Next, let us exclude those who judged a nonstandard 4-[nák] "correct" and we have 247 respondents left. Then exclude those who judged a nonstandard 5-t-final verb "correct", then another such verb "correct", then exclude those who judged nonstandard 9-[az miatt] "correct", also exclude those who judged a standard (hypercorrection-inducing) 6-t-final verb as "incorrect". After the seventh hurdle, nonstandard 7-[adverb+that-clause], we have 102 respondents left, after the eighth 93, after the ninth 67, and finally, when those who judged a hypercorrect 2-[bVn] "correct" are also eliminated, we are left with 64 respondents or 7.7% of the country-wide representative sample. This figure shows that, as far as grammaticality judgments are concerned, Hungarian language cultivators promulgate a set of rules that only 8% of the population adheres to, even when they are on their best linguistic behavior, as they are when answering questions on linguistic correctness posed by a social scientist. In other words, the correctness judgments of 92% of the adult population of Hungary differ from those prescribed by the language cultivators.

If we use the same linguistic hurdle race for the oral sentence-completion data, we see a similar picture, but the loss of respondents is on a smaller scale, see Figure 2. When all seven sentences have been completed in accordance with CSH, we have 290 respondents left, which is 34.8% of the representative sample. Consequently, we can say that Hungarian language cultivators "target" the speechways of two-thirds of the country's adult population.

As can be readily seen, the grammaticality judgments show the sample to be much less standard than the oral sentence-completion tasks. This is not only because the number of variables used in the two "hurdle races" is different, but also because respondents demonstrated more linguistic awareness (audio-monitoring) during oral sentence-completion than during grammaticality judgments. For instance, the nonstandard 7-[adverb+that-clause] variant was used by 22.5% of the sample in oral sentence-completion, it was judged "grammatically correct" by 52%, and it was left uncorrected in a written correction task by 73%. Most of the other variables show the same hierarchy or task effects: more respondents are standard in oral sentence-completion than in grammaticality judgments, and more are standard in judgments than in written correction.[10] The fact, however, remains that advocates of CSH have many millions of unruly Hungarians to tame.

---

[10] In a way, these results remind us of Labov's audio-monitoring hypothesis (the more attention paid to speech, the more standard performance). However, if we assume that the least audio-monitoring occurs during oral sentence-completion, more occurs during grammaticality judgments, and the most during the written correction exercise, then the results are the exact opposite of what we would expect. Thus it appears that Labov's audio-monitoring hypothesis, if accepted, may not be applicable to large-scale sociolinguistic surveys like the HNSS. Such a reversal of 'the more attention, the more target-like (standard) performance' is common in second language acquisition as well. For example, Preston (1989: 257-259) shows that in Tarone's study of Arabic and Japanese learners of English, for one linguistic factor (3rd singular indicative marker on the verb) accuracy increases with attention or monitoring; for another (articles), it decreases.

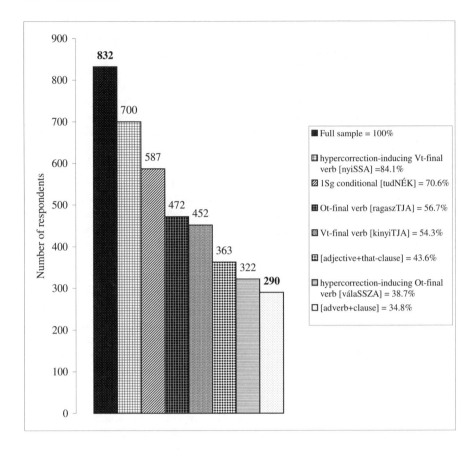

Figure 2: *Respondents who orally completed 1, 2, ..., 7 sentences in accordance with CSH*[11]

6. Learnability

Language guardians often charge that sloppy or lazy speech is produced by sloppy or lazy people, or, as Lesley Milroy (1999: 175) characterizes the attitudes of language regulators, "dim-witted speech of the kind characterised by glottal stops is inevitably produced by dim-witted speakers". Milroy and Milroy (1999: 219) summarize such beliefs this way:

> "Language guardians always consider non-standard usage (and sometimes standard colloquialisms) to arise from the perversity of speakers or from cognitive deficiency (an inability to learn what is 'correct')".

---

[11] The sixth and eighth bars in Figure 2 show those respondents who used the two standard variants of the variable 7-(adjective+*that*-clause). In the former task, respondents could insert an adjective or an adverb before a *hogy* "that"-clause, while in the latter they could insert an adverb or an adverb+*hogy* "that" before a clause without *hogy* "that".

The Milroys must have based their statement on their British experience, but Hungary is just like Britain in this respect, as can be illustrated by what a professor of Hungarian linguistics said on Hungarian National Radio on 4 January 1999, when linguists were discussing the (t-final verbs in the indicative) variable in a phone-in program (my translation from Kontra 2003b: 179):

> "There are people who are grammatically cultured, and there are those who are grammatically uncultured. What we see here is mistaking the imperative for the indicative forms. If you ask me, the fact that many people do this, intellectuals included, is something the schools deserve to be blamed for. Schools can teach one not to do this, and they should. After all, keeping the two forms apart is a sign of correct speech."

This cognitive deficiency argument is a little different, in that it assumes that nonstandard speakers could learn standard speech, if only they were not too lazy, or if the schools were not that inefficient. Advocates of standard language ideology, such as, for instance, the linguists Stein and Quirk (1995: 63) believe that "a standard language vastly enhances individual liberty by moving towards the ideal of universal empowerment." Sociolinguists have serious doubts.

Chambers (1992/1998) has shown that rule complexity plays a significant role in how successful second-dialect acquisition can be. For instance, it is easy for Canadian youths moving to England to learn the t-unvoicing rule in English (to pronounce letter with a [t] in place of the usual flapped Canadian [ɾ]), but it is difficult to learn the vowel backing rule, e.g. [dæns] → [daːns] (see Figures 9.5 and 9.6, pp. 154 and 155 in Trudgill & Cheshire, eds., 1998). The reasons are linguistic: t-unvoicing is a simple rule which admits no exceptions, whereas vowel backing is a complex rule with exceptions, hence it is difficult to learn.

Some standard variants are easier to learn for nonstandard speakers than others, and some nonstandard variants are harder to unlearn than others. Take the example of short u in British English dialects. As is well known, ME ŭ, phonetically [ʊ], developed an unrounded variant [ʌ] in certain words. However, as Chambers & Trudgill (1998: 106) state, "the occurrence of either variant, [ʊ] or [ʌ], is not predictable anywhere today, and all standard accents of English have contrasting pairs like *put* and *putt*, *butcher* and *butter*, and *cushion* and *cousin*." In other words, it is fairly easy for a southern speaker to learn northern speech: all s/he needs to do is replace [ʌ] with [ʊ]. But for a northern speaker to learn southern speech is (next to) impossible because the occurrence of the unrounded vowel is unpredictable. This then means that a standard (southern) speaker would find it easy to learn nonstandard (northern) speech, but the latter is in a no-win situation if s/he wants to learn to use [ʌ] as southerners do. In this case, phonological predictability plays a major role in distributing the burden of learning difficulty among speakers of the two dialects when they learn each other's variety.

Let us now examine the Hungarian variables from the point of view of learning difficulty. It is assumed that the learning of one's vernacular from birth is unproblematic even if it involves learning structural irregularities. However, learning the structural irregularities of a second dialect in school or later in life may present problems. In other words, linguistic variants can be easy to learn if they are part of one's vernacular, but they can be nearly impossible to learn when they are imposed on people whose vernacular does not have the variants in question, especially when their distribution is irregular and thus structurally unpredictable.

A speaker who uses the stigmatized 3-[k] variant of the 3-(m) variable needs to learn to use 3-[m] for 3-[k] as in high-prestige *eszem* "I eat (something)" for lower-prestige *eszek*. This would appear to be a fairly simple thing to learn.

A user of the stigmatized 1-[bV] variant of the inessive 1-(bVn) variable needs to restore the regularity of formally marking the functional difference between 'at rest' and 'motion to' for the interior cases, something s/he does anyway for the exterior and surface cases (see Fenyvesi 1998: 235). The semantic functions are crystal clear for all speakers of Hungarian. Dropping the *n* from the standard 1-[bVn] variant is the result of a natural process which occurs variably in the speech of all native speakers. Although 'putting the *n* back' at the end of nouns is not unproblematic (as is shown by the high percentage of respondents [51 and 53%] who judged our two hypercorrect sentences with 2-[bVn] for standard 2-[bV] grammatically correct), many speakers use the standard variant near-consistently – at least in contextual styles with high audio-monitoring (see Váradi 1995–1996).

Speakers who use the nonstandard variant 4-[nák] of the 1Sg conditional 4-(nVk) variable with back-vowel root verbs do nothing else but obey the rules of vowel harmony. Standard speakers, who use 4-[nék] with all verbs, violate vowel harmony, which is an all-pervasive characteristic of Hungarian morphonology. That the use of the standard variant is the result of blocking vowel harmony is shown by the occasional occurrence of the nonstandard variant in the speech of standard speakers (who have learned to block harmony in just this one case as part and parcel of their vernacular) as a result of lapses or fatigue. It is hard to learn to suspend vowel harmony in just one case (the 1Sg conditional form of back-vowel root verbs) when one had already learned to speak Hungarian obeying vowel harmony all the time.[12]

Nonstandard speakers who attach the question particle -*e* to a preverbal focused constituent or to a preverbal negative particle as in 8-[nem+-e], do so in conformity with "a natural tendency of speakers to append the interrogative particle directly to the communicatively marked sequence" (Kassai 1995: 28). Kiss (2004: 20) notes that the rule for -*e* placement in standard Hungarian is a

---

[12] Gósy (1989: 96) has shown that Hungarian children tend to observe the general vowel harmony rule and use 4-[nák] with back-vowel roots, which she explains by timing: harmony rules are learned much earlier than conditional forms. The strength of vowel harmony rules is shown by her summary statement: "The data in the literature almost unambiguously support the claim that *a Hungarian child will never violate VH*" (emphasis in the original).

disjunctive rule, i.e. it operates differently on different sentence types,[13] hence it burdens the memory of speakers, who try to avoid such rules.

Speakers of standard Hungarian maintain a formal distinction between some indicative and imperative forms of t-final verbs, e.g. *látjuk* "we see, definite conjugation" and *választjuk* "we choose, definite conjugation" vs. *lássuk* "let us see (it)" and *válasszuk* "let us choose (it)". Nonstandard speakers use the latter forms in both indicative and imperative. With verbs not ending in -t, standard speakers do the same as nonstandard speakers when they use t-final verbs: they use the same forms in both indicative and imperative, e.g. *hozza* "s/he brings (it)" and "let him/her bring it", *mondja* "s/he says (it)" and "let him/her say (it)". Other back-vowel roots in standard Hungarian have the same dual-function use for definite conjugation forms, e.g. *használjuk* "we use (it)" and "let us use (it)", *olvassuk* "we read (it)" and "let us read (it)", etc. The influence of analogy in the speech of nonstandard speakers was readily acknowledged even by such a highly respected language cultivator as Lőrincze (1961). He maintained, however, that "dialect speakers should be taught to speak standard Hungarian rather than we should accept their nonstandard verbal conjugation." Without showing the details, let us note that in Sándor's analysis (see Kontra 2003a: 139–141) nonstandard speakers (who never maintain the indicative vs. imperative distinction formally) have four rules in their grammar, semistandard speakers (who maintain it with verbs ending in Vt, but not in Ot) have six rules, and standard speakers (who maintain it with all verbs ending in t) have eight.[14] Table 1 summarizes what we need to know about t-final verbs:

---

[13] The rules of CSH require that the question particle *-e* be cliticized
(a) to the finite verb in a simple predicate as in
    Tamás   dolgoz-ik-e?
    Thomas   work-3SG-particle
    "Does Thomas work?"
to the verbal part of a complex predicate as in
    Nem tud-om, hogy Tamás   lázas   volt-e.
    not   know-1SG that   Thomas   feverish be.PAST.3SG-particle
    "I don't know whether Thomas had a fever."
(b) to the nonfinite auxiliary in a complex conditional predicate as in
    Nem tud-om, hogy Tamás   dolgoz-ott volna-e.
    not   know-1SG that   Thomas   work-PAST.3SG COND-particle
    "I don't know whether Thomas would have worked."

[14] As mentioned in note 7, due to an oversight we did not include Rt verbs in the HNSS; therefore we cannot say anything about them.

Table 1: *Hungarian lects with regard to* t-*final verbs. The indicative vs. imperative distinction is formally maintained (+) or not (–). Percentages do not add up to 100.*[15]

Lects	Distinction in standard maintained		Percent of speakers		Number of rules needed
	Vt	Ot	Judgments (N = 784)	Oral completions (N = 743)	
Nonstandard	–	–	25.8%	5.0%	4
Semistandard	+	–	29.8%	14.0%	6
Standard	+	+	39.9%	79.8%	8

The data in Table 1 are in line with the task effects mentioned at the end of Section 5: more informants are standard in oral sentence-completion (namely 79.8% of the total) than in judgments (39.9% of the total), and more are nonstandard in judgments (25.8%) than in oral completions (5%).

7. Multi-generational effects in second-dialect acquisition

Just as features of a second dialect may be easy or difficult to learn, so features of a first dialect may be easy or difficult to unlearn. Some of these features may be stigmatized, others may be unnoticed. Chambers (1992/1998: 163) notes that "Though Intrusive /r/ is stigmatized [in Southern England English], it appears to be almost impossible to suppress completely, even by the most self-conscious RP speakers."

One obvious measure of learning difficulty is the number of generations of speakers needed for learning a new feature. Payne (1980) has described the extremely troublesome case of "short-a" in the Philadelphia suburb King of Prussia, which Chambers (2003: 109) has summarized this way:

– none of the out-of-state children mastered the complex Philadelphia system
– children of out-of-state parents failed to master it even if they were born in King of Prussia
– the subjects who did master it were those born there of parents who were born and raised in Philadelphia.

---

[15] The HNSS data do not completely agree with the implicational relationships shown in Table 9–1 in Chambers & Trudgill (1998: 131). According to that table, we would expect that those speakers who maintain the non-distinction with Vt verbs also maintain it with Ot verbs, but not vice versa. This could be formalized as (Vt verbs): [indicative = imperative] implies (Ot verbs): [indicative = imperative]. In other words, there should not be any respondents who maintain the indicative vs. imperative distinction with Vt verbs, but not with Ot verbs. However, the judgment data show that 4.5% of the respondents did exactly that, and the oral completion data show that 1.2% did the same. I have only a very tentative explanation for this: the small percentage of responses violating the implicational relationship might be due to the large size of the data set gathered from a large country-wide representative sample like that of the HNSS. In our study, not even the most blatantly ungrammatical sentences were rejected by all the respondents, e.g. 4.8% judged *Add ide aztatat a könyvet!* "Give me that book" 'grammatically correct', despite the three accusative markers in *aztatat* (as opposed to standard *az-t* "that-ACC").

The acquisition of Philadelphia 'short-a' then takes at least two generations born in King of Prussia. It is a multi-generational job, in terms of geographic mobility.

The HNSS offers a unique opportunity to measure the effect of another kind of mobility, educational, on language use.

8. The effects of educational mobility

Like in all schools the world over, mother-tongue education takes place in Hungarian schools as well. The stated aim of this education is to teach the standard variety of Hungarian. The question we pose here is this: To what extent is this goal realizable? According to a naive view, the goal is indeed realizable. According to the professor of Hungarian linguistics cited in Section 6, people speak "incorrect" Hungarian only because schools do not do what they should. If schools did what they should, people would not use nonstandard forms of t-final verbs, would not use nonstandard forms of 1Sg conditional verbs, etc. In other words, high educational levels and standard speech would co-occur. This is actually true for many variables. As is shown in Table 2, a larger proportion of the less educated groups judged the nonstandard sentences "grammatically correct" than the more educated groups, and the same holds for oral sentence-completions[16] (see Kontra 2003b: 170 ff.).

Table 2: *The effect of education on judging nonstandard sentences "grammatically correct"*

	< 8 years	8 years	12 years	coll/univ	N	χ^2	df	p
1-[bV]	81%	69%	36%	21%	805	135.32	3	< .01
4-[nák]	60%	57%	25%	13%	792	99.10	3	< .01
5-Ot non-distinction	81%	64%	38%	17%	809	125.97	3	< .01
5-Vt non-distinction	61%	34%	8%	4%	798	146.06	3	< .01
7-[adverb+that-clause]	75%	64%	35%	25%	781	96.12	3	< .01
8-[nem+-e]	66%	42%	16%	9%	810	128.62	3	< .01
3-[k]	77%	59%	29%	17%	800	126.66	3	< .01
hypercorrect 2-[bVn]	76%	68%	26%	6%	805	198.37	3	< .01
9-[az miatt]	48%	37%	14%	8%	787	70.77	3	< .01

After World War II, education in Hungary became much more socially widespread and educational mobility increased a great deal; that is, large numbers

---

[16] These data are very different from an earlier publication of mine (Kontra 1992), which has also been quoted by Chambers (1995: 54–55) in the section on Hungarian imperative declaratives. Unfortunately, that analysis was carried out using an erroneous data file, hence the two-dimensional data reported there, e.g. "sentence judged correct" by education, are incorrect. The error was discovered and fixed in May 2002. It is only since that discovery that we have known that education has the expected effects on Hungarian judgments and oral sentence-completions (see Kontra 2003).

of Hungarians became more highly educated than their parents.[17] Thus, we can test the following *hypothesis*:

> Language use becomes more standard not as a result of speakers' higher educational levels, but as a result of educatedness accumulated through several generations of being part of the intelligentsia.

Thus the null hypothesis will be this: in a group of people with the same level of education, there will be no linguistic differences correlated to educational mobility.

As stated above, our Mobility variable grasps the difference in education between a child and his/her father. Those with an educational level higher than their fathers' are upwardly mobile, those with the same education or with less education (the latter comprise only 6% of the respondents) are called immobiles. In a few cases Mobility has a significant effect on judgments and production. Out of the 68 tasks in the survey, Mobility has a statistically significant effect on five judgment tasks, two of which concern nonstandard 3-[k],[18] one oral sentence-completion concerning 4-(nVk), and three written correction items (two of which concern 3-[k] again). It is always the upwardly mobile who are more standard, but the differences between the two groups are small, for instance, the low-prestige form *iszok* "I drink" was judged correct by 56% of the immobile but by 48% of the upwardly mobile group. These results would prompt one to discard the null hypothesis. They suggest that the beneficiaries of educational mobility are, at least in a few cases, more standard. Such an effect should not surprise us if we take into consideration the fact that Mobility is "a simple variable based on educational difference between the respondent and his/her father" (my translation, Angelusz & Tardos 1991: 110). This implies that the upwardly mobile group contains those who completed 8 years of school but their fathers less, as well as those who completed a university education but their fathers less. In other words, Mobility grasps educational mobility but does so in a crude way, as it is insensitive to the differences among various educational levels. However, this problem can be handled by including the independent variable Education in the analysis. We can compare the immobiles and the upwardly mobiles from one educational level to the next. When we do this, the number of significant correlations between educational mobility and language judgments/use greatly increases, and the direction also changes: in all cases the upwardly mobile are less standard than the immobile, see Figures 3 and 4. The differences are always significant at the .01 or .05 level, and it is always the upwardly mobile who are much less standard.

---

[17] Frans Hinskens (personal communication) reports to me that this also holds for several west European countries. For instance, in the Netherlands only 42% of the adults had more than elementary education before World War II, but this percentage grew to well over 80% by 1958.

[18] The other three tasks concern variables not analyzed in this paper (see Kontra 2003b: 173 ff.).

	JUDGED "CORRECT":	N	f	χ^2	p
1	Nonstandard 1-[bV]	368	1	14.845	< 0.01
2	Nonstandard 5-Ot verb elhalasszák	369	1	22.176	< 0.01
3	Nonstandard 5-Vt verb láthassák	366	1	7.269	< 0.01
4	Nonstandard 7-[adverb+that-clause]	364	1	6.817	< 0.01
5	Nonstandard question particle 8-[nem+-e]	369	1	8.118	< 0.01
6	Nonstandard SENTENCE COMPLETION 3-elkése[k]	355	1	16.526	< 0.01
7	Nonstandard 5-Vt verb lássa LEFT UNCORRECTED	348	1	20.493	< 0.01

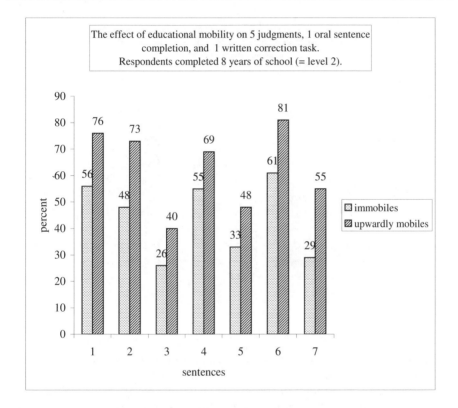

Figure 3: *The effect of educational mobility on judging 5 nonstandard sentences "grammatically correct", and on an oral completion and a written correction task. The respondents have completed 8 years of school (= level 2).*

	JUDGED "CORRECT":	N	f	χ^2	p
1	Nonstandard 1-[bV] (12 years)	192	1	7.452	< 0.01
2	Nonstandard 4-[nák] (12 years)	192	1	6.832	< 0.01
3	Nonstandard question particle 8-[nem+-e] (12 years)	195	1	6.006	< 0.05
	LEFT UNCORRECTED:				
4	Nonstandard 1-[bV] (coll/university)	76	1	10.130	< 0.01
5	Nonstandard 7-[adverb+that-clause] (coll/university)	76	1	5.684	< 0.05

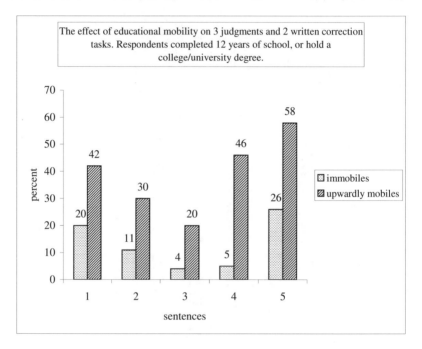

The effect of educational mobility on 3 judgments and 2 written correction tasks. Respondents completed 12 years of school, or hold a college/university degree.

Figure 4: *The effect of educational mobility on judging nonstandard sentences "grammatically correct", and on leaving nonstandard written sentences uncorrected. The respondents have completed 12 years of school (= level 3, sentences 1 to 3), or hold a college / university degree (= level 4, sentences 4 and 5).*[19]

[19] The different N's for sentences 1 to 3 vs. 4 and 5 are due to the educational stratification of Hungarian adults in 1988. Twenty-one percent of the sample (N=832) had less than 8 years of education, 45% had 8 years, 24% had 12 years, and 10% had a college/university degree.

The effects are statistically significant (consequently we can generalize to the entire adult population of Hungary when it was about to change from a communist to a post-communist country), and the differences are fairly big. For instance, among those with 8 years of education, the nonstandard 5-Ot-final form *elhalasszák* "they postpone (it)" was judged "grammatically correct" by 48% of the immobile but by 73% of the upwardly mobile (Figure 3), and, in the college/university-educated group, the nonstandard 1-*mostanába* "nowadays" (for standard 1-*mostanában*) was left uncorrected by 46% of the upwardly mobile group but by only 5% of the immobile group (Figure 4).

We conclude that there are linguistic differences among Hungarians with the same education which are correlated to their educational mobility, and the upwardly mobile are less standard than the immobile (meaning a greater proportion of the upwardly mobile group have nonstandard features in their speech than the immobile group). Higher educational levels (and a university education) most probably covary with reduced levels of nonstandard language use, but they certainly do not eliminate it. There are linguistic variables whose nonstandard variants will not be eliminated by increasing educational levels of speakers.[20] The data in Figures 3 and 4 appear to support the hypothesis at the beginning of this section.

9. How to officially ratify societal prejudice

In a highly illuminating study, Myhill (2004) shows that a great many sociolinguists have been victims of unintentionally ethnocentric models of prescriptivism and its social consequences. We tend to assume that prescriptivism necessarily reinforces social inequalities. However, there are languages where this is not the case. For instance, Myhill (2004: 398) has observed that "ordinary users" of Hebrew "express very little in the way of hostility towards prescriptivism," whereas "there are groups of 'ordinary' English speakers, for example among speakers of Black English, who regard the imposition of prescriptive norms as oppressive." In cases like Hebrew, the correctness of a linguistic form is determined by factors which are independent of the social status of the people who use it, hence prescriptivism causes little social damage, it is not discriminatory.

Myhill distinguishes three distinct understandings of the notion 'correctness':
– textual correctness, which is based on the written form of valued texts in the language, e.g. the Bible and Mishna in Hebrew or the Koran in Arabic
– prestige-based correctness, which is based on the usage of the representatives of the elite whose behavior is generally regarded as the model for society, and

---

[20] One could also interpret these findings as evidence of the educated people in Hungary being more tolerant of certain variants than are the prescriptivists. As Jack Chambers observed (personal communication), this might be an indication that the next generation will encode more resilient rules and greater linguistic tolerance.

– prescriptive correctness, which is determined by some recognized body of authorities. Such recognition can be official as in France or Hungary, or informal as in England.

Myhill calls these kinds of 'correctness' parameters, and shows that there are cases in which they are not necessarily aligned together. In most European societies we are used to situations where prestige-based correctness supports textual and prescriptive correctness. However, in a number of languages (such as Hebrew, Arabic, Icelandic, or Sinhala) the 'standard' or 'correct' variety is not based on the everyday language of the social elite, but rather on a body of authoritative texts (the Bible, the Koran, etc). In these languages and societies, 'correctness' is not generally related to social class.[21] Myhill (2004: 396) makes an astonishing statement: "There are a number of cases in which the form generally associated with higher-status speakers is in fact the prescriptively 'incorrect' one, a situation which is by definition impossible in a language like English." English and Hebrew prescriptivism are equally unscientific, "but only English prescriptivism can also be considered to be discriminatory because only English prescriptivism is based upon following the usage of the highest-status speakers" (p. 398). After analyzing a number of languages and their societies (e.g. Arabic, Greek, and Norwegian), Myhill (2004: 413) arrives at the following generalization:

> It is only prestige-based 'correctness' which is inherently discriminatory; prescriptive 'correctness' is only discriminatory if it is an imitation of prestige-based correctness, while textual 'correctness' is only discriminatory if the model texts follow norms of prescriptive 'correctness' which have been devised as an imitation of prestige-based 'correctness' (in other words, if the ultimate source is prestige-based 'correctness'). Prescriptive 'correctness' and textual 'correctness' are not in themselves inherently problematic; they only become problematic if they imitate prestige-based 'correctness', thereby officially ratifying societal prejudice.

For the typical European reader, Myhill's points are hard to digest. "Why wouldn't the social elite force its language norms to be adopted by all others?" is the highly 'sensible' question which must be answered somehow. According to Myhill, Arabic, Hebrew, Icelandic and Sinhala are all languages whose written varieties have been the property of all speakers, rather than a social elite. However, in Christianity and Hinduism, for example, a priestly caste had practically exclusive control of literacy until modern times, and when that caste was overthrown, it was natural that their archaic language, which was based upon

---

[21] One might ask whether it is not the case that higher social classes have better access to the authoritative texts (because they have better access to education), so that there is an *indirect* relationship between this type of norm and social class. Myhill (personal communication) regards this as a relatively small problem in Hebrew but a significant one in Arabic. He does not think unequal access to education has a great effect on pronunciation or verb conjugations in spoken language, but it would affect vocabulary usage in writing. Myhill views this as a separate phenomenon from the nature of the prescriptive norm itself because unequal access to education will *always* cause inequality.

textual correctness, would be replaced with a prestige-based norm based on the usage of the new social elite. In the societies associated with Arabic, Hebrew, Icelandic and Sinhala, there was no language associated with the religious establishment, and consequently there was no reason for modernization to involve overthrowing the language of the religious establishment.[22]

Hungarian offers a perfect demonstration of how prescriptive correctness can be supported by prestige-based correctness (or vice versa). As stated above, in the 1988 Hungarian National Sociolinguistic Survey our independent variable 'Occupation'[23] has four levels. Table 3 demonstrates the judgments and oral sentence-completions of the highest and lowest occupational group. In some cases there is hardly any difference between the two extreme groups, while in others the differences can be huge. For instance, 97% of the highest group judged the form 3-*iszom* "I drink something" grammatically correct and 93% of the lowest group did the same, which shows that the standard 3-[m] variant has high prestige among all speakers. However, the judgments of nonstandard 3-[k] are very different: 26% of the highest group, but 64% of the lowest group judged it "correct".[24]

Table 3: *Judging different variants "grammatically correct", and using them in oral sentence-completion tasks by two extreme occupational groups*

	upper-level managers and college/university-trained intellectuals	unskilled workers
Nonstandard 1-[bV]	28%	70%
Nonstandard 4-[nák]	24%	60%
Nonstandard 5-Ot verb	30%	66%
Nonstandard 5-Vt verb	7%	41%
Nonstandard 7-[adverb+that-clause]	29%	63%
Nonstandard 8-[nem+-e]	10%	45%
Nonstandard 3-[k]	26%	64%
Standard 3-[m]	97%	93%
Hypercorrect 2-[bVn]	13%	69%
Hypercorrect 6-Vt verb in oral sentence-completion	3%	18%
Nonstandard 5-Ot verb in oral sentence-completion	5%	27%

[22] This is a simplified paraphrase of Myhill's much more detailed explanation, for which the reader is referred to Myhill (2004: 410-411).

[23] Occupation has almost as strong effects on grammaticality judgments and oral sentence-completions as Education. The former has a significant effect (at .01 or .05) on 20 out of 34 judgment tasks and 13 out of 16 oral completion tasks, whereas the latter has a significant effect on 27 judgments and 15 oral completions (see Kontra 2003b: 209). The tasks mentioned here contain one or more variants of all the 9 variables described in Section 3, and variants of four more variables, which are irrelevant in this paper.

[24] One intriguing question to ask is: Has this situation in Hungary changed since the demise of communism? Unfortunately, I do not know the answer. I conducted a restudy with the Budapest subsample in November 2005 (N=200), but the data are inconclusive because 70% of the respondents are eliminated when the highest and lowest occupation levels are compared, which then yields too few respondents for a cell.

The N's for each variant in Table 3 are between 229 and 241, and the chi-square results are significant at p < .001 for all but two variants. The result for standard 3-[m] is not significant, and that for hypercorrect 6-Vt verb in oral sentence-completion is significant at p < .01.

10. Linguicism at its worst

Myhill's focus was on establishing a basic framework and, for that reason, he did not consider "the particular motivation within each society for conceptualizing 'correctness' in one way rather than another" (p. 394). What I propose to do here is to highlight one aspect of prescriptivism which may aggravate social discrimination when prescriptive correctness and prestige-based correctness support each other: the requirement to learn linguistic variants which are difficult or (next to) impossible to learn in school or later in life.

Perhaps the first seriously argued alternative to what Milroy & Milroy (1999) call the language guardians' cognitive deficiency argument (an inability to learn what is 'correct') was Kroch's (1978) paper. Briefly, Kroch proposed that the public prestige dialect of the elite in a stratified community differs from the dialect(s) of the non-elite strata in resisting "normal processes of phonetic conditioning (both articulatory and perceptual) that the speech of the non-elite strata regularly undergo", and that the cause of such stratification is in ideology rather than in purely linguistic factors:

> "Dominant social groups tend to mark themselves off symbolically as distinct from the groups they dominate and to interpret their symbols of distinctiveness as evidence of superior moral and intellectual qualities. [...] in the case of pronunciation they also mark their distinctiveness in a negative way — that is by inhibiting many of the low level, variable processes of phonetic conditioning that characterize spoken language and that underlie regular phonological change". (Kroch 1978: 18)

Kroch also notes that "there is both experimental and historical evidence that prestige dialects require special attention to speech, attention motivated not by the needs of communication but by status consciousness" (p. 19). He speaks of "a particular ideological motivation at the origin of social dialect variation" (p. 30), which causes the prestige dialect speaker "to expend more energy in speaking than does the user of the popular vernacular."

On the basis of the HNSS data, Pléh & Bodor (2000) propose a metaphoric psychological model of standardization, stigmatization and hypercorrection, which is in some ways fairly similar to Kroch's (1978). Pléh & Bodor (2000: 124) claim that in Central Europe "the social idea of an 'educated person' is someone who is not easily trapped by naturally occurring simplification tendencies in language." Prototypical educated speakers have control over their 'linguistic instincts'. The concept of norm following "assumes a continuous metacontrol, a replacement of automatic information processing by controlled processing"

(p. 126). Finally, Pléh and Bodor advance motivations similar to those cited by Kroch when they claim the following:

> "In these communities [in which the supremacy or viability of a national standard variety has been established, M.K.] there is more at stake than 'merely' understandability: what is at issue is the distinctiveness of one language community from other neighboring language communities, and also the distinctiveness of the literate intelligentsia not only from several types of aristocracy (old, inherited, and the new rich, cosmopolitan or national) but also from the lower classes. This is the driving force behind the central and emotionally laden role of language cultivation in all of these communities." (Pléh and Bodor 2000: 135)

Kroch's argument hinges on attention to speech and effort, but Lippi-Green (1997: 241) goes further: she brings into the discussion the limits of effort:

> "A person's accent (the bundle of distinctive intonation and phonological features) is fixed or hard-wired in the mind, and once past a certain age it can only be very laboriously changed, to a very limited degree, regardless of commitment, intelligence, and resources. [...]"

The process of language subordination is so deeply rooted, so well established, that we do not see it for what it is. We make no excuses for preferences which exclude on the basis of immutable language traits.

"Exclusion on the basis of immutable language traits" is similar to exclusion on the basis of sex or skin color.[25] My point is that the typical European situation where prescriptive correctness supports prestige-based correctness can be analyzed further in terms of the learning difficulty placed on nonstandard speakers. As I have shown in Section 6 above, some nonstandard variants may be replaced with standard variants relatively easily, others may be difficult or impossible to replace. Here are three more examples:

– It is extremely hard for someone born and raised in the south of the USA to produce an [ɛ] in front of nonback nasals, e.g. to pronounce *pen* and *pin* differently.
– "Speakers of Broad Scots find it very difficult to use the standard strong past tense forms in speech correctly over an extended period." (Miller 1999: 119)
– Propagators of the English prescriptive rule which requires the nominative pronouns (*I*, *s/he* etc) in constructions where a personal pronoun follows *to be*, as in *It's I* rather than *It's me*, "have created considerable insecurity in the minds of many speakers about the "'correctness' of their language" (Andersson and Trudgill 1990: 117). The prescriptive rule seems to be very

---

[25] In an interview I conducted with Peter Trudgill (Kontra and Trudgill 2000: 23), he said: "And it seems to me that the correct way to counter discrimination is not to say, well… if Black people are being discriminated against, you don't say, 'Well, you should become white,' or if women are being discriminated against, you don't say, 'Well, you should become a man,' and if non-standard speakers are being discriminated against, why should you say 'Well, you should speak Standard English'? What you should actually attack is the discrimination."

difficult for most speakers, to the extent that even prescriptivists get it wrong, witness the now very common *between you and I*.

In his study of the principles of language change, Labov (2001: 415 ff.) confronts the problem of transmission and states that the general condition for linguistic change can be stated in a simple way: children must talk differently from their mothers. He calls this process vernacular reorganization and states that age is a crucial factor in it. The reorganization must take place "sometime between first learning and the effective stabilization of the linguistic system" (2001: 416). Payne (1980: 144) suggests that there may be a borderline, at about age 6-8, between early acquisition and later acquisition. After the initial learning of one's vernacular is completed (whenever it may be), changes become difficult. As Wolfram & Schilling-Estes (1998: 287) say, "Once a linguistic structure is entrenched, it is difficult to break out of the pattern without paying focused attention to the details of the pattern. The special attention needed to do this, referred to as MONITORING, is actually somewhat unnatural, given the fact that we do not ordinarily have to think about the structures of language in order to speak a language."

If we add to the learnability problem and the age problem the fact that linguistic changes often "extend across three, four, or more generations of speakers" (Labov 2001: 416), it becomes abundantly clear that the cognitive deficiency argument, or the requirement of standard speakers that others also should speak like them, is absolutely unrealistic.

We have seen that three Hungarian variables, (t-final verbs in the indicative), (nVk), and (e), have badly stigmatized variants which are natural in the sense that they observe the deeper linguistic regularities or non-prescriptive rules of Hungarian. To learn the standard variants requires great effort, and to use them requires constant monitoring (as in the case of violating vowel harmony). If a Hungarian uses t-final verbs in the stigmatized way, s/he reduces the variability in the verbal conjugation system, and thereby increases his/her linguistic security (Kassai 1998: 24). As Kassai remarks, it would be a miracle if Hungarians did not use t-final verbs in the nonstandard way. We have also seen that these nonstandard variants are fairly static, in the sense that a significantly greater proportion of educationally upwardly mobile people use them than speakers with the same education who are educationally static.

11.   Teachers

In many societies, teachers from kindergarten to university have a decisive role in shaping language attitudes and maintaining and re-creating linguicism. Many of them practice subtractive teaching, that is, they are teaching standard X at the expense of dialects of X, rather than in addition to them. Standard English, to take an example from Wolfram & Schilling-Estes (1998: 285), is often taught in the United States as a replacive dialect; that is, teachers aim to eradicate nonstandard dialects and replace them with standard English. Typically, I will add, they don't

This chapter is a little oddly structured, but the bit about difficulty is interesting/relevant & good questions & good range of ideas. Good questions

Sustainable Linguicism   123

even know why they are so unsuccessful. But standard X can also be taught as an additive dialect, one which is added to the learners' vernacular to increase their linguistic repertoire.

Subtractive teaching and teachers increase linguistic and social conflicts, and play into the hands of those who maintain and benefit from linguistic discrimination. Subtractive teachers multiply the social occasions that cause embarrassment. They encourage the insecure and the disadvantaged to remain silent rather than risk embarrassing themselves by using the wrong verb form or case ending. Such silence, of course, is a sign of oppression (Chambers, personal communication). Additive teaching and teachers, on the other hand, decrease conflicts and increase linguistic security. I would also like to claim that subtractive teachers commit educational malpractice (see Baugh 1999) and should perhaps have their teaching licenses temporarily suspended, for the simple reason that they increase social conflicts, rather than decrease them. However, this "radical" position of mine may need to be softened in at least some cases: Wolfgang Wölck (personal communication) has commented that suspending the licenses of teachers who teach subtractively may well result in removing all the teachers from the inner-city schools in the United States, which would aggravate the educational plight of inner-city schoolchildren.

12. Conclusions

Language subordination tactics (Lippi-Green 1997) work best when prescriptive correctness and prestige-based correctness go hand in hand, and the linguistic variants at issue are hard or impossible to learn in school or later in life. For language mavens, the most lucrative prescriptive rules are those that will always be violated. For linguicist societies, such prescriptive rules ensure sustainable linguicism. For sociolinguists and school teachers, the challenge is to make linguicism unsustainable.[26]

References

Andersson, L.-G. & P. Trudgill. 1990. Bad Language. London: Penguin.
Angelusz, R. & R. Tardos. 1991. Hálózatok, stílusok, struktúrák [=Networks, styles, and structures]. Budapest: ELTE Szociológiai Intézet.
Angelusz, R. & R. Tardos. 1995. "Styles of knowledge and interactive habits". International Journal of the Sociology of Language 111. 57-78.
Baugh, J. 1999. Out of the mouths of slaves: African American language and educational malpractice. Austin, TX: University of Texas Press.
Cameron, D. 1995. Verbal hygiene. London/New York: Routledge.
Chambers, J.K. 1992/1998. Dialect acquisition. The sociolinguistics reader: Multilingualism and variation ed. by P. Trudgill & J. Cheshire, 145-178. London: Arnold.
Chambers, J.K. 1995. Sociolinguistic theory: Linguistic variation and its social significance. Oxford: Blackwell.

---

[26] I am fully aware of how great a challenge this is. See, for instance, Wallace and Wray (2002), Hudson (2004), and the Dialogue section in the Journal of Sociolinguistics 5 (2001): 575–631.

Chambers, J.K. 2003. Sociolinguistic theory: Linguistic variation and its social significance. Second edition. Oxford: Blackwell.

Chambers, J. K. & P. Trudgill. 1998. Dialectology. Second edition. Cambridge: CUP.

Cseresnyési, L. 2004. Nyelvek és stratégiák avagy a nyelv antropológiája [=Languages and strategies, or the anthropology of language]. Budapest: Tinta Könyvkiadó.

Cseresnyési, L. 2005. "Review of Miklós Kontra (ed.) Nyelv és társadalom a rendszerváltáskori Magyarországon [= Language and society in Hungary at the fall of communism]. Budapest: Osiris Kiadó, 2003". Journal of sociolinguistics 9. 307-313.

Fenyvesi, A. 1998. "Inflectional morphology". Hungarian ed. by I. Kenesei, R.M. Vago & A. Fenyvesi, 191-381. London/New York: Routledge.

Fenyvesi, A. (ed.). 2005. Hungarian language contact outside Hungary: Studies on Hungarian as a minority language. Amsterdam/Philadelphia: John Benjamins.

Gósy, M. 1989. "Vowel harmony: interrelations of speech production, speech perception, and the phonological rules". Acta Linguistica Hungarica 39. 93-118.

Halliday, M.A.K., A. McIntosh & P. Strevens. 1964. The linguistic sciences and language teaching. London: Longmans.

Hudson, R. 2004. "Why education needs linguistics (and vice versa)". Journal of Linguistics 40. 105-130.

Johnson, S. 2001. "Who's misunderstanding whom? Sociolinguistics, public debate and the media". Journal of Sociolinguistics 5. 591-610.

Kálmán L. 2005. "A pincei bogár. A hiszékenység nyelvészbőrbe bújt vámszedőiről. [On the exploiters of credulousness who masquerade as linguists]". Élet és Irodalom, 13 May 2005, pp. 3-4.

Kassai, I. 1995. "Prescription and reality: the case of the interrogative particle in Hungarian". International Journal of the Sociology of Language 111. 21-30.

Kassai, I. 1998. Csoda-e, ha suksükölünk? [=Is it a miracle that we use Vt verbs in the nonstandard way?] Nyelvi változó - nyelvi változás ed. by K. Sándor, 23-25. Szeged: JGYF Kiadó.

Kenesei, I., R.M. Vago & Anna Fenyvesi. 1998. Hungarian. London/New York: Routledge.

Kiss, K.É. 2004. Anyanyelvünk állapotáról [=On the state of our mother tongue]. Budapest: Osiris Kiadó.

Kontra, M. 1992. "Class over nation - linguistic hierarchies eliminated: the case of Hungary". Multilingua 11: 217-221.

Kontra, M. 1997. "Hungarian linguistic traitors champion the cause of contact dialects". Recent studies in contact linguistics ed. by W. Wölck & A. de Houwer, 181-187. Bonn: Dümmler.

Kontra, M. 2001. "Hungarian verbal puzzles and the intensity of language contact". Journal of Sociolinguistics 5. 163-179.

Kontra, M. 2003a. "Vizsgálati eredmények: a független változók hatásai a nyelvi változókra". Nyelv és társadalom a rendszerváltáskori Magyarországon [= Language and society in Hungary at the fall of communism], ed. by M. Kontra, 85-168. Budapest: Osiris Kiadó.

Kontra, M. 2003b. "A független változók hatásainak összegzése". Nyelv és társadalom a rendszerváltáskori Magyarországon [= Language and society in Hungary at the fall of communism] ed. by M. Kontra, Miklós, 169-228. Budapest: Osiris Kiadó.

Kontra, M. 2003c. Changing mental maps and morphology: Divergence caused by international border changes. Social Dialectology: In honour of Peter Trudgill ed. by D. Britain & Jenny Cheshire, 173-190. Amsterdam/Philadelphia: John Benjamins.

Kontra, M. & P. Trudgill. 2000. "If women are being discriminated against, you don't say "You should become a man": An interview with Peter Trudgill on sociolinguistics and Standard English". novELTy (A Journal of English Language Teaching and Cultural Studies in Hungary) 7:2. 17-30.

Kontra, M. (ed.). 2000. Language contact in East-Central Europe (= Multilingua 19-1/2).

Kontra, M. (ed.). 2003. Nyelv és társadalom a rendszerváltáskori Magyarországon. [= Language and society in Hungary at the fall of communism]. Budapest: Osiris Kiadó.

Kontra, M. & C. Pléh (eds.). 1995. Hungarian Sociolinguistics (= International Journal of the Sociology of Language No. 111).

Kroch, A.S. 1978. "Toward a theory of social dialect variation". Language in Society 7. 17-36.

Labov, W. 2001. Principles of linguistic change, Volume 2: Social factors. Oxford: Blackwell.

Lanstyák, I. 2003-2004. "Helyi "értékes" nyelvváltozatok, "tisztes" idegen szavak, "visszás" jelentések, "agresszív" rövidítések, "kevercs" nyelv és társaik. Válogatás a nyelvmûvelõi csacskaságok gazdag tárházából. I-II. [=A selection from the rich storehouse of silly claims in Hungarian language cultivation]". Fórum Társadalomtudományi Szemle 2003/4: 69-98, and 2004/1: 51-76.

Laforest, M. 1999. "Can a sociolinguist venture outside the university?". Journal of Sociolinguistics 3. 276-282.

Lippi-Green, R. 1997. English with an accent: Language, ideology, and discrimination in the United States. London/New York: Routledge.

Lõrincze, L. 1961. "A "suksük"-özõ igeragozásról [=On the nonstandard use of verbs ending in Vt]". Édes anyanyelvünk ed. by L. Lõrincze, 378-379. Budapest: Akadémiai Kiadó.

Mendoza-Denton, N. 2002. Language and identity. The handbook of language variation and change ed. by J.K. Chambers, P. Trudgill & N. Schilling-Estes, 475-499. Oxford: Blackwell.

Miller, J. 1999. "Review of Cheshire, Jenny and Dieter Stein, eds., Taming the Vernacular: From Dialect to Written Standard Language (London: Longman, 1997)". Language and speech 42. 117-125.

Milroy, J. 1999. "The consequences of standardization in descriptive linguistics". Standard English: The widening debate ed. by T. Bex & R.J. Watts, 16-39. London/New York: Routledge.

Milroy, L. 1999. Standard English and language ideology in Britain and the United States. Standard English: The widening debate ed. by T. Bex & R.J. Watts, 173-206. London/New York: Routledge.

Milroy, J. & L. Milroy. 1999. Authority in language: Investigating Standard English. Third edition. London/New York: Routledge.

Myhill, J. 2004. "A parametrized view of the concept of 'correctness'". Multilingua 23. 389-416.

Papp, I. 1935. A magyar nyelvtan nevelõereje [= The educational side of Hungarian grammar]. Budapest: Királyi Magyar Egyetemi Nyomda.

Payne, A.C. 1980. "Factors controlling the acquisition of the Philadelphia dialect by out-of-state children". Locating language in time and space ed. by W. Labov, 143-178. New York: Academic Press.

Pintzuk, S., M. Kontra, K. Sándor & A. Borbély. 1995. The effect of the typewriter on Hungarian reading style (=Working Papers in Hungarian Sociolinguistics, No. 1). Budapest: Linguistics Institute, Hungarian Academy of Sciences. <http://www.nytud.hu/buszi/wp1/index.html> (30 July 2006).

Pléh, C. & P. Bodor. 2000. "Linguistic Superego in a normative language community and the stigmatization-hypercorrection dimension". Multilingua 19. 123-139.

Preston, D.R. 1989. Sociolinguistics and second language acquisition. Oxford: Blackwell.

Preston, D.R. 2001. "Style and the psycholinguistics of sociolinguistics: the logical problem of language variation". Style and sociolinguistic variation ed. by P. Eckert & J.R. Rickford, 279-304. Cambridge: CUP.

Sándor, K. 2001a. "'A nyílt társadalmi diszkrimináció utolsó bástyája': az emberek nyelvhasználata ['The last bastion of overt social discrimination": people's use of language]". Replika Nos 45/46. 241-259.

Sándor, K. 2001b. Language cultivation in Hungary: further data. Issues on language cultivation ed. by K. Sándor, 43-61. Szeged: JGYF Kiadó.

Sherwood, P. 1996. "'A nation may be said to live in its language': Some Socio-historical Perspectives on Attitudes to Hungarian". The Literature of Nationalism: Essays on East European Identity ed. by R.B. Pynsent, 27-39. London: School of Slavonic and East European Studies, University of London.

Siptár, P. & M. Törkenczy. 2000. The phonology of Hungarian. Oxford: Oxford University Press.

Skutnabb-Kangas, T. 1988. "Multilingualism and the education of minority children". Minority Education: From Shame to Struggle ed. by T. Skutnabb-Kangas & J. Cummins, 9-44. Clevedon/Philadelphia: Multilingual Matters.

Stein, G. & R. Quirk. 1995. Standard English. The European English Messenger IV/2: 62-63.

Váradi, T. 1995-1996. "Stylistic variation and the (bVn) variable in the Budapest Sociolinguistic Interview". Acta Linguistica Hungarica 43. 295-309.

Váradi, T. & M. Kontra. 1995. "Degrees of Stigmatization: t-final Verbs in Hungarian". ZDL-Beiheft 77: Verhandlungen des Internationalen Dialektologenkongresses Bamberg 1990. Band 4 ed. by W. Viereck, 132-142. Franz Steiner Verlag Stuttgart.

Wallace, M. & A. Wray. 2002. "The fall and rise of linguists in education policy-making: From "common sense" to common ground". Language Policy 1: 75-98.

Wiley, T.G. 1996. "Language planning and policy". Sociolinguistics and language teaching ed. by S.L McKay & N.H. Hornberger, 103-147. Cambridge: CUP.

Wolfram, W. & N. Schilling-Estes. 1998. American English: Dialects and variation. Oxford: Blackwell.

Good demonstration of the illogicality of linguicism based on correctness equated with social factors — more educated people in Hungary more tolerant of "nonstandard/incorrect" forms. Structure a bit odd, perhaps.

Phonetic variation in Tyneside
Exploratory multivariate analysis of
the Newcastle Electronic Corpus of Tyneside English

Hermann Moisl, Warren Maguire & Will Allen
Newcastle University

Abstract: The newly-created Newcastle Electronic Corpus of Tyneside English (NECTE) offers an opportunity to study a recent sample of English spoken in the Tyneside region of North-East England. This paper describes an exploratory multivariate analysis of phonetic data derived from NECTE that was undertaken with the aim of generating hypotheses about phonetic variation among speakers and speaker groups in the corpus, and how this variation correlates with social factors. The discussion is in four main parts. The first part outlines exploratory multivariate analysis in general and hierarchical cluster analysis in particular, the second describes the NECTE phonetic data used in the analysis, the third carries out a hierarchical cluster analysis of that data, and the fourth interprets the cluster analysis and relates the result to existing work on Tyneside English. The interpretation of the cluster analysis result is that phonetic variation among the NECTE speakers correlates strongly with gender and to a lesser extent with socio-economic status, but a correlation with age could not be demonstrated. The conclusion, finally, indicates directions for future work.

1. Exploratory multivariate analysis

1.1   Introduction to multivariate analysis

The proliferation of computational technology has generated an explosive production of electronically encoded information of all kinds. In the face of this, traditional paper-based methods for search and interpretation of data have been overwhelmed by sheer volume, and a wide variety of computational methods has been developed in an attempt to make the deluge at least tractable. As such methods have been refined and new ones introduced, something over and above tractability has emerged — new and unexpected ways of understanding the data. The fact that a computer can deal with vastly larger data sets than a human is an obvious factor, but there are two others of at least equal importance: one is the ease with which data can be manipulated and reanalyzed in interesting ways without the often prohibitive labour that this would involve using manual techniques, and the other is the extensive scope for visualization that computer graphics provide.

These developments have clear implications for the analysis of large bodies of text in corpus-based linguistics. On the one hand, large electronic text corpora potentially exploitable by the linguist are being generated as a by-product of the many kinds of daily IT-based activity worldwide, and, on the other, more and more application-specific electronic linguistic corpora are being constructed.

Effective analysis of such corpora will increasingly be tractable only by adapting the interpretative methods developed by the statistical, information retrieval, and related communities (Tabachnik & Fidell 2001, Hair et al. 1998, Baeza-Yates & Ribeiro-Neto 1999, Belew 2000). In the present paper we are interested in one particular type of tool: multivariate analysis. What is multivariate analysis?

Observation of nature plays a fundamental role in science. In current scientific methodology, an hypothesis about some natural phenomenon is proposed and its adequacy assessed using data obtained from observation of the domain of inquiry. But nature is dauntingly complex, and there is no practical or indeed theoretical hope of being able to observe even a small part of it exhaustively. Instead, the researcher selects particular aspects of the domain for observation. Each selected aspect is represented by a variable, and a series of observations is conducted in which, at each observation, the values for each variable are recorded. A body of data is thereby built up on the basis of which an hypothesis can be assessed. One might choose to observe only one aspect — the height of individuals in a population, for example, in which case the data set consists of more or less numerous values assigned to one variable; such a data set is referred to as univariate. If two values are observed — say height and weight — then the data set is said to be bivariate, if three — height, weight, age — trivariate, and so on up to some arbitrary number n. Strictly speaking, any data set where n is greater than 1 is multivariate, though in practice that term is normally used only when n is greater than 2 or 3 (Hair et al. 1998, Tabachnik & Fidell 2001).

As the number of variables grows, so does the difficulty of understanding the data, that is, of conceptualizing the interrelationships of variables within a single data item on the one hand, and the interrelationships of complete data items on the other. Multivariate analysis is the computational use of mathematical and statistical tools for understanding these interrelationships in data.

Numerous techniques for multivariate analysis exist. They can be divided into two main categories which are usually referred to as 'exploratory' and 'confirmatory'. Exploratory analysis aims to discover regularities in data which can serve as the basis for formulation of hypotheses about the domain from which the data comes; such techniques emphasize intuitively accessible, usually graphical representations of data structure. Confirmatory analysis attempts to determine whether or not there are significant relationships between some number of selected independent variables and one or more dependent ones. These two types are complementary in that the first generates hypotheses about data, and the second tries to determine whether or not the hypotheses are valid. Exploratory analysis is naturally prior to confirmatory; this discussion is concerned with the former.

1.2   Hierarchical cluster analysis

Hierarchical cluster analysis is a variety of exploratory multivariate analysis. To understand how it works and how the results it gives should be interpreted, it is first necessary to understand the concept of distance between data points in vector space.

Assume a domain of inquiry, say a linguistic corpus, which will be studied using six variables. If the six-dimensional data is to be analyzed using an exploratory method, it has to be represented mathematically. This is done in the form of vectors, where a vector is a sequence of values indexed by the positive integers 1, 2, 3.... Thus, Figure 1 is a length-6 vector v of numerical values in which the value of v_1 is 1.6, the value of v_2 is 2.4 and so on.

$$v = \begin{array}{|c|c|c|c|c|c|} \hline 1.6 & 2.4 & 7.5 & 0.6 & 0.1 & 2.6 \\ \hline \end{array}$$
$$\quad\; 1 \quad\; 2 \quad\; 3 \quad\; 4 \quad\; 5 \quad\; 6$$

Figure 1: *Example of a vector*

Where the data consists of more than one case, which it usually does, then each case is represented by a vector, and the set of vectors is assembled into a matrix, which is a sequence of vectors arranged in rows and the rows are indexed by the positive integers 1, 2, 3... . In matrix M, case 2 is at row M_2 and the value of the third variable for that case is at $M_{2,3}$, that is, 0.1.

$$M = \begin{array}{c|c|c|c|c|c|c|} 1 & 1.6 & 2.4 & 7.5 & 0.6 & 0.1 & 2.6 \\ \hline 2 & 3.4 & 6.2 & 0.1 & 1.1 & 0.1 & 1.1 \\ \hline 3 & 10 & 9.1 & 9.0 & 5.2 & 9.0 & 5.2 \\ \hline \end{array}$$
$$\qquad 1 \quad\; 2 \quad\; 3 \quad\; 4 \quad\; 5 \quad\; 6$$

Figure 2: *Example of a matrix*

A vector space is a geometrical interpretation of a set of vectors:

- The dimensionality n of the vectors, that is, the number of its elements, defines an n-dimensional space
- The indices of the vectors define the coordinates of the space
- The values in the vector define the coordinates of a point in that space

For example, a bivariate data set defines a 2-dimensional space in which each vector specifies the coordinates of a point in that space. Take a data set consisting of vectors that specify the age and weight of some number of individuals. A single such vector might be $v = (36,160)$. In geometrical terms, the x or age axis is 0..100, the y or weight axis is 0..200, and any vector in the data set can be plotted in the (x,y) space, as in Figure 3:

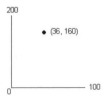

Figure 3: *A vector in 2-dimensional space*

If more vectors are plotted in the space, nonrandom structure may or may not emerge, depending on the interrelationships of the real-world characteristics that the variables represent. Where there are no structured real-world interrelationships, the result will look something like the plot of random points in Figure 4a. If there is structure, the plot might look something like 4b, where two clusters have clearly emerged; these clusters tell us something about the interrelationships of the represented entities.

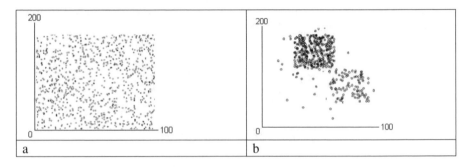

Figure 4: *Plots of random and nonrandom data vectors*

Analogously, a trivariate (age, weight, height) vector $v = (36, 160, 71)$ from a data set of length-3 vectors defines a point in 3-dimensional space, as shown in Figure 5:

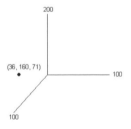

Figure 5: *A vector in 3-dimensional space*

A length-4 vector defines a point in 4-dimensional space, and so on to any dimensionality n. Mathematically there is no problem with spaces of dimension greater than 3: the conceptual and formal frameworks apply to n-dimensional spaces, for any n, as straightforwardly as to 2 or 3 dimensional ones. The only problems lie in the possibility of visualization and intuitive understanding. As the number of variables, and thus dimensions, grows beyond 3, graphical representation and intuitive comprehension of it become impossible — who can visualize points in a four-dimensional space, not to speak of a 40-dimensional one?

Given that the structure of data with dimensionality higher than 3 cannot be directly visualized, how is it to be understood? The various exploratory multivariate methods provide indirect visualizations. Hierarchical cluster analysis, in particular, constructs 'dendrograms' or trees that show the constituency structure of clusters using relative distance between and among points in the high-dimensional data vector space, where 'distance' can for present purposes be understood quite literally: distance between points A and B in Figure 6 can be measured, and it is less than the measured distance between, say, A and C.

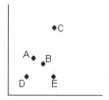

Figure 6: *Vectors with various relative distances in 2-dimensional space*

These relativities can be represented as a tree in which the horizontal lines represent distance: the longer the line, the greater the distance. Knowing this, it is easily seen that, in Figure 7, there are two main clusters, (C) and (ABDE), the latter of which itself has internal structure.

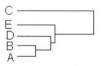

Figure 7: *Tree representation of relative vector distances in Figure 6*

Given a set of data vectors, hierarchical cluster analysis generates the corresponding distance-based tree. Details of distance measures and how these are used to generate such cluster trees are available in a wide variety of textbooks, for example Everitt (2001).

all very clear
(useful too) so far.

2. The NECTE data

2.1 Overview of the NECTE corpus

The NECTE corpus is based on two pre-existing corpora of audio-recorded speech, one of them gathered by the Tyneside Linguistic Survey (TLS) undertaken in the late 1960s (Strang 1968, Pellowe et al. 1972, Pellowe & Jones 1978, Jones-Sargent 1983), and the other between 1991 and 1994 for the 'Phonological Variation and Change in Contemporary Spoken English' (PVC) project (Milroy et al. 1994, Docherty & Foulkes 1999). The aim of the NECTE project has been to enhance, improve access to, and promote the re-use of the TLS and PVC corpora by amalgamating them into a single, TEI-conformant electronic corpus. The result is now available to the research community in a variety of formats: digitized sound, phonetic transcription, and standard orthographic transcription, all aligned and accessible on the Web (Corrigan, Moisl & Beal 2005).

The TLS component of NECTE includes phonetic transcriptions of about 10 minutes of each of 63 recordings. It is with these transcriptions that the remainder of this discussion is concerned.

2.2 The TLS phonetic transcriptions

One of the main aims of the TLS project was to see whether systematic phonetic variation among Tyneside speakers of the period could be significantly correlated with variation in their social characteristics. To this end they developed a methodology which was radical at the time and remains so today: in contrast to the then-universal and still-dominant theory driven approach, where social and linguistic factors are selected by the analyst on the basis of some combination of an independently-specified theoretical framework, existing case studies, and personal experience of the domain of enquiry, the TLS proposed a fundamentally empirical approach in which salient factors are extracted from the data itself and then serve as the basis for model construction.

To realize its research aim using its empirical methodology, the TLS had to compare the audio interviews it had collected at the phonetic level of representation. This required that the analog speech signal be discretized into phonetic segment sequences, or, in other words, to be phonetically transcribed. Details of the TLS transcription scheme are available in Jones-Sargent (1983) and Corrigan, Moisl & Beal (2005). For present purposes, it is sufficient to note that two levels of transcription were produced, a highly detailed narrow one designated 'State', and a superordinate 'Putative Diasystemic Variables' (PDV) level which collapsed some of the finer distinctions transcribed at the 'State' level.

3. Hierarchical cluster analysis of the TLS phonetic transcriptions

This section applies hierarchical cluster analysis to the TLS phonetic transcriptions at the PDV level of phonetic representation.

3.1   Data construction

The analyses are based on comparison of profiles associated with each of the TLS speakers. A profile for any speaker S is the number of times S uses each of the PDV codes defined by the TLS transcription scheme in his or her interview. More specifically, the profile P associated with S is a vector having as many elements as there are codes such that each vector element P_j represents the j'th PDV, where j is in the range 1..number of codes in the TLS scheme, and the value stored at P_j is an integer representing the number of times S uses the j'th PDV code. There are 156 PDVs, and so a PDV profile is a length-156 vector.

There are 63 TLS speakers, and their profiles are represented in a matrix having 63 rows, one for each profile. At the PDV level, therefore, the data used in this study is a 63 x 156 matrix M.

3.2   Data preprocessing

Prior to analysis, M was transformed in two ways.

i. Normalization for text length
The number of codes per transcription varies significantly. This variation in length has to be taken into account when conducting the analyses in order to avoid skewed results. The following function was applied to the raw PDV frequency matrix M:

$$freq'(M_{ij}) = freq(M_{ij}) \times \left(\frac{\mu}{l}\right)$$

Figure 8: *Text length normalization function*

where *freq'* is the adjusted frequency, M_{ij} is the value at the (i,j) coordinates of the data matrix M, *freq* is the raw frequency, μ is the mean number of codes per interview across all 63 interviews, and l is the number of codes in interview *i*. This function increases the frequency values for relatively shorter interviews in proportion to the mean interview length, and decreases frequency values for relatively longer interviews relative to the mean.

ii. Dimensionality reduction
Since there are 156 PDVs, there are 156 criteria for distinguishing the 63 speakers. It is, however, easy to show that many of these criteria are superfluous. The key to doing so is the statistical concept of variance, which measures the range of variation of values that a variable takes. Each of the columns in M is a

variable; the variances of the columns were calculated, sorted by decreasing magnitude, and plotted, and the result is shown in Figure 9:

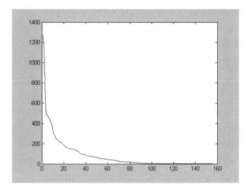

Figure 9: *Variance profile of the 156 PDV variables in the data matrix M*

Relative to the variance range 0..1300 there are a few very high-variance PDVs, a moderate number of middling-variance PDVs, and a majority of low-variance ones. Low variance says that the values a variable takes do not vary a great deal. This makes them unimportant for distinguishing the cases that the variable describes. In the present case, the PDVs to the right of — generously — the 80th have such low variance that they can be eliminated from consideration. They were, therefore, removed from M, resulting in a reduced-dimensionality 63 x 80 matrix.

3.3   Data analysis

Hierarchical cluster analysis is not a single method but a family of closely related ones which offer a range of ways to measure distance between vectors in *n*-dimensional space and of defining what constitutes a cluster in terms of those distance measures. Details can be found in any multivariate analysis or cluster analysis textbook; a standard account is in Everitt (2001). M is here analyzed using one particular combination of distance measure and cluster definition: squared Euclidean distance and increase in sum of squares clustering, also known as Ward's Method. This combination was chosen to facilitate comparison with earlier work on the data being analyzed here, on which more later. A standard caution in hierarchical cluster analysis applies, however. Relative to a given data matrix, different distance measure/cluster definition combinations can and usually do generate different trees. This leads to an obvious question: what are these methods really telling us about the structure of the data they describe — how reliable, in other words, are they, and are they in fact any use at all if they cannot be relied on to reveal the true structure of the data? The answer is that this is the wrong way of looking at what these methods are useful for. A set of vectors in *n*-dimensional space has a 'true' structure in the sense that the relative distances among the vectors exist independently of the observer and can be determined to arbitrary accuracy using an appropriate measure. Cluster membership, however, is not latent in the data. It is a matter of definition: each clustering method defines a cluster in its own way and then describes the data in terms of that definition, giving its own characteristic view of it. When faced with different analyses of the same data, it is up to the analyst to understand their artifactual nature, to realize that none is necessarily more 'true' of the data than any other, and to select those that are most useful for hypothesis generation, which is the object of the exploratory multivariate analysis.

Two analyses of the PDV frequency data are presented: the first (Figure 10a) includes all 63 speakers, that is, 7 Newcastle and 56 Gateshead speakers in the sample, and the second (Figure 10b) looks in detail at the Gateshead speakers.

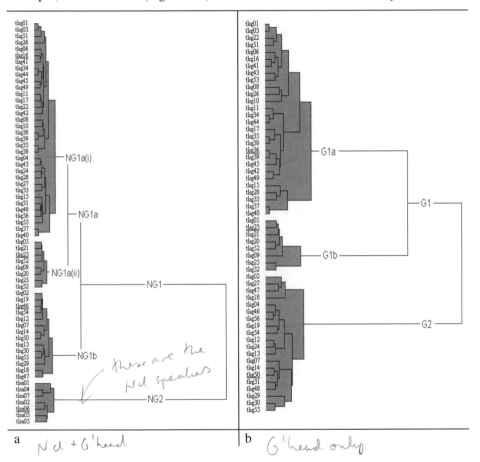

Figure 10: *Cluster trees of the NECTE data matrix*

Analysis 1: All speakers
There are two main clusters, labelled NG1 and NG2, and NG1 has subclusters with labels indicating constituency. NG2 clusters markedly against the rest, and comprises the Newcastle group. On the basis of the phonetic segment frequency distribution evidence at the PDV level, therefore, Newcastle speakers are strongly distinguished from Gateshead ones.

Analysis 2: Gateshead speakers only
The purpose of this second analysis is to examine in detail the structure of the cluster of Gateshead in Analysis 1, and to see if that structure correlates interestingly with social characteristics such as gender, age, and socio-economic status of the TLS speakers. We were primarily interested in the vowel variables, and so looked only at the vowel PDVs, though a similar analysis could be done for the consonants. The PDV frequency matrix M was re-calculated using vowel-PDV frequency data for the Gateshead speakers only, length-normalized, and dimensionality reduced as above to a 56 x 40 matrix. The result was two main clusters, labelled G1 and G2, and G1 itself comprises two subclusters G1a and G1b.

In the following table, the cluster labels are given in the first column, followed by the NECTE speaker ID and social variables selected from those included in the NECTE corpus.

Table 1: *Correlation of clusters with social variables*

Cluster	ID	Sex	Age	Education	Employment	Cluster	ID	Sex	Age	Education	Emplo-ment
G1a	tlsg01	F	31-40	Minimum	Skilled manual	G1b	tlsg05	F	21-30	Day release	Lower admin
G1a	tlsg03	F	41-50	Minimum	Semi-skilled manual	G1b	tlsg23	M	21-30	Tertiary	Higher admin
G1a	tlsg22	F	41-50	Minimum	Skilled manual	G1b	tlsg21	F	17-20	Night school	Skilled manual
G1a	tlsg51	F	21-30	Minimum	Skilled manual	G1b	tlsg20	M	21-30	Tertiary	Skilled manual
G1a	tlsg06	F	61-70	Minimum	Semi-skilled manual	G1b	tlsg52	F	31-40	Night school	Skilled manual
G1a	tlsg16	F	41-50	Minimum	Unskilled manual	G1b	tlsg09	F	21-30	Day release	Higher admin
G1a	tlsg41	F	51-60	Minimum	Unskilled manual	G1b	tlsg25	F	41-50	Night school	Skilled manual
G1a	tlsg43	M	21- 30	Minimum	Skilled manual	G1b	tlsg32	F	51-60	Minimum	Lower admin
G1a	tlsg53	M	16-20	Day release	Skilled manual						
G1a	tlsg08	F	17-20	Minimum	Unskilled manual	G2	tlsg02	M	31-40	Minimum	Skilled manual
G1a	tlsg26	F	41-50	Minimum	Unskilled manual	G2	tlsg27	M	21-30	Minimum	Skilled manual
G1a	tlsg10	F	17-20	Minimum	Unskilled manual	G2	tlsg47	M	21-30	Minimum	Unskilled manual

G1a	tlsg11	F	31-40	College	Semi-skilled manual	G2	tlsg18	M	31-40	Minimum	Unskilled manual
G1a	tlsg34	F	31-40	College	Lower admin	G2	tlsg04	M	61-70	Minimum	Skilled manual
G1a	tlsg44	F	51-60	Night school	Unskilled manual	G2	tlsg46	M	31-40	Minimum	Lower admin
G1a	tlsg17	F	51-60	Minimum	Semi-skilled manual	G2	tlsg56	M	21-30	Night school	Skilled manual
G1a	tlsg35	F	31-40	Minimum	Unskilled manual	G2	tlsg19	M	41-50	Minimum	Semi-skilled manual
G1a	tlsg38	F	31-40	Minimum	Unskilled manual	G2	tlsg54	M	21-30	Day release	Skilled manual
G1a	tlsg36	F	31-40	Minimum	Unskilled manual	G2	tlsg12	M	21-30	Minimum	Semi-skilled manual
G1a	tlsg39	F	31-40	Minimum	Unskilled manual	G2	tlsg24	M	61-70	Minimum	Skilled manual
G1a	tlsg45	F	41-50	Minimum	Unskilled manual	G2	tlsg13	M	61-70	Minimum	Unskilled manual
G1a	tlsg42	F	21-30	Minimum	Skilled manual	G2	tlsg07	M	31-40	Minimum	Skilled manual
G1a	tlsg49	F	41-50	Minimum	Unskilled manual	G2	tlsg14	M	41-50	Minimum	Semi-skilled manual
G1a	tlsg15	F	21-30	Minimum	Skilled manual	G2	tlsg50	M	31-40	Minimum	Skilled manual
G1a	tlsg28	M	61-70	Minimum	Unskilled manual	G2	tlsg31	M	31-40	Minimum	Unskilled manual
G1a	tlsg33	M	61-70	Minimum	Unskilled manual	G2	tlsg48	M	51-60	Night school	Skilled manual
G1a	tlsg37	F	41-50	Minimum	Unskilled manual	G2	tlsg29	M	41-50	Minimum	Skilled manual
G1a	tlsg40	F	41-50	Minimum	Unskilled manual	G2	tlsg30	M	41-50	Minimum	Skilled manual
						G2	tlsg55	M	21-30	Minimum	Skilled manual

The clearest correlation is between cluster structure and sex: G2 consists entirely of men, and G1 mainly though not exclusively of women. With a few slight exceptions, the men in G2 have the minimum legal level of education, and all are in unskilled - skilled manual employment. In G1 there is a clear split between a cluster consisting mainly of women with minimum education in unskilled - skilled manual employment, and one consisting of men and women with a slightly higher educational and employment level. Finally, there is no obvious correlation between cluster structure and age.

3.4   Assessment of results relative to existing work on Tyneside English

The TLS project culminated in Jones-Sargent (1983), who performed cluster analyses based on the segmental phonological data and on the social data we have been dealing with, and then attempted to relate the two in a sociolinguistically meaningful way. In order to derive social and linguistic classifications, Jones-Sargent used hierarchical cluster analysis, and squared Euclidean distance and

Ward's method more specifically. We chose that combination in our own analyses to facilitate comparison with Jones-Sargent's work. Direct comparison is nevertheless complicated, for several methodological reasons:

- The data that Jones-Sargent used for one speaker (in her analysis, labeled STEPH5M3) is no longer directly available, while data for 12 speakers (tlsg31-tlsg40, tlsg55, tlsg56) included in the present analysis were not analyzed by Jones-Sargent.
- Jones-Sargent analyzed the detailed State rather than the PDV level used in the present study.
- A different length normalization method was used (Jones-Sargent 1983:93-94)
- The data was not dimensionality-reduced.
- Due to computational hardware and software limitations when the analysis was done in the early 1980s, the TLS data had to be partitioned into three groups — monophthongs, diphthongs, and consonants — and analyzed separately (Jones-Sargent 1983:105 & 195-199), and the cluster trees for the groups differ among themselves.

Jones-Sargent's tree for the diphthong group is given in Figure 11. To facilitate comparison, we have inserted to the left of Jones-Sargent's labels at the leaves of the tree our own cluster labels from Figure 10a showing, for each speaker, the cluster to which that speaker belongs in our own analysis. The sharp distinction we found between the Newcastle and Gateshead speakers is evident here, as well as in Jones-Sargent's analyses of the TLS monophthong and consonant groups. Apart from this, however, it is difficult to see anything but a random match between our results and Jones-Sargent's.

As regards the correlation between phonetic clusters and social factors, Jones-Sargent's results are very different from our own: her conclusion is "that there is no simple relationship between the social classification and this linguistic classification" (1983:249). A full explication of this disparity in results would require engagement with the details of Jones-Sargent's methodology for social classification of the TLS speakers (1983, chs. 5 & 7), which is not possible within the space constraints on this discussion. It must therefore suffice to note that she clustered speakers on 38 social variables using a methodology closely analogous to that used for the phonetic data, and then attempted to correlate the social and phonetic cluster results. We took the far less complex approach of manually identifying the social variables for which a correlation with the phonetic cluster results could be demonstrated or seemed likely.

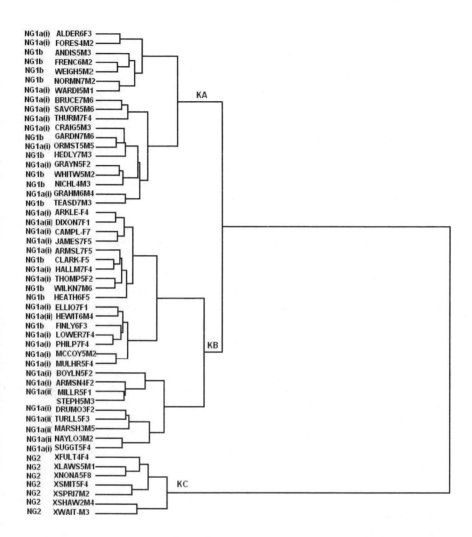

Figure 11: *Cluster tree for diphthong data from Jones-Sargent (1983: 198)*

More generally on the relationship between phonetic clusters and social factors, previous analysis has found a consistent correlation between a number of social variables and phonetic / phonological variation in Tyneside English. Milroy et al. (1994), Docherty et al. (1997) and Watt & Milroy (1999), analyze the social distribution of variants of a small number of linguistic variables (/p/, /t/ and /k/, and the FACE, GOAT and NURSE vowels), and they all find that gender, in particular, plays a central role in determining the distribution of linguistic variables in the dialect. So important is this social factor that Watt & Milroy (1999:42) suggest that that "Differentiation by gender … seems in fact to be tantamount to a sociolinguistic priority" in their data. The distribution of male and

confirm our finding

female speakers in the present analysis suggests that gender is a centrally important factor in determining the distribution of a wide range of linguistic variants, of which the small number of variables previously examined are only a small part. Similarly, Milroy et al. (1994), Docherty et al. (1997) and Watt & Milroy (1999) all find that social class and age have an important effect on the distribution of the linguistic variants that they examine. For example, Watt & Milroy (1999) found that highly localized, traditional pronunciations of the FACE, GOAT and NURSE vowels are most characteristic of older working class speakers, whilst "non-traditional supra-local" variants (p.40) are most characteristic of younger middle class speakers.

4. Conclusion

The aim of the research reported in this paper was to generate hypotheses about phonetic variation among speakers and speaker groups in the NECTE corpus, and how this variation correlates with social factors, using exploratory multivariate analysis and cluster analysis more particularly. The result was a clearly-defined classification of speakers on the basis of their phonetic usage that has a strong correlation with the speakers' social characteristics, and generally agrees with existing work on Tyneside English.

Future work based on this result will consider the following:

a. The cluster analysis presented above does not give the 'true' analysis of the data, as already noted: other distance measure / cluster definition combinations in hierarchical analysis as well as completely different analytical methods such as self-organizing maps (Kohonen 2001) can and do yield different results (Jones & Moisl 2005). The aim is therefore to try a variety of other types of analytical method to determine the degree to which they agree with one another.
b. The above analysis says *that* the NECTE speakers fall into particular clusters, but not *why*. We aim to establish this by examining the clusters with a view to identifying the phonetic variables that are most important in determining the cluster structure.

References

Baeza-Yates, R. & B. Ribeiro-Neto. 1999. Modern information retrieval. Addison Wesley.
Belew, R. 2000. Finding Out About: a cognitive perspective on search engine technology and the WWW. Cambridge: CUP.
Corrigan, K., H. Moisl & J. Beal. 2005. "The Newcastle Electronic Corpus of Tyneside English". http://www.ncl.ac.uk/necte/> (10 July 2006).
Docherty, G. J. & P. Foulkes. 1999. "Sociophonetic variation in 'glottals' in Newcastle English". Proceedings of the 14th International Congress of Phonetic Sciences, 1037-1040. University of California, Berkeley.
Docherty, G. J., P. Foulkes, J. Milroy, L. Milroy & D. Walshaw. 1997. "Descriptive adequacy in phonology: a variationist perspective". Journal of Linguistics 33. 275-310.
Everitt, B. 2001. Cluster Analysis. London: Arnold.

Hair, J., R. Anderson, R. Tatham & W. Black. 1998. Multivariate data analysis. Prentice-Hall.

Jones, V. 1985. "Tyneside syntax: A presentation of some data from the Tyneside linguistic survey". Focus on England and Wales ed. by W. Viereck, 163-177. Amsterdam: John Benjamins.

Jones, V. & H. Moisl. 2005. "Cluster analysis of the *Newcastle Electronic Corpus of Tyneside English*: A comparison of methods". Web X: A Decade of the World Wide Web, Proceedings of the Joint International Conference of the Association for Computers and the Humanities and the Association for Literary and Linguistic Computing. Athens: University of Georgia. Literary and Linguistic Computing 20. 1-22.

Jones-Sargent, V.1983. "Tyne Bytes. A computerised sociolinguistic study of Tyneside". Bamberger Beiträge zur englischen Sprachwissenschaft. Frankfurt am Main: Peter Lang.

Kohonen, T. 2001. Self-organizing maps, 3rd ed. New York: Springer.

Milroy, J. et al. 1994. "Local and supra-local change in British English: the case of glottalisation". English World-Wide 15:1. 1-32.

Milroy, L., J. Milroy, G.J. Docherty, P. Foulkes & D. Walshaw. 1997. "Phonological variation and change in contemporary English: evidence from Newcastle-upon-Tyne and Derby". Variation and linguistic change in English ed. by S. Conde & J.M. Hernandez-Compoy, 35-46. London: Cuadernos de Filolog'a Ingelsa.

Pellowe, J., G. Nixon, B. Strang & V. McNeany 1972. "A dynamic modelling of linguistic variation: the urban (Tyneside) Linguistic Survey". Lingua 30. 1-30.

Pellowe, J., & V. Jones. 1978. "On intonational variety in Tyneside speech". Sociolinguistic patterns of British English ed. by P. Trudgill, 101-121. London: Arnold.

Strang, B. 1968. "The Tyneside linguistic survey". Zeitschrift für Mundartforschung, NF 4 (Verhandlungen des Zweiten Internationalen Dialecktologenkongresses). 788-794.Wiesbaden: Franz Steiner Verlag.

Tabachnik, B. & L. Fidell. 2001. Using multivariate statistics. Boston: Allyn & Bacon.

Watt, D. & L. Milroy. 1999. "Patterns of variation and change in three Newcastle vowels: is this dialect levelling?". Urban voices: accent studies in the British Isles ed. by P. Foulkes & G. Docherty, 25-47. London: Arnold.

Production and judgment in childhood
The case of liaison in French

Aurélie Nardy & Stéphanie Barbu
Université Stendhal & Université Rennes1

Abstract: Sociolinguistic studies show that adult speakers' behaviour does not necessary reflect their evaluation of linguistic variants. The present study investigated the influence of children's social backgrounds on both production and evaluation of two types of liaison: the variable or optional liaison, which is a sociolinguistic variable, and the obligatory liaison, which does not vary with social characteristics in adults. Informants were 188 French native speakers, aged from 2 to 6 years, using a transversal study. Social differences were found both in children's productions and judgments. Furthermore, the two types of liaison followed different developmental courses. Significant social differences in production of variable liaison appeared late in development, whereas differences concerning obligatory liaison appeared at an early age but decreased with age. Social differences in children's evaluations of variable liaison were recorded in late development, whereas the differences observed in evaluations of obligatory liaison were only temporary, during the fifth year of age. These findings are discussed by integrating psycholinguistic and sociolinguistic perspectives, as both have stressed the importance of the frequency of exposure to linguistic forms in the speaker input.

1. Introduction[*]

Adult speakers often attribute social values to linguistic variants; they can evaluate them in either positive or negative ways. However, sociolinguistic studies have shown that speakers' behaviour does not necessary reflect their judgment. For instance, speakers may produce variants they evaluate negatively (Labov 1976). Although some previous work has examined the production of sociolinguistic variables by children (Labov 1964, Roberts 1994, 1997, Chevrot Beaud & Varga 2000, Días-Campos 2005), to our knowledge, no studies have investigated both the production and the judgment of linguistic variants during language acquisition. Therefore, the present study aimed to examine how young children produce and evaluate a variable phonological phenomenon: liaison in French.

Liaison is a sandhi phenomenon which consists of the production of a consonant between two words (word₁ and word₂) in connected speech. For this consonant to appear, word₂ must begin with a vowel when it is pronounced in

[*] This research was supported by the program Systèmes Complexes en Sciences Humaines et Sociales proposed by the French Centre National de la Recherche Scientifique and the Ministry of Research.

isolation. For instance, when the French determiner *les* "the" is combined with the noun *ours* "bear" in fluent speech, the sequence is pronounced [lezurs]. Thus, the liaison consonant /z/ appears when the two words *les* and *ours* are combined. The most frequent liaison consonants (99.7% of the realized cases) are the apical consonants /n/, /z/ and /t/ (Boë & Tubach 1992). Word$_1$ determines which of these consonants appears. For example, the word$_1$ *un* "a"/"one" activates the liaison consonant /n/, the word$_1$ *deux* "two" activates the liaison consonant /z/ and the word$_1$ *petit* "little" activates the liaison consonant /t/.

French liaison can be divided into two categories: obligatory liaison and variable or optional liaison. Our study was based on the classification established by Booij & de Jong (1987). By studying 38 adult French native speakers from three age groups and five socio-economic classes (approximately equal numbers of men and women), they established contexts in which liaison appeared to be obligatory. They found that obligatory liaison contexts (i.e., when the rate of realization is 100%) are not frequent: "after determiners and in the combinations 'personal pronoun + verb' and 'verb + pronoun', as well as in certain frozen expressions" (Booij & de Jong 1987: 1010). Other liaison contexts appear to be variable, having rates of realization below 100%. Previous studies have shown that optional liaison involves a stratified linguistic variable. The frequency of realization of this type of liaison varies with *speech style* — greater variable liaison realizations in careful style (Ågren 1973) —, *age* — lower variable liaison realizations in young people (Ashby 1981) — and *gender* — divergent findings: more realizations in males (de Jong 1991), more realizations in females (Ashby 1981; Green & Hintze 1990). Moreover, another factor influencing the realization of variable liaison is *social status* (Moisset 2000; Armstrong 2001). Several studies have presented evidence that upper-class adult speakers realize more optional liaison than lower-class speakers,[1] but little is known about children's productions. Thus, this study investigated the influence of children's social backgrounds on both the production and evaluation of these two types of liaison. In this perspective, we examined whether the social differences evidenced in adults in the production of variable liaison are observed in children of 2 to 6 years old and whether children's evaluations of variable liaison differ according to their social backgrounds.

Several sociolinguistic principles have been established on the basis of adult speaker data (Labov 2001). Concerning the production of variable liaisons, Bloomfield's Principle of Density (Bloomfield 1933), updated by Labov, suggested that "the more often people talk to each other, the more similar their speech will be" (Labov 2001: 228). As adults present in the environment of children from upper-class backgrounds produce variable liaison more frequently (de Jong 1991), upper-class children were expected to realize variable liaison more frequently than lower-class children. Thus, on the assumption that children behave like grown-ups, social differences should be observed in children's

---

[1] Delattre (1966), Alécot (1975), Ashby (1981), Booij & de Jong (1987), de Jong (1994).

production of optional liaison (hypothesis 1). Regarding the judgment of acceptability of variable liaison, the Principle of Uniform Evaluation (Labov 2001, 2003) postulated that all speakers evaluate a stratified linguistic variable in the same way, although speakers use linguistic variants differently. Thus, social differences are not expected to occur in children's judgments. Children are expected to evaluate the two variants of optional liaisons (i.e., whether liaison is realized or not) in the same way (hypothesis 2). Finally, we studied children's production and evaluation of obligatory liaison. All speakers realize them categorically, whatever their social characteristics and the communication setting. Given the fact that obligatory liaison is not subject to variation in adult speech, no social differences were expected to emerge either in production or in judgment (hypothesis 3). Therefore, our general aim was to examine how variation or non-variation of linguistic forms in child input influences the acquisition of this particular French phenomenon. The three hypotheses that we proposed are summarized in the table below (Table 1).

Table 1: *Social differences expected in the production and the judgment of variable and obligatory liaisons*

| | Social differentiation? | |
	Variable liaison	Obligatory liaison
Production	yes (hyp.1)	no (hyp.3)
Judgment	no (hyp.2)	no (hyp.3)

2. Methods

2.1   Subjects

188 children of 2 to 6 year-old took part in this study. They were divided into four age groups and two social backgrounds: upper-class and lower-class (Table 2).

Table 2: *Age group and social background distribution*

Age groups	Social backgrounds	N
Age group 1 (2-3 years old)	Upper-class	22
	Lower-class	19
Age group 2 (3-4 years old)	Upper-class	25
	Lower-class	20
Age group 3 (4-5 years old)	Upper-class	27
	Lower-class	27
Age group 4 (5-6 years old)	Upper-class	25
	Lower-class	23

Social backgrounds were based on their parents' occupations following the INSEE[2] nomenclature (Desrosières & Thévenot 1988). Children whose two parents were from group 3 of the INSEE nomenclature (e.g., professors and scientific professions, senior managers, engineers) were considered to belong to the upper-class. Children whose two parents were from group 6 (i.e., all types of workers: industrial, artisanal, agricultural workers and drivers) were classified in the lower-class. When one of the parents was unemployed (i.e., did not work outside the household), only the occupation of the other working parent was considered.

2.2   Experimental tasks

Two tasks were designed to induce children to produce and to evaluate obligatory and variable liaison. The production task was a picture naming task. Children were asked to produce 24 word$_1$-word$_2$ sequences from 24 pictures of objects or animals with nouns starting with a vowel : *ours* "bear" - *arbre* "tree" - *avion* "plane" - *escargot* "snail" - *éléphant* "elephant" - *ordinateur* "computer" (n word$_1$ = 6). According to Booij & de Jong's classification (1987), liaison following determiners such as *un* "a"/"one" and *deux* "two" is obligatory, whereas the liaison after prenominal adjectives such as *petit* "little" and *gros* "big" is variable (n word$_2$ = 4). To elicit the production of obligatory liaison after the words$_1$ *un* "a"/ "one" and *deux* "two", the objects/animals were drawn once on six pictures and twice on six others. To induce optional liaison, 12 pictures of the same objects/animals were presented to children: six were large (word$_1$: *gros* "large") and six were small (*petit* "little"). In all, children had to produce 24 word$_1$-word$_2$ sequences: 12 inducing obligatory liaison and 12 inducing variable liaison. For both variable and obligatory liaison, a case was considered to be correctly realized when the children produced the appropriate liaison consonant.

In the judgment of acceptability task, children had to determine which one of the two linguistic forms they heard was correct. The two forms were produced by the experimenter who made two puppets talk. Children had to show which puppet they guessed was speaking more correctly. For obligatory liaisons, one puppet produced an utterance with liaison correctly (e.g., [œ̃nuʀs]) and the other produced liaison incorrectly (e.g., [œ̃zuʀs], which is a recurring error in child speech, cf. Chevrot, Dugua & Fayol (2005). For the variable liaison, children heard an utterance with liaison (e.g., [pətituʀs]) and an utterance without liaison (e.g., [pətiuʀs]). Words$_1$ and words$_2$ used in the judgment task were the same as in the production task. Thus, children had to evaluate 24 word$_1$-word$_2$ sequences: 12 including obligatory liaison (6 were correct and 6 were not) and 12 including variable liaison (6 with a correct liaison, i.e. with the correct liaison consonant, and 6 with no liaison; for more details about the procedure, see Nardy 2003).

---

[2] INSEE : *Institut National de la Statistique et des Etudes Economiques* (French National Institute of Statistic and Economic Studies).

3. Results

3.1   Production of variable liaison

Whatever the age group, upper-class children realized variable liaison correctly more often than lower-class children (Figure 1) (ANOVA, $F_{1,179}$ = 11.123, p = 0.001).[3] The effect of social background was significant only for age group 4 (Holm-Sidak, p = 0.001). Five to six year-old upper-class children produced approximately 40% of the variable liaison, whereas the mean rate of realization by lower-class children did not exceed 21%. In age group 3, upper-class children also tended to produce variable liaison correctly more often (28.40%) than lower-class children (15.80%) (Holm-Sidak, p = 0.061). No significant differences were found in age groups 1 and 2.

very low even here

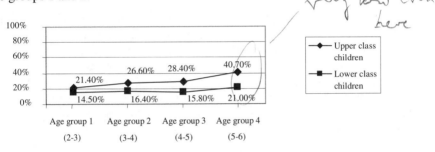

Figure 1: *Percentages of correctly realized variable liaison*

Congruent with the prediction based on the Principle of Density (Bloomfield 1933; Labov 2001), we evidenced significant social differences in the production of variable liaison by the oldest children. After several years of exposure to the different linguistic uses, the variable liaison scores of upper- and lower-class children diverged, while children's rates of realization converged toward adult rates.

3.2   Production of obligatory liaison   *rather a loaded term*

Obligatory liaison was produced correctly in greater proportions by upper-class children than by lower-class children (Figure 2) (ANOVA, $F_{1,179}$ = 32.511, p< 0.001). Social differences in success rates were significant for age group 1 (Holm-Sidak, p<0.001) and age group 3 (p=0.019) and marginally significant for age group 2 (p=0.087), but in age group 4 no social differences were observed.

---

[3] For statistical analyses, 2 way ANOVAs (social class x age) were used after making transformations to normalize data (Sokal & Rohlf 1981).

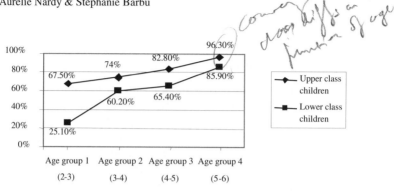

Figure 2: *Percentages of correctly realized obligatory liaisons*

Contrary to our assumption, social differences were found in children's production of obligatory liaison, although no such differences exist in adults. Nevertheless, the social differentiation shrank in the course of development (the differences are 42, 14, 17, 10 percentage points, respectively). However, the children's environments may have had an impact on the acquisition of this type of liaison. Although obligatory liaison does not show any sociolinguistic variation in adults (i.e., the production rate is 100%), we could suppose that other kinds of differences may influence acquisition processes. This issue is discussed below.

3.3   Developmental paths of the production of variable and obligatory liaisons

We found that the production of variable and obligatory liaison did not follow the same developmental courses. Upper- and lower-class age group 1 children (i.e., from 2 to 3 years old) produced variable liaison correctly with similar rates, but the rates diverged gradually during further development (Figure 1). On the other hand, the greatest difference for the production of obligatory liaison appeared in age group 1, and then differences decreased while rates for upper- and lower-class children converged gradually during development (Figure 2). Therefore, following these developmental paths, the production of children aged 5 to 6 years matched the performance of adult speakers, which results in social heterogeneity in variable liaison and social homogeneity in obligatory liaison.

3.4   Judgment of acceptability of variable liaison

We found a significant effect of social background in the evaluation of variable liaison (ANOVA, $F_{1,179} = 5.426$, p=0.021). Until they are 4 to 5 years old, children from both social backgrounds did not judge utterances produced with optional liaison to be more acceptable than those produced without liaison (Figure 3). Indeed, they judged both linguistic forms to be the correct form at similar rates (i.e., approximately 50%). Thus, we found no significant social differences from age group 1 to age group 3. However in age group 4, upper-class children favoured the realization of variable liaison significantly more frequently than lower-class children (Holm-Sidak, p=0.004). Only upper-class children progressed between age groups 3 and 4, leading to the late emergence of social differences.

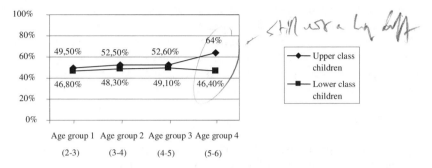

Figure 3: *Percentages of judgments in favour of realized variable liaison*

Contrary to our prediction based on the Principle of Uniform Evaluation (Labov 2001), social differences were observed in the judgment of variable liaison at the age of 5-6 years when significant social differences were also found in production. The fact that social differences appeared at roughly the same time both in production and in judgment suggests that a period of exposure to the linguistic forms encountered in the environment may be necessary before social background influences both child use and evaluation of the variants.

3.5   Judgment of acceptability of obligatory liaison

We found a significant effect of social background in the judgment of obligatory liaison (ANOVA, $F_{1,179}$ = 5.612, p=0.019). However, the difference between upper- and lower-class children was significant only for one age group (viz. age group 3) when children were between 4 and 5 years old (Holm-Sidak, p = 0.001) (Figure 4).

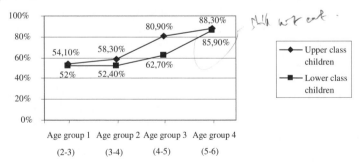

Figure 4: *Percentages of judgments in favour of correctly realized obligatory liaisons*

Our assumption that no social differences should occur in the judgment of obligatory liaison is partially supported by our findings. Indeed, the youngest children from both social backgrounds selected utterances produced with correct or incorrect liaison at similar rates (i.e., approximately 50%). As children grew up, they gradually judged the realization of obligatory liaisons more accurately. Nevertheless, upper-class children progressed faster than lower-class children, leading to the significant temporal difference reported above. Although no social value is assigned to obligatory liaison, a temporary difference between the social groups appeared during development. As this difference cannot be explained by differences in adult uses and evaluation, we discuss other explanations below.

4. Discussion

Our findings support only one of the two predictions we drew from sociolinguistics to investigate production and judgment of acceptability of variable liaison, namely the prediction concerning their production. Congruent with previous evidence for adult speakers, we found social differences in the production of variable liaison by the oldest children of our sample. Thus, the Principle of Density (Bloomfield 1933; Labov 2001) appears to apply to children's uses. Nevertheless, the second prediction regarding variable liaison (i.e. no social differentiation in evaluation) was not confirmed. Our results suggest that children's judgments of optional liaison do not fit the Principle of Uniform Evaluation (Labov 2001). Contrary to our hypothesis, variable liaison was evaluated differently by the oldest children of the study. Our findings suggest that this principle may require time to emerge during development. As Labov noticed, "if the dominant prestige norms are concerned, one can expect to find the rate of acquisition to be socially stratified" (Labov 2001: 215). Finally, our assumption that no early social differences in obligatory liaison would be observed was not confirmed. Unexpectedly, we found that this type of liaison shows social differences in childhood, although no variations has been reported in adults, neither in production, nor in evaluation.

A solution to account for all our findings would be to consider the frequency of usage of linguistic forms in child input. This has been shown an important factor by psycholinguistic researchers.[4] Indeed, this perspective provides some fruitful insights into our findings for the two types of liaison, even if optional liaison provides variable input whereas obligatory liaison results in invariable sequences.

The fact that social background influenced children's uses of obligatory liaison was surprising, as children from all social classes are exposed to categorical realization of this type of liaison in their environment. However, Hoff and her colleagues have shown that the quantity of input provided to a child varies according to social background (Hoff-Ginsberg 1994; Hoff et al. 2002; Hoff 2003). They have presented evidence that upper-class mothers provide a greater quantity of input to their children by using more complex sentences and a larger lexicon than lower-class mothers. Thus, upper-class children may produce

---

[4] Bybee & Hopper (2001); Huttenlocher et al. (2002); Lieven, Behrens, Speares & Tomasello (2003); Tomasello (2003).

obligatory liaison more accurately because they are more familiar with these linguistic forms, given their higher frequency in the input. A greater quantity of input may also facilitate children's evaluations of obligatory liaison, as they have greater perceptive familiarity with such forms. In the long run, the cumulative effects of input may induce the differences recorded between 2 and 6 years old to develop until the acquisition curves of children from both backgrounds converge toward adult uses.

Frequency and familiarity with some variants can also explain our results concerning variable liaison. Inputs of this type of liaison will equally differ according to social background. Indeed, upper-class adults realize optional liaison more often than adults from other backgrounds. Thus, upper-class children are more familiar with the realized variants as these variants are more frequent in their environment. Contrary to our findings concerning obligatory liaison, for variable liaison, the cumulative effects of input lead to the late emergence (i.e., at 5-6 years old) of social differences for both production and judgment. In this case, the longer the exposure, the greater the social differences. Therefore, social differences in obligatory liaison may result from differences in the pace of the learning process which, in turn, depends on the quantity of the input received, whereas social differences in variable liaison may result from the progressive learning of different social dialects, induced by inputs that are qualitatively different. Although variable and obligatory liaisons provide different kinds of inputs, frequency effects seem to play an important role in the learning process.

Considering either the psycholinguistic or the sociolinguistic perspective, our interpretation remains compatible with the Principle of Density (Bloomfield 1933, Labov 2001), albeit in a different way. Studying the density of interactions is another way of studying frequency and familiarity effects. Finally, the challenge of an integrative perspective between sociolinguistic and psycholinguistic approaches is all the more important in order to elaborate developmental sociolinguistics, which would account for children's acquisition of language variation.

References

Ågren, J. 1973. Étude sur quelques liaisons facultatives dans le français de conversation radiophonique. Uppsala: Uppsala University Press.

Armstrong, N. 2001. Social and stylistic variation in spoken French: A comparative approach. Amsterdam, Philadelphia: John Benjamins.

Ashby, W. 1981. "French Liaison as a Sociolinguistic Phenomenon". Linguistics Symposium on Romance Languages 9th ed. by W. W. Cressey & D. J. Napoli, 46-57. Washington, DC: Georgetown University Press.

Bloomfield, L. 1933. Language. London: G. Allen and Unwin.

Boë, L.-J. & J.-P. Tubach. 1992. "De A à Zut". Dictionnaire phonétique du français parlé. Grenoble: Ellug.

Booij, G. & D. de Jong. 1987. "The domain of liaison: Theories and data". Linguistics 25: 5. 1005-1025.

Bybee, J. & P. Hopper. 2001. "Introduction to frequency and the emergence of linguistic structure". Frequency and the emergence of linguistic structure ed. by J. Bybee & P. Hopper, 1-24. Amsterdam, Philadelphia: John Benjamins.

Chevrot, J.-P., L. Beaud & R. Varga. 2000. "Developmental data on a French sociolinguistic variable: The word-final post-consonantal /R/". Language Variation and Change 12:3. 295-319.

Chevrot, J.-P., C. Dugua & M. Fayol. 2005. "Liaison et formation des mots en français: Un scénario développemental". Langages 158. 38-52.

de Jong, D. 1994. "La sociophonologie de la liaison orléanaise". French Generative Phonology: Retrospective and perspectives ed. by C. Lyche & E. Salford, 95-130. Association for French Language Studies in association with the European Studies Research Institute.

de Jong, D. 1991. "La liaison à Orléans France et à Montréal Québec". Mimeo of paper presented at the XIIth international congress of phonetic sciences, Aix-en-Provence.

Delattre, P. 1966. Studies in French and comparative phonetics: Selected papers in French and English. The Hague, London, Paris: Mouton.

Desrosières, A. & L. Thévenot. 1988. Les catégories socioprofessionnelles. Paris: La Découverte.

Días-Campos, M. 2005. "The emergence of adult-like command of sociolinguistic variables: A study of consonant weakening in Spanish-Speaking children". Selected Proceedings of the 6th Conference on the Acquisition of Spanish and Portuguese as First and Second Languages ed. by D. Eddington, 56-65. Somerville, MA: Cascadilla Proceedings Project.

Green, J.-N. & M.-A. Hintze. 1990. "Variation and change in French linking phenomena". Variation and change in French: Essays presented to Rebecca Posner on the occasion of her sixtieth birthday ed. by J.-N. Green & W. Ayres-Bennett, 61-88. London, New York: Routledge.

Hoff, E. 2003. "The specificity of environmental influence: Socioeconomic status affects early vocabulary development via maternal speech". Child Development 74:5. 1368-1378.

Hoff, E., B. Laursen & T. Tardif. 2002. "Socioeconomic status and parenting". Handbook of parenting ed. by M. H. Bornstein, 231-252. Mahwah: Lawrence Erlbaum

Hoff-Ginsberg, E. 1994. "Influences of mother and child on maternal talkativeness". Discourse Processes 18. 105-117.

Huttenlocher, J., M. Vasilyeva, E. Cymerman & S. Levine. 2002. "Language input and child syntax". Cognitive Psychology 45. 337-374.

Labov, W. 1964. "Stages in the acquisition of Standard English". Social dialects and language learning ed. by R. Shuy, A. Davis & R. Hogan, 77-104. Champaign: National Council of Teachers of English.

Labov, W. 1976. Sociolinguistique. Paris: Editions de Minuit.

Labov, W. 2001. Principles of linguistic change, vol. 2: Social factors. Oxford: Blackwell.

Labov, W. 2003. "Some sociolinguistic principles". Sociolinguistics: The essential reading ed. by C. B. Paulston & G. R. Tucker, 234-250. Malden: Blackwell Publishing.

Lieven, E., H. Behrens, J. Speares & M. Tomasello. 2003. "Early syntactic creativity: A usage-based approach". Journal of Child Language 30. 333-370.

Malécot, A. 1975. "French liaison as a function of grammatical, phonetic and paralinguistic variables". Phonetica 32. 161-179.

Moisset, C. 2000. Variable liaison in Parisian French. Ph.D. diss., University of Pennsylvania.

Nardy, A. 2003. Production et jugement d'acceptabilité entre 2 et 6 ans: Aspects psycholinguistiques et sociolinguistiques de l'acquisition de la liaison. Université Stendhal: Mémoire de Diplôme d'Etudes Approfondies.

Roberts, J. 1994. Acquisition of variable rules: -t,d deletion and ing production in preschool children. Ph.D. dissertation, University of Pennsylvania.

Roberts, J. 1997. "Acquisition of variable rules: A study of -t,d deletion in preschool children". Journal of Child Language 24. 351-372.

Sokal, R. R. & J.F. Rohlf. 1981. Biometry: The principles and practice of statistics in biological research. New York: W.H. Freeman and Company.

Tomasello, M. 2003. Constructing a language: A usage-based theory of language acquisition. Cambridge: Harvard University Press.

Stereotypes and /n/ variation in Patra, Greece
Results from a pilot study

Panayiotis A. Pappas
Simon Fraser University

Abstract: This paper discusses the variation in coronal nasals in the Patra variety of Greek. The variable is defined as the realization of /n/ in (C)ni(C) syllables which comprises three variants: alveolar, palatal and palatalized. The most important factors affecting the variation are age, gender, and—as revealed in interviews—lifestyle preference, as well as awareness of the negative stereotypes that the palatal regional pronunciation carries. An investigation of the different phonological systems that underlie the variation suggests that the difference between alveolar and palatal users is based on the different ranking of the constraints *C-i and Ident-IO (Place) and that the former have borrowed the ranking system of Standard Modern Greek. The palatalized variant has most likely emerged as a way of avoiding the palatal [ɲ] and the social stigma that accompanies it.

1. Introduction[*]

In this paper I present the results of a pilot study about coronal nasal variation and the attitudes towards it in the city of Patra Greece. In the next section, I define the variable as the realization of /n/ in (C)ni(C) syllables and demonstrate that it comprises three variants: alveolar, palatal and palatalized. In the third section, I discuss the non-linguistic parameters affecting the variation. I show that there has been change in apparent time as the palatalized and alveolar variants have emerged in the younger generations (younger than 55). I present evidence that women are leaders in this change as well as evidence that the use of the alveolar variant is associated with speakers who prefer an urban lifestyle to a provincial or rural one. I also discuss speakers' attitudes towards the variation and will show that the older generation is generally unaware of it, while in the two younger groups the palatal variant is stigmatized. Once again women seem to have a higher sensitivity towards this stigmatization. In the final section, I present a phonological account of the variation in which the difference between alveolar and palatal users is explained as a difference in ranking of the constraints *C-i and Ident-IO (Place) in the grammars of the two varieties. Successful users of the alveolar have borrowed the ranking system of Standard Modern Greek (SMG),

---

[*] I am grateful to SFU for supporting this research with a Small SSHRC grant, to Alexei Kochetov for discussing the OT analysis with me, and to two anonymous reviewers for their helpful suggestions. I would also like to thank Dimitri Papazachariou, Frans Hinskens, Yue Wang, Arne Mooers, Dora Antonakopoulou, Niki Efstathopoulou, Caitlin MacRae, Lilian Pappas, the anonymous reviewers and of course all participants in Patra. I am solely responsible for any errors.

while the emergence of the palatalized nasal appears to be mainly the result of speakers' articulatory efforts to avoid using the stigmatized palatal variant.

2. Background information

The city of Patra is located in the northwest part of the Peloponnesus, approximately 217 kilometers west of Athens. Patra is the third largest city of Greece after Athens and Thessaloniki. However, it is much smaller than either of these two cities with a population of approximately 250,000 while the metropolitan areas of Athens and Thessaloniki have 4 million and 2 million people respectively.

In the past, the population of Patra had enjoyed a high standard of living, as the city was the trading center for the agricultural production of the most fertile part of the Peloponnesus. Especially in the last half of the 19th century and the first half of the 20th century, the export of currants brought significant wealth to the city (Bakounakis 1995). At the turn of the century, Patra had banks, courthouses, conservatories and a Philharmonic Orchestra, dozens of newspapers, an airport, and was connected to many cities in Europe and America via ocean liners (Brettos 1998). The city's carnival, which is the biggest in Greece and one of the biggest in Europe, has been organized since 1860. In the second half of the 20th century the city was a major center of Greek industry. However, ever since the 1980s, the city has been facing a major recession, and currently has an unemployment rate of 16%, which is almost double that of Greece in general (9%) and is the highest among 200 cities surveyed by the European Commission's Urban I project (1994-1999). During the interviews the participants talked of Patra as a city that has suffered devastating financial damage and has lost its grandeur, and frequently mentioned the existence of important families that have only kept their name (i.e., they have status without wealth). Yet it must still be noted that in addition to the Carnival, Patra also hosts an international arts festival and is home to over twenty, theatrical, musical, and literary associations. The status of Patra as the impoverished grande dame who still must keep up appearances is one that is still very salient in the lives of its inhabitants.

2.1   Methodology

The data was collected during the month of May 2004 in the city of Patra. By making use of personal and family connections in the city I was able to recruit 21 participants. The participants were both female and male, their ages range from mid-twenties to early seventies, and they come from a variety of educational and occupational backgrounds. In the older group, participants have had only a few years in middle school at most, and have been employed as laborers. In the younger groups, all participants have at least graduated from high school and several even have postsecondary degrees. Some are unemployed, which is typical for Greek society, but most hold a variety of white-collar jobs (pharmacist, veterinarian, civil servant). Several female participants are teachers.

Data were elicited in four different ways: group discussion, interview, reading a short passage, and reading a word list. All data elicitation sessions were recorded using a SONY PCM-M1 digital audio recorder on HHB 125 digital audiotapes at a sampling rate of 44.1 kHz. A Shure SM58 microphone was used during the group discussions while a Sony electret condenser microphone ECM 44B was used in all other recordings. The data were first transferred from the audiotapes to CDs via a Pioneer Compact Disc Recorder PDR 509 and then converted in .wav files for acoustic analysis. The program used for this analysis was Praat 4.2.19. All statistical tests were conducted on JMP 5.1.1.

2.2   Defining the linguistic variable and its variants

In SMG, most consonants have palatal or palatalized realizations when followed by a front vowel, especially /i/. For example, the root of 'have' is /ex/ but in the first two persons of the singular there is alternation between ['exo] and ['eçis]. In the case of /n/ and /l/ the allophonic distribution is slightly more complicated, as the palatal nasal or lateral appears only when the high front vowel is followed by another tautosyllabic vowel (Arvaniti 1999). For example, the plural of /pa'ni/ "rag", after the suffixation of /a/, is [paɲa], a two-syllable form with a palatal nasal, while in the three-syllable adverb ['spania] "rarely", the nasal is alveolar.

In some dialects of Greek, however, these segments have palatal realizations even when /i/ is the only vowel in the syllable. To use the same example, in these dialects both [pa'ɲi] and ['spaɲia] are pronounced with a palatal nasal. The isogloss of this variation has not been determined—Kontosopoulos (1980) does not mention this variable, while Holton, Mackridge & Philippaki-Warburton (1997) mention it in their grammar but do not provide any geographical information. Newton (1972: 137-141) does refer to this variation in the section on dental palatalization (5.2). Although he is careful to stress that "Much careful work must be done before a detailed and accurate survey of dental palatalization in Greek will be possible" (p. 137) he does comment on /n/ (and /l/—see below) palatalization in three different areas. For the northern dialects and the dialect of Zakinthos, which is located near Patra in the Ionian Sea, he claims that the degree of palatalization of /n/ before /i/ is the same as the degree of palatalization before tautosyllabic /iV/. For the southern dialects, which he exemplifies by reference to "normal Peloponnesian pronunciations" (p. 138), he claims that /n/ in the sequence (C)ni(C) is either not palatalized at all or only slightly palatalized by a "late phonetic rule": "Otherwise the final syllable of [/xoni/ "funnel"] would be homophonous with the word [/nii/ "youths"] and, as far as my observations allow me to judge, this does not appear to be the case." (*ibid*). Finally my own impression is that speakers from the city of Patra and the island of Lesvos are stereotyped for having this feature, but it is also present in other areas, such as Kefalonia, Kriti, Thasos, Volos and Chalkidike.

It is important to note that the coronal lateral /l/ is characterized by the same distribution. Papazachariou (2003) examines the variation with respect to (C)li(C) in Patra and demonstrates that there are three variants and not just two as had been generally thought. He describes these variants as the standard alveolar, the laminal post alveolar and the apical post alveolar. I hesitate to proceed to the articulatory description of these sounds based simply on acoustic characteristics, especially in the case of nasals, because their formants tend to be quite weak in laboratory conditions, and even more so in field recordings (Ladefoged 2003). Despite these reservations, the prior findings can still serve as a springboard for a less specific question: Are there also three variants of /n/ in Patra?

This study revealed that there are, indeed, three variants, which I broadly characterize based on their acoustic signature as alveolar [n], palatal [ɲ] and palatalized [nʲ], and which probably correspond to Papazachariou's alveolar, laminal post alveolar and apical post alveolar laterals. Figure 1 depicts the spectrograms of the first two segments of the word /ˈanisos/ "unequal" as it is pronounced by three different speakers. Notice the change in F2 during the transition from the vowel /a/ into the following /n/ for each token. The leftmost spectrogram shows a standard alveolar nasal with the F1 and F2 in parallel position throughout the preceding vowel. In the central spectrogram, typical of a palatal [ɲ], the F2 rises sharply, while in the rightmost spectrogram, which is typical of the palatalized [nʲ], the F2 rises gradually.

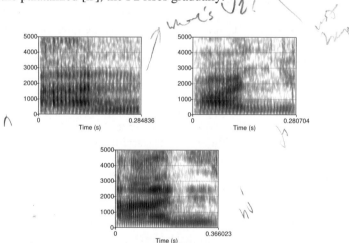

Figure 1: *Spectrograms of the first two syllables of /ˈanisos/ as pronounced by three different speakers*

Ideally, the tokens would have been coded acoustically (Thomas 2001), but determining the place of articulation for voiced nasals based on their acoustic signal is quite complicated even when data are collected in a controlled environment. Ladefoged and Maddieson (1995: 117), following Recasens (1983), argue that the difference in place of articulation affects the mean value of the nasal zero, when "[n]asal zero [is] considered to be the largest negative peak located between F1 and F2 in the spectral display." However, Ladefoged (2003:144), claims that the higher formant frequencies of nasals cannot be measured in a reliable way because their amplitudes are very low. Instead he recommends examining the transition or movement of formants in the vowels that follow the nasal. One such approach highlighted (*ibid*: 163) is the use of locus equations, which require measuring the F2 of several vowels once at the onset and then during the steady state of the vowel. The two values are plotted against each other on a grid, yielding a point for each vowel. A straight line can be fitted between these points and its y-intercept defines the abstract locus of the consonant. Unfortunately, neither of these two methods could be employed in a straightforward fashion. The data were recorded in environments with some ambient noise making it effectively impossible to locate the nasal zero, while the plotting technique could not be used because the following vowel in this variation is always /i/.

In order to overcome these difficulties, a compromise was implemented. First, word list tokens that include the sequence /ani/ were isolated and coded impressionistically by the author and a research assistant. Then, I independently measured the value of the offset for /a/ in each token, and tested the correlation between our perception of the variants and this acoustic measure. The one-way ANOVA test and the post hoc Tukey-Kramer test, seen in Figure 2, confirm that—for both men and women—differences between the F2 offset values for each variant are statistically significant, and provide justification for coding the data set impressionistically which I then did for all other occurrences of (C)ni(C). (Male and female speakers were tested separately because there is considerable variation in the onset and offset values of /a/ based on sex).

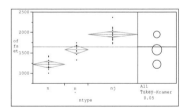 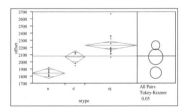

Figure 2: *Offset values of the three variants for male (left) and female speakers*

3. Description of the variation

Overall, 21 participants were interviewed for this study, but only 16 of them are natives of Patra. The other five have grown up in the surrounding provinces of the Peloponnesus or in Athens. Of these 16 participants from Patra, 9 are male and 7 female. They were categorized into three age groups:

1. Group A: speakers between the ages of 25 and 35; 5 male participants and 1 female.
2. Group B: speakers between 36 and 55; 3 female participants and 3 male.
3. Group C: speakers between 56 and 71; 3 female participants and 1 male.

The participants in Group A come from various backgrounds. Among the males were an unemployed web designer with a Masters degree, an unemployed high school graduate, a civil servant with a high school degree, a restaurant owner with a junior college degree and a veterinarian. The female works as a German language instructor and holds a BA in German literature. In Group B, the males are all civil servants with high school degrees, while the female participants are elementary school teachers. In Group C, 3 of the speakers have minimal education (not past elementary) and have worked blue collar jobs (truck driver, seamstress). One of the female participants had a high school education but had not worked outside the house.

As the contingency table in Figure 3 shows, there is a clear change in the use of the variants in apparent time. (ChiSq = 53.459, df = 4, p <.0001). In Group C (older than 56) there is near categorical use of the palatal variant (80%). In Group B (36-55) we see use of the palatal variant (56%) and the palatalized variant (38%), while in Group A the variation exists between the alveolar variant (51%) and the palatal one (40%).

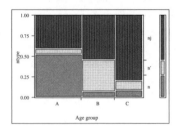

Figure 3: *Distribution of variants by age*

One interesting observation about the variation in groups A and B concerns the source of the variation. In Group B (Figure 4, right) there is intra-speaker variation for most participants; two of the males use both the palatal and the palatalized variants while among the females two of the participants use all three variants. Even though the use of the alveolar variant in the female group is limited, its existence is significant as an indication that the women are leaders in this change and the ensuing discussion will provide corroborating evidence. In Group A on the other hand, intra-speaker variation is limited to one speaker (TS), a male who uses both the alveolar and palatalized variant. The other speakers use either the alveolar or the palatal variant.

In the following sections, I will discuss evidence collected in one-on-one and group interviews. The ethnographic information provided by the participants indicates that the variation is in great part determined by a speaker's attitude not only towards the city of Patra but also towards the variants themselves.

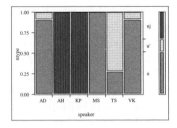 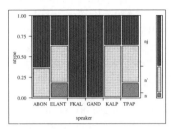

Figure 4: *Intra-speaker variation in Groups A (left-VK is female) and B (AB, FK and KK are male)*

3.1   Attitudes towards the city of Patra

The fact that the attitude of speakers towards their community plays an important role in the linguistic variation has been known since Labov's (1963) study in Martha's Vineyard. Labov was able to classify participants as positively, neutrally or negatively oriented toward the island community and demonstrated that there was a strong correlation between these attitudes and the degree of nucleus centralization among speakers. In the present study, the responses to questions about life in Patra do not seem, at first glance, to yield any revealing information as speakers with similar attitudes use different variants and vice versa. For example, both AH, who uses the palatal [ɲ], and AD, who uses the alveolar [n], enjoy their life in the city.

(1)   Personally I believe that Patra is a place for a family. I am over thirty and I Imagine I can't...I don't have plans to move to another city...Except New York, where I lived for a while, but for that to happen many things would have to change. (AH, male 33)

(2)   I like Patra as a city I want to live here...there are opportunities...and the lifestyle is more relaxed. (AD, male 30)

On the other hand, both TS who uses the alveolar and palatalized realizations and TP who uses all three variants are not so thrilled with life in Patra:

(3)   As a city, I like it [Patra]. As far as lifestyle, I would like to live somewhere else in a larger city, with a more intense lifestyle. I find life here too calm. (TS, male 30)

(4)   As I told you before, I don't like living in Patra at all...Patra could never shake off the complex of a grand city that lost its glamour... I would like to live in a smaller place, I would be ecstatic if I could work in a remote area, like an island...because the relationships that are developed in smaller places are different from those that develop in a city (TP, female 40)

However, what differentiates these speakers from one another are the reasons behind their like or dislike of life in Patra. Although AH and TP have different feelings towards the city, the reasons for these feelings are the same: a fondness for provincial life, expressed in the idealized characteristics of quietness, simplicity, and proximity to nature. The only difference is that AH finds Patra provincial enough, while TP does not.

Similarly, AD and TS are interested in the same lifestyle, the urban one, but their needs are not similarly fulfilled by living in Patra. AD likes the city because it can offer similar opportunities as Athens, while TS does not like what it has to offer and would like to move to larger city. The use of the palatal and palatalized variants appears to be associated with an ideological attachment to provincial life, while the alveolar variant is associated with a preference for the urban lifestyle. Broce and Cacoullos (2002: 348) arrive at similar conclusions about the variation between /r/ and /l/ in the rural community of Coclé in Panama, where participants' attitude towards Panama City is a significant factor.

3.2   Awareness of the variation

Speakers' awareness of the variation depends on their age. In the oldest group, speakers are unaware that their pronunciation of /l/ and /n/ differs from the standard. The following quote is an exchange between EFA (female 68) who was born and raised in Athens before moving to Patra at the age of 23, and KA (female 58) who is a Patra native.

(5)   EFA: ...and the lu [l], the lu here, the lu, the lamda, which they accent, here in the area
       KA: here? they accent it?
       EFA: ...yes, you don't realize this...
       KA: ba? [really?]

In Group B, speakers are either unaware of the local pronunciation, or they were introduced to the difference at a later age, usually when they left Patra to go to another city for University.

(6)   ...[when I was at University] my friends made fun of me... about my [ʎi] and my [ɲi]... (EA, female 37)

In the youngest group the situation is more complex. Those who use the alveolar variant claim to have been aware of it since they were young (early teens), while the users of the palatal one were made aware of the variation after they left Patra for University. Quite interestingly, the one speaker that varies between the alveolar variant and the palatalized one is aware of all three variants:

(7)   …and I don't like to hear *ni* and *li* so strong. I prefer it when it is softer…even though I don't believe I say it correctly, exactly, I hear people who say it even stronger (TS, male 30)

3.3   Attitudes towards the variation

As I have already mentioned, speakers in the oldest group are generally unaware of the difference between the Patra pronunciation and the standard. In those cases where they have become aware of it, it is the *alveolar* pronunciation that strikes them as novel. The following excerpt is from my conversation with EA who is describing her parents' reaction when her boyfriend, an Athenian, would call for her. Notice that she uses the alveolar [n] in the pronunciation of her name in order to demonstrate how her father would ridicule the standard pronunciation.

(8)   …or my father and my mother…he [boyfriend from Athens] would call, and ask for me, and they would say "mmm… the [eˈleni] guy called." (EA female 37, emphasis original)

In Group B, the male speakers who are unaware of the difference in pronunciation also believe that their local variety is almost identical to the standard. The two female speakers who are aware of the variation and use all three variants expressed a different sentiment. At first they were disturbed to find out that they spoke with an accent, and they tried to change their pronunciation, so that it would be closer to the standard. It is interesting that both of them used the same verb to describe this effort: [maˈzevo] which literally means "to collect" or "to gather" and in this case means "to reign in". However, both admitted that they were not very successful and abandoned the effort.

(9)   …it didn't bother me too much, because some times, when I caught myself trying to reign in the [ʎi] a little bit, I couldn't do it, so OK, I relaxed. (EA, 37)

The third female teacher, TP, as she was getting ready to read the scripted passage that I had given her, asked me how I would like her to read it: in Greek or in *Patrina* (the Patra variety). Seeing my surprise, she went on to explain that in formal situations and especially when she is teaching her elementary students how to read, she concentrates more and can avoid using the palatal pronunciation, because as she put it, "I want to teach them what is correct." She then gave two readings, a formal one and a 'natural' one, the difference between which will be discussed in the next section.

   In the youngest group, there is of course a split between those who use the alveolar variant and those who use the palatal. The men who use the alveolar express a dislike for how the palatal sounds, but are adamant that they do not judge people by it.

(10) …it has nothing to do with education, nothing. You could be the smartest person in the world, and still have the [ɲi]. I don't judge him… (TS, male 30)

The female participant had stronger views:

(11) I don't like it as a sound, and if I had it, I would try to correct it…It's a little *vlahiko* [peasant-like], if I may use that term. (VK, female 28)

And later on:

(12) …a friend of mine, her mother uses this [ʎi] and [ɲi] a lot and I have told her, me and her daughter —you [polite] should not use it…it does not sound so nice. [pretending to be the friend's mother]—And why not? This is how I was brought up, this is how I will speak. I like it. If you like it, listen to me, if you don't, don't listen…So yes, some people do take it as a matter of patriotism, they want to preserve this characteristic of Patra, which is not bad. But for me, OK, I don't like how it sounds. (VK, female 28)

The two men who use [ɲ] and are aware of the variation have different perspectives. AH, a restaurant owner, believes that it's a characteristic of Patra speech that everyone shares, and is favorable towards local varieties from all over Greece.

(13) …if you go to a different place in Greece, the way you talk, and someone recognizes where you are from, that is not a reason for insult, nor is it an ugly thing… (AH male 30)

KP, a teacher, on the other hand, was left with some troubling questions:

(14) …they were making fun of me, and I said, what do you mean guys, what is it? I had never heard of this being the case, not even as a rumor, that in Patra I speak like this…I could not understand what they were talking about…it makes you think, is it so much different from common speech? You want to understand how foreign you sound. (KP male 28)

The existence of a strong correlation between speakers' attitude towards their dialect and the degree of convergence to the standard has also been observed since Labov's early work (1963, 1966). In a more recent study, Gerritsen (1999: 58-61) was able to confirm this by comparing the use of dialect forms among young girls from three different towns on the borders of Belgium, Germany and the Netherlands. She demonstrates that the highest percentage of standard forms were used in the town of Waldfeucht where attitude towards the local dialect was the most negative. Similarly in Patra the highest use of the innovative variants (palatalized, alveolar) is found in speakers who have the most negative attitude towards the Patra variety. In the next section, I discuss in more detail the speech pattern of a particular individual, which shows that the two types of attitude (towards the city and towards the dialect) can affect the linguistic variation in discrete ways.

3.4   Performance Speech

In the previous section, it was mentioned that one of the teachers, TP, expressed the sentiment that although she was not ashamed or embarrassed by her use of the palatal [ɲi], she did take care to use the standard alveolar variant when teaching students to read or in formal situations. She claimed that she had total control over her pronunciation and offered to demonstrate it by reading the same passage twice, once naturally, as it occurred to her, and once using the alveolar (standard) pronunciation only. One might expect that TP has overstated her code-switching abilities, since another early finding of Labov's research (1966, 1972) is that there exists a significant difference between speakers's perception of their pronunciation and their actual production (notably speaker Steve K, cf. Labov 1972: 104-5). What is surprising is that none of the tokens produced is an actual alveolar nasal, as Figure 5 shows. Instead, the majority of tokens in TP's performance reading are palatalized nasals, indicating that she must perceive this variant as equivalent to, or at least passable as, the standard pronunciation.

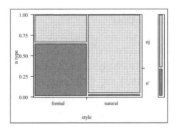

Figure 5: *Distribution of variants in formal and natural speech by speaker TP*

However, as the spectrograms in Figure 6 show, there is a clear difference between what she perceives as a standard pronunciation on her part, and what speakers of the standard actually produce. On the left is what TP claims is [liˈmani] but is actually [liˈmanʲi], while on the right is VK's alveolar pronunciation.

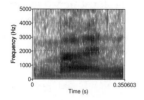 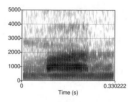

Figure 6: *Spectrograms of palatalized (left) and alveolar /n/*
in the word /li'mani/ "port"

What is most interesting about the case of TP is that it allows us a glimpse into the multi-faceted nature of personal identity, how the different facets of identity interact with attitude, and how the overall combination affects linguistic variation (cf. Eckert 1996, 2000). As a private person, TP is negatively disposed towards Patra because it is too urban, but positively disposed towards its variety, which for her is linked to the provincial or rural aspect of life there, and she is therefore comfortable with the palatal pronunciation. As a public person, however, as a teacher, TP has a negative attitude towards the local variety, because she sees it as part of her duties to promote the standard — in her mind the "correct" — pronunciation. In the next section I will look at a possible phonological interpretation of the variation and propose an explanation for why speakers such as TP produce a palatalized variant instead of the alveolar one.

4. An OT account of the variation

One possible approach to understanding the phonological system behind the variation would be to follow Newton's (1972: 137-9) insight that the dialects of Modern Greek exhibit two types of palatalization. In dialects such as SMG, palatalization is caused by the palatal glide [j] only, while in others the high front vowel /i/ also has a palatalizing effect. A formalization of this approach would first have to address glide formation, since glides are not phonemes in Newton's account. I treat this as a prosodically-driven process, which is the result of *Onset* ("Onsetless syllables are prohibited", cf. Kager 1999: 93) being ranked higher than *Dep-IO (μ)* ("Do not delete moras", *ibid*: 156) in all SMG varieties. As a result, forms like [pa.ni.a] and [pa.ɲi.a] are starred while forms with glides or palatals (through fusion) like [pa.nja], [paɲ.ja] or [paɲ.a] are favored.[1] Both types of palatalization and glide absorption are motivated by the fact that

---

[1] Due to considerations of space, certain aspects of this proposal cannot be fully explored. Among these is the status of [j] in SMG and the related issue of hiatus in /iV/ sequences in words of learned origin (cf. Newton 1972: 31-40), as well as the question of how the constraints proposed can be integrated in the more general phonological system. It should also be noted that even though the constraint Onset prohibits onsetless syllables, one could still allow for the existence of vowel-initial words in SMG by ranking it lower than *Align-Left*, a constraint which requires that left edges of grammatical and prosodic words are aligned (Kager 1999: 111).

sequences where consonants are followed by palatal glides or front vowels are marked. Cross-linguistically, these are often repaired by palatalization, especially when the consonant is an anterior coronal. The consonant assimilates fully or partially to the place of articulation of the glide or the vowel (Bhat 1978: 52). In addition, when sequences of a consonant and palatal glide are repaired by palatalization, the glide is often 'absorbed' by the palatal(ized) consonant; Newton (1972: 138) handles the absorption with a rule of post-palatal yod deletion. Since in the varieties of Modern Greek different coronal consonants pattern differently with respect to palatalization the constraints have to be feature-specific. In the current case, they refer to coronal sonorants only. Following Rubach (2000), I propose these constraints:

(15) *C-i: A sequence of an anterior coronal consonant and a high front vowel is prohibited.

(16) *C-j: A sequence of a coronal consonant and a palatal glide is prohibited.

These constraints are in conflict with the faithfulness constraint *Ident-IO (Place)*, which prohibits any changes in place of articulation. In a form such as [paˈɲa], [ɲ] is a result of a fusion of /n/ and /i/ (or [j]). This does not violate the faithfulness constraint *Max-IO* ("Do not delete segments"), since both /n/ and /i/ of the input have a correspondent segment in the output, [ɲ]. However, the form violates *Linearity-IO* ("Do not change the precedence structure of the input"; Kager 1999: 63) and Ident-IO (Place) (the [+ant] of the input has been changed to [-ant]). I suggest that the difference between [ni] users and [ɲi] users in Patra rests in the ranking of *C-i and Ident-IO (Place) as illustrated below.

Tableau 1: *A grammar of [ni] users: Ident-IO (Place) » *C-i*

a. /pani/	Onset	*C-j	Ident-IO (Place)	*C-i	Lin-IO	Dep-IO (μ)
☞ paˈni				*		
paˈɲi			*!			
b. /pani-a/	**Onset**	***C-j**	**Ident-IO (Place)**	***C-i**	**Lin-IO**	**Dep-IO (μ)**
paˈnia	*!					
paˈɲia	*!		*			*
paˈnja		*!	*			*
paˈɲja		*!	*			*
☞ paˈɲa			*		*	*

Tableau 2: *A grammar of [ɲi] users: *C-i » Ident-IO (Place)*

a. /pani/	Onset	*C-j	*C-i	Ident-IO (Place)	Lin-IO	Dep-IO (μ)
pa'ni			*!			
☞ pa'ɲi				*		
b. /pani-a/	**Onset**	***C-j**	***C-i**	**Ident-IO (Place)**	**Lin-IO**	**Dep-IO (μ)**
pa'nia	*!		*			
pa'ɲia	*!			*		*
pa'nja		*!				*
pa'ɲja		*!		*		*
☞ pa'ɲa				*	*	*

In the case of speakers who use the palatalized variants ([lʲ], [nʲ]) it is clear that they have the same constraint rankings as older speakers. The evidence that points to this is that most speakers vary between the palatalized variant and the palatal one, not the alveolar. In addition, we have seen that for at least two speakers (TP and EA) the palatalized variant is the result of a conscious effort to produce an alveolar instead of a palatal sound. This would not be necessary if the constraints were ranked as in SMG. One should also keep in mind that palatalized variants are similar to alveolar ones in that they both have a tongue tip constriction. As a result of this, the F2 values of their transitions are more similar to the F2 values of the transitions of plain alveolars than those of palatals. It is reasonable then to suggest that the palatalized variant is the result of speakers trying to approximate [l]/[n] in terms of articulation and acoustics rather than an adjustment of constraint rankings. Finally, for TS (group A) who varies between the palatalized and the alveolar variant, the most likely explanation is that there is competition between the two grammars in Tableaux 1 and 2 as well as articulatory/acoustic approximation of their distinct outputs.

5. Conclusion

In this paper I have discussed the variation between the alveolar, palatalized and palatal realization of a nasal in (C)ni(C) syllables in the Patra variety of Greek. The distribution of the variants by age indicates that the regional palatal pronunciation is being replaced by a palatalized or alveolar one. The latter is the result of younger speakers borrowing the ranking of constraints from SMG. The palatalized variant emerged in the group of speakers that are between 36 and 55 years old as a way of avoiding the palatal variant, which is negatively stereotyped, not only outside of Patra, but also *within* the speech community by younger speakers. Further research is needed to determine whether the palatalized nasal has the status of a social marker or an indicator. Finally, an examination of similar variation patterns in the nasal and lateral realization of other, non-stigmatized, varieties can test the hypothesis that the emergence of the palatalized variant in Patra is associated with the stigmatization of the palatal pronunciation.

References

Arvaniti, A. 1999. "Standard Modern Greek". JIPA 29. 167-172.

Bakounakis, N. 1995 (2nd edition). Patra 1828-1860: Mia Eliniki Protevusa ston 19o Eona [Patra 1828-1860: A Greek capital in the 19th century]. Athens: Kastaniotis.

Bhat, D.N.S. 1978. "A general study of palatalization". Universals of human language. Vol. 2: Phonology ed. by J. H. Greenberg, 47-91. Stanford, CA: Stanford University Press.

Brettos, L.S. 1998. Patra, Odigos Pliroforisis [Patra, an information guide]. Patra: Achaikes ekdosis.

Broce, M. & R. Torres Cacoullos. 2002. "'Dialectología urbana' rural: la estratificatión social de (r) y (l) en Coclé Panamá" [Rural 'Urban Dialectology': The social stratification of (r) and (l) in Coclé, Panama]. Hispania 85. 342-353.

Eckert, P. 1996. "(ay) Goes to the City: Exploring the expressive use of variation". Towards a social science of language: papers in honor of William Labov, vol. 1: Variation and change in language and society (= Current Issues in Linguistic Theory, 127) ed. by G.R. Guy, C. Feagin, D. Schiffrin & J. Baugh, 47-68. Amsterdam: Benjamins.

Eckert, P. 2000. Linguistic variation as social practice. Oxford: Blackwell.

European Commission. 1994-1999. Urban I. <http://europa.eu.int/comm/ regional_policy> (19 July 2006)

Gerritsen, M. 1999. "Divergence of dialects in a linguistic laboratory near the Belgian-Dutch-German border: Similar dialects under the influence of different standard languages". Language Varation and Change. 43-65.

Holton, D., P. Mackridge & I. Philippaki-Warburton. 1997. Greek: A comprehensive grammar of the modern language. London: Routledge.

Kager, R. 1999. Optimality theory. Cambridge: CUP.

Kontosopoulos, N. 1980. Dialekti kai idiomata tis Neas Elinikis [Dialects and varieties of Modern Greek]. Athina.

Labov, W. 1963. "The social motivation of a sound change". Word 19. 273-309.

Labov, W. 1966. "The social stratification of English in New York City". Washington, DC: Center for Applied Linguistics.

Labov, W. 1972. Sociolinguistic patterns. Philadelphia: University of Pennsylvania Press.

Ladefoged P. 2003. Phonetic data analysis: An introduction to fieldwork and instrumental techniques. Malden, MA: Blackwell.

Ladefoged, P. & I. Maddieson. 1995. Sounds of the world's Languages. Oxford, Cambridge, MA: Blackwell.

Newton, B. 1972. The generative interpretation of dialect: a study of modern Greek phonology. Cambridge: CUP.

Papazachariou, D. 2003. "I pragmatosi tis phonologikis monadas /l/ tis Patrinis dialektu [The realization of the phoneme /l/ in the Patra dialect]". Proceedings of The 6th International Conference of Greek Linguistics (University of Rethymno, September 20, 2003).

Recasens, D.R. 1983. "Place cues for nasal consonants with special reference to Catalan". JASA 73. 1346-53.

Rubach, J. 2000. "Backness switch in Russian". Phonology 17. 39-64.

Thomas, E.R. 2001. "Instrumental phonetics". The handbook of language variation and change ed. by J.K. Chambers, P. Trudgill & N. Schilling-Estes, 168-200. Malden, MA: Blackwell.

Modelling linguistic change
The past and the present of the future
in Brazilian Portuguese

Shana Poplack & Elisabete Malvar
University of Ottawa

Abstract: Examining an apparently abrupt change in the expression of future temporal reference in Brazilian Portuguese, we trace the trajectory of its exponents over five centuries of development. Focusing specifically on the variability inherent in the system, we document the means by which the incoming form gradually expropriates the preferred contexts of the older variants, prior to ousting them from the sector. We thus confirm that the transition period in linguistic change is not abrupt. Rather, change proceeds as a series of small adjustments, as incoming and outgoing variants accommodate each other in the system. As a variant recedes, constraints on its selection do not remain constant, though the distinctions it conveyed may be transferred to another exponent. These findings challenge some widely-held assumptions about the nature of linguistic change.

1. Introduction[*]

In this paper we revisit a fundamental question first raised by Weinreich et al. (1968:100) in their seminal work on language change: If a language must be structured to function efficiently, what happens to its functions as structure changes? In contrast to accounts which construe change as *abrupt*, and therefore unobservable during its course, we focus on the *process* of replacement, exemplifying with a spectacular change in the expression of future time in Brazilian Portuguese which took over five centuries to achieve completion. In so doing, we shed light on two of the key problems in the study of linguistic change: the 'transition' problem, i.e. the means by which a language moves from state to state, and the "embedding" problem, i.e. the effects of this process on the surrounding system of linguistic relations (Weinreich et al. 1968, Labov 1982).[1] Because future temporal reference was variable from its earliest attestations, we

[*] The research on which this paper is based is part of a larger project entitled *Confronting prescription and praxis in the evolution of grammar*. We gratefully acknowledge the support of the Social Science and Humanities Research Council of Canada and the Killam Foundation to Poplack, and the Conselho Nacional de Desenvolvimento Científico e Tecnológico (CNPq) and the University of Ottawa to Malvar. We thank David Sankoff for enlightening discussion of many of the issues treated here. Audiences at SS15, LSRL 34, WECOL 2004 and ICLaVE 3 offered useful comments and critiques. Some of the material in this paper is treated in more detail in Poplack & Malvar (in press). We are grateful to Frans Hinskens for his careful reading of the manuscript.
[1] Both problems obviously include a social dimension, which will not be the focus here.

make use of variationist methodology to trace over time the trajectory of its competing expressions across the functions and contexts constituting this domain. Claims in the prescriptive and descriptive literature about which conditions favored the choice of one variant over another at each stage are operationalized as factors and tested against contemporaneous usage. The diagnostic is the *constraint hierarchy*, construed as the grammar giving rise to variant selection. Independent multivariate analyses of the contribution of these factors in each time period reveal how the labor of expressing future temporal reference is divided. Comparison of significant effects across variants and over time enables us to trace the progress of the change in considerable detail, charting the behavior of variant forms as they accommodate to incoming and outgoing counterparts, and thereby bringing new data to bear on the transition and embedding of linguistic change.

In this paper we first sketch out the facts of future expression in Portuguese (Sections 2 and 3), then describe a method for studying language change capable of accounting for rampant variability over long periods of time (Section 4). In so doing, we develop novel uses of traditional data sources, and an analysis that confronts standard accounts of these phenomena with the facts of actual usage. Section 5 presents the results of these analyses century by century. In Section 6 we offer some conclusions on the nature of the transition and embedding of linguistic change.

1.1   Future temporal reference in Portuguese

The lexico-grammatical apparatus associated with the future is never limited to a single exponent, and nowhere is this more evident than in Portuguese. Most accounts identify four variant expressions: the synthetic future (SF), as in (1), the *haver-* (lit. "have to") periphrasis (HP), as in (2); the futurate present (P; (3)) and the *ir-* ("go") periphrasis (IR; (4)). The synthetic future (1) appears in conjugation tables, and is typically identified as the "default" form conveying primary future meaning; the other variants are associated with a wide array of modalities (e.g. certainty, doubt, resolution, necessity, probability) and/or contexts of use (e.g. affirmative sentences, monosyllabic verbs, proximity in the future).

(1)   Senhor, eu o *servirei* **(SF)** e não quero outro senhor. (Vicente 1526/1975. Ourives:83)[2]
       "Sir, I *will serve* you and I do not wish another master".
(2)   Pois aonde o *hei de pôr* **(HP)**? (Silva 1737/1980. Semicúpio:54)
       "Well, where *shall* I *put* it?"
(3)   São nove horas e o oficio de ramos *principia* **(P)** às dez e meia. (Pena 1853/1972. Ambrósio:12)
       "It's nine o'clock and the Palm procession *begins* at ten-thirty."

---

[2] Codes in parentheses indicate the source of the example: Playwright, year of publication, character and page number in the *Corpus of popular Portuguese plays* (Malvar 2003); speaker, counter number and date of recording in the *Corpus of vernacular Brazilian Portuguese* (ibid.).

(4)   Ano que vem eu *vou tirar* **(IR)** a Cleide dessa escola e colocar na escola
        pública. (Vânia/B:30/1992)
        "Next year I'm *going to take* Cleide out of this school and put her in a
        public school."

Analysis of a large corpus of 20th-century Brazilian Portuguese (Malvar 2003),
however, revealed almost no variation at all. On the contrary, nearly all references
to future time were expressed by the *ir*-periphrasis (4). The synthetic future (1) is
vanishingly rare, the futurate present (3) at best a minor contender, and the *haver*-
periphrasis (2) is virtually non-existent. How can these contradictory accounts be
reconciled? Are they due to abrupt linguistic change? The gulf between
prescription and usage? Divergence between speech and writing? To answer these
questions, we investigate how future temporal reference was expressed at earlier
stages of the language.

1.2   A method for studying language change

The empirical study of linguistic change has always represented one of the
linguist's greatest challenges. Though this is sometimes overlooked, a basic
requirement is that the outcome be compared with an initial (or at least a prior)
stage, but locating the relevant diachronic evidence is no easy matter. Since most
putative changes originate in spoken vernaculars, the most appropriate
comparison point would logically be a precursor to those vernaculars. Written
documents, even the most 'speech-like', often turn out to be poor approximations
of speech, either because they lag far behind or fail to represent it at all (e.g. van
Herk & Poplack 2001).[3]
    Data representing both an "earlier" stage *and* vernacular speech necessarily
offer a time depth too shallow to assess the full course of change. Thus most
available materials are not pertinent to the goal of tracing variable usage over long
periods of time. In this paper we describe the methods we have been
experimenting with at the University of Ottawa Sociolinguistics Laboratory to
make the best of the "poor data" (Labov 1994) of language history. We show that
access to sufficient time depth, coupled with the tools of variation theory, reveal
unexpected facts about the transition period in linguistic change.

2. Data

Our confrontation of the present with the past is based on three complementary
sources of data, diachronic and synchronic, prescribed and used, spoken and
modeled after speech. Assessment of the normative treatment of future temporal
reference is based on a corpus of grammars published between the 16th and 21st

---

[3] This problem is exacerbated in colonial situations. In Brazil, for example, only European
Portuguese was recognized for literary and official purposes until the early 19th century. As a
result, the first bona fide Brazilian plays and grammars (i.e. written by a Brazilian and written,
published and/or produced in Brazil) date only from that time.

centuries (Malvar 2003; Poplack & Malvar in press), details of the contemporaneous spoken vernaculars are inferred from analysis of a corpus of popular theatre, and both of these are validated through comparison with data on late 20th-century spoken Brazilian Portuguese. Though none of these data sets in and of itself is ideally suited to address the questions we raised in the introduction to this paper, comparison amongst them validates each as a valuable source of information on language variation and change.

2.1   Diachronic data

2.1.1 Popular theatre
To tap into the spoken Portuguese of earlier centuries, we compiled a corpus of 22 comedies, farces and satires, published between 1509 and 1999, specifically intended for popular consumption. We sampled the *oeuvre* of (largely social realist) playwrights like Gil Vicente, Martins Pena and França Júnior, among others, reputed for their ability to represent the everyday speech of their lower- and working-class characters (e.g. Entwistle 1973:351-352, Hamilton-Faria 1976:75-96, Sletsjöe 1965:13, Ferraz 1980:29-30, Veríssimo 1998:361-362, Prado 1999:56-59). But the main criterion for retention in our corpus was explicit linguistic evidence in the dialogue of the social origins of the character. Much of this involved non-standard lexical or phonological features, as in (5) and (6) respectively. Particularly revealing were the (relatively rarer) morphosyntactic features, like lack of pronominal infixation with SF, as in (7), or nonstandard preposition usage, as in (8). Among the well-documented nonstandard morphosyntactic features of 20th-century vernacular Brazilian Portuguese, we find lack of subject-verb agreement (9), nonstandard pronoun placement (10), and 3rd person subject/object pronoun alternation (11).

(5)   Se o doente estivesse em tuas mãos, já há muito que tinha *espichado a canela.* (Pena 1844/1968. Cautério:271)
       "If the patient had been in your hands, he would have *croaked* a long time ago."
(6)   Ou você consegue um lugar *num* [< em um] desses prédios da Coorporação, *pra* [< para] essa gente se abrigar ou eles vão morrer de frio, de fome. (Labaki 1999/2000. Verônica:55)
       "Either you find shelter in one of the Corporation buildings for those people, or they're going to die of cold, of starvation."
(7)   *Dará-se* [< *dar-se-á*] caso que eu tenha dito alguma asneira?! (França Júnior 1870/1980. Matias:115)
       "Will anyone notice that I said something stupid?"
(8)   Chega *na* [< à] porta e acena com lenço. (Pena 1837/1968. Narrador:39)
       "Come into [to] the door and wave with a handkerchief."
(9)   Olha, Tião, são dois anos que *tu* não *acerta* [< *tu acertas*] as contas comigo. (Buarque 1978. Max:57)
       "Look Tião, you haven't paid me back for two years."

(10) *Me* deixa [< *deixa-me*], Cipriano! E fica sabendo, não vou a passeata
      nenhuma!
      (Guarnieri 1961. Américo:71)
      "*Me leave* [*leave me*] alone, Cipriano! I'm not going to any protest, and
      that's that!"
(11) Olha, lá, tá sangrando! Vamos tirar *ele* [< tirá-*lo*] de lá.
      (Guarnieri 1961. Américo:76)
      "Look, he's bleeding! Let's take *he* out of there."

To what extent, if any, does the language contained in these plays represent the
vernacular(s) spoken at the time they were written and/or performed? A
reasonable working hypothesis, based on the facts that the plays targeted popular
audiences, featured characters from the same social classes and the non-standard
linguistic forms associated with them, is that the language of the performers bore
at least some resemblance to that of the intended audience. As we show in Section
5.4, explicit comparison of 20th-century popular theatre with 20th-century popular
speech supports this assumption.

2.1.2 Normative discourse
A second window on the past comes from a meta-analysis of the evolution of
normative discourse on the expression of the future, culled from a corpus of 41
Portuguese grammars and usage manuals published between 1536 and 2005. We
use this material to: 1) infer the existence of prior variability (from citations of
alternative forms), 2) trace the evolution of grammatical dictates associated with
each, and perhaps most revealing, 3) discern hints of the linguistic conditions
contributing to their selection. In the case at hand, for example, in addition to the
plethora of semantic readings assigned to each of the future temporal reference
variants, we learn that grammarians have at one time or another associated SF
with monosyllabic verbs, HP with relative clauses, and P with disambiguating
temporal adverbs. We can incorporate these conditions as factors in a multivariate
analysis of variable usage over time, and use them not only to test whether older
constraints remain operative in contemporary varieties (i.e. whether change has
taken place), but equally instructive for present purposes, to elucidate the
transition from one stage to the next.

2.2   Synchronic data

As a check on both of these diachronic data sources, 20th-century spontaneous
speech data were collected from 34 urban working-class residents of Brasília, the
capital of Brasil, using standard sociolinguistic techniques (Malvar 2003). Built as
recently as the 1960s and settled by immigrants from various parts of the country,
the speech of the capital is often regarded as a microcosm of Brazilian Portuguese
(Bortoni-Ricardo 1991).[4] Detailed comparison of constraint hierarchies enables us

---

[4] Our references to these data in what follows as 20th-century speech are meant to distinguish
them from the writings of previous centuries. However, to the best of our knowledge, the only

to validate the diachronic data as representations of contemporaneous spoken vernaculars.

3. The trajectory of the future variants throughout the Portuguese grammatical tradition

Our meta-analysis (Poplack and Malvar in press) of the treatment of the variants throughout the Portuguese normative tradition confirms that alternate expressions of the future have been attested in grammars since the earliest times. But beyond acknowledging the variant forms, grammarians never explicitly identify them as alternate expressions of the same referential meaning. On the contrary, by ascribing to each a specific nuance or context of occurrence, they effectively rule out the possibility of variability. Thus SF has always been viewed as the basic exponent of futurity, while the other variants are prescribed to convey secondary readings, which only parenthetically occur in future time.

The temporal category of future is traditionally associated with a variety of irrealis or nonfactive modalities (Fleischman 1982: 14, Poplack & Turpin 1999), so it is not coincidental that many of the readings invoked refer to the speaker's psychological state at the time of the utterance. This of course cannot be tested, let alone confirmed. This indeterminacy explains the persistent lack of agreement over which forms convey which readings. Each of SF, HP and P has been assigned the reading of probability. HP, P and IR have all been assigned readings of proximity/imminence and necessity. All four of the variants have been associated with certainty and intention. Why is there so little agreement on what these readings are, and which forms convey them, whether from one period to the next or even within the same period (or occasionally, grammarian)? All of these facts, taken together, suggest the existence of prior variability, whether acknowledged or not.

4. A variationist perspective on the alternation among SF, HP, P and IR

Even if the different readings played a role in variant selection, the distinctions they imply need not be operative every time one of the variant forms is used. Indeed, the hypothesis underlying the study of morphosyntactic variability within the variationist framework is that "for certain identifiable sets of alternations, these distinctions come into play neither in the intentions of the speaker not in the interpretation of the interlocutor" (Sankoff 1988:153). This is because distinctions in referential value or grammatical function among different surface forms can be neutralized in discourse. Such neutralization is the fundamental mechanism of variation and change.

After a brief discussion of a number of methodological considerations regarding the variable context (Section 4.1), we introduce competing hypotheses

---

substantive differences with respect to the expression of future temporal reference in Brazilian Portuguese are register, rather than dialect, differences.

about variant selection (Section 4.2), and test them (Section 5) by means of systematic analysis of the distribution and conditioning of SF, HP, P and IR in Portuguese, diachronic and synchronic, written and spoken. We will demonstrate that within the specific domain of future temporal reference, they function as classical variants of a linguistic variable. These variants gradually enter and exit the sector, assuming the functions of their erstwhile counterparts in the process, or abandoning them altogether. As in other well-documented situations of variability, at no time during the development of the Portuguese future temporal reference system was variant selection free or idiosyncratic; on the contrary, each was regularly conditioned by elements of its preferred context(s) of occurrence. Nearly all of these have now been colonized by IR, which represents the new, though largely unacknowledged, default future.

4.1   Circumscribing the variable context

The systematic study of inherent variability requires that not only the variant forms, but also the contexts in which differences among them are neutralized, be identified. Our analysis takes as its point of departure, not the forms themselves, but rather the future temporal reference sector per se. By examining the distribution and use of forms across the different configurations of contexts constituting this sector, we can ascertain not only which of the variants are used preferentially in each, but also the nature of the factors promoting or inhibiting their selection. This requires that the locus of variation be carefully defined. We thus begin by circumscribing the variable context (i.e. the context(s) in which all variants may co-occur): any and all unambiguous reference to a state or event occurring posterior to speech time.

   This entails excluding from the quantitative portion of the analysis false futures (which may feature future morphology, but do not refer to future time), as well as true future contexts which admit no variation. False futures include imperatives, hypothetical questions, and use of *ir* + infinitive to indicate movement in space or to denote habitual actions or general truths, in the 1st p. pl. present (*vamos*), corresponding to English adhortative "let's", and in protases of hypothetical *se* ("if") complexes (where future subjunctive is prescribed). Such uses were not considered here. Non-productive uses of future morphology, e.g. in frozen expressions, proverbs and quotations from or allusions to the Bible, were also not considered in the quantitative analysis. Retained for this study were a total of 2365 tokens of verbs making unambiguous reference to future time via one of the four morphological forms exemplified in (1-4).

4.2   Operationalizing motivations for variant choice

As noted earlier, study of the evolution of the prescriptive treatment of the variants revealed that the lion's share of variant choice is ascribed to subtle semantic or pragmatic distinctions in the message the speaker wishes to convey. As already observed by Poplack & Turpin (1999) with regard to an analogous situation in French, however, such distinctions are difficult, if not impossible, to operationalize: psychological notions like 'intention', 'certainty', 'probability' and 'doubt' cannot be identified in the absence of some overt contextual clue. Distinctions that *can* be operationalized are those based not on the meaning said to be embodied by a variant (which would be circular), but on supporting contextual indicators of that meaning, where present. Thus for example, notions like agentivity, subjectivity and volition, often associated with selection of future variant, can be captured by factors like grammatical person and animacy.

Accordingly, the linguistic hypotheses we investigate instantiate a number of lexico-semantic and morphosyntactic properties of the contexts in which the variants appear. Some relate to the verb (lexical identity, stativity, number of syllables); others to the subject (grammatical person and number, animacy). At the syntactic level, we investigate type of sentence (declarative, interrogative, negative), type of clause (main, subordinate, relative). At a broader semantic/discourse level, we examine the temporal distance between speech time and the event predicated (distal, proximal), contingency of the future eventuality (contingent, assumed), polarity (negative vs. affirmative), and presence and type of disambiguating adverbial specification (specific vs. non-specific). Each of these has been claimed, historically, synchronically or both, to affect variant choice, as explained below.

4.2.1 Factors relating to the subject.
Each of HP, IR and P has been associated with readings of certainty, conviction, intention and volition.[5] Certainty has also been cited as a reading of SF.[6] Assuming that these are related to agentivity, one way of operationalizing these notions is by distinguishing subjects according to animacy. Human subjects exercise the highest degree of agentivity, and could thus be expected to favor the variants associated with these attitudes.

Likewise, to the extent that variant choice is related to speaker intent, grammatical person/number of the subject should also play a role, with 1st p. subjects favoring the relevant variants (as found by Baleeiro (1988) and Santos (1997) for formal Brazilian Portuguese). We tested these hypotheses by distinguishing, for each subject of a verb referring to future time, humanness, animacy, number (singular, plural) and grammatical person (first, second, third). Because there is so much overlap amongst these factors (virtually all 1st and 2nd persons are human; inanimates occur only in 3rd p.), we collapsed them into 1st p. animate (12), 2nd p. animate (13), 3rd p. animate (14), and 3rd p. inanimate (15).

(12)   Quando eu for em Petrópolis, <u>eu</u> *vou gostar* (IR). (Cláudio/A:02/1992)
       "When I go to Petrópolis, I'*m going to like* it."

---

[5] Arruda (2000), Bechara (1968), Cipro Neto & Infante (2004), Corrêa (1964), Cunha & Cintra (1984/1999), Kury (1989), Lapa (1968), Mateus et al. (1983), Said Ali (1964), Sardinha & Ramos (2000), Soares Barboza (1852), Thomas (1969), van Achter et al. (1996).
[6] Azeredo (2000:130), Cipro Neto & Infante (2004), Cunha & Cintra (1984/1999), Kury (1989).

(13) Mas já que sua filha casou mesmo, <u>você</u> não *vai dar* (IR) um presentinho?
      (Buarque 1978. Geni:39)
      "But since your daughter did get married, aren't <u>you</u> *going to give* her a
      little gift?"

(14) O presidente lançou um comunicado lá dizendo que [<u>ele</u>] não *vai
      reclassificar* (IR) ninguém. (Alessandra/A:04/1992)
      "The president sent a memo saying that [<u>he</u>] *is not going to promote*
      anybody."

(15) Se eu fizer isso, <u>a notícia</u> *vai se espalhar* (IR) e em menos de uma semana
      vai ter uma multidão querendo entrar aqui. (Labaki 1999/2000. Ricardo:58)
      "If I do that, <u>the news</u> *is going to spread*, and in less than a week, there's
      going to be a mob trying to get in here."

4.2.2 Factors relating to the verb.
Because even forms that are not otherwise productive may persist in specific types
of lexical hosts,[7] we pursued this possibility in three ways. We first noted the
lexical identity of each verb separately to determine whether there were
associations between specific verbs and variants. Perhaps the best known lexical
effect in the future temporal reference sector involves avoidance of the *go*-future
with verbs of motion until the former has been bleached of its original semantic
content of movement toward a goal, and grammaticized as a future marker. If, as
some grammarians (e.g. Bechara 1968, Said Ali 1969, Thomas 1969) claim, the
Portuguese IR-periphrasis retains its original meaning of movement, it should be
less likely to occur with other verbs of motion (see Poplack & Tagliamonte 2001
for such a finding in Early African American English). We therefore distinguished
verbs of motion, as in (16), from other verbs, as in (17):

(16) *Vão <u>vir</u>* (IR) agora em abril pra nos visitar, devem passar um mês, um mês e
      meio, entendeu? (Rodrigo/B:185/2003)
      "[They] *are going to <u>come</u>* in April to see us, [they] are supposed to stay a
      month, a month and a half, see?"

(17) Só que tem muita gente que *vai <u>reprovar</u>* (IR), por causa de bagunça e de
      nota. (Priscila/A:14/1992)
      "But there are a lot of people that *are going to <u>fail</u>*, because of behavior and
      grades."

4.2.3 Syntactic factors
Sentence type has also been considered relevant to the selection of the future
forms: SF is said to express uncertainty, doubt, and politeness in questions (e.g.
Amaral 1920; Said Ali 1964). Soares Barboza (1852) ascribed an affirmative

---

[7] Two well-documented examples are the retention of French subjunctive morphology (Poplack
1992) and English irregular past-tense morphology (Bybee et al. 1994, Poplack & Tagliamonte
2001) with a small set of verbs.

reading to SF. Poplack & Turpin (1999) found that the single strongest predictor of SF in Canadian French was negative polarity. Accordingly, we distinguished each token according to whether it occurred in an affirmative declarative sentence, as in (18), an interrogative (19), or a negative (declarative or interrogative) sentence (20).

(18) Marido, *sairei* (SF) eu agora/ que há muito que não saí.
      (Vicente 1523/1998. Inês:226)
      "Husband, I *will go out* now/ because I haven't been out for a long time."
(19) E eu como é que fico? *Vou virar* (IR) Teresinha Pinto? Deus me livre!
      (Buarque 1978. Teresinha:58)
      "And what about me? I'*m gonna turn into* Teresinha Pinto? God forbid!"
(20) Daqui a dois dias não *sabe* (P) mais falar Português.
      (Pena 1842/2000. Clemência:47)
      "In another two days he *does*n't [*won't*] *know* how to speak Portuguese anymore."

Though 'type of clause' in which the future forms appear is not typically considered relevant by grammarians to variant selection, HP was originally said to be used to translate the Latin active future participle (e.g. Barros 1540/1971: 93-94; Leão 1608/1983: 298), corresponding to a relative clause in Portuguese. Tokens were distinguished according to whether they occurred in a main (21), subordinate (22) or relative (23) clause.

(21) Eu *salvarei* (SF), mas debaixo de certas condições. (Pena 1853/1972. Carlos:96)
      "I *will save* [you], but only on certain conditions."
(22) Então diga ao teu marido que nós não *vamos precisar* (IR) do dinheiro dele, não. (Buarque 1978. Terezinha: 74)
      "Then tell your husband that we'*re* not *going to need* his money."
(23) Tolerância demais das autoridades que *vão permitir* (IR) essa imoralidade. (Gomes 1963/1990. Padre:446)
      "Too much lenience from the authorities who *are going to allow* this immorality."

Infixation of clitic pronouns with SF is a distinctive feature of Portuguese (cf. Cunha & Cintra 1984/1999, Figueiredo 1941, Huber 1933, Melo 1957, Machado Filho 1938, Williams 1944, 1968). Prescriptive grammar dictates that clitic pronouns be inserted between verb stem and SF inflection in some contexts (e.g. *dar-lhe-ei*, literally "give -to you - I will"). But as this construction is viewed as pompous and artificial (e.g. Nunes 1910), we test the hypothesis that SF might in fact be avoided here. Accordingly, we distinguished among tokens occurring with direct object clitics, as in (24); indirect object clitics, as in (25); neither, as in (26); both, as in (27), and reflexive or passive pronouns, as in (28):

(24) Mais quero eu quem me adore/ que quem faça com que chore./ *Chamá-lo-ei*
      (SF), Inês. (Vicente 1523/1998. Leonor:189)
      "I prefer someone who adores me/ to someone who makes me cry./ I *will*
      call him, Inês."
(25) Ela lhe *dará* (SF) o recado. (Silva 1737/1980. Periandro:34)
      "She *will give* you the message."
(26) Eu que falo com ela, e muito, sei que ela não *há de aceitar* (HP) proposta de
      casamento sem estar muito bem coberta. (Buarque 1978. Vitória:32)
      "Since I talk to her a lot, I know she *won't accept* a marriage proposal
      without guarantees."
(27) Não vo-lo *hei de negar* (HP): fazei-me uma petição. (Vicente 1526/1975.
      Fidalgo:176)
      "I *won't deny* it to you: make your request."
(28) Ora, faça-me um favor! Então esse pessoal que já enfrentou metralhadora
      vai se assustar (IR) por causa de cinco tiras! (Guarnieri 1961. Agileu:28)
      "Oh, please! Guys who've stood up to machine-guns *are going to be scared*
      of five cops?!"

4.2.4 Semantic/discourse factors
One of the most persistent readings of both *go*-periphrases and the futurate present
is that of proximity in the future.[8] To test these claims, we distinguish proximal
events and states (here defined as those predicted to occur within the same day of
the utterance), as in (29), from distal events and states (occurring thereafter), as in
(30):

(29) Aí agora, eu num sei hoje, né, não, porque hoje eu num *vou* (P) pra escola.
      Vou fazer (IR) o exame no ouvido. (Ana/A:13/1991)
      "Well, today I don't know, no, because today I'*m not going* to school. [I'm]
      going to have an ear exam."
(30) Ano que vem eu *vou tirar* (IR) a Cleide dessa escola e colocar na escola
      pública, do governo. (Vânia/B:30/1992)
      "Next year, I'*m going to take* Cleide out of this school and put her in a
      public school, a government school."

Future variants are often associated with different degrees of specificity. Soares
Barboza (1852) ascribes to SF a reading of indeterminacy. Thomas (1969, 1974),
Cunha & Cintra (1984/1999), Mateus et al. (1983) and van Achter et al. (1996)
claim that P conveys specific future time when accompanied by a temporal
adverb. If this is the case, specific adverbs could be expected to favour selection
of P, and non-specific (or no) adverbs should favour SF. To test this hypothesis,

---

[8] E.g. Arruda (2000), Cegalla (2005), Cipro Neto & Infante (2004), Cunha & Cintra, (1984/1999),
Kury (1986), Said Ali (1969), Silva Junior (1887), Silveira Bueno (1968), and Thomas (1969) for
Portuguese; Bentivoglio and Sedano (1992) for Spanish; Poplack & Turpin (1999) for French;
Poplack & Tagliamonte (2001) for English.

we coded for type of adverbial specification, distinguishing among specific, non-specific and no modification, as in (31) - (33) respectively.

(31) Tá certo. Hoje eu faço vista grossa, mas <u>amanhã</u> eu te *caço* (P), viu?
      (Buarque 1978. Max:57)
      "OK, today I'm letting it go, but <u>tomorrow</u> I *catch* you, see?"
(32) Periandro, <u>logo</u> *falaremos* (SF), não te ausentes.
      (Silva 1737/1980. Filena:39)
      "Periandro, [we] *will talk* <u>soon</u>. Don't leave."
(33) Não tou pagando nada, então não *vou estudar* (IR) não. Num precisa.
      (Salvador/A:24/1992)
      "I'm not paying anything, so no way I'm *going to study*. I don't have to."

It has often been noted that SF expresses notions of doubt, probability and possibility,[9] readings which have also been assigned to HP (Barreto 1944, Thomas 1969). In addition, Thomas (1969) claims that P conveys the sense of promise in future contexts (e.g. *se você me ajudar, eu lhe* **pago** *bem* "If you help me, I'll pay you well"). We may capture these observations by distinguishing events assumed to have a high likelihood of occurring from those whose occurrence is contingent on other events. Following Fleischman (1982) and Poplack & Turpin (1999), we coded as contingent events whose realization is dependent upon the fulfillment of a condition, as in (34), in contrast to those whose realization is assumed, as in (35):

(34) Se eu fugir, eles me *alcançam* (P) em dois tempos.
      (Labaki 1999/2000. Ricardo:65)
      "If I run away, they'*ll get* me in a minute".
(35) Ninguém *vai saber* (IR). Você sabe. A imprensa só publica o que deixam
      publicar. (Labaki 1999/2000. Verônica:59).
      "Nobody *is going to know*. You know. The press only publishes what they
      <u>let them</u> publish."

4.2.5 Medium
In addition, where possible (i.e. in the 20th century), we examine the contribution of the extralinguistic factor of medium (spoken vs. written). According to Santos (1997), SF is the preferred variant in formal written Brazilian Portuguese. If the (written) plays retained for this study are representative of the spoken language, their use of the variants should reflect that of speech. We test this hypothesis statistically by comparing rates and conditioning of variant selection in theatre

---

[9] E.g. Amaral (1920), Arruda (2000), Azeredo (2000), Bechara (1968), Cegalla (2005), Cipro Neto & Infante (2004), Cunha & Cintra, (1984/(1999), Kury (1989), Rossi (1945), Said Ali (1969), van Achter et al. (1996).

and speech of the 20th century, the only century for which spoken data is available.

Each of the 2365 tokens retained for analysis was coded for each of the factors introduced in Sections 4.2.1 through 4.2.5. In this way we test claims about the uses of the exponents of future temporal reference against the way they are actually employed unreflectingly by speakers.

4.3 Coding and analysis

The coding system described above represents a series of hypotheses, relating mainly to the meaning and/or function of specific variants, about the choice mechanism. To determine which of these factors contribute a statistically significant effect to variant choice when all are considered simultaneously, we analyzed the materials using Goldvarb 2.0 (Rand & Sankoff 1990), a variable-rule application for the Macintosh. Variable rule analysis helps determine how the choice process is influenced by the factors constituting the environment in which the variant form occurs. We adduce two lines of evidence deriving from variable rule analysis in interpreting the results: statistical significance (at the .05 level) of the effect, and constraint hierarchy, or direction of effect, as inferred from the ordering of factor weights within a factor group. We interpret the detailed picture afforded by variable rule analysis as a snapshot of the way the variants divide up the labor of expressing the future at a particular stage in the course of the development of this grammatical sector. Comparison of these snapshots reveals the movements of the variants both over time and across the contexts constituting the future temporal reference domain. In ensuing sections, we review the results of these analyses.

5. Results

Table 1 displays the distribution of the future temporal reference variants by century.

Table 1: *Distribution of future temporal reference variants by century*

	Synthetic future		*Haver -* periphrasis		*Present*		*Ir -* periphrasis		
Century	N	%	N	%	N	%	N	%	Total
16th	198	66	91	30	10	3	3	1	302
18th	169	57	103	35	19	6	5	2	296
19th	276	53	104	20	66	13	72	14	518
20th Plays	46	9	5	1	93	18	384	73	528
Speech	4	1	—	—	104	14	613	85	721
Total	693	30	303	13	292	12	1077	45	2365

In contrast to what could be inferred from grammarians' characterizations , Table 1 shows that at any given period, most reference to the future is made by only two variants, one analytic and one synthetic. During the 16th and 18th centuries, these are SF and HP, which represent over 90% of the data in each period. They continue to predominate throughout the 19th century, though by this point IR has infiltrated the system, and together with P, now accounts for nearly a third of the temporal reference contexts. The 20th century sees an abrupt reversal: IR has virtually replaced the older variants, with P continuing to play the same (minor) role as in the previous century, returning full circle to a two-variant system. Comparison of 20th-century popular plays with speech confirms that this dramatic change cannot be attributed solely to differences in medium. Although the older variants still persist in the plays, albeit at very low rates, variant proportions follow those of speech remarkably closely. This is a first suggestion that the dialogues in our popular theatre corpus do in fact represent contemporaneous speech, despite the lag in rate of the incoming variant.

How was this change implemented? To answer this question we examine the state of the future temporal reference sector period by period, performing independent multivariate analyses of the factors contributing to variant selection in each. Comparison across periods yields a graphic view of the role of each variant over the course of the change. We make use of this information to determine the trajectory by which the incoming variants infiltrated the system, eventually to oust their older counterparts. In each of Tables 2-6, the higher the figure, the greater the probability the variant in question will be selected in the environment under consideration.

5.1   Period I: 16th and 18th centuries

Table 2 shows the results of three independent variable rule analyses of the contribution of linguistic factors selected as significant to choice of SF, HP, and P in the 16th and 18th centuries. 17th-century plays are not included here because 1) during the Spanish rule of Portugal (1580-1640) most Portuguese literature was written in Spanish or Latin (Rebello 1989), 2) few comedies corresponding to our criteria were produced in Portugal (*ibid.*) and 3) there is no record of play production or performance in Brazil during this period (Prado 1999). We note first that of the nine linguistic factors originally investigated, only two or three were found to be significant to the choice of each variant.[10]

---

[10] The factor lexical identity was investigated independently; the outcomes are not presented here. Two factors, *type of clause* and *presence of clitics*, were not selected as significant to the choice of any variant at any time period.

Table 2: *Variable rule analyses of the contribution of factors selected as significant to variant choice: 16th/18th centuries*[11]

	SF	HP	P	IR
Total N:	367	194	29	8
Corrected mean:	.63	.32	.05	-
Sentence Type				
Declarative	.55	.44	[ ]	-
Negative	.37	.62	[ ]	-
Interrogative	.31	.70	[ ]	-
Contingency				
Contingent	.68	.30	[ ]	-
Assumed	.48	.52	[ ]	-
Verb Type				
Non-motion	.54	[ ]	.37	-
Motion	.35	[ ]	.88	-
Temporal Distance				
Distal	[ ]	[ ]	.36	-
Proximal	[ ]	[ ]	.71	-
Grammatical Person/Animacy				
1st Animate	[ ]	[ ]	.70	-
2nd Animate	[ ]	[ ]	.21	-
3rd Animate	[ ]	[ ]	.39	-
3rd Inanimate	[ ]	[ ]	.58	-
Adverbial Specification				
Non-Specific	[ ]	[ ]	[ ]	-
No Adverbial	[ ]	[ ]	[ ]	-
Specific	[ ]	[ ]	[ ]	-
Type of Clause				
Subordinate	[ ]	[ ]	[ ]	-
Main	[ ]	[ ]	[ ]	-
Presence of Clitics				
No clitic	[ ]	[ ]	[ ]	-
Object clitic	[ ]	[ ]	[ ]	-
Reflexive/passive clitic	[ ]	[ ]	[ ]	-
Factors not selected as significant				
Sentence Type			X	-
Contingency			X	-
Verb Type		X		-
Temporal Distance	X	X		-
Grammatical Person/Animacy	X	X		-
Adverbial Specification	X	X	X	-
Type of Clause	X	X	X	-
Presence of Clitics	X	X	X	-

Comparison of factor weights across analyses confirms that in Period I, the task of expressing future temporal reference is largely divided between SF and HP. With a corrected mean (or overall tendency of occurrence) of .63, at this stage SF does in fact appear to be the default variant it has been characterized as for so long.

---

[11] For the statistical analyses in this and ensuing tables, the 16th and 18th centuries are treated together, as are reflexives and passives (due to sparse data).

Consistent with this role, it is preferred in frequent, neutral or unmarked contexts, such as declarative sentences (probability .55) and with most lexical verbs (.54). But SF is also clearly favoured in contingent contexts, as in (36), while HP is favored in assumed contexts, as in (37), as well as in negative (38) and interrogative (39) sentences.

(36) Não senhora; eu *virei* (SF) logo nessora, se m'eu lá não detiver.
       (Vicente 1509/1975. Moça:382)
       "No mother; if I don't have to stay there, I *will come* right at that time."
(37) Aqui te *hei de fazer* (HP) em picado com os dentes.
       (Silva 1734/1957. Eurípedes:61)
       "Here [I] *will tear* you to shreds with my teeth."
(38) Porém não *hei de casar* (HP)/ senão com homem avisado;/ ainda que pobre
       e pelado,/ seja discreto em falar. (Vicente 1523/1998. Inês:186)
       "But I *will* not *get married*/ except to an educated man;/ even if poor and
       naked,/ as long as he is discreet."
(39) Pois aonde o *hei de pôr* (HP)? (Silva 1737/1980. Semicúpio:54)
       "Well, where *shall* I *put* it?"

P is very rare in the early popular plays we have studied, accounting for no more than 6% of all future temporal reference throughout the 18th century (cf. Table 1). Despite its rarity, however, it can be seen from Table 2 to have already staked out its preferred loci of occurrence. The most important factor conditioning its selection is verb type: motion verbs favor P highly, with a probability of .88. (Indeed, well over half the verbs instantiated as P correspond to main verb *ir* "to go", a harbinger of what would develop into a categorical association between verb and variant.) Proximal future contexts, traditionally associated with futurate presents, and 1st (animate) and 3rd person inanimate subjects (not so associated) also favor P. The example in (40) illustrates the basic future temporal reference uses of P until he 19th century. At this stage, the *ir*-periphrasis was barely incipient (N=8), and so does not figure in the quantitative portion of the analysis. One of the few examples of IR in this period is reproduced in (41).

(40) Vai tu, filho Joane, e dize que logo *vou* (P), que não faz tempo que cá estou.
       (Vicente 1512/1998. Velho:83)
       "Go, my son Joane, and say that I *go* soon, because I haven't been here
       long."
(41) Deixe-o enforcar, que eu também *vou fazer* (IR) o mesmo.
       (Silva 1734/1957. Esopo:132)
       "Let him hang himself, for I am also *going to do* the same thing."

5.2   Period II: 19th century

We now examine the variable expression of future temporal reference in the 19th century (the first period in which specifically Brazilian Portuguese is represented in popular theatre). Recall from Table 1 that while SF and HP continue to predominate, all four variants are clearly in competition at this time. Note that IR, only incipient in previous centuries, has undergone a substantial rate increase, and together with P now accounts for nearly a third of the future temporal reference data.

Table 3, which displays four independent variable rule analyses of the factors selected as significant to variant choice in the 19th century, reveals the first subtle shifts the future temporal reference sector underwent to accommodate the new variant. The factors examined are the same as for previous centuries.

Focusing first on the emergent variant, we see that like other *go*-periphrases, IR also entered the system via proximate future contexts, as in (42). In Period I, these were the domain of P; with a probability of .79, selection of IR is now strongly favored here.

(42)   Aí a mãe dela falou assim, "pois <u>agora</u> você *vai levar* (IR) uma surra, menina; porque eu não disse que não era pra você sair?!" (Tiago/B:189/1991)
   "Then her mother said, "<u>now</u> you're going to get it, girl, because didn't I tell you not to go out?!""

Though IR accounts for less than 15% of the data at this time, it is noteworthy that proximity in the future represents the only 'specialized' context of occurrence for this variant. Elsewhere, the distribution of IR foreshadows its eventual role as default future marker: it is preferred in the more frequent, less marked contexts of declarative affirmative sentences (the former domain of SF), as well as those with no adverbial specification. These are exemplified in (43).

(43)   *Vou transmitir* (IR) essa ordem ao porteiro porque eu posso não estar na ocasião. (Azevedo 1897/1965. Gerente:23)
   "I'*m going to give* this order to the doorman, because I may not be here for the occasion."

How did P react to the incursion of IR? Although the two variants are now quantitatively on par, comparison of their variable conditioning reveals that the former remains more structurally restricted than its emergent counterpart. The fact that P is heavily constrained to co-occur with specific adverbs (probability .89), as in (44), suggests that it is still necessary to disambiguate its temporal reference.

(44)   O livro que te prometi, *mando* (P) <u>amanhã.</u> (Pena 1842/2000. Cecília:50)
   "The book I promised you, I *send* <u>tomorrow</u>."

Table 3: *Variable rule analyses of the contribution of factors selected as significant to variant choice: 19th century*

	SF	HP	P	IR
Total N:	268	104	48	72
Corrected mean:	.55	.21	.10	.15
Sentence Type				
Declarative	[ ]	[ ]	[ ]	.59
Negative	[ ]	[ ]	[ ]	.10
Interrogative	[ ]	[ ]	[ ]	.31
Contingency				
Contingent	[ ]	.26	.85	[ ]
Assumed	[ ]	.52	.47	[ ]
Verb Type				
Non-motion	.52	[ ]	.44	[ ]
Motion	.31	[ ]	.87	[ ]
Temporal Distance				
Distal	.56	.54	[ ]	.36
Proximal	.38	.40	[ ]	.79
Grammatical Person/Animacy				
1st Animate	[ ]	[ ]	[ ]	[ ]
2nd Animate	[ ]	[ ]	[ ]	[ ]
3rd Animate	[ ]	[ ]	[ ]	[ ]
3rd Inanimate	[ ]	[ ]	[ ]	[ ]
Adverbial Specification				
Non-Specific	.70	[ ]	.46	.15
No Adverbial	.46	[ ]	.45	.62
Specific	.43	[ ]	.89	.27
Type of Clause				
Subordinate	[ ]	[ ]	[ ]	[ ]
Main	[ ]	[ ]	[ ]	[ ]
Presence of Clitics				
No clitic	[ ]	[ ]	[ ]	[ ]
Object clitic	[ ]	[ ]	[ ]	[ ]
Reflexive/passive clitic	[ ]	[ ]	[ ]	[ ]
Factors not selected as significant				
Sentence Type	X	X	X	
Contingency	X			X
Verb Type		X		X
Temporal Distance			X	
Grammatical Person/Animacy	X	X	X	X
Adverbial Specification		X		
Type of Clause	X	X	X	X
Presence of Clitics	X	X	X	X

Moreover, in addition to co-occurring almost categorically with main verb *ir*,[12] as in example (40) above, it continues to entertain a strong association with other motion verbs, as in (45). Finally, it appears to have inherited from the receding SF

---

[12] It was therefore excluded from the calculations in Table 4.

the role of expressing contingent events (as in example (34)), in contrast with HP, which continues to be the variant of choice in assumed/certain contexts.

(45) Se fô possível, muito que bem, se não fô, paciência; a gente arruma as mala e amanhã memo _volta_ (P) pra fazenda. (Azevedo 1897/1965. Eusébio:94)
"If it's possible, fine, if not, so be it; we pack our bags and tomorrow we _return_ to the farm."

Summarizing, rates of P have doubled since the 16/18th centuries, but rather than spreading across the future temporal reference domain, the use of this variant has become more entrenched in the relatively infrequent, more specialized contexts of motion verbs, contingent contexts and disambiguating adverbs. As for the older exponents of future temporal reference, with one exception each (non-motion verbs in the case of SF, and assumed contexts in the case of HP), as SF and HP recede from the sector, their erstwhile preferred domains either disappear, are transferred to another variant, or are replaced by new domains. Sentence type, which distinguished between SF and HP in the 16/18th centuries, no longer plays a role in their selection. Contingent predications, formerly the domain of SF, have now been transferred to P. Incursion of P and IR into contexts with specific (44, 45) and no adverbial (43) modification respectively, relegated SF to the remaining contexts, those modified by non-specific adverbs (46). Likewise, the novel but strong association of IR with proximal eventualities left both SF and HP to express distal states and events.

(46) Que impertinência! <u>Logo</u> _conversaremos_ (SF) (Pena 1842/2000. Mariquinha:25)
"What nerve! We'_ll talk_ <u>later</u>."

Only one relationship, the propensity of P to co-occur with motion verbs, and the resulting (weak) association of SF with the remaining verbs, has remained unchanged since preceding centuries. The future temporal reference system of the 19th century is one in which the variants are in opposition in almost all contexts. They are not necessarily the same variants as those competing in these very contexts in previous centuries, but the constraints on their selection remain in place.

5.3   Period III: 20th-century theatre

Table 4 compares the results of three independent variable rule analyses of the contribution of the same factors to variant selection in 20th-century popular plays. These results, when compared with those of Table 1, illustrate the trajectory by which the expression of future temporal reference resolved itself in contemporary usage.

Table 4: *Independent variable rule analyses of the contribution of factors to the probability that SF, P and IR will be selected in future temporal reference contexts in 20th-century popular plays.*

	SF	HP	P	IR
Total N:	35	5	61	373
Corrected mean:	.08	-	.13	.81
Sentence Type				
Declarative	[　]	-	[　]	[　]
Negative	[　]	-	[　]	[　]
Interrogative	[　]	-	[　]	[　]
Contingency				
Contingent	[　]	-	.73	.27
Assumed	[　]	-	.48	.52
Verb Type				
Non-motion	[　]	-	.47	.52
Motion	[　]	-	.78	.29
Temporal Distance				
Distal	[　]	-	[　]	[　]
Proximal	[　]	-	[　]	[　]
Grammatical Person/Animacy				
1st Animate	[　]	-	.65	.39
2nd Animate	[　]	-	.14	.72
3rd Animate	[　]	-	.46	.54
3rd Inanimate	[　]	-	.51	.50
Adverbial Specification				
Non-Specific	.70	-	.61	.33
No Adverbial	.48	-	.45	.55
Specific	.30	-	.76	.33
Type of Clause				
Subordinate	[　]	-	[　]	[　]
Main	[　]	-	[　]	[　]
Presence of Clitics				
No clitic	[　]	-	[　]	[　]
Object clitic	[　]	-	[　]	[　]
Reflexive/passive clitic		-	------*	------
Factors not selected as significant				
Sentence Type	X	-	X	X
Contingency	X	-		
Verb Type	X	-		
Temporal Distance	X	-	X	X
Grammatical Person/Animacy	X	-		
Adverbial Specification		-		
Type of Clause	X	-	X	X
Presence of Clitics	X	-	X	X

* no data

Of the outgoing variants, HP has disappeared altogether. The use of SF, now very rare, is also highly constrained. First, the 19th-century association of SF with distal future has disappeared, as inferred from the result that temporal distance is not a statistically significant predictor of variant choice (itself a likely consequence of the fact that P is no longer associated with proximity). Likewise, the longstanding association of SF with non-motion verbs, dating back to its earliest (16th century) uses, is no longer operative either. Only the propensity of SF to occur with non-specific adverbs remains. Thus, as SF nears extinction in the 20th century, it is relegated (in popular plays) to only one of its former preferred contexts, those with non-specific adverbial modification. Closer inspection of the data (not shown here) suggests that SF also tends to occur in *be*-passive constructions, as in (47), which are rare in speech.

(47)   a. Isso *será esclarecido* (SF) no decorrer da nossa estória. (Gomes
           1963/1990. Malta: 382)
           "This *will be clarified* as our story plays out."
       b. Me liberte e todos os seus pecados *serão perdoados*. (Labaki 1999/2000.
           Ricardo: 68)
           "Free me and all your sins *shall be pardoned*".

By way of contrast, despite little more than a marginal rate increase over the centuries, P not only retains all of its earlier associations (i.e. with motion verbs, contingent predications and specific adverbs), it is now also associated with the non-specific adverbs formerly the domain of SF. In addition, P now displays the same distinct tendency to co-occur with 1st p. subjects (and an even stronger avoidance of 2nd p. subjects) that was last seen to be operative in the 16/18th centuries (Table 2). It disappeared in the interim, only to reemerge now, for reasons which are unclear. IR occurs everywhere else.

5.4   Period III: 20th-century speech

Having reviewed the constraints on variant selection in 20th-century plays, we are now in a position to validate them with 20th-century speech, the first period for which we have access to such data (Table 5).

Table 5: *Variable rule analyses of the contribution of factors selected as significant to variant choice: 20th century speech*

	SF	HP	P	IR
Total N:	4	0	47	611
Corrected mean:	-	-	.07	.93
Sentence Type				
Declarative	-	-	[ ]	[ ]
Negative	-	-	[ ]	[ ]
Interrogative	-	-	[ ]	[ ]
Contingency				
Contingent	-	-	.87	.13
Assumed	-	-	.45	.55
Verb Type				
Non-motion	-	-	[ ]	[ ]
Motion	-	-	[ ]	[ ]
Temporal Distance				
Distal	-	-	[ ]	[ ]
Proximal	-	-	[ ]	[ ]
Grammatical Person/Animacy				
1st Animate	-	-	[ ]	[ ]
2nd Animate	-	-	[ ]	[ ]
3rd Animate	-	-	[ ]	[ ]
3rd Inanimate	-	-	[ ]	[ ]
Adverbial Specification				
Non-Specific	-	-	.57	.43
No Adverbial	-	-	.42	.58
Specific	-	-	.80	.20
Type of Clause				
Subordinate	-	-	[ ]	[ ]
Main	-	-	[ ]	[ ]
Presence of Clitics				
No clitic	-	-	[ ]	[ ]
Object clitic	-	-	[ ]	[ ]
Reflexive/passive clitic	-	-	-------	------
Factors not selected as significant				
Sentence Type	-	-	X	X
Contingency	-	-		
Verb Type	-	-	X	X
Temporal Distance	-	-	X	X
Grammatical Person/Animacy	-	-	X	X
Adverbial Specification	-	-		
Type of Clause	-	-	X	X
Presence of Clitics	-	-	X	X

Comparison of Tables 1 and 5 shows that of the outgoing variants, HP has disappeared from speech as well, and at 1% of the data, SF is vanishingly rare. With few exceptions, the expression of future temporal reference has by now basically been assumed by IR, which has infiltrated all the contexts formerly dominated by other variants. As a result, most of the factors once implicated in variant selection no longer contribute statistically significant effects to variant choice. The only two barriers to the colonization by IR of the entire future sector are those in which P has become entrenched: contingent contexts, and those modified by specific adverbials, as exemplified in (41), (42) and (43). Contingent contexts, once the domain of SF, were transferred to P in the 19th century. Those modified by specific adverbs have been associated with P since then as well. The strong preference for P with motion verbs, dating back to its earliest (16th century) uses, has now resolved itself in a near-categorical association with main verb *ir*, as illustrated in Figure 1.

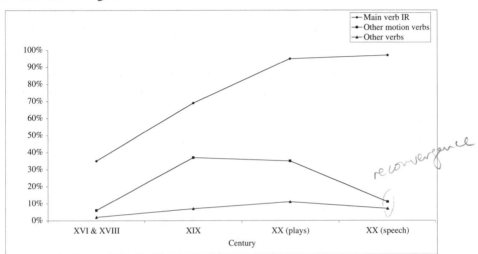

recovergence

Figure 1: *Association of lexical verbs with P*

Though all other motion verbs can occur freely with the IR-periphrasis in contemporary Brazilian Portuguese, as can be seen in (48a) and (48b), there remains a widespread, albeit informal, constraint against collocating main verb *ir* with the IR-periphrasis ("go$_{fin}$ (to) go"). Such constructions are heavily stigmatized and overtly corrected. The utterance in (49), of a 10-year old boy, is the only such example in more than 650 references to the future in 20th-century speech.

(48)   a.   Isso é um pesadelo. Eu *vou correr* (IR) aqui e vou ver até onde vou
            (Eduardo/B:39/1992)
            "This is a nightmare. I'*m going to run* and [I'm] going to see how far I
            get."
      b.   Você não pensa muito assim: ah, eu *vou sair* (IR) na rua. Não *vou sair*
            (IR) com roupa de marca porque se não ali na esquina vão me roubar
            (IR). (Érica/A:27/1992)
            "You don't really think: oh, I'*m going to go out*, but I'*m not going to go
            out* in designer clothes because if I do, [they're] going to rob me, right on
            the corner."

(49) Aí, agora, a gente *vai ir* (IR) agora é num do bombeiro. Conhecer lá uns negócios que o bombeiro usa pra apagar o fogo. (Tiago/A:67/1991)
"Now where we're *going to go* now is to the fire station. See the stuff the fireman uses to put out the fire."

In view of the assumption by the IR-periphrasis of virtually all the contexts and functions of its erstwhile competitors, its aversion to main verb *ir* is curious at best. *Go*-futures tend not to co-occur with motion verbs early in the grammaticization process (Bybee et al. 1994), while lexical identity of the verb has little effect on variant selection at later stages (Poplack & Tagliamonte, 1999). There can be little doubt that IR has now grammaticized into the major (and for many speakers, virtually the *only*) exponent of future temporal reference, and our analyses reveal no constraint against its co-occurrence with other motion verbs. Yet in contrast to French, where the periphrastic *go*-future is also on the rise (Poplack & Turpin 1999), and even English, where its use is far more moderate (Poplack & Tagliamonte 1999; Poplack, Walker & Malcolmson in press), the Portuguese IR-periphrasis is still avoided in conjunction with main verb *ir*.

5.5   Speech and the representation of speech

We may now ask what relationship, if any, spoken Brazilian Portuguese entertains with the facsimiles of speech instantiated by dialogues of popular plays written in the same century. Table 1 shows remarkable parallels in rates of variant use (despite some overrepresentation of the outgoing variants and concomitant underrepresentation of the emergent variant). The variable rule analysis in Table 6 reveals that there are also remarkable parallels in conditioning of variant selection. This emerges from comparing, across media, the hierarchy of constraints, which reveals the underlying structure of the variability, even when the factor is not statistically significant.[13] Note the remarkable parallels between the patterning of variation in the plays and speech. The only discrepancy involves the effect of grammatical person/animacy, noted in Section 5.3. This effect, manifested as a strong aversion to P in 2nd p. animate contexts (*você(s)*), is not relevant to speech; it neither constrains variant selection nor shows consistent effects. The fact that IR has advanced further in actual usage than in the dialogue of the plays explains why variant choice is less constrained in the former.

---

[13] Weights for non-significant factor groups are derived from an analysis in which all factors are included in the regression (the first 'stepdown' run in Goldvarb 2.0), not shown here.

Table 6: *Variable rule analyses of the contribution of factors selected as significant to variant choice: 20th-century plays vs. speech*

	P		IR	
	Plays	**Speech**	**Plays**	**Speech**
Total N:	61	47	373	611
Corrected mean:	.13	.07	.81	.93
Sentence Type				
Declarative	[ ]	[ ]	[ ]	[ ]
Negative	[ ]	[ ]	[ ]	[ ]
Interrogative	[ ]	[ ]	[ ]	[ ]
Contingency				
Contingent	.73	.87	.27	.13
Assumed	.48	.45	.52	.55
Verb Type				
Non-motion	.47	[.48]	.52	[.52]
Motion	.78	[.62]	.29	[.38]
Temporal Distance				
Distal	[ ]	[ ]	[ ]	[ ]
Proximal	[ ]	[ ]	[ ]	[ ]
Grammatical Person/Animacy				
1st Animate	.65	[.44]	.39	[.56]
2nd Animate	.14	[.56]	.72	[.44]
3rd Animate	.46	[.46]	.54	[.54]
3rd Inanimate	.51	[.69]	.50	[.31]
Adverbial Specification				
Non-Specific	.61	.57	.33	.43
No Adverbial	.45	.42	.55	.58
Specific	.76	.80	.33	.20
Type of Clause				
Subordinate	[ ]	[ ]	[ ]	[ ]
Main	[ ]	[ ]	[ ]	[ ]
Presence of Clitics				
No clitic	[ ]	[ ]	[ ]	[ ]
Object clitic	[ ]	[ ]	[ ]	[ ]
Reflexive/passive clitic	------	-------	------	------
Factors not selected as significant				
Sentence Type	X	X	X	X
Contingency				
Verb Type		X		X
Temporal Distance	X	X	X	X
Grammatical Person/Animacy		X		X
Adverbial Specification				
Type of Clause	X	X	X	X
Presence of Clitics	X	X	X	X

6. The transition period in language change

Examining an apparently abrupt change in the expression of future temporal reference, we traced the trajectory of its exponents over five centuries of development. We documented a system which was overwhelmingly dominated by

SF and HP until the 19th century, at which time the emergent IR began infiltrating the sector, predictably, via proximate future contexts. Although accounting for no more than 15% of the data at that time, IR had also already established a foothold in unmarked affirmative and adverbially unspecified contexts. By the 20th century, it had expanded into *all* of the contexts formerly associated with the older and far more robust variants, effectively ousting them from this domain. We showed how this change was driven by the gradual expropriation of the preferred contexts of the older variants by the incoming IR, and how it culminated in the contemporary situation in which the latter has become the default choice everywhere but in the few remaining bastions of the (rare but incredibly tenacious) P: contingent and adverbially specified contexts and the lexical verb *ir* "to go".

Our focus on the variability inherent in the system confirms that the transition period in linguistic change is not abrupt, as most generative (and some historical) accounts portray it to be. Rather, change proceeds as a series of small adjustments, as incoming and outgoing variants jockey for position in the system. In support of this claim, we summarize the trajectory of the outgoing variants from Period I, when they accounted for nearly all (95%) of the data, through their disappearance in Period III (Tables 2-5).

SF, initially favored in contingent constructions and affirmative declarative sentences, had by Period II lost both effects (transferring the first to P, and the second to IR). Despite substantial reduction in frequency, SF was still the majority variant at this time; this may explain why it also acquired new constraints: an aversion to proximate contexts, (now transferred to IR from P), and an association with non-specific adverbials. As we suggested earlier, however, SF was more likely simply relegated to the residual contexts created once the other variants had staked out their respective niches (IR with proximity; P with motion verbs). Its novel association with non-specific adverbs now places it in opposition to the other two variants in this context. Thus, over the duration of the change, SF lost, transferred, and acquired constraints, the latter mostly as a reaction to the activity in the remainder of the future temporal reference system. By Period III, it had disappeared.

HP followed a similar trajectory. In Period I, it was favored in assumed and negative/interrogative contexts. As it receded (Period II), it lost the latter, but acquired a novel association with distal future (likely, as with SF, in response to the strong propensity of the incoming IR to occur in proximal contexts). By Period III, HP too was lost. The proximity distinction, formerly captured by the opposition between SF and HP (expressing distal future) on the one hand, and IR (proximal future) on the other, had no further *raison d'être* once the variants associated with one pole of the opposition had disappeared. In Period III, IR does basically all the work of future temporal reference, except in the two contexts in which P has remained entrenched: overt adverbials and contingent contexts.

A widely documented characteristic of the development of the Romance languages is the replacement of Classical Latin synthetic structures with analytic structures. The developments detailed above shed light on how this came about.

The change from synthetic to analytic was not abrupt. Setting aside P, the only variant to have persisted over the duration, the competition may be seen to occur between the analytic forms, with the emergent IR driving out its older counterpart, HP. SF, the older synthetic form, disappears thereafter. As a result, the Portuguese future temporal reference sector, initially constituted of a synthetic and analytic form, has come full circle, with variant proportions now reversed. Only the exponents are not the same![14]

Such accommodations to variant movements over time do not exhibit the Constant Rate Effect (Kroch 1989, 2001). According to the latter account of the transition between language states in linguistic change, when one variant replaces a competitor across a set of linguistic contexts, the rate of replacement is the same in all. Some contexts may favor the incoming form over its competitors; others disfavor, but they all acquire it at the same time (albeit at different initial frequencies), and crucially, they maintain the same pattern of favoring and disfavoring effects as the change proceeds. Thus, "a constant rate of change across contexts is mathematically equivalent to fixity of contextual effects, in direction and size, across time periods" (Kroch 1989: 206).

The trajectory of change presented here is at odds with this view. Contextual effects on variant choice, as expressed by the constraint hierarchies associated with each variant and context in the multivariate analyses we have presented, rarely remain constant across time. And this result is not merely an effect of loss of statistical significance; even when factors no longer significant are "forced" into the regression, they do not display the same constraint hierarchies as previously, tending instead toward .5, or reversing direction altogether. Rather, four variants, each with its own characteristic propensity of occurrence, enter and exit the system at different periods and different speeds (as measured by the increase, from one period to the next, in the corrected means, or overall rates of variant use, in Tables 2-5). As a variant disappears, the constraints on its selection (whether assessed by statistical significance or factor values after they have lost significance) do not remain the same. Nonetheless, the important distinctions conveyed by a factor group by and large perdure, though they may eventually come to be expressed by different variants, or as is presumably the case for IR, by the same one.

The Constant Rate Effect is an outgrowth of the general principle that contextual effects are independent. Whether or not this is true of the two-variant situations generally adduced in its support (e.g. Kroch 1989, Santorini 1993, Taylor 1994, Shi 1989), it cannot be projected onto the complex multi-variant case we have examined. Here the binary system is perturbed each time a variant appears or disappears. And since such cases are far from uncommon — TMA distinctions, for example, are frequently expressed by three or more competing variants — the applicability of the Constant Rate Effect must be restricted to periods in which the repertoire of variants remains stable, i.e. periods which

---

[14] We are grateful to Mary Kato for calling this pattern to our attention.

feature neither incipient nor moribund forms. To generalize to the multi-variant situation studied here, the requirement that constraint remain associated with variant would have to be relaxed, and transfer of constraints from outgoing to incoming variants be permitted.

Kroch (1989: 237) further invokes the Constant Rate Effect to reject the (widely accepted) idea that language change proceeds context by context, with new forms appearing first in a restricted context and spreading to others only later. Instead, Kroch claims, all contexts acquire the new form at the same rate, favoring ones as well as disfavoring ones, albeit at lower initial frequencies in the latter case. Our results contradict this claim. They show that forms *do* appear first in restricted contexts. They may proceed to spread to others, as eventually happened with IR, or they may remain entrenched in their restricted contexts (as occurred with P). Indeed, this study suggests that the type of contexts associated with a variant can provide valuable information about their trajectory. For example, the fact that IR entered via (or quickly infiltrated) unmarked contexts was a harbinger of its eventual assumption of the role of default future marker. P, on the other hand, has remained entrenched in the same restricted contexts for over five centuries! Two other related assumptions of the Constant Rate Effect will need to be reconsidered in light of the findings presented here. One is the claim that grammar remains homogeneous during the course of change. It may contain a variable structure (as instantiated by the constraint hierarchy of favoring and disfavoring factors), but this structure remains constant, because the factor weights remain the same. We have shown that constraints on variant selection do not remain fixed as the repertoire of competing forms changes. This is of course not visible in the cases studied by Kroch and associates, precisely because the repertoire consists of the same two variants at all times. And contrary to the claim that only when one form displaces the others *entirely* will there be a reorganization of the grammar (Kroch 1989: 133), we have seen that in fact, the grammar continues to reconfigure each time a variant enters or exits the system. To the objection that the replacements we have documented are not properly syntactic changes, we would counter that removing such a spectacular change such as this, involving the total disappearance of forms, from the purview of the Constant Rate Effect would be like throwing out the baby with the bath water.

These results suggest that if the grammar does remain fixed (in Kroch's sense) over the course of change, it is only while the set of variants remains stable. Nonetheless, it is clear that reference to the future has been made in essentially the same way over the duration: the major distinctions (semantic, contextual) continue to be expressed, albeit by different exponents! This is evidenced by the transfer of constraints amongst variants in successive centuries. Thus, in response to Weinreich et al. (1968)'s question posed at the outset regarding the effects on linguistic structure of language change, we can confirm that there is nothing dysfunctional about the process.

References

Amaral, A. 1920. O Dialecto Caipira. São Paulo: Casa Editora "O Livro".

Arruda, L. 2000. Gramática de Português para Estrangeiros. Porto: Porto Editora.

Azeredo, J.C. 2000. Fundamentos de Gramática do Português. Rio de Janeiro: Jorge Zahar Editor.

Azevedo, A. 1897/1965. A Capital Federal. Rio de Janeiro: Editora Letras e Artes.

Baleeiro, M.I. 1988. O Futuro do Presente do Português Culto Falado em São Paulo. State University of Campinas: Master's Thesis.

Barreto, M. 1944/1980. Novos Estudos da Língua Portuguesa. 3rd ed. Rio de Janeiro: Instituto Nacional do Livro e Fundação de Rui Barbosa/ MEC - Presença.

Barros, J. 1540/1971. Gramática da Língua Portuguesa: cartinha, gramática, diálogo em louvor da nossa linguagem e diálogo da viciosa vergonha. 3rd ed. Lisboa: Publicações da Faculdade de Letras da Universidade de Lisboa.

Bechara, E. 1968. Moderna Gramática Portuguesa: Curso Médio. 13th ed. São Paulo: Companhia Editora Nacional.

Bentivoglio, P. & M. Sedano. 1992. "Morfosintaxis". El idioma español de la Venezuela actual. Caracas: Editorial Arte S.A.

Bortoni-Ricardo, S.M. 1991. Dialect Contact in Brasilia. Ms. University of Brasilia.

Buarque, F. 1978. Ópera do Malandro. Lisboa: Editora 'O Jornal'.

Bybee, J.L., R.D. Perkins & W. Pagliuca. 1994. The evolution of grammar: Tense, aspect, and modality in the languages of the world. Chicago: University of Chicago Press.

Cegalla, D. 2005. Novíssima Gramática da Língua Portuguesa. 46th ed. revised. São Paulo: Companhia Editora Nacional.

Cipro Neto, P. & U. Infante. 2004. Gramática da Língua Portuguesa. 2nd ed. São Paulo: Scipione.

Corrêa, G.G. 1964. O Programa de Vernáculo: Curso Ginasial. 2nd ed. Rio de Janeiro: Livraria Francisco Alves.

Cunha, C. & L. Cintra 1984/1999. Nova Gramática do Português Contemporâneo. 15th ed. Lisboa: Edições João Sá da Costa.

Entwistle, W. 1973. Las lenguas de España: castellano, catalán, vasco y gallego-portugués. Madrid: Ediciones Istmo.

Ferraz, M. 1980. "Apresentação crítica, notas, glossário e sugestões para análise literária". Guerras do Alecrim e da Mangerona ed. by A. Silva. Lisboa: Seara Nova.

Figueiredo, C. 1941. Falar e Escrever - Novos Estudos Práticos da Língua Portuguesa ou Consultório Popular de Enfermidades da Linguagem.vol. 2. 4th ed. Lisboa: Livraria Clássica Editora - A.M. Teixeira & Cia.

Fleischman, S. 1982. The future in thought and language: Diachronic evidence from romance. Cambridge: CUP.

França Júnior, J. 1870/1980. "O Defeito de Família". Teatro de França Júnior ed. by C. Gadelha & M. Saadi, vol. 1. Rio de Janeiro: Ministério da Educação e Cultura, Fundação Nacional de Arte.

Gomes, D. 1963/1990. "O Berço do Herói". Os Falsos Mitos ed. by A. Mercado. vol. 2.: Rio de Janeiro: Bertrand Brasil.

Guarnieri, G. 1961. A Semente: peça em 3 atos. São Paulo: Massao Ohno.

Hamilton-Faria, H. 1976. The farces of Gil Vicente: a study in the stylistics of satire. Spain: Playor S.A.

Huber, J. 1933. Gramática do Português Antigo. Lisboa: Fundação Calouste Gulbenkian.

Kroch, A.S. 1989. "Reflexes of grammar in patterns of linguistic change". Language Variation and Change 1. 199-244.

Kroch, A.S. 2001. "Syntactic change". Handbook of syntax ed. by. M. Baltin & C. Collins. Cambridge: Blackwell Publishers.

Kury, A. 1986. Novas Lições de Análise Sintática. São Paulo: Editora Ática.

Kury, A. 1989. Para Falar e Escrever Melhor o Português. 2nd ed. Rio de Janeiro: Nova Fronteira.

Labaki, A. 1999/2000. A Boa. São Paulo: Boitempo Editorial.

Labov, W. 1982. "Building on empirical foundations". Perspectives on historical linguistics ed. by W. Lehmann & Y. Malkiel, 17-92. Amsterdam/Phila: John Benjamins.

Labov, W. 1994. Principles of linguistic change: Internal factors. Vol. 1. Cambridge: Blackwell Publishers.

Lapa, M.R. 1968. Estilística da Língua Portuguesa. 5th ed. Rio de Janeiro: Acadêmica.

Leão, D. 1608/1983. Ortografia e Origem da Língua Portuguesa. Portugal: Imprensa Nacional-Casa da Moeda.

Machado Filho, A. 1938. Escrever Certo. 2nd ed. Rio de Janeiro: Editora ABC.

Malvar, E. da Silva. 2003. Future temporal reference in Brazilian Portuguese: Past and present. University of Ottawa: Ph.D. dissertation.

Mateus, M.H., A.M. Brito, I. Duarte & I. Faria. 1983. Gramática da Língua Portuguesa: Elementos para a descrição da estrutura, funcionamento e uso do português actual. Coimbra: Almedina.

Melo, G. 1957. Iniciação à Filologia Portuguesa. 2nd ed. Rio de Janeiro: Livro Técnico.

Nunes, J. 1910. Compêndio de Gramática Histórica Portuguesa: Fonética e Morfologia. 8th ed. Lisboa: Clássica Editora.

Pena, M. 1837/1968. O Juiz de Paz da Roça. In Comédias de Martins Pena. Rio de Janeiro: Tecnoprint Gráfica.

Pena, M. 1842/2000. Os Dous ou O Inglês Maquinista. Rio de Janeiro: Civilização Brasileira.

Pena, M. 1844/1968. Os Três Médicos. In Comédias de Martins Pena. Rio de Janeiro: Tecnoprint Gráfica.

Pena, M. 1853/1972. O Noviço. In Comédias. Rio de Janeiro: Agir Editora.

Poplack, S. & E. Malvar (in press). "Elucidating the transition period in linguistic change: the expression of the future in Brazilian Portuguese". Probus 19.1.

Poplack, S. & S. Tagliamonte. 1999. "The grammaticalization of going to in African American English". LVC 11. 315-342.

Poplack, S. & S. Tagliamonte. 2001. African American English in the Diaspora. Oxford: Basil Blackwell.

Poplack, S. & D. Turpin 1999. "Does the FUTUR have a future in Canadian French?" Probus 11. 133-164.

Poplack, S., J. Walker & R. Malcolmson (in press). "An English "like no other"?: Language contact and change in Quebec". Canadian Journal of Linguistics.

Prado, D.A. 1999. História Concisa do Teatro Brasileiro: 1570-1908. São Paulo: Editora da Cidade de São Paulo.

Rand, D. & D. Sankoff. 1990. GoldVarb: A variable rule application for the Macintosh. Montreal, Canada: Centre de recherches mathématiques, Université de Montréal.

Rebello, L.F. 1989. História do Teatro Porguguês. 4th Ed. Portugal: Publicações Europa-América.

Rossi, C. 1945. Portuguese: The Language of Brazil. New York: Henry Holt and Company.

Said Ali, M. 1964. Gramática Secundária e Gramática Histórica da Língua Portuguesa. 3. Brasília: Ed. Universidade de Brasília.

Said Ali, M. 1969. Gramática Secundária da Língua Portuguesa. 8. São Paulo: Edições Melhoramentos.

Sankoff, D. 1988. "Sociolinguistics and syntactic variation". Sociolinguistics and syntactic variation ed. by F.J. Newmeyer, 140-161. CUP: Linguistics: The Cambridge Survey: Cambridge.

Santorini, B. 1993. "The rate of phrase structure change in the history of Yiddish". Language variation and change 5. 257-283.

Santos, A. 1997. O Futuro verbal no Português do Brasil em variação. Brasilia: University of Brasilia, Master's Thesis.

Sardinha, L. & L. Ramos 2000. Prontuário e Conjugação de Verbos. Lisboa: Didáctica Editora.

Shi, Z.-Q. 1989. "The grammaticalization of the particle le in Mandarin Chinese". Language variation and change 1. 99-114.

Silva Junior, M. 1887. Noções de Grammatica Portugueza. Rio de Janeiro: J. G. de Azevedo Editor.

Silva, A.J. O Judeu. 1734/1957. "A Vida de Esopo". In: Duas Comédias de Antônio José, O Judeu. Rio de Janeiro: Editora Civilização Brasileira.
Silva, A.J. O Judeu. 1737/1980. Guerras do Alecrim e Mangerona. Lisboa: Seara Nova.
Sletsjöe, L. 1965. 0 Elemento Cénico em Gil Vicente. Lisboa: Casa Portuguesa.
Soares Barboza, J. 1852. Compendio de Grammatica Portugueza. 2nd ed. Pernambuco: Dos Editores Propietarios Santos & C.ª.
Taylor, A. 1994. "The change from SOV to SVO in Ancient Greek". Language variation and change 6. 1-37.
Thomas, E. 1969. The Syntax of Spoken Brazilian Portuguese. Nashville: Vanderbilt University Press.
Thomas, E. 1974. A Grammar of Spoken Brazilian Portuguese. Nashville: Vanderbilt University Press.
van Achter, E., J. Monteiro, J. Teixeira & M. Duarte. 1996. Estudar o Verbo - Exercícios Práticos para Estrangeiros. Coimbra: Minerva.
van Herk, G., & S. Poplack. 2001. "Rewriting the past: Zero marked verbs in Early African American letters". Paper presented at 30th Conference on New Ways of Analyzing Variation, Raleigh, North Carolina.
Veríssimo, J. 1998. História da Literatura Brasileira: de Bento Teixeira 1601 a Machado de Assis 1908. 7th. Rio de Janeiro: Topbooks Editora.
Vicente, G. 1509/1975. Auto da Índia. In Sátiras Sociais. Edição Anotada. Publicações Europa-América.
Vicente, G. 1512/1998. O Velho da Horta. In Gil Vicente. São Paulo: Ateliê Editorial.
Vicente, G. 1523/1998. Farsa de Inês Pereira. In Gil Vicente. São Paulo: Ateliê Editorial.
Vicente, G. 1526/1975. Farsa dos Almocreves. In Sátiras Sociais Edição Anotada. Publicações Europa-América.
Weinreich, U., W. Labov & M. Herzog. 1968. "Empirical foundations for a theory of language change". Empirical Foundations for a theory of language change. Directions for historical linguistics ed. by W.P. Lehmann & Y. Malkiel, 95-188. Austin: University of Texas Press.
Williams, E. 1944. An Introductory Portuguese Grammar. 5th ed. New York: F. S. Crofts & CO.
Williams, E. 1968. From Latin to Portuguese: Historical Phonology and Morphology of the Portuguese Language. 2nd ed. Philadelphia: University of Pennsylvania Press.

This chapter is rather longer than it needs to be (30 pages). It's poorly proofread, like the rest of the book (e.g. "21th century" on back cover).

The role of linguistic factors in the process of second dialect acquisition

Kathy Rys & Dries Bonte
University of Ghent

Abstract: This paper reports on the secondary acquisition of the Maldegem dialect by children and adolescents who have Standard Dutch as their home language. The acquisition of about 26 phonological variables was examined in the language of children of 9, 12 and 15 years old. The basic assumption is that second dialect learners form correspondence rules between their first and second language in order to facilitate the learning process. In this paper, a number of hypotheses are developed regarding a range of factors which enhance the intersystemic strength of those correspondence rules, and thus improve second dialect acquisition.

1. Introduction[*]

Whereas in the early days the study of dialectology focused mainly on geographical patterns of variation, now its main focus is on processes of dialect loss and dialect change. Local dialects are affected more and more by structural and functional dialect loss. Structural dialect loss involves changes in the linguistic system of the dialect itself. Functional loss brings with it a decline in the number of situations in which dialect is used (see Hoppenbrouwers 1990, Hinskens 1993). Often this deterioration begins in formal situations and gradually starts to affect dialect in more informal situations. Perhaps the most informal occasion on which dialect is used, is the home situation. Even there, however, dialect eventually loses its function in favour of a standardized variant.

Even when children no longer learn the local dialect during primary socialization, they often come into contact with this dialect at a later stage in their lives. Under the pressure of the peer group, these children often attempt to learn the local dialect as a second language. This process of second dialect acquisition is the subject of the research reported on. The acquisition of dialect as a second language has only seldom been studied. Payne (1980) and Chambers (1992) focused on the dialect acquisition of children who had moved from one dialect region to another. Vousten's research (1995) into the acquisition of a Limburg dialect by children who were brought up in Standard Dutch, probably comes closest to the research reported on in this contribution. Unlike Payne and

---

[*] We would like to thank Frans Hinskens, Gunther De Vogelaer, Liselotte van Vlem and the anonymous reviewers for their comments.

Chambers, the present research as well as that of Vousten do not involve children who were raised in another dialect but in the standard language.

This paper is a report of an investigation into second dialect acquisition of children living in the Flemish village of Maldegem who were raised in Standard Dutch or a standardized variant by their parents. The process of second dialect acquisition will be approached from a language-internal point of view, focusing on the extent to which the several phonological correspondences are acquired and on the factors which favour the acquisition of one correspondence above another. First, we will describe the location of the research, the parameters for selecting the informants and the method used to gather the data (Section 2). Then, we will briefly explain the concept of intersystemic correspondences, which is fundamental in our research (Section 3). Next, four factors which relate to the intersystemic strength of correspondences and which are assumed to influence the process of dialect acquisition will be discussed; the discussion will be supported by actual research results (paragraphs 3.1-3.4).

2. Location, informants and questionnaire

The geographical setting is the East-Flemish village of Maldegem. This village is situated besides the border between the provinces of East- and West-Flanders and just south of the border between Belgium and the Netherlands. Consequently, a transitional dialect is spoken there, sharing some phonological features with the neighbouring West-Flemish and some others with the surrounding East-Flemish dialects. The Maldegem dialect has also developed some idiosyncratic phonological features (see Versieck 1989).

Maldegem has a population of about 22,000 with the localities Kleit, Donk, Middelburg and Adegem included. Since the dialects of these localities differ from that of the centre of Maldegem with respect to some phonological features, informants were mainly selected from the centre of Maldegem.[1] The requirement was that the informants had lived in Maldegem for their entire lives and that they went to school there. Further criteria for the selection of the informants were age, gender and home language.[2] Therefore, one controlled variable and three systematically manipulated variables were integrated in the research design. In the end, 164 informants were selected. They are categorized by the different parameters as shown in Table 1. The 128 children who were raised in Standard Dutch or a standardized variety will be referred to as the 'second dialect learners', while the 36 informants who were brought up in the Maldegem dialect represent the 'control group'.

---

[1] Only a few children lived in one of these localities, but they all went to school in the centre of Maldegem.

[2] Next to these main parameters, the informants can also be divided into different groups on the basis of the origin of their mother and father. Although this factor is only of secondary importance, it will be taken into account as well.

Table 1: *Categorization of the informants by the parameters*
home language, age and gender

Home language	Age	Gender	Number of informants
	9	Male	28
		Female	27
Standard Dutch	12	Male	30
(or standardized		Female	21
variety)	15	Male	9
		Female	13
	9	Male	5
		Female	3
Dialect	12	Male	13
		Female	4
	15	Male	6
		Female	5

Spoken data were elicited from the informants by way of an interview. A questionnaire asking for 167 words was used. This questionnaire was representative of 26 phonological variables.[3] Before the interview, the subjects were told that we were interested in their knowledge of the Maldegem dialect. During the recordings, the interviewer (K.R.) spoke the Maldegem dialect — of she is a native speaker — in order to create a more or less 'informal' environment in which the subjects would speak as 'natural' as possible. The words were elicited by showing picture cards and by a sentence completion task.

The speech material was phonetically transcribed in PRAAT (version 4.2.05; Paul Boersma and David Weenink) by the first author of this paper. Doubtful cases were transcribed by a second listener as well. In addition, acoustic measurements of F_1, F_2 and F_3 were carried out in case of doubt. For each realization of each informant, the relevant phonological variable was scored binomially, with each dialect realization being given a score of 1 and each realization deviating from the Maldegem dialect (as it was described by Taeldeman 1975 and Versieck 1989) being given a score of 0.

3. Intersystemic correspondences

Children who are acquiring a dialect as their second language, starting from Standard Dutch as their language of primary socialization, will unconsciously form intersystemic correspondences between equivalent elements of the two language systems (see also Taeldeman 1993, Rys 2003). This concept of intersystemic correspondences is fundamental in our research. Auer (1993) proposed a two-dimensional phonological model in which the horizontal

---

[3] Apart from the 26 phonological variables that were related to the most salient intersystemic correspondences, 16 lexical exceptions to some of these correspondences were also represented in the questionnaire.

dimension is made up of correspondence rules between equivalent elements of L1 and L2. Auer describes these rules as follows:

> "Jeder lexikalischen Form, die ein dialektales Phonem enthält, wird ihre korrespondierende Standard-Form zugeordnet bzw. umgekehrt. Die Regeln, durch die diese Zuordnung geschieht [...] sollen hier Korrespondenzregeln [...] genannt werden. Korrespondenzregeln beziehen morphologische Formen [...] aufeinander." (Auer 1993: 8)
> [roughly: "Every lexical form that contains a dialect feature is matched with the corresponding standard form and vice versa. The rules that express this matching [...] will be referred to as correspondence rules [...]. Correspondence rules relate morphological forms [...] to one another."]

Auer's notion of 'correspondence rules' is crucial in our research. We assume that the formation of correspondence rules is the basic learning strategy of second dialect learners. These correspondence rules can always be formulated as follows: "The Standard Dutch (SD) sound x is realized as y in the Maldegem dialect (DIA)". Correspondence rules of this kind are formed in the mental grammar of second dialect learners but are not 'rules' governing the second language: there is no 'rule' that turns SD x into DIA y in the mental grammar of a (hypothetical) monolingual speaker of the Maldegem dialect, because SD is not the starting-point for this speaker (see also Rys to appear: 61-62). The research reported on in this paper suggests that the correspondence rules between the mother tongue, the standard language and the interlanguage of dialect learners differ in their intersystemic strength, depending on several factors. In what follows, we will discuss four factors which are assumed to influence the intersystemic strength.

3.1   Incidence

All of the 26 variables that were surveyed, can in principle be formulated as a correspondence rule of the shape: "SD x is pronounced as DIA y". An example is the correspondence "SD /ɛ^1/ → DIA [Ø], except preceding a laryngeal or velar consonant", which applies to words such as *wijn* "wine", *prijs* "price", *bijten* "to bite". All cases involved in this research concern correspondence rules between phoneme values.

Correspondence rules differ with respect to the number of words they apply to. This number of words determines the incidence (cf. "type frequency", Bybee 2001) of a correspondence rule, which presumably plays a role in the degree of acquisition of the correspondence. Each of the 26 variables involved was measured for incidence. In order to do so, an existing word list was consulted: the 'Unaniemenlijst voor België' from the *Streeflijst woordenschat voor 6-jarigen* ("Unanimity[4] List for Belgium". In: *Target Vocabulary List for Six-year-olds*. Schaerlaekens et al. 1999). This list contains 1903 words which are expected to be known by six-year-old Dutch-speaking children in Belgium. From these, 1810

---

[4] The 'Unanimity list' is a list of words which 90 % of the jury considers necessary to be known to six-year-old children. There is a list for Belgium (Flanders) as well as one for the Netherlands. These two lists differ in a few details.

words were selected that could possibly be used in a Maldegem context. The incidence of each correspondence rule was measured by calculating the sum of all the words from this selection to which the relevant correspondence rule applies.

In what follows, we will test the hypothesis that: "The higher the incidence of a correspondence rule, the better this correspondence will be acquired by the second dialect learners."

The different hypotheses discussed in this paper were tested by carrying out statistical analyses in the SAS program. The database on which these analyses were performed is built up as follows:

Table 2: *Extract from the database*

Informant	Rule	Nr. of successes	Nr. of Trials	Score	Indep. var. 1 (e.g. incidence)	Etc.
1	$\varepsilon^i \to \text{ø}$	7	10	0.70	50	...
1	$\text{o:} \to \text{ø}$	5	7	0.71	99	...
...	...	...	...	...	...	...
164	$\varepsilon^i \to \text{ø}$	4	10	0.40	50	...
164	$\text{o:} \to \text{ø}$	4	7	0.57	99	...
...	...	...	...	...	...	...

Each phonological correspondence rule (table 2, 2nd column) considered in the research was retrieved from the informants (1-164, Table 2, 1st column) by asking for several words (= number of trials; Table 2, 4th column). The correspondence rule 'SD $\varepsilon^i \to$ DIA ø' for instance, was elicited in the questionnaire by means of 10 words (i.e. *zwijn* "swine"; *ijs* "ice"; *prijs* "price"; *bijten* "to bite"; etc.). For each word, a particular informant may either use the dialect variant ø or another variant. In the first case, the relevant realization of this informant is coded 1 (= success in realizing the 'correct' dialect variant), in the latter case, the realization is coded 0 (= failure to realize the 'correct' dialect variant). The actual dependent variable in our analyses is the result of the division (nr. of successes : nr. of trials), represented in Table 2 by 'Score'. This implies that the dependent always takes on a value between 0 and 1. This kind of data allows for logistic regression. Logistic regression is a statistical method for describing the relationships between a dependent variable that has only two possible values (i.e. 'success' = 1 or 'failure' = 0) and one or more independent/explanatory variables which can either be categorical (i.e. have discrete values) or quantitative. Since our dependent variable ('score') is derived from such a binary variable (i.e. dialect variant vs. not a dialect variant), logistic regression is allowed, on the condition that a logarithmic function is applied. In general, the dependent variable ('score') is expressed by the logarithm (ln) of 'the *odds* of a respondent realizing the correct dialect variant'; the *odds* are defined as the probability divided by the not-probability, i.e. p/(1-p), in which p represents the probability of 'success' (= 1; i.e. realizing the 'correct' dialect variant) and (1-p) represents the probability of 'failure' (= 0; i.e. not realizing the 'correct' dialect variant). We applied the logistic model ln(p/(1-p)) =

int. + b_1x_1 + b_2x_2 + ε. In this formula, 'int.' represents the intercept or constant, i.e. the point at which the graph cuts the Y-axis; b_1 and b_2 are the regression coefficients of the independent variables x_1 and x_2 respectively, which indicate whether there is a positive or negative effect of the independent on the dependent variable. ε stands for 'error'.

In order to test the hypothesis on the effect of incidence, we performed a mixed logistic regression model (SAS 9.2, procedure glimmix). This means that we have analyzed whether our dependent variable (use of the 'correct' dialect variant on N trials) can be explained by the independent variable 'incidence of the correspondence'. Next to incidence, the variable 'home language' is also integrated (as fixed effect) in the model, to investigate whether individuals from the control group on the one hand and the dialect learners on the other hand, show different reactions towards incidence. The results of the logistic regression analysis are shown in Table 3.

Table 3: *Logistic regression model analyzing the effects of incidence and home language on dialect proficiency*

Effect	B	Standard Error	df	F	p
Incidence	0.01911	0.006431	1,6845	9.88	0.0017
HomeLanguage	1.8949	0.2270	1,6845	69.69	<.0001
Incidence*HomeLanguage	0.002305	0.001303	1,6845	3.13	0.0771

s^2_{rule} = 2.5126 ± 0.5922 (p < 0.0001); s^2_{resp} = 1.3561 ± 0.1591 (p < 0.0001)[5]

Table 3 visualizes the regression coefficients (B) for logistic regression of dialect proficiency — as expressed by the number of successes on N trials — as a function of incidence and home language (the independent variables). From the table it appears that the degree of dialect acquisition/proficiency is affected most by home language; F indicates the strength of the effect (F = 69.69). The incidence of the correspondences also seems to have a significant positive effect: the acquisition of the relevant correspondence increases as its incidence becomes higher (F = 9.88; p = 0.0017). In general, whether the effect of the independent variable on the dependent variable is positive or negative can be deduced from the parameter estimates or regression coefficients, B (second column in Table 3). These estimates indicate the direction of the association between the dependent and independent variables. A negative estimate indicates a negative association between the variables, which implies that the value of the dependent variable decreases if that of the independent variable increases (and vice versa). A positive estimate indicates a positive association between the dependent and independent

---

[5] These figures indicate that the random variation due to rule and respondent is significantly different from zero. This can be deduced from the fact that the standard errors on the mean variation (0.5922 and 0.1591) are very small compared to the mean values of the variation (2.5126 and 1.3561, respectively). This random variation is variation that is caused by differences among individual respondents and among individual rules, which is not accounted for by the independent variables in the analysis.

variables, which means that the values of both variables increase or decrease simultaneously (e.g. 'dialect proficiency' (dep.) and 'age' (indep.)). A positive value of the parameter estimate for 'home language' (e.g. 1.8949), however, indicates that the value of the dependent variable (i.e. the degree of success in dialect acquisition) increases if 'home language' has code 1 or, in other words, if the home language is the Maldegem dialect. This interpretation is due to the fact that 'home language' is a 'dummy variable', which is coded as 1 if the home language is dialect and coded as 0 if the home language is Standard Dutch.

So, as we hypothesized, a high incidence improves the acquisition of a correspondence rule and this effect can be seen in the dialect learners as well as in the control group.

Figure 1 reveals the exact nature of the effect of incidence on dialect proficiency.

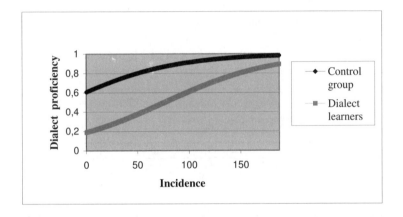

Figure 1: *Effect of incidence and home language on dialect proficiency*

The graph[6] shows that even the native speakers do not control the correspondences with a very low incidence perfectly (± 60% 'correct' dialect variants used). The dialect learners are much more impeded by a low incidence in their acquisition (± 20% 'correct' dialect variants used). So it is clear that home language has an important effect on the proficiency of a speaker in the Maldegem dialect. Further, the fact that both the curve representing the control group as well as that representing the dialect learners is rising, shows that incidence has a positive effect on the dialect of both groups.

There is, however, no significant effect of the interaction between incidence and home language (= 'Incidence*Home language'). This implies that the factor incidence exerts an overall positive influence on the realization of the Maldegem

---

[6] Because we are dealing with logit functions, the regression cannot be expressed by a straight line (regression line), but has to be expressed by a curve which turns off at 0 and 1. This mirrors the fact that the dependent variable (number of successes on N trials) always takes on values between 0 and 1, since it is the logarithm of the probability divided by the not-probability (i.e. p/(1-p)).

variants, irrespective of whether these realizations come from the second dialect learners or from the control group. So incidence is not a variable which allows us to distinguish the language behaviour of dialect learners from that of native dialect speakers.

3.2   Word Frequency

Word frequency is another factor that has to be considered when investigating the different influences on dialect acquisition and dialect proficiency. Probably, the frequency of usage of the words (cf. 'token frequency') that are involved in measuring the incidence of correspondence rules also plays a role in the degree of acquisition of the relevant correspondence rule. In order to find out the frequency of those words, the Spoken Dutch Corpus,[7] which consists of about seven million words, was consulted. With respect to word frequency, we formulate the following hypothesis: "The higher the frequency of usage of the words to which an intersystemic correspondence rule applies, the better this correspondence rule is acquired."

In order to test the above hypothesis, a mixed logistic regression model was conducted. The results are shown in Table 4.

Table 4: *Logistic regression model analyzing the effects of word frequency and home language on dialect proficiency*

Effect	B	St. Error	df	F	P
Word frequency	0.000042	0.000020	1,6845	4.21	0.0403
HomeLanguage	1.8978	0.2249	1,6845	71.17	<.0001
Word frequency *HomeLanguage	9.196E-6	3.223E-6	1,6845	8.14	0.0043

$s^2_{rule} = 2.7917 \pm 0.6537$ ($p < 0.0001$); $s^2_{resp} = 1.3565 \pm 0.1592$ ($p < 0.0001$)

In Table 4, the regression coefficients (B) for logistic regression of dialect proficiency as a function of word frequency and home language are given. Again, the factor home language has the strongest influence on dialect proficiency (F = 71.17). The chart also indicates a positive (B = 0.000042) significant (p < 0.05) effect of word frequency, which confirms our hypothesis. Even the interaction between word frequency and home language (= 'Word frequency*Home language') has a significant effect (p < 0.01). The nature of this effect can be seen in Figure 2.

---

[7] Spoken Dutch Corpus (CGN): http://lands.let.kun.nl/cgn/home.htm, http://www.tst.inl.nl/

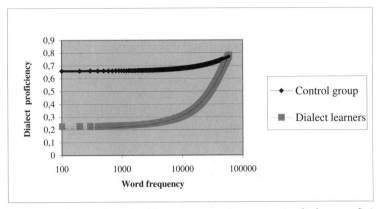

Figure 2: *Effect of word frequency and home language on dialect proficiency*

The fact that the interaction between home language and word frequency is significant, makes the latter factor an interesting one in the light of second dialect acquisition. The interaction implies that word frequency distinguishes the control group from the second dialect learners. In other words, the effect of word frequency on dialect acquisition is of another nature among the second dialect learners than among the native speakers. Figure 2 shows that word frequency has much more impact on the dialect acquisition of the dialect learners (lower curve) than on the dialect of the control group (upper curve). As can be seen, a low word frequency blocks good dialect acquisition among the dialect learners (± 20% 'correct' dialect variants used), while it only does so to a small extent among the control group (± 65% 'correct' dialect variants used). The chart also reveals that if the word frequency of the words to which a correspondence applies, is extremely high, the dialect learners get to grips with the correspondence rule equally well as the native speakers.

3.3 Predictability: number of realizations

The predictability of an intersystemic correspondence rule between Standard Dutch (SD) and the Maldegem dialect (DIA) works in two directions. Starting from SD, the predictability of the correspondence 'SD x → DIA y' depends on the number of different dialect realizations of SD x. If fewer dialect realizations of SD x are possible, a one-to-one relationship between SD x and DIA y is increasingly approached and a correspondence rule becomes more predictable. Reversely, starting from the Maldegem dialect, the predictability of a correspondence rule increases if the number of possible realizations in SD is low (and thus, a negative association between the two variables is expected).

Let us illustrate this with an example of predictability from SD to DIA. SD /ε^1/ can be realized in six different ways in the Maldegem dialect:

a vowel?

1) SD /ɛ^i/ → DIA [Ø], except preceding a laryngeal or velar consonant (e.g. wijn "wine" → w[Ø]n)
2) SD /ɛ^i/ preceding a laryngeal or velar consonant → DIA [e] (e.g. zwijgen "to be silent" → zw[e]gen)
3) SD /ɛ^i/ → DIA [i^ə] (e.g. klein "small" → kl[i^ə]ne)
4) SD /ɛ^i/ → DIA [æ^i] (e.g. kei "boulder" → k[æ^i])   *sic?*
5) SD /ɛ^i/ → DIA [ɛ̞^{i}] (e.g. blij "happy" → bl[ɛ̞^{i}]e)
6) SD /ɛ^i/ → DIA [i], only in the lexical exceptions *bij* "bee" and *tijger* "tiger"

For a child acquiring the Maldegem dialect as a second language, it is relatively difficult to predict what dialect realization will match SD /ɛ^i/. There is no one-to-one relationship between SD and DIA, but a one-to-six relationship.

In order to measure the predictability of a correspondence rule, it does not suffice to count the possible SD- or DIA-realizations which are involved in the correspondence rule. Let us illustrate this problem with an example. SD /œ^y/ has five different realizations in the Maldegem dialect, that is: [ø], [œ^y], [i], [æ^i] and [i^ə]. The last three realizations concern lexical exceptions such as *kuiken* "chick", *ruiken* "to smell", *fornuis* "cooker" and *spuit* "needle". These words are lexical exceptions to the correspondence rule "SD /œ^y/ → DIA [ø]" seeing that this correspondence is normally applied in contexts preceding a velar (/k/) or alveolar (/s/, /t/) consonant (e.g. *buik* "belly" → [bøk]; *huis* "house" → [øs]; *ruit* "window" → [røtə]). The second realization ([œ^y]) only applies in final position (e.g. in *trui* "jumper", *lui* "lazy"). Since Dutch has only a few words with /œ^y/ in final position, the correspondence SD /œ^y/ → DIA [œ^y] has a very low incidence. Consequently, the correspondence SD /œ^y/ → DIA [ø] will have a high degree of predictability, since the incidence of this correspondence is much higher than that of the other correspondences that start from SD /œ^y/. The example reveals that the predictability cannot be expressed by the number of realizations alone, because the incidence of the different correspondences involved also plays a role. Therefore, we do not concentrate on the effect of the number of realizations on its own, but we try to find out the effect of the interaction between the number of realizations and the incidence of each realization.

Our twofold hypothesis about the influence of the number of realizations on the degree of dialect acquisition can be formulated as follows: (a) "If a SD element x has fewer dialect realizations, the correspondence rule between SD and dialect becomes more predictable and the correspondence rule will be more easily acquired. On the other hand, if the number of dialect realizations increases, the learnability of the correspondence rule will decrease." (b) "The predictability from dialect to SD plays a less important role in the acquisition of the second dialect learners, since all learners depart from SD as their first language. However, we do not exclude an influence of this kind of predictability on the dialect proficiency of the control group."

To find out the effect of the interaction between incidence and number of dialect realizations, we performed a multiple logistic regression, in which non-significant contributions were eliminated by backward stepwise-procedure. The results are presented in Table 5.

Table 5: *Logistic regression model analyzing the effects of incidence, home language and number of dialect realizations on dialect proficiency (backward, stepwise)*

Effect	df	F	p
Incidence	1,6846	9.06	0.0026
HomeLanguage	1,6846	76.80	<.0001
Number of DIA realizations	1,6846	0.22	0.6380
Incidence*HomeLanguage	1,6845	3.11	0.0778
Incidence*Number of DIA realizations	1,6845	0.60	0.4389
Number of DIA realizations*HomeLanguage	1,6844	0.21	0.6505
Incidence*Number of DIA realizations*HomeLanguage	1,6843	3.44	0.0637

$s^2_{rule} = 2.5984 \pm 0.6281$ (p < 0.0001); $s^2_{resp} = 1.3561 \pm 0.1591$ (p < 0.0001)

Table 5 reveals that only the variables 'incidence' and 'home language' have probability values lower than 0.05 (actually < 0.01)[8] and are therefore retained in the model. As we can see, the factor 'home language' contributes most to the overall model (F = 76.8; p<.0001). Furthermore, incidence has a positive, significant effect on dialect proficiency (F = 9.06; p <0.01). However, neither the number of dialect realizations, nor the interaction of this factor with incidence, has a significant effect on the degree of dialect acquisition. Consequently, the first part of our twofold hypothesis is not confirmed.

In the second part of our hypothesis we proposed that the predictability from DIA to SD should also be taken into account when investigating dialect acquisition. We hypothesized that the number of SD realizations would mainly have an influence on the dialect of the native speakers, since they revert to the Maldegem dialect to a larger extent than the dialect learners. In order to test this hypothesis, we performed a mixed logistic model again. The results can be seen in Table 6.

Table 6 visualizes the regression coefficients (B) for logistic regression of dialect proficiency as a function of the number of SD realizations and home language. As the coefficients of 'number of SD realizations' and of its interaction with 'home language', have a negative sign, a negative association between this factor and the number of 'correct' dialect variants (dependent variable) can be assumed. This implies that the proficiency score of the informants on a particular phonological variable will decrease, as the number of SD realizations of the dialect variant involved increases.

---

[8] Backward stepwise regression removes all the variables with a p-value higher than 0.05 from the model.

Table 6: *Logistic regression model analyzing the effects of number of Standard*
Dutch realizations and home language on dialect proficiency

Effect	B	St. Error	df	F	p
Number of SD realizations	-0.2328	0.1863	1,6845	2.23	0.1352
HomeLanguage	2.2450	0.2377	1,6845	89.23	<.0001
Number of SD realizations*HomeLanguage	-0.09163	0.02539	1,6845	13.03	0.0003

$s^2_{rule} = 2.9826 \pm 0.6953$ (p < 0.0001); $s^2_{resp} = 1.3583 \pm 0.1594$ (p < 0.0001)

The table further reveals that the number of SD realizations has no significant effect (p=0.1352) as a variable on its own, but it does have a significant effect in interaction with the variable 'home language' (p=0.0003). A significant interaction between home language and another variable implies that the control group and the dialect learners show a different reaction towards this other variable. This is the case with the variable 'number of SD realizations'. Table 6 shows us that the interaction between home language and number of SD realizations is highly significant (p=0.0003). This interaction is visualized in Figure 3.

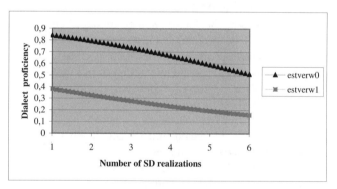

Figure 3: *Effect of number of SD realizations and home language*
on dialect proficiency

Figure 3 shows that the control group (upper curve) scores better for dialect proficiency than the dialect learners (lower curve). In addition, we see that the more realizations a dialect sound has in Standard Dutch, the worse the relevant correspondence rule is acquired (i.e. there is a negative association between dependent and independent variables). As expected, this effect manifests itself more strongly in the language of the control group than in that of the dialect learners. This is visualized by the fact that the curve representing the control group has a steeper slope than the one representing the dialect learners. So, as we hypothesized, the factor 'number of SD realizations' has more influence on the control group than on the dialect learners. Probably this can be explained by the fact that the latter group cannot rely on their knowledge of the Maldegem dialect as much as the control group and therefore cannot use the dialect as a starting-point to the same degree as the native speakers do.

3.4   Regularity

A fourth factor that may be influence the degree of acquisition of phonological correspondence rules is the regularity of those rules. Some intersystemic correspondences are characterized by a high incidence and a relatively low number of dialect realizations, but cannot be defined by a 'rule'. An example is the correspondence that turns SD /o:/ into DIA [uᵊ]. This correspondence rule has an incidence of 104 (out of 1810) and SD /o:/ has three possible realizations, that is: DIA [uᵊ], DIA [ø.] and DIA [ø]. Still, it is impossible to predict with any certainty which of the three realizations is the right one for a given word, since no rule can be applied to the relevant correspondence rules. On the other hand, the reverse situation also exists. An example can be found among the previously mentioned correspondences that take SD /ɛⁱ/ as their starting-point. One of these, 'SD /ɛⁱ/ → DIA [ɛ]', has an incidence of 10. This is considerably lower than the incidence of SD /o:/ turning into DIA [uᵊ] which we just discussed (104 items). Further, SD /ɛⁱ/ has six possible dialect realizations, which is twice as many as the number of possible realizations of SD /o:/. However, the correspondence 'SD /ɛⁱ/ → DIA [e]' is distinguished from the correspondence 'SD /o:/ → DIA [uᵊ]' in being defined by a rule, that is to say, 'SD /ɛⁱ/ → DIA [e] *if preceding a laryngeal or velar consonant*'.

All the correspondences involved in our research were checked for being defined by a rule or not; that is to say: is there a 'deterministic' rule that refers to the environment of the segment as the condition or one of the conditions for the correspondence — relevant to that segment — to take place? An example of such a deterministic rule is the part of the correspondence "SD /ɛⁱ/ → DIA [e]" which refers to the environment, that is: preceding a velar or laryngeal consonant. In this case the 'environment' is the condition for the correspondence to take place. We hypothesize that: "Correspondences which can be defined by a rule (from SD to DIA) will be acquired more easily than those which cannot."

A logistic regression analysis renders the results given in Table 7.

Table 7: *Logistic regression model analyzing the effects of regularity from SD to DIA and home language on dialect proficiency*

Effect	B	St. Error	df	F	p
Rule SD → DIA	0.6926	0.4646	1,6845	3.35	0.0672
Home Language	2.0304	0.2353	1,6845	71.17	<.0001
Rule* Home Language	0.08908	0.08803	1,6845	8.14	0.0043

$s^2_{rule} = 2.9238 \pm 0.6823$ (p < 0.0001); $s^2_{resp} = 1.3564 \pm 0.1592$ (p < 0.0001)

Table 7 represents the number of 'correct' dialect variants used, in function of the variables 'regularity' (i.e. 'rule': yes = 1; no = 0) and 'home language'. It shows that the effect of regularity from SD to DIA is not significant when viewed separately (p > 0.05), but the interaction between regularity and home language does have a significant effect (p < 0.01). Figure 4 illustrates the nature of this effect.

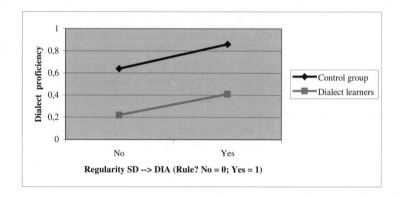

Figure 4: *Effect of regularity SD → DIA and home language on dialect proficiency*

Figure 4 reveals that, as expected, the control group (upper line) scores better than the dialect learners (lower line) as for dialect proficiency. Further, the chart shows that regularity induces a positive effect for both groups, that is: when there is a rule from SD to DIA (= 1), the correspondences are more easily acquired than in the absence of a rule (= 0). This implies that our hypothesis is confirmed. The interaction between regularity and home language is revealed by the fact that the line representing the control group and the one representing the dialect learners are not completely parallel. v. small diff tho

4. Discussion and conclusion

In this paper, we have discussed four factors which influence the degree of intersystemic strength of correspondence rules, and we have looked into their influence on the process of second dialect acquisition in dialect learners as well as on dialect proficiency in native speakers. So far, we have learnt that dialect acquisition is influenced significantly and positively by incidence, word frequency, number of SD realizations and regularity from SD to DIA. While incidence did not interact with home language, the other factors did. This implies that there is a general effect of incidence on the dialect of the native dialect speakers as well as that of the control group, while both groups are influenced to a different degree by the other three factors.

128 SD children
36 Maldegem kids control group

In order to find the most important factor in the process of dialect acquisition, we applied a multiple logistic model to our data. By forward stepwise-procedure, every independent variable which was significant at the 5% level ($p < 0.05$), was admitted in the model. Only the factors 'home language' and 'incidence' could thus be admitted. This implies that the combination of the variables 'home language' and 'incidence' significantly predicts dialect proficiency, while the factors 'word frequency', 'number of SD realizations' and 'regularity from SD to DIA' do not significantly contribute to the prediction. However, when these other factors are entered separately in a logistic model, they all turn out to be significant predictors of dialect proficiency.

To conclude, except for the number of dialect realizations, all factors discussed in this paper have a significant and positive effect on second dialect acquisition to some extent and these factors have similar but less pronounced effects on the dialect proficiency of native dialect speakers (i.e. the control group) as well. The effect of the incidence of the correspondences, however, overrides the effects of all the other variables.

References

Auer, P. 1993. "Zweidimensionale Modelle für die Analyse von Standard/Dialekt-Variation und ihre Vorläufer in der deutschen Dialektologie". Verhandlungen des internationalen Dialektologenkongresses ed. by W. Viereck. Bamberg. 3-22.

Bybee, J. 2001. Phonology and language use. Cambridge: CUP.

Chambers, J.K. 1992. "Dialect Acquisition". Language 68. 673-705.

Hinskens, F. 1993. "Dialectnivellering en regiolectvorming; bevindingen en beschouwingen". Dialectverlies en regiolectvorming ed. by F. Hinskens, C. Hoppenbrouwers en J. Taeldeman [Taal en Tongval 46]. 40-61.

Hoppenbrouwers, C. 1990. Het regiolect. Van dialect tot Algemeen Nederlands. Muiderberg: Dick Coutinho.

Payne, A.C. 1980. "Factors controlling the acquisition of the Philadelphia dialect by out-of-state children." Locating language in time and space ed. by W. Labov, 143-178. New York, London, Toronto, Sydney, San Francisco: Academic Press.

Rys, K. 2003. "Secundaire verwerving van fonologische elementen van een dialect." Taal en Tongval 55:1. 68-108.

Rys, K. (to appear). "Overgeneralisatie als proces bij de secundaire verwerving van een dialect". Handelingen van het colloquium georganiseerd door de Koninklijke Zuid-Nederlandse Maatschappij voor Taal- en Letterkunde en Geschiedenis op 16 oktober 2004. 57-75.

Schaerlaekens, A., D. Kohnstamm & M. Lejaegere (eds.). 1999. Streeflijst woordenschat voor 6-jarigen. Derde herziene versie. Gebaseerd op nieuw onderzoek in Nederland en België. Lisse: Swets & Zeitlinger.

Taeldeman, J. 1975. De klankstructuur van het Kleitse dialekt. Een synchrone studie met referenties aan het diachrone en geografische kader. Unpublished PhD diss., University of Ghent.

Taeldeman, J. 1993. "Dialectresistentie en dialectverlies op fonologisch gebied". Taal en Tongval, Themanummer 6. 102-119.

Versieck, S. 1989. Het Maldegemse klanksysteem in het heden en honderd jaar geleden. Unpublished PhD diss., University of Ghent.

Vousten, R. 1995. Dialect als tweede taal. Linguïstische en extra-linguïstische aspecten van de verwerving van een Noordlimburgs dialect door standaardtalige jongeren. Unpublished PhD diss., University of Nijmegen.

A bit tricky on the statistical detail, perhaps, but impressively systematic in terms of working out what makes dialect acquisition successful

Folk views on linguistic variation and identities in the Belarusian-Russian borderland

Marián Sloboda
Charles University, Prague

Abstract: Belarus has been described as the most Russified 'national republic' of the former Soviet Union. The Belarusians are also known for the fact that their nation-building has not been completed. In addition, two closely-related languages, Belarusian and Russian, are used, sharing the 'state language' status. In such a context, focus on the Belarusian-Russian borderland, where an international border appeared as late as 1991 with the dissolution of the USSR, is pertinent. This study in folk linguistics deals with non-expert linguistic identities and perceptions of linguistic variation by the borderland population. It discusses the social meaning of the emic category 'mixed language' and four types of perceived (socio)linguistic differences in connection with the processes of language shift and convergence to Russian.

1. Introduction

The Belarusian-Russian borderland is a territory where Belarusian and Russian, two closely related and socially imbalanced languages, have been in intensive contact since the emergence of the Belarusian linguistic identity in the 19th century. This study in "folk linguistics" (Niedzielski & Preston 2003) concerns folk or emic perceptions and constructions of linguistic variation in this region. It touches on the field of perceptual dialectology, but focuses more widely on non-expert linguistic identities and perceived linguistic variation in connection with its social meanings and processes of language shift and convergence.

2. The language situation in Belarus

Belarus (or in the Russianized form 'Belorussia/Byelorussia') is an East European country with a population of about 10 million people and an area of 208,000 sq. kms. It became independent in 1991 as a result of the disintegration of the Soviet Union. In contrast to Ukraine and the Baltic neighbors, the Russian language in Belarus has maintained its position in all domains of social life as opposed to the indigenous language, Belarusian (see Zaprudski 2002, on language policy in Belarus in the 1990s). The majority of the population perceives Russian as superior, better, refined or as offering more prospects than Belarusian (see Woolhiser 2001, for a detailed discussion of language ideologies in Belarus). Both languages are *de jure* official, but the relationship between them is not legally regulated, so the decision to use one or the other language usually depends on personal preferences and power/status relations in social groups and organizations. Most of the population chooses Russian, which is related to several factors, e.g., Soviet language policy or the fact that cities have linguistically been mostly Russian. Prior to World War II, Yiddish also played an important role.

Although Belarusian is typically used in certain types of situations by certain groups of people,[1] language alternations in discourse are widespread, especially language mixing (in the sense of interactionally non-functional language alternation of Auer 1999). Due to speakers' incomplete acquisition of Russian in the process of shifting toward it, mixed varieties have also appeared. Soviet linguists have identified the so-called "Belarusian natiolect of Russian" (Mikhnevich 1985b: 11), a variety of Russian with borrowings, especially phonetic ones, from Belarusian. Dialectologists mention "mixed dialectal speech" (Kurtsova 1990: 57), i.e. traditional Belarusian dialects heavily populated with Russian lexical items, with some morphological and phonetic borrowings as well. The widely used term "trasianka" refers to Belarusian-Russian mixed discourse or varieties in general (cf. Tsykhun 2000; Liskovets 2002; Hentschel & Tesch 2006). Bilingual discourse takes more varied forms in Belarus, but it has not been systematically studied from the perspective of contact linguistics or sociolinguistics (see Woolhiser 1995, for an overview; cf. the theory and methodology used in Bulyko & Krysin 1999).

Belarusian and Russian are closely related, and are more or less mutually intelligible languages. In Heinz Kloss' terms, they are *ausbau* languages, that is, languages that are so similar that they could be considered one language, had one of them (in our case Belarusian) not been consciously developed as a separate language for the purpose of literary expression (Kloss 1967). In the Belarusian-Russian borderland, there is a dialect continuum as well as dialects that cross the Belarusian-Russian political border (Kryvitski 2003: 196). In such a context, it is interesting to examine how the *ausbau* bilinguals of that borderland region categorize linguistic phenomena and which linguistic identities they construct.[2] In addition, the Belarusian national identity has been rather ambiguous and indistinct, and the folk perception of a border of any kind between Belarus and Russia is unclear. This raises further questions concerning language attitudes, convergence and shift to Russian.

---

[1] By a great part of the political opposition and by people whose work is related to the national culture, while Belarusian dialects are spoken by some villagers.

[2] As regards the expert view, Belarusian dialectologists, as if by collective tacit agreement, demarcate the "Belarusian national language" and the "Russian national language" with the *political* border in spite of their awareness of the border-crossing dialects (Kryvitski 2003: 196; Avanesaŭ et al. 1963, 1968-9).

3. Region and respondents

3.1   A profile of the borderland region

A major part of the data was generated during the field research that was carried out by an international and multidisciplinary group of researchers in the Belarusian-Russian borderland in July 2004.[3] The fieldwork took place mainly in two districts on the Belarusian side of the border: the districts of Horki (or Gorki — ed.) and Drybin (hereafter 'the Region'; see Map 1).

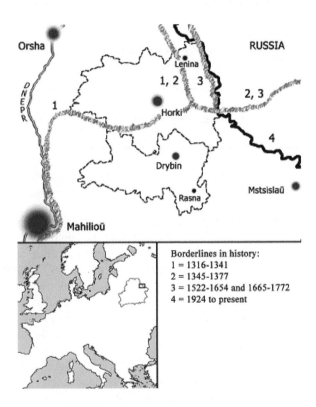

Map 1: *The districts of Horki and Drybin, and borderlines in history*
Sources: Avanesaŭ et al. (1963: maps II and IV), Nasevich (1996)

The town of Horki and the town of Drybin are the district centers and the only urban settlements in the Region. The districts have 67,000 inhabitants, 55% of whom belong to the urban and 45% to the rural population (*Regiony* 2004: 621);

---

[3] The research has been part of the larger Polish project 'Belarus and its borderlands', directed by Elżbieta Smułkowa and organized by OBTA, Warsaw University. A collection of papers based on this project is in preparation.

90% declared Belarusian and 8% Russian ethnicity in the 1999 Census (*National* 2001: tab. 7.6). Table 1 provides some statistics about the usage of Belarusian and Russian languages in the Mahilioŭ (or Mogil'ov — ed.) region, to which the districts belong (the information for the separate districts is not available). Note the difference between the urban and rural population and the disparity in the declaration of Belarusian and Russian as the 'language usually spoken at home' and as the 'native language' (*rodnoi iazyk*). The term 'native language', widely used in the post-Soviet territory, does not usually mean 'the first acquired language' or 'the best spoken language' but it rather refers to the language of one's ethnic heritage or cultural identification (for more details, see Woolhiser 2001: 97ff; Brown 2005).

Table 1: *The 'native language' and the language usually spoken at home in the Mahilioŭ region (1999 Census)*

	urban		rural	
	Belarusian	Russian	Belarusian	Russian
'native'	71%	27%*	91%	9%
usually spoken at home	14%	86%	69%	31%

* The remaining 2% declared another language as their "native language".
(National 2001: table 11.7)

The Region was borderland territory for most of its history (see Map 1). The local dialects formed during feudal times (Avanesaŭ et al. 1968-9: 220ff.), when the Region bordered with Muscovy on the east for three centuries with a 150-year break from the end of the 14th to the beginning of the 16th century, when the borderline ran further in the east. The border was unstable, because the Region was often a battlefield in the wars between the Grand Duchy of Lithuania and Muscovy. The state border disappeared in 1772, when the Russian Empire annexed the territory, but it was re-established in 1991 with the disintegration of the USSR. Internal administrative borders changed several times through history (cf. Nasevich 1996), but the current border between Belarus and Russia had already been established in 1924 as an internal (and permeable) border within the Soviet state. The Region has been heterogeneous in terms of religion, with the predominance of Orthodox Christians (and Jews until World War II), but the territory has not been divided along religious lines.

The Belarusian dialects of the Region share many features with the southwestern Russian dialect group and differ from other Belarusian dialects (see Orlova 1961). Several isoglosses run east of the border with Russia, thus uniting the eastern Belarusian dialect group with the southwestern Russian dialect group (Avanesaŭ et al. 1968-9: 216ff.). The Region is internally diversified, although its dialects belong to one dialect group, viz. the East Mahilioŭ subgroup of the Vitsebsk-Mahilioŭ group.

While several isoglosses distinguish the Region from *neighboring* Belarusian territories, others run through it and define local territorial ('horizontal') variation *within* the Region (Avanesaŭ et al. 1968-9; Ramanaŭ 1928). However, as can be seen in the dialect atlas of Belarusian (Avanesaŭ et al. 1963), only a few transitions represented there are abrupt: the Atlas documents also a number of variants that occur in one place, thus representing intrasystemic variation. The three types of variation (distant territorial, local territorial and intrasystemic) include the following:

(1) presence of the distinction [r] : [r'] vs. absence of it (i.e. only non-palatalized [r]);

(2) preservation of the feature [voiced] before the word ending and unvoiced consonants vs. devoicing in these positions, e.g. *xl'eb#* ("bread"/"grain"), *horad#* ("town"/"city"), *nož#* ("knife"), *ložka* ("spoon"), *kazka* ("fairy-tale") vs. *xl'ep#, horat#, noš#, loška, kaska*;

(3) verbs with *-e-* stems only vs. *-i-* and *-e-* stems (e.g. *dreml'-e.š* vs. also *drem'-i.š*, "doze-PRS.2SG");

(4) verb infinitive endings without *-i* (*s'es'-ts'*, "sit-INF"; *n'es'-ts'*, "carry-INF") vs. both the infinitives with and without *-i* (i.e. also *s'es'-ts'i, n'es'-ts'i*);

(5) verb infinitive endings: only without *-y* (*p'e-tš*, "bake-INF"; *b'areš-tš*, "defend-INF") vs. both the infinitives with and without *-y* (i.e. also *p'a-tšy, b'erax-tšy*; note: the stems *p'é-* vs. *p'a-* and *b'aréš-* vs. *b'erax-* are accentual variants; the first variants are stressed, the second ones are unstressed);

(6) adjectival ending for nominative singular masculine: *-yj* only vs. both *-y* and *-yj* (*nov-yj* vs. also *nov-y*, "new-NOM.MSG");

(7) adjectival ending for dative singular feminine: -oj vs. -ej (malad-oj vs. malad-ej, 'young-dat.Fsg');

(8) instrumental of the pronoun *t-aja* ("that-NOM.FSG"): *t-ej* vs. *t-oj* ("that-INST.FSG");

(9) denominations for "fence": *plot* vs. *zharoda*;

(10) denominations for "potatoes": *bul'ba* vs. also *kartoška* / *kartofl'a* / *kurdopy*.

Variants under (1), (2), (6) and (7) contribute to geographical variation that distinguishes the Region from a neighboring region (in each case the former variant is used in the Region and the latter one in a neighboring region); variants under (3)-(5) and (8)-(10) contribute to geographical variation within the Region (one variant is used in one part of the Region, the other(s) in another part); and variants included in (3)-(6) and (10) also contribute to intrasystemic variation (they all occur in the same place).[4]

In addition to the Belarusian dialectal basis, Standard Russian has also contributed considerably to the formation of the language of the Region (but the extant literature does not document its influence well). To sum up, variation in the

---

[4] Numbers (1), (2), (4)-(9): Avanesaŭ et al. (1968-9): maps 36, 37, 45 and 55; numbers (3) and (10): Avanesaŭ et al. (1963): maps 159, 277, and p. 860.

Region is reported to be high, both within its borders and in contrast to the neighboring regions.

3.2   A profile of the respondents

Our team carried out semi-structured qualitative interviews with about 250 respondents in total. From these, I have selected interviews at which I was present. These include 24 respondents. Their average age was, however, quite high and there was only one respondent from an urban settlement among them. Therefore, I later interviewed (in May 2005) five young people who came from the town of Horki. The whole group of 29 respondents thus consisted of 22 women and 7 men (with an age range of 8-92, average age ca. 57, median 64). At the time of the interviews they lived in Horki, villages north of Horki, near Lenina, near Drybin, in Rasna (cf. Map 1) and in Minsk, the capital.[5] Their education varied from none to tertiary. Their recruitment for an interview in selected villages was usually coincidental; with some respondents, the 'snowball' or 'friend-of-a-friend technique' was used.

The respondents showed high sensitivity to differences in speech, which we could experience directly as they commented spontaneously on our pronunciation. Their linguistic experience and awareness expressed in their accounts drew on several sources, as can be reconstructed from the accounts and literature (e.g. Grigor'eva & Kasperovich 2004; Lapitskaia-Antipova 1985; Bulyko & Krysin 1999: 184-202). In their family and village community, most of them acquired the local dialect with Russian elements, most of all lexical ones. Those respondents who grew up in towns or ethnically heterogeneous families acquired mostly Russian, probably with regional features. In the workplace, they were usually exposed to Russian more than at home. The respondents had attended elementary school (with the exception of one illiterate respondent) and some of them had also attended secondary school and university. Belarusian or Russian was the medium of instruction at lower-level schools, with the other language taught as a subject. Russian (and, in some rare instances, Belarusian as well) was the language of instruction at universities. A small number of the respondents were immigrants to the Region, and most of the native respondents had lived or spent a longer period of time outside of the Region (the men had served in the Soviet army outside of the Region). Many respondents read newspapers and magazines, watched television or listened to the radio both in Russian and Belarusian. Subscribing to one or several newspapers in Russian and/or Belarusian has been common practice even among the rural population.

The respondents were in contact with several varieties of Belarusian and Russian and, indeed, their speech displayed high levels of variation. This concerned, for example, pronunciation of unstressed vowels (dissimilation, raising, reduction), palatalization of prealveolar fricatives, verb morphology, etc.

---

[5] More specifically, they live(d) in: Andrukhi (2 respondents), Hantoŭlia (2), Horki (6), Iurkava (3), Krasulina (1), Minsk (1), Pakutstse (1), Patashy (1), Rasna (9), Sysoieva (2), Vishnia (1).

The respondents also usually accommodated to the language of the interviewer, and alternations between Belarusian and Russian took place. Local inhabitants' speech contains many variants which may potentially be associated with various social identities. The question is, then, which of these were used for the construction of social and linguistic identities in the respondents' accounts.

4. Perceptions and categorizations of linguistic phenomena and differences

Our first question about language was usually: "What language do you speak?" The typical answer was "mixed language" or "mixture" (*smeshanyi iazyk,* *meshanka, smes'*; see Section 4.1). Our next questions led to more detailed formulations of the linguistic differences between the respondents' language use and the language use

- in other villages, towns or areas of their region or a neighboring one (local territorial differences; Section 4.2);
- in other parts of Belarus (distant territorial differences; Section 4.3);
- of the Russians (Section 4.4).

Finally, Section 4.5 deals with
- the linguistic differences between social groups (sociolinguistic differences).

In the rest of the paper, I will elaborate on these topics and try to relate them to their social background and meanings (Section 5).

4.1   "Mixed language"

The answer "We speak a mixed language" or "Our language is mixed" was not the respondents' only answer, but it was the most frequent one. This answer need not be surprising because of the borderland nature of the Region. It is, however, typical not only of the borderland but for nearly the entire Belarusian countryside. The categories the respondents used to define their "mixed language" were "Russian" and "Belarusian". Education, and possibly also TV, seems to be at play here. The respondents might have learned to match the categories "Belarusian" and "Russian" with standard varieties of these languages in school, or with the speech on TV, which differs from theirs. Indeed, some of the respondents added that the local language was not "pure" Belarusian or Russian. At the same time, they usually did not conceive of their language as a *Belarusian* dialect, and even considered old dialect features as elements that cause the mixture, e.g., palatalized [r'] (which is typical of Russian and atypical of Belarusian). The reason for this may be that the respondents were probably not given information about Belarusian dialects in school.

Interestingly, some respondents specified their "mixed language" as "neither Belarusian nor Russian" (cf. the appended extract) while others specified it as "both Belarusian and Russian". In a few cases, the same respondent gave the former characterization in one part of the interview and the latter in another part. Only one respondent mentioned a *local* linguistic particularity: an 80-year-old woman in Iurkava told us that in the local "mixed language" there are also a few "before-the-Flood" words (*dapatopnyie slava*). She gave the example of *kurtopy* ("potatoes" — cf. (10) in Section 3.1 above) and contrasted it to "*kartoshka* in Russian" and "*bul'ba* in Belarusian" (which is, in fact, the case in the standard varieties).

Although many respondents declared that they spoke a "mixed language", it is noteworthy that in the 1999 Census the majority of population categorized their "native language" and the language they use at home as "Russian" or "Belarusian". The category "mixed" did not appear in the census results (Grigor'eva & Kasperovich 2004: 57-58; cf. Table 1 above).

4.2   Local territorial differences

To learn about local territorial differences as perceived by the respondents, we usually asked if other villages in the Region differed in regard to language ("How do other villages differ as to language?" or "Does the language of other villages differ, or not?"). Although the respondents showed a high sensitivity to linguistic differences in speech and the territorial linguistic variation is high (see Section 2.1 above), the typical answer to this question was that the language in their area is the same. Some of the respondents explicitly related the absence of local differences to intelligibility or based it implicitly on the "recognizability" of discourse as belonging to the same variety (Kloss 1967: 36f.). We were told about certain differences only later in the interviews, e.g. two respondents, from Iurkava and Andrukhi, distinguished their region from the one to the north (which, according to dialectologists, indeed belongs to a different dialect group, viz. the Vitsebsk group). Although the respondents mentioned some local territorial differences in their accounts, neither was constructed as salient.

4.3   Distant territorial differences

The respondents spoke about linguistic differences rather in comparison to more distant places and areas of Belarus. This happened in the context of their definitions of the local "mixed language", so the comparisons concerned the question of where "Belarusian" or "pure Belarusian" was spoken if not in the Region. In particular, the respondents mentioned regions and places in the western, but also the central, part of the country, thus drawing a linguistic boundary between the Region and other parts of Belarus. In the appended extract, two women from Rasna (cf. Map 1) discuss where the 'hard' *r* (typical of Belarusian) is pronounced, in contrast to the local use of the 'soft' (palatalized) *r'*. Its use is sometimes hypercorrect in this area (noted already by Ramanaŭ 1928: 142; see the isogloss in Avanesaŭ et al. 1968-9: 59), which I recorded in the speech of a 92-year-old woman from Andrukhi who had started saying *pr'aznyvali* before she corrected to *praznyvali* ("they celebrated"; cf. *prazdnovali* in Standard Russian, *s'v'atkavali* in Standard Belarusian). Only one of the respondents (in Rasna) mentioned this hypercorrect use explicitly, but as she was a teacher of Belarusian and provided the textbook-example *r'iba* ("fish", cf. *ryba* in both languages), this knowledge can be that of an expert.

One of the respondents in the extract also gives the reason why people in the west speak Belarusian: she states that they live near the border (with Ukraine), whereas she lives in the center. Thus she disregarded the political border with Russia, which runs only about 25 kilometers northeast of her village.[6]

4.4   Differences from the Russians

Although the Region shares a border with Russia, differences from Russians were usually not spontaneously mentioned in the respondents' accounts, and we asked about them. The respondents often answered that there are none, especially as regards the rural Russian population on the other side of the border. They often made intelligibility the criterion, adding: "everyone understands Russian." Some of them, however, admitted that Russians spoke a bit differently — they speak "Russian," or "better" or "purer" Russian. A respondent of Grigor'eva and Kasperovich (2004), who lived on the Russian side of the border, said "the 'mixed' language unites us with the Belarusians. In the town, they often take us to be Belarusians" (p. 59). However, only older people speak the "mixed language" on the Russian side of the border (ibid.).

4.5   Sociolinguistic differences

The respondents ascribed linguistic differences to certain local social groups. An interesting group whose members' speech is perceived as different are the *perasialentsy* ("resettlers"), the refugees from the area contaminated by the nuclear fallout from the Chernobyl power station (some 350 km to the south, in northern Ukraine — ed.). They had lived in the southeastern districts of the Mahilioŭ region before they moved to the Belarusian-Russian borderland Region in 1989 (Dribinskii 1999: 2). They usually live in separate parts of villages or towns, but respondents often mentioned that they were part of the local community and spoke the same language, although they were said to use specific words, have an 'accent', or speak more Belarusian. Respondents did not relate the differences with the ethnicity of *perasialentsy*, as they often considered them Belarusians since they usually knew where they had lived before their resettlement, that is, in the same (Mahilioŭ) region just around 70 km to the south. In addition to the general statements about the linguistic differences of *perasialentsy*, a young respondent from Rasna provided an example of a morphological difference in a verb ending (3rd person singular): "An'i gavar'at *budz'e*, my *bud(z)'et*" ("They say *it will₁*, we say *it will₂*"; cf. the correspondence with dialectological data in Avanesaŭ et al. 1968-9: map 49, and Ramanaŭ 1928: 145). Nevertheless, the two Chernobyl refugees interviewed, who had settled in the same village, denied any difference between their speech/language and the speech/language of the local population. When we asked them about the

---

[6] The border regime is loose (see Grigor'eva & Kasperovich, 2004: 8), but international roads do not pass through the Region and the closest one is as far as the town of Mstsislaŭ, i.e. 50 kilometers away (cf. Map 1). Old respondents have crossed it rarely or not at all but their adult children find better-paid work in Russia nowadays.

morphological difference, they denied its importance and stated that they "speak the same way". Interestingly, they differed considerably from one another in their speech during the interview itself.

The respondents mentioned a few other groups whose language differed from their own. Among them are former artisans who used to produce felt boots, hats and caps before the industrialization — the so-called *shapovals*. They were concentrated in the town of Drybin and several neighboring villages and used their own secret language (see its description in Romanov 1901; cf. also Liŭshyts & Tsyhanaŭ 1999). The ethnic groups were, e.g., Lithuanians in Mal'kaŭka (cf. Kinduris 1956) and Jews in Rasna before World War II. However, none of these groups were widely known.

"Belarusian", often presented as a different language, was attributed to schoolteachers and sometimes to elderly people as well. However, the most frequent and significant construction of linguistic difference was that between the villagers and people in cities and towns. Respondents said that the latter spoke "the urban way" (*pa-haradskomu*). They used this category spontaneously when they were defining their "mixed language". Many of them further equated "the urban way" of speaking to "Russian". They named several cities in their definitions, particularly Minsk and Mahilioŭ, which are regional centers, but also the town of Horki. Nevertheless, a respondent who grew up in this town and now studies in Minsk said that even in Horki people do not speak correct Russian, but a "mixed language".[7] According to her and another respondent from Horki, Russian in Minsk differs from Russian in Horki.

Not only villagers perceived the speech of the town/city as different, but also the respondents from the town of Horki said that they were able to recognize villagers by their speech. They added, however, that they were unable to identify precisely which village or area of the Region a speaker came from.

In spite of the major perceived distinction 'rural-urban' and the few other perceived sociolinguistic differences mentioned above, many linguistic variants that are documented in the literature (cf. Section 3.1 above; Avanesaŭ et al. 1963) were not presented as socially marked in the respondents' accounts.

5. Discussion and conclusion

The Dutch linguist Antonius Weijnen (1999/1968) wrote that dialectologists should ask their respondents which people in the neighboring villages speak the same, because in his opinion the question if there are any differences will always have an affirmative answer (p. 132). In the Belarusian-Russian borderland, this was not quite the case, and the question is why and what this means in the context of Belarusian-Russian relations.

The respondents of the two borderland districts showed high sensitivity to discourse differences and the dialectological literature described the districts as

---

[7] According to a survey from the 1980s (Bulyko & Krysin 1999), 40.5% of respondents from Horki self-reported the use of "mixed language" (p. 95).

internally highly variable. Nevertheless, the respondents stated that there were no local territorial differences, or considered those they mentioned to be unimportant, often from the point of view of intelligibility or "recognizability" (Kloss 1967).

The feeling that there are no differences also concerned the relationship between the respondents and the Russians. This is probably due to the fact that they are not aware of any serious problems in the relations with Russians (and neither with local villages, towns and social groups, for that matter). The most important causes of this may include Soviet communist indoctrination, weak memory of forced collectivization in the 1930s, which restructured social networks concentrating people in collective state farms and factories, war migrations, the Region's traditional cultural orientation to the Russian city of Smolensk and later to Russia as a whole, the spatial diffusion of families within Belarus and also into Russia, and rapid urbanization of some family members who often maintain contacts with those who have stayed.

The question about local differences followed the respondents' answer to the question of what language they spoke, and the respondents seemed to have "erased" perceived differences as irrelevant with respect to the category "mixed", which they had chosen in their previous answer (cf. Gal & Irvine 1995, on "erasure" in identity construction). In creating the category "mixed", the respondents overcame the difference between Belarusian and Russian, the languages that they think are typically spoken in distant parts of Belarus or in large urban centers and Russia, respectively. The respondents were either uniting the two categories or excluding them, creating, at the same time, the new category "mixed", which distinguishes only the local population. Linking the absence of local differences with intelligibility or "recognizability" was another way of overcoming the difference between Belarusian and Russian.

For comparison, as early as the 1980s, Lapitskaia-Antipova (1985) reported that the majority of her respondents from a village in the Horki district (Aŭsianka) said they spoke a "mixed Belarusian-Russian" language (45 of 50 do so in the family and 27 of 40 at work; p. 32f.). At the same time, however, Voinich (1985) mentioned that the folk term for local language in the *western*, Belarusian-*Polish*, borderland (the village of Beniakoni, Hrodna region) was "plain/simple language" (*prostyi iazyk*; p. 56). Bulyko & Krysin (1999) show that the self-reported "mixed speech" was, generally, far more common in the eastern part of Belarus than in the western part in the 1980s (pp. 95 190). Belarusian and Russian are East Slavic languages, whereas Polish belongs to the West Slavic group. Although this might have played a role in the different folk categorizations, the fact that the political and sociocultural history of Western Belarus is different and that it became part of the USSR later than Eastern Belarus has brought along different language ideologies, and thus the different folk categorizations, in the west and the east of Belarus.

Twenty years later, Elżbieta Smułkowa and Curt Woolhiser confirm the folk categorization "plain/simple language" in the western borderlands, but add that we are witnessing a shift to the category "mixed" nowadays (Smułkowa 2003: 53;

Woolhiser 2001: 112, 2005: 260). Woolhiser further specifies that the category "plain/simple" is typically used by older people, esp. those born prior to 1940, whereas the younger generations increasingly categorize their local language as "mixed" (ibid., see Woolhiser 2003 for details). In the eastern Belarusian-Russian borderland, we did not notice different categorizations made by the elderly.

The borderlands of Belarus can also be compared to the western borderland of Slovakia, as there are a number of similarities, e.g., former political unity; contact of closely-related "ausbau" languages (Belarusian-Russian and Slovak-Czech); border-crossing dialects and dialect continuum; a weak folk perception of a linguistic border and asymmetry in trans-border sociocultural exchange. On the other hand, there are also substantial differences, such as the fact that the language policy of Czechoslovakia did not aim at *productive* bilingualism, in contrast to the USSR. Only Standard Slovak has roofed the Slovak side of the border since 1918 (with the exception of Czech as the language of religion among the Slovak Lutheran minority), whereas in eastern Belarus it has been both Belarusian and Russian (except in the period 1990-1995). Thus, for example, in Skalica, a small Slovak town near the border with the Czech Republic, the respondents of Bosničová (in press) consider their local dialect to be *Slovak*, i.e. they do not regard it as "mixed" but as *part* of the *national* language, and converge on Standard Slovak. This takes place despite the fact that precisely the Skalicians are known for their pride of their local Skalician identity and dialect, and that some eastern Slovaks, unlike the Skalicians, categorize the dialect as "Czech" (ibid.). Thus the Slovak side of the Slovak-Czech border seems to be much more integrated into the national community than the Belarusian side of the Belarusian-Russian border.

The folk conception of the inherently variable "mixed language" can have far-reaching consequences for language processes in the Belarusian-Russian borderland. The respondents presented the variation within their "mixed language" as unconstrained and irrelevant, which must facilitate further language mixing and convergence towards Russian. If the local language were conceived of as "Belarusian with Russianisms" it might be purged or cultivated, but this is hardly imaginable for a "mixed language". Similarly, shifting from the "mixed language," which does not have any literary tradition or institutional support, seems to be easier than if it were considered "Belarusian".

In spite of the orientation to Standard Russian (or the "urban way" of speaking), low attractiveness of Standard Belarusian, and the deconstruction of the border with the Russians, convergence to Standard Russian on the Belarusian side of the border is slower than on the Russian side (Section 3.4, Grigor'eva & Kasperovich 2004: 59). The inhabitants of the Region seem to feel and maintain a certain distinction from the Russians (cf. ibid., pp. 33-43) but it also seems that they want to be similar to them. While the populations on the two sides of the Belarusian-*Polish* border, as shown in Woolhiser (2005), converge towards two different national communities (those of Belarus and Poland), the effect of the Belarusian-*Russian* border is weaker and the convergence, for the time being, seems to be moving in the same direction. As it is not a problem, according to respondents, to be *Belarusian* and use only *"mixed"* language or *Russian* in everyday life, the situation described in this paper inclines toward the convergence and shift to Russian even after the (re)establishment of the state border. Because of its 'urban' connotations, Russian is attractive.

References

Auer, P. 1999. "From codeswitching via language mixing to fused lects: Toward a dynamic typology of bilingual speech". The International Journal of Bilingualism, 3 (2 & 3). 309-332.

Avanesau et al. 1963. = Аванесаў, Р. I., i інш.: Дыялекталагічны атлас беларускай мовы [Dialectological atlas of the Belarusian language]. Мінск: Акадэмія навук Беларускай ССР.

Avanesau et al. 1968-9. = Аванесаў, Р. I., i інш.: Лінгвістычная геаграфія i групоўка беларускіх гаворак [Linguistic geography and the classification of Belarusian dialects]. 2 vols. Мінск: Навука i тэхніка.

Bosnièová, N. (in press). "Náreèie mesta Skalice [The dialect of the town of Skalica]". Èeská slovakistika a èesko-slovenské vztahy v aktuálních souvislostech ed. by M. Nábìlková (Slavica Pragensia XLII.) Praha: Univerzita Karlova.

Brown, A.N. 2005. Language and identity in Belarus. Language Policy 4. 311-332.

Bulyko & Krysin. 1999. = Булыко, А. Н. - Крысин, Л. П. (eds.): Типология двуязычия и многоязычия в Беларуси [Typology of bilingualism and multilingualism in Belarus]. Минск: Беларуская навука

Dribinskii. 1999. = Дрибинский район: история и день сегодняшний [The Drybin district: its history and present]. Могилев.

Gal, S., & J. Irvine. 1995. "The boundaries of languages and disciplines: How ideologies construct difference". Social Research 62:3. 967-1001.

Grigor'eva & Kasperovich. 2004. = Григорьева, Р. А., - Касперович, Г. И.: Население белорусско-русского пограничья: Демография, язык, этническая идентификация [The population of the Belarusian-Russian borderlands: Demography, language, ethnic identity]. Минск: Право и экономика.

Hentschel, G. & S. Tesch. 2006. "'Trasjanka': Eine Fallstudie zur Sprachmischung in Weissrussland". Marginal linguistic identities: Studies in Slavic contact and borderland varieties [= Eurolinguistische Arbeiten 2] ed. by D. Stern & C. Voss, 213-243. Wiesbaden: Harrassowitz.

Kinduris. 1956. = Киндурис, М. К.: Литовский говор в белорусском окружении (Говор дер. Мальковка в БССР) [A Lithuanian dialect in the Belarusian environment (The dialect of the village of Mal'kovka in the BSSR)]. PhD diss. Ленинград: ЛГУ.

Kloss, H. 1967. "'Abstand languages' and 'ausbau languages'". Anthropological Linguistics 9. 29-41.

Kryvitski. 2003. = Крывіцкі, А. А.: Дыялекталогія беларускай мовы [Dialectology of the Belarusian language]. Мінск: Вышэйшая школа.

Kurtsova. 1990. = Курцова, В. М.: Стан i праблемы беларускай сельскай гаворкі (сацыялінгвістычны аспект) [The state and problems of the Belarusian rural dialect (sociolinguistic aspects)]. Беларуская лінгвістыка, 1990, вып. 38, 50-58.

Lapitskaia-Antipova. 1985. = Лапицкая-Антипова, И. Н.: Деревня Овсянка Горецкого района Могилевской области [The village of Ausianka, Horki district, Mahiliou region]. In Mikhnevich 1985a, 29-35.

Liskovets 2002. = Лисковец, И. В.: Трасянка: происхождение, сущность, функционирование [Trasianka: its origin, nature and functioning]. Антропология, фольклористика, лингвистика, вып. 2. Санкт-Петербург: Европейский университет в Санкт-Петербурге, 329-343.

Liushyts & Tsyhanau. 1999. = Ліўшыц, У. - Цыганаў, А.: Дрыбінскія шапавалы i iх мова (катрушніцкі лемезень) - унікальная з'ява беларуска-расійскага памежжа [The Drybin shapovals and their language - a unique phenomenon of the Belarusian-Russian borderland] In Культура беларускага пагранічча, кн. VI. Горкі/Брэст: Беларуская сельскагаспадарчая акадэмія / Міжнародная акадэмія вывучэння нацыянальных меншасцей, 48-50.

Mikhnevich. 1985a. = Михневич, А. Е. (ed.): Русский язык в Белоруссии [The Russian language in Belarus]. Минск: Наука и техника.

Mikhnevich. 1985b. = Михневич, А. Е.: Основные аспекты проблемы [Basic aspects of the problem]. In Mikhnevich 1985a: 3-12.

Nasevich. 1996. = Насевіч, В.: З сівой даўніны [From bygone times]. In Памяць: Горацкі раён [Memory: Horki district]. Мінск: Вышэйшая школа, 26-37.

National Composition of Population of the Republic of Belarus and Languages Used by the Population: Statistical Book, vol. I. 2001. Minsk: Ministry of Statistics and Analysis of the Republic of Belarus.

Niedzielski, N.A. & D.R. Preston. 2003. Folk linguistics. Berlin/New York: Mouton de Gruyter.

Orlova.1961. = Орлова, В. Г.: Русско-белорусские языковые отношения по данным диалектологических атласов [Russian-Belarusian linguistic relations in the light of the data in dialect atlases]. In Материалы и исследования по русской диалектологии, 2. Москва: Издательство академии наук СССР, 3-14.

Ramanau. 1928. = Раманаў, Е.: Гаворкі Магілёўскае губэрні [The dialects of the Mahiliou gubernia]. In Запіскі аддзелу гуманітарных навук, кн. 2., Працы клясы філёлёгіі, том 1. Менск: Інстытут беларускай культуры, 121-147.

Regiony. 2004. = Регионы Республики Беларусь: Статистический сборник [The regions of the Republic of Belarus]. Минск: Министерство статистики и анализа Республики Беларусь.

Romanov. 1901. = Романовъ, Е. Р.: Катрушницкій лемезень (условный языкъ дрибинскихъ шаповаловъ) [The secret language of the Drybin shapovals]. In Сборникъ Отделенія русскаго языка и словесности Императорской Академіи Наукъ, т. 71, № 3, 1-44.

Smułkowa, E. 2003. Badanie pograniczy językowych - uwagi metodologiczne [Studies on linguistic borderlands - methodological comments]. In J. Sierociuk (ed.). Gwary dziś, 2. Poznań: Wydawnictwo PTPN, 45-56.

Tsykhun. 2000 = Цыхун, Г. А.: Креалізаваны прадукт (трасянка як аб'ект лінгвістычнага даследвання) [A creolized product (trasianka as an object of linguistic inquiry)]. Arche - Пачатак, 11, № 6, 2000, <http://arche.home.by> (29 July 2006).

Voinich. 1985. = Войнич, И. В.: Деревня Бенякони Вороновского района, Гродненской области [The village of Beniakoni, Varona district, Hrodna region]. In Mikhnevich, 1985a 51-59.

Weijnen, A.A. 1999/1968. On the value of subjective dialect boundaries. Handbook of perceptual dialectology, vol. 1 ed. by D. Preston, 131-133. Amsterdam/Philadelphia: John Benjamins.

Woolhiser, C. 1995. The sociolinguistic study of language contact and bilingualism in the former Soviet Union: The case of Belarus. When East met West: Sociolinguistics in the former socialist bloc ed. by J. Harlig & C. Pléh, 63-88. Berlin / New York: Mouton de Gruyter.

Woolhiser, C. 2001. Language ideology and language conflict in post-Soviet Belarus. Language, ethnicity and the state, vol. 2: Minority languages in Eastern Europe post-1989 ed. by C.C. O'Reilly, 91-122. Palgrave.

Woolhiser, C. 2003. Constructing national identities in the Polish-Belarusian borderlands. Ab Imperio No. 1. 293-346.

Woolhiser, C. 2005. Political borders and dialect divergence/convergence in Europe. Dialect change: Convergence and divergence in European languages ed. by P. Auer, F. Hinskens & P. Kerswill, 236-262. Cambridge: CUP.

Zaprudski, S. 2002. Language policy in the Republic of Belarus in the 1990s. Belarus - The Third Sector. People - Culture - Language ed. by P. Kazanecki & M. Pejda, 33-40. Warsaw/Minsk: East European Democratic Centre.

Appendix: interview extract

Transcription notation

( )	unintelligible piece of talk (to the transcriber)
(word)	unsure transcription, possibly uttered
(( ))	commentary of the transcriber
[ ]	stretch of talk that overlaps with the talk of another speaker
=	the speaker's turn continues below the line(s) of another speaker's turn
(0.6)	pause (measured in seconds)
. , ?	final falling, non-final, and final question intonation
a:	prolongation of a sound (here of *a*)
hhh .hhh	audible out-breath and audible in-breath

Y = younger woman (born 1981), O = older woman (born 1957), I_1 = interviewer$_1$, I_2 = interviewer$_2$. (Translated from Belarusian, Russian and/or Belarusian-Russian.)

```
1   Y:    we have neither Russian nor Belarusian here, it's a mixed language.
2   I₁:   uh huh, and why it [happened that-?
3   Y:                       [.hhhh well in the cities (yeah) they speak the Russian
4         language a::nd (as for our village), they speak, (0.2) mixed (language).
5   I₁:   and Belarusian then?
6         (0.5)
7   Y:    .hhhhh [(in our country) in Palessie, some]where. no, where?
8   O:           [(s o r t  o f)  t e a c h e r s,  h e r e.]
9         (0.3)
10  Y:    somewhere, far away, where in Belarus are they c[alled-?
11  O:                                                    [well the Palessians.
12        in the west.
... ((9 lines skipped))
22  O:    that's the Hrodna region (that's there,)
23  Y:    yes, there they have, kind of, r, (0.2) sort of hard r,
24  I₁:   uh huh,
25  Y:    somewhere there's the soft on[e,
26  O:                                 [well, I know also, more or less my-, my
27        stepfather himself-, (0.6) Klichaŭ district, there's also that (hard) r
28        [there they have the same language as we have.]
29  Y:    [(                          ) we say] Riasna, and (others)
30        say Ra::sna. that's [it. (   )
31  O:                        [(and) in Klichaŭ there's sort of hard (  ).
... ((13 lines skipped))
45  I₁:   .hhh and why is it so that there, in the west they speak uh::, Belarusian
46        and here they spe[ak, (0.2) mixed (          )?]
47  Y:                     [.hhh because they live on the] border, there.
48        [(       ) Ukraine, .h]hh Ukraine and Belarus and (somewhere) they=
49  I₁:   [but here's border too.]
50  I₂:                   [((l a u g h s))]
51  Y:    =speak more Ukrain[ian somewhere mixed. [the Belarusian Ukrainian=
52  O:                      [mm hm,               [and there in (      )(but)=
53  Y:    =languages are (mixed) .hhh] we're sort of (  ) in the center, so, ((laughs))
54  O:    =(that's also) (    ) (Poland)]
```

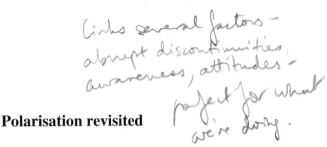

links several factors –
abrupt discontinuities,
awareness, attitudes –
perfect for what
we're doing.

Polarisation revisited

Johan Taeldeman
Universiteit Gent

Abstract: In Flanders, abrupt dialect transitions are marked, whereas gradual scenarios are unmarked. Yet, a thorough exploration of the Flemish dialect landscape presents quite a lot of abrupt transitions and, more generally, cases of polarisation. All cases of polarisation display the following characteristics:
- on the spatial level there are abrupt transitions and at least one of the polarised variants has a small-scale diffusion;
- on the linguistic level: a deepening of the linguistic contrast occurs as well as a maximisation of the linguistic scope;
- on the mental and socio-psychological level we find (a) a high degree of awareness and (b) a strong (positive or negative) attitudinal position towards the home variant.

These characteristics strongly parallel Schirmunski's (1930) distinction between 'primary' and 'secondary' dialect features. In his work, and also in more recent literature so-called 'primary' features are considered to be more liable to change. From my observations it appears that 'primary' features are indeed easy to suppress but whether they _will_ be suppressed will depend on socio-psychological factors: in case of a negative attitude they may and even will disappear quickly, but in case of a positive attitude they are very likely to survive.

1. Introduction[*]

The oldest branch of variation linguistics, pre-sociolinguistic 'dialectology', and more specifically 'dialect geography', displayed an interesting paradox with respect to language variation. On the one hand, it concentrated on spatial variation (_ein räumliches Nebeneinander_) as an instantaneous exposure of an ongoing or completed language change (_ein zeitliches Nacheinander_), but on the other hand classical dialect geographers started from a monolithic concept of dialects: every place of investigation (a bigger or smaller residential nucleus) was represented by a kind of 'ideal (stable-system) native speaker'. This concept resulted in the view — or shall I call it a 'working hypothesis' — that dialect transitions take place abruptly, and this was made concrete in the classical (linear) 'isogloss'.

This is represented schematically in 1:

[*] I thank Valérie Bouckaert and Chris Dewulf for their technical assistance.

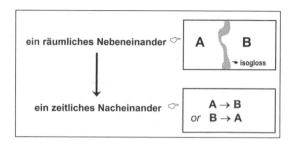

Figure 1

Dialect geographers were convinced of, and/or preoccupied with, the primordiality or even the monopoly of the spatial dimension of language variation.

In more recent times, this practice has been strongly criticised (for the most part on good grounds) by a very strong generation of sociolinguists (e.g. Trudgill 1983). But also in scientific disciplines reactions may be too extreme or exaggerated. In this case, it led to a degradation of the spatial dimension that was too strong and to these two postulates:

– dialect transitions basically occur gradually
– in transition areas, variation is conditioned by social factors rather than by spatial ones.

This paper is concerned with the spatial dimension of language variation and — related to this — the way in which dialect transitions occur: gradually or abruptly. Explicit attention will be paid to the Flemish dialect landscape and more particularly to the types of dialect transitions (cf. Taeldeman 1986 and 2000). The paper will report and comment more deeply on findings regarding a typology of dialect transitions. The focus will be on the dialects of the former County of Flanders (nowadays the provinces of West- and East-Flanders) and on phonological aspects of variation.

2. Polarisation

Also in Flanders the abrupt transition represents a marked situation, whereas the gradual scenario is the unmarked state of affairs. This is all the more expected, as — also in Flanders — the factors that provoke graduality have become more and more important since the end of the 1960s. These factors include:

1. People have become more and more mobile. The factor of mobility has always strongly influenced the configuration of dialect landscapes as they are reflected on dialect maps. The importance of this factor is clear from the configuration of the transition zone between the West- and the East-Flemish

dialect areas: in areas with more intensive interlocal traffic, the transition zone is broader (cf. Map 1):

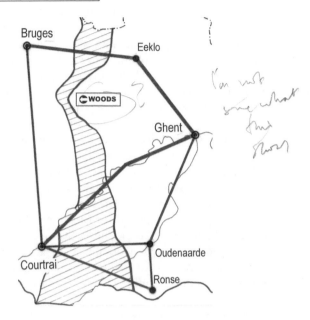

Map 1: *The transition zone between West- and East-Flanders*

The relative thickness of the lines connecting the main towns and cities represents the relative intensity of interlocal traffic.

2. The educational level has grown steadily in recent decades and this implied (among other things) a more frequent contact with other lects, and more particularly with the standard variety and its levelling influence.
3. Social control, has decreased as a result of the fact that the social networks of the average Fleming continually become looser and looser.

And yet, as was shown in Taeldeman (2000), we are still confronted with quite a lot of cases of polarisation in the Flemish dialect landscape. In all cases polarisation shows a remarkable set of abruptness features:

– Space: polarisation implies fairly abrupt transitions.
– Linguistic distance: although polarisation presupposes oppositions that are liable to gradation (e.g. the aperture of vowels), the opposition is deepened to the extreme: a closed vowel will contrast with an open one, and there are no 'intermediate' forms: 'les extrêmes se touchent'

- Linguistic scope: every linguistic element that can take part in the (polarised) opposition, will do so, hence there is no lexical diffusion, and there are no exceptions.
- On the mental level: there is (at least on one side of the two conflicting areas, but in most cases on both sides) a very high degree of awareness of the opposition.
- On the socio-psychological level: polarisation typically goes hand in hand with a strong positive attitude towards one's own variant and towards the place where this variant is being used (usually the speaker's place of birth or the place where he/she was socialised), and with a strong negative attitude towards the competing variant and (most of the times and to a certain extent) also the place(s) where it is used. The user of a polarised feature has therefore developed a strong loyalty towards that feature and the linguistic community (a village or a town) that uses it (cf. Mattheier's notion of '*Ortsloyalität*'; see Mattheier 1980). In general, we may say that socio-psychological divergence often results in, or at least surfaces as linguistic divergence (see also Hinskens, Kallen & Taeldeman 2000: 6-7). There is, of course, a strong interaction between the five features mentioned above, which often coincide. Looking at the classical ingredients of a dialect landscape, we see that these features (and their interaction) are typical of real 'transition zones' (between two rather homogeneous dialect areas; see for example the Map in 1) and the zones where urban and rural dialects meet.

3. Some Flemish cases of polarisation

The Flemish dialect landscape displays some striking examples of (phonological) polarisation.

3.1   East-Flemish and Brabantine dialects

The transition zone between the East-Flemish and the Brabantine dialect areas is located completely in a rural area without any natural obstacles (which in Flanders are always rivers).

As the map may suggest, this transition zone coincides with the intersection of the socio-economical hinterland of (on the right-hand side) Brussels and its satellite towns on/near the border of the province of East-Flanders (Dendermonde, Aalst, Ninove and Geraardsbergen), and (on the left-hand side) Ghent and its satellite towns Wetteren and Zottegem. SN stands for Sint-Niklaas, a town which takes an intermediate position between Ghent and Antwerp, which is on the right (i.e. Brabantine) bank of the river Scheldt.

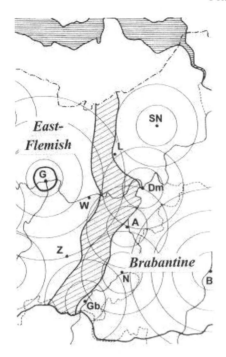

Map 2: *The transition zone between the East-Flemish and (South-)Brabantine dialects*

3.1.1. In this transition zone, there are two small villages, Vlekkem (300 inhabitants, Vl. on Map 3) and Ottergem (500 inhabitants, Ot. on Map 3), which are 2 kms apart.

One of the 'deep' phonological oppositions between the (East-)Flemish and the Brabantine dialects relates to the aperture of short front vowels: these are much higher in Brabant than in Flanders, but within the Flemish area the short front vowels have their most open realisation in Vlekkem and some neighbouring East-Flemish places (including Wetteren and Vlierzele): so [vis] ′fish′ and [pyt] ′pit′ in the Brabantine dialect of Ottergem contrast with [vɛs] and [pœt] in Vlekkem. In most areas the transition is more gradual (with intermediate forms), but in and around the two villages mentioned the phonetic distance is extremely large. Exactly at this point we encounter the five dimensions of polarisation that we already mentioned: an abrupt transition (spatially), extreme phonetic contrasts, no exceptions, extreme awareness and a very high degree of *Ortsloyalität*/"local loyalty".

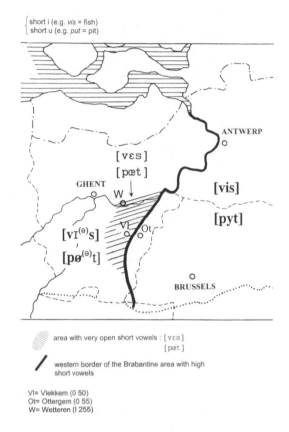

Map 3: *Polarisation of aperture in short palatal vowels*

3.1.2. In the same zone, but in a somewhat bigger area, there is another striking case of polarisation. One of the most salient phonological features of the Brabantine dialects in the contact area (see Keymeulen 1993) is the palatalisation of most postvocalic coronal clusters:

e.g.　Brabantine [winʲtʲ]　vs. Flemish [wɛnt] "wind"
　　　Brabantine [wilʲtʲ]　vs. Flemish [wɛlt] "wild"
　　　Brabantine [plɔtʲsʲ]　vs. Flemish [plɔts] "place"

The Flemish reaction (see Map 4) resulted in the opposite development: depalatalisation of historically palatal clusters:

e.g.　[be.tsə]　vs. [betʃə] "a bit"
　　　[strɔtsə] vs. [strɔtʃə] "small street"
　　　[tsips]　 vs. [tʃips] "chips"
　　　[finis]　 vs. [finiʃ] "finish"

East-Flemish area with weak(er) depalatalisation

East-Flemish area with strong depalatalisation

South-West-Brabantine area with palatalisation

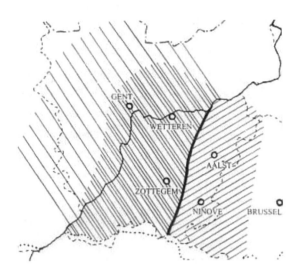

Map 4: *Palatalisation and depalatalisation*

3.2   East- and West-Flemish dialects

Turning to the transition zone between West- and East-Flemish (see Map 1 above), we should mention first of all the very interesting phenomenon of overdiphthongisation in the southern half of that zone (see Map 5).

[α] from Middle Dutch *ii* (e.g. *ijs* / 'ice')

—

[β] from Middle Dutch *uu* (e.g. *huis* / 'house')

—

[γ] from Middle Dutch *oe* (< Gm. *ô*) before [-alv.] C (e.g. *broek* / 'trousers')

to the east: diphthongisation

area with overdiphthongisation

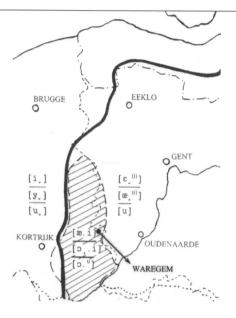

Map 5: *Overdiphthongisation*

It is a well-known characteristic of the West-Flemish dialects that, unlike Standard Dutch and most of the Dutch dialects, they did not take part in the diphthongisation of Middle Dutch *ii* and *uu*:

	West-Flemish	Standard Dutch + East-Flemish	
e.g.	[is]	[ɛ.ⁱs]	"ice"
	[ripə]	[rɛ.ⁱpə]	"ripe"
	[ys]	[(h)œ.ʸs]	"house"
	[kypə]	[kœ.ʸpə]	"tub"

The East-Flemish dialects did take over diphthongised vowels from the Brabantine dialects. This happened in two ways: (a) by a gradual infiltration from east to west and (b) by the hierarchical diffusion pattern, in which the East-

Flemish cities and towns (especially Ghent) played an important role (see Taeldeman 2005a and 2005b for details). Yet, between the two rather homogeneous areas of West-Flemish and East-Flemish there is a small transition zone which displays a number of symptoms of polarisation (over-diphthongisation):

- the presence of very heavy diphthongs (e.g. in Waregem: $ii \rightarrow \varepsilon^i \rightarrow \mathrm{æ}^i$, uu $\rightarrow \mathrm{œ}^i \rightarrow \mathrm{ɔ}^i$) and hence a deepened phonetic distance to non-diphthongising West-Flemish;
- a broader scope of diphthongisation, spreading to historical categories of vowels that did not diphthongize elsewhere in Flanders (e.g. Middle Dutch *oe* (= [u]) followed by a non-coronal consonant):

	Waregem	elsewhere	
e.g.	brouk	broek	"trousers"
	roup'm	roep'm	"to call"
	prouv"n	proev"n	"to taste"

- a high awareness of the phenomenon. In Waregem, the largest place in this transition zone, forms such as *brouk, roup'm* and *prouv'n* still reach(ed) a frequency of usage of more than 75% (albeit under strong monitoring (cf. Staelens 2004)). In Waregem even very young informants 'know' that *brouk* is the 'real' Waregem pronunciation.
- At least in Waregem and in some other smaller places (though not in Deerlijk, cf. Vandekerckhove 2000) polarised forms such as [æ^{i}s] "ice", [ɔ.^{i}s] "house" and [brɔ^{u}k] "trousers" are still felt as symbols of local authenticity and of loyalty to the home place.

3.3   Urban and rural East-Flemish dialects

We continue our round of Flanders and turn to an area where a real urban dialect (Ghent) and East-Flemish rural dialects meet.

The most prominent phonological peculiarity of the rural East-Flemish dialects in the near hinterland of Ghent, is the deletion of non-plosive [+high] consonants in intervocalic position, which is accompanied by compensatory lengthening of the preceding vowel:

		rural East-Flemish	Ghent	
e.g.	*liegen*	[li:^{ə}n]	[li.ɣ^ə]	"to lie"
	(hij) *liegt*	[liχt]	[liχt]	"he lies"
	zingen	[ze:^{ə}n]	[zɛ^{i}ŋɣ^ə]	*"to sing"
	(hij) *zingt*	[zɪŋt]	[zɛ^{i}ŋχt]	*"he sings"
	groeien	[ɣru:^{ə}n]	[ɣru.jə]	"to grow"
	('t) *groeit*	[ɣrujt]	[ɣʀujt]	"it grows"
	oude (d → w)	[a:^{ə}]	[æ.^{u}w^ə]	"old ones"
	oud	[awt]	[æ^{u}wt]	"old"

Map 6 shows that in the urban dialect of Ghent, none of these intervocalic consonants are deleted and, as a consequence, there is no compensatory vowel lengthening. With intervocalic [ŋ] even hypercorrect reintroduction of [ŋɣ] occurs (marked by * in the above examples), which occurs nowhere else in Flanders, but which increases the distance between the rural dialects and Ghent. In the deleting dialects these consonants are, as the examples show, still consciously present (i.e. they occur in the underlying form), as they reappear in the non-intervocalic positions.

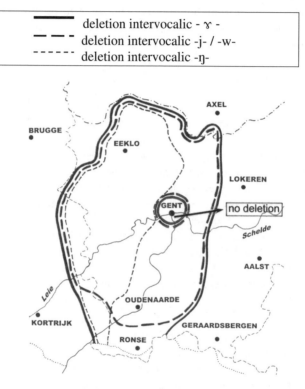

Map 6: *Deletion of intervocalic consonants in the East-Flemish dialects*

In fact this observation confronts us, at first sight, with a mystery: for a radical change such as intervocalic consonant deletion and compensatory vowel lenghtening, one might be inclined to suggest an urban origin. Yet, the only big town in this area (Ghent) is also the only place in the East-Flemish dialect area where C-deletion and V-lenghtening are absent in the local dialect. In view of the fact that linguistic innovations normally arise in urban areas (see also Taeldeman 2005a: 276-277), the following development seems plausible (see also Taeldeman 2005b):

Phase (1): C-deletion starts in and spreads through the urban dialect of Ghent.
Phase (2): The surrounding countryside (= the hinterland of Ghent) adopts the innovation.
Phase (3): People from Ghent, when hearing that country folk speak the same way as they do, dissociate themselves from their own innovations and (in this case) reintroduce the deleted — but underlyingly still present — consonant, sometimes even in a hypercorrect way, as in the case of [ŋɤ].

This outline of the presumed development presupposes at least three elements: *i.* a large linguistic (in this case phonological) distance between the two competing forms, *ii.* a high degrees of awareness of the opposition, *iii.* a strong attitudinal opposition between city dwellers en country folk and, in combination with this, a marked loyalty to the (kind of) place where one lives.

   By now it be clear that, when looking at the three classical ingredients of dialect landscapes, viz.
– relatively homogeneous central areas,
– prototypical transition zones (where several dialect oppositons meet),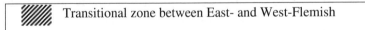
– island-like urban dialects and the area(s) where they meet the surrounding rural dialects,
polarisation is naturally related with areas (b) and (c).

4. Kleit vs. Landegem

Kleit (3,000 inhabitants) clearly belongs to a real transition zone (= the above type b), in this case between the West-Flemish dialect group and the East-Flemish one. See Map 7.

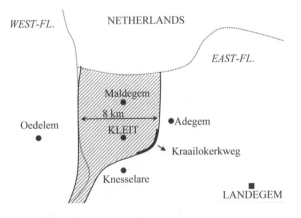

Map 7: *Kleit and Landegem*

There are enormous phonological differences between the Kleit dialect and those of the neighbouring villages: in the west Oedelem (at 5 kms., a real West-Flemish dialect) and in the east Adegem (at 3 kms., a real East-Flemish dialect). In the middle of the relatively homogeneous East-Flemish dialect area (= the above type a) lies the village of Landegem (2,500 inhabitants). Micro-research into linguistic variation and its significance in and around both villages (Kleit and Landegem) brought to light astonishingly large differences between the two places. The findings are summarised in Table 1:

Table 1: *Kleit vs. Landegem*

Kleit	Landegem
(a) transition zone	(a) relatively homogeneous central area
(b) variation prevails	(b) uniformity prevails
(c) mainly abrupt transitions	(c) gradual transitions
(d) the spatial parameter of variation prevails (→ dialects)	(d) the social parameter of variation prevails (→ sociolects)
(e) linguistic variation is primarily associated with a place + *Ortsloyalität* (you choose form X to indicate that you belong to place A)	(e) linguistic variation is primarily associated with social position; little or no *Ortsloyalität*
(f) a very high degree of linguistic awareness	(f) a very low degree of linguistic awareness

In and around the northern part of the transition zone between West- and East-Flemish, Kleit (together with Maldegem) takes such a marked position that around and within the village a kind of 'internal' norm has arisen. This norm has been stabilised by the high degree of awareness of its ingredients and by the high degree of *Ortsloyalität* that has become associated with this local norm, so there is a mutual fortification between linguistic awareness and local loyalty on the one hand and the local dialect features on the other. The same factors may be held responsible for the fact that, within Kleit, the degree of social variation has remained so low.

To illustrate this last point, I refer to the results of the 1985 fieldwork project in the south-eastern periphery of Kleit (presented in Taeldeman 1986). 25 local people (either born in Kleit or Adegem, all of whom lived in a street separating the two villages) completed a questionnaire of 44 items that were representative of the systematical phonological oppositions between both local dialects. The results were astonishing: 14 informants almost exclusively (i.e. between 83.9% and 97.7%) followed the Kleit 'norm', whereas 11 informants hardly ever (i.e. between 0 and 11.5%) mentioned a feature of the Kleit dialect. *None* of the informants seemed to speak a real interlect, a 'fudged lect' (cf. Chambers & Trudgill 1998), in which both dialects had an almost equal share. My informants apparently chose to speak either the Kleit dialect or the Adegem one. The deciding factors were: (a) the dialect of the parents (and more particularly the dialect of the mother) and (b) the place where they (had) attended primary school.

5. Polarisation revisited

What can we learn from this 'polarisation tour' through Flanders?

5.1   Ingredients of polarisation

1. Polarisation and its spatial correlate, abrupt transitions,   goes hand in hand with at least two other polarisation phenomena on the linguistic level:
   - linguistic distance tends to be deepened/maximised and no intermediate forms arise;
   - linguistic scope (= the linguistic material that takes part in the opposition) also tends to be maximised, so there are no exceptions, and there is no lexical diffusion.
2. On the spatial level, at least one of the participating variants has a small-scale diffusion.
3. On the mental level, there is a high degree of awareness of the opposition.
4. On the socio-psychological level, people take a strong attitudinal position towards the variant of the home place. The positive association of one or more linguistic forms with the home place may become so strong, that a kind of 'Ortsloyalität' may stabilise the opposition.

5.2   Polarisation ingredients in a dynamic perspective

In this section I shall try to give an answer to the next question: how can we put the features discussed above in a dynamic perspective, i.e. with respect to the changeability of dialect features (which as a matter of fact should never be considered in isolation, but as members of an opposition)?

Of course I am not the first to ask this question, but this paper might give a new impetus to this issue. An interesting stimulus is the work by Schirmunski (1930), who introduced the notions primary and secondary dialect features as a conglomerate of factors, the primary dialect features (unlike the secondary ones) implying a small-scale spatial diffusion, a remarkable structural distance to competing forms and a high degree of salience (which in fact also implies an amount of awareness). Schirmunski's conclusion was that primary features are more liable to change than secondary ones.

Some twenty years ago (or fifty years after Schirmunski) a new generation of variation linguists rediscovered this issue and in fact renewed (at least partially) Schirmunski's question, e.g. Hinskens 1986. Thelander 1982 and Hinskens 1993 offered convincing evidence for the proposition that features with a small-scale diffusion are more liable to change than features with a wide diffusion. Trudgill (1986) should also certainly be mentioned here because of his introduction of the notion of 'salience' and the discussion it aroused (see Hinskens, Auer and Kerswill 2005: 43-45).

In order to re-open the debate on what factors may affect the liability to change of dialect elements (or rather, dialect oppositions), I propose to depart from Table

2, which comprises the features that normally co-occur with polarisation(s) and to create a trichotomy:

Table 2: *Ingredients of polarisation*

Polarisation	primary *vs.*	secondary features
(1) *spatial diffusion*:	small-scale	large-scale
(2) *linguistic distance*:	large (no intermediate forms) no	rather small
(3) *linguistic scope*:	exceptions, no lexical diffusion	exceptions + lexical diffusion
(4) *awareness*:	high	low
(5) *attitudinal effect*:	strong	weak
(6) *Ortsloyalität*:	strong	weak
	↓	↓
	PRIMARY	SECONDARY
liability to linguistic change	quite liable to change unless socio-psychological factors have a blocking effect	less liable to change/more resistent
modality of change	rather abrupt changes	rather gradual changes

For a linguist, features (1) - (3) — although they are of a scalar kind — can be measured fairly objectively. Bearing in mind the results of previous investigations (including the investigations in Flanders mentioned above), we may say that the characteristics of the primary features (1), (2) and (3) normally imply a higher liability to change. Combined, they also result in (4): a high degree of salience, a high(er) awareness of the feature and the opposition in which is takes part. At that point, the socio-psychological factors (5) and (6) may start to intervene. If there is a strong interaction between these two factors on the one hand, and the factors (1), (2) and (3) on the other, there can be two paths of evolution. See Table 3:

Table 3: *Attitude towards the home variant*

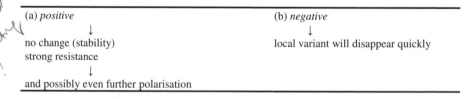

(a) *positive*	(b) *negative*
↓	↓
no change (stability) strong resistance	local variant will disappear quickly
↓	
and possibly even further polarisation	

Bearing in mind that the features involved are of a scalar kind, it is clear that we have to adopt a continuum. Yet, if only for the sake of clarity, or as a kind of working hypothesis (but certainly as a kind of idealisation), we wish to point out more or less stationary phases on that continuum: a three-step scheme could be considered, rather than the two-step one that was inherent to the opposition primary vs. secondary features. So we add a tertiary type of features, which, as a whole, constitute what we commonly call a 'regional' accent. Walsh and Diller

(1981) gave a clear description of this term: "Low order processes such as pronunciation are dependent on the early maturing and less adaptive macro-neural circuits, which makes a foreign accent difficult to overcome after childhood." Table 4 comprises an overview of the characteristics of these three   types of dialect features:

Table 4: *Overview of the characteristics of tertiary, secondary and primary features*

TERTIARY (accent)	SECONDARY	PRIMARY
– a relatively big area	– intermediate	– a relatively small area
– gradual transitions	– intermediate	– sharp transitions
– very stable	– changes are possible	– strong liability to change
– if any changes, then very slowly, gradually in all respects (distance, lexically, intermediate forms)	– changes are more gradual in nature	– changes are absolute in all respects (distance may be big, no intermediate forms)
– a very low degree of awareness (if any)	– an intermediate degree of awareness	– a very high degree of awareness
– no attitudinal engagement with respect to the home form	– no attitudinal engagement with respect to the home form	– a high attitudinal markedness – high (chance of) Ortsloyalität
– no *Ortsloyalität*	– (almost) no *Ortsloyalität*	
↓	↓	↓
difficult to suppress	not difficult to suppress	easy to suppress

The analysis of the seven characteristics involved leads at least to the following conclusions:

1. Tertiary features are very difficult to suppress and are thus marked by a high degree of stability.
2. Secondary features are not difficult to suppress; hence their liability to change depends on all kinds of mainly external factors.
3. Primary features are easy to suppress, but whether they *will* be suppressed, will mainly depend on socio-psychological factors: in case of a negative attitude they may or will disappear quickly, but in case of a positive attitude, they are very likely to survive.

An investigation of the use of *shibboleths* in the Dutch and Flemish dialects (see Taeldeman 2003) makes clear that shibboleths always relate to dialect features on the right-hand side of Table 4, the primary features.

6. To conclude

Polarisation involves a very strong interaction of linguistic, spatial, social, mental and socio-psychological factors. When studying processes of language change or remarkable cases of resistance to change, we should continually bear this interaction in mind. We have to consider not only the linguistic facts and the linguistic factors behind them, but also the speaking human being with his or her lectic metaknowledge and language attitudes.

References

Chambers, J.K. & P.J. Trudgill. 1998. Dialectology. 2nd edition. Cambridge: CUP.

Hinskens, F. 1986. "Primaire en secundaire dialectkenmerken: een onderzoek naar de bruikbaarheid van een vergeten (?) onderscheid". Werk-in-uitvoering: momentopname van de sociolinguïstiek in België en Nederland ed. by J. Creten, G. Geerts & K. Jaspaert, 135-158. Leuven/Amersfoort: ACCO.

Hinskens, F. 1993. "Dialectnivellering en regiolectvorming: bevindingen en beschouwingen". Dialectverlies en regiolectvorming (= themanummer Taal en Tongval 46) ed. by F. Hinskens, C. Hoppenbrouwers & J. Taeldeman, 40-61.

Hinskens, F., J.L. Kallen & J. Taeldeman. 2000. "Merging and drifting apart. Convergence and divergence of dialects across political borders". Dialect convergence and divergence across European borders (= International Journal of the Sociology of Language 145) ed. by J. Kallen, F. Hinskens & J. Taeldeman, 1-28.

Hinskens, F., P. Auer & P. Kerswill. 2005. "The study of dialect convergence and divergence: conceptual and methodological considerations." Dialect change. convergence and divergence in European languages ed. by P. Auer, F. Hinskens & P. Kerswill, 1-48. Cambridge: CUP.

Keymeulen, L. 1993. "De Zuidwestbrabantse mouillering en de umlaut". Handelingen Koninkijke Commissie voor Toponymie en Dialectologie LXV. 115-142.

Mattheier, K. 1980. Pragmatik und Soziologie der Dialekte: Einführung in die kommunikative Dialektologie des Deutschen. Heidelberg: U.T.B./Quelle & Meyer.

Schirmunski, V.M. 1930. "Sprachgeschichte und Siedlungsmundarten". Germanisch-Romanische Monatschrift XVIII. 113-122 (Teil I). 171-188 (Teil II).

Staelens, L. 2004. Klanksysteem en klankvariatie in het Waregems. Unpublished Masters Thesis. University of Ghent: Department of Dutch Linguistics.

Taeldeman, J. 1986. "Dialekt versus Soziolekt in Übergangsgebieten". Kontroversen, alte und neue (Band 4), 263-272. Tübingen: Niemeyer.

Taeldeman, J. 2000. "Polarisatie". Taal en Tongval 52. 227-244.

Taeldeman, J. 2003. "Aan uw taal heb ik u herkend. Over sjibboletvorming in de Nederlandse dialecten". Het Dialectenboek 7: Aan taal herkend. Het bewustzijn van dialectverschil ed. by V. De Tier & R. Vandekerckhove, 14-43. Stichting Nederlandse Dialecten.

Taeldeman, J. 2005a. "The influence of urban centres on the spatial diffusion of dialect phenomena". Dialect change. Convergence and divergence in European languages ed. by P. Auer, F. Hinskens & P. Kerswill, 263-283. Cambridge: CUP.

Taeldeman, J. 2005b. Taal in stad en land: Oost-Vlaams. Tielt: Lannoo.

Thelander, M. 1982. "A qualitative approach to the quantitative data of speech variation". Sociolinguistic variation in speech communities ed. by S. Romaine, 65-83. London: Edward Arnold.

Trudgill, P.J. 1983. On dialect. Oxford: Blackwell.

Trudgill, P.J. 1986. Dialects in contact. Oxford: Blackwell.

Vandekerckhove, R. 2000. Structurele en sociale aspecten van dialectverandering. Gent: Koninklijke Academie voor Nederlandse Taal- en Letterkunde.

Walsh, T.M. & K.C. Diller. 1981. "Neurolinguistic considerations on the optimum age for second language learning". Individual Differences and Universals in Language Learning Aptitude ed. by K.C. Diller, 3-21. Rowley, MA: Newbury House.

Ethnicity as a source of changes in the London vowel system

Eivind Torgersen, Paul Kerswill & Susan Fox
Lancaster University, Queen Mary & University of London

Abstract: Previous acoustic analyses of the short monophthongs of younger and older speakers in south-east England demonstrate a convergence in the vowel systems (Torgersen & Kerswill 2004). Following Wells's (1982) claim that London is the centre of accent innovation in the south-east, we suggested that the change was driven by diffusion from London. Analyses of vowels of young and elderly informants in inner and outer London boroughs suggest that, in fact, many young Londoners are engaged in a process of innovation and divergence, not levelling. We find variation between ethnic groups, and this points to inter-ethnic relations as a source of innovation in London English.

1. The short vowel systems in London and south-east England

This paper attempts to relate developments in the short vowel system in London to general developments in south-east England. London supposedly has a major influence on spoken English: "its working-class accent is today the most influential source of phonological innovation in England and perhaps in the whole English-speaking world" (Wells 1982: 301). However, there has so far has been little detailed sociolinguistic or phonetic investigation of London vowels. We plug this gap with analyses of existing and newly collected datasets.

Descriptions of the London vowel system can be found in Wells (1982) and Hughes & Trudgill (1996). Qualities for the short vowels do not differ much from the ones given for RP. Acoustic measurements of British English vowels are also few in number[1] and, for London, so far no measurements have been published; all descriptions are impressionistic.[2] These descriptions suggest that the short front vowels (KIT, DRESS and TRAP) previously (i.e. in the first half of the twentieth century) had qualities that were more close (Trudgill 2004, Wells 1982). The STRUT vowel was more front and the FOOT vowel further back (Sivertsen 1960). A current trend in London English is a lowering of the short front vowels, at least for DRESS and TRAP (Tollfree 1999: 165, Wells 1982: 128-129). The STRUT vowel may also be in a process of backing; Kerswill & Williams (2000) found few examples of a fronted vowel in the new town of Milton Keynes, though Tollfree (1999: 166), investigating London does describe a more fronted quality, similar to earlier descriptions.

---

[1] Bauer (1985), Bauer (1994), Fabricius (2002), Torgersen & Kerswill (2004), Watt & Tillotson (2001).
[2] Beaken (1971), Hurford (1967), Sivertsen (1960), Tollfree (1999).

Partly similar developments are noted outside London. In a study of Ashford and Reading, Torgersen & Kerswill (2004) argue for a dialect contact model for changes in the short vowel systems; see Figure 1 for the positions of the four locations mentioned in this article: Ashford, Reading, Milton Keynes and London.

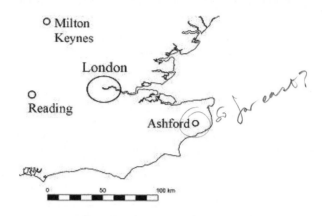

Figure 1: *Location map*

In Ashford, the vowel change appeared to take the form of an anti-clockwise (chain) shift, while Reading showed vowel movements in directions running counter to the chain shift idea. Ashford had backing and raising of STRUT, as part of a chain shift, while Reading had lowering of the same vowel from a central position.

Figure 2 shows the vowel qualities in Ashford. Our 2004 data are here presented as mean F1 (first formant) and F2 (second formant) values using normalised formant data (Lobanov 1971). The ellipses show the standard deviation from the mean within the set of data points (Plichta 2004: 24). It has to be said that this mode of display, which involves normalising and then averaging data for several speakers, does not show any clear lowering of DRESS and TRAP, even though this was clear from non-normalised individual plots given in the 2004 paper.[3] However, the backing of TRAP, the backing and raising of STRUT, the raising of LOT and the fronting of FOOT are all clear from Figure 2. These changes are very much in line with the south-eastern chain shift described by previous authors. STRUT, however, is generally not mentioned as being part of this chain shift. In fact, Trudgill appears to contradict this finding when he refers to a "change in the realisation of /ʌ/, in that the fronting of this vowel, which is typical of London and the Home Counties" as "on the increase" in East Anglia (1986: 51). We refer again to Trudgill's observation below. Our data gives a more complete picture of the shift, showing that all the short vowels are implicated, and

---

[3] Lowering, if any, was probably not significant for these vowels.

that DRESS and TRAP, as evidenced by their very slight shift at least in Ashford, had largely completed their shift before that of the other vowels.

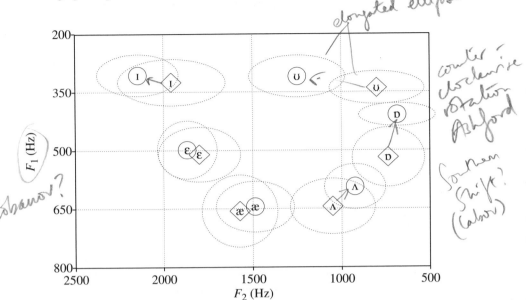

Figure 2: *F1-F2 plot showing Ashford elderly (diamonds) and young (circles) normalised vowel data*

These results for the front vowels KIT, DRESS and TRAP, along with earlier descriptions of these vowels, go against Labov's (1994) claim that London short front vowels are rising. On the other hand, they are fully in line with the south-eastern drag chain as described by Trudgill (2004). This process started with the lowering of TRAP (from [ɛ] to [æ]) and DRESS and KIT follow on in a drag-chain. Some traditional dialects in the south-east (in East Anglia) have partly retained the older qualities where only TRAP has been lowered. Trudgill (2004: 43) argues that Cockney has a system where DRESS has been lowered, but not KIT (it retains an [i] quality). Our older Ashford speakers are at this stage of the chain shift: they show shifted DRESS and TRAP, but unshifted STRUT, LOT and FOOT.

As we have suggested, the changes in Reading short vowels do not represent a clear chain shift. Figure 3 shows the short vowels there.

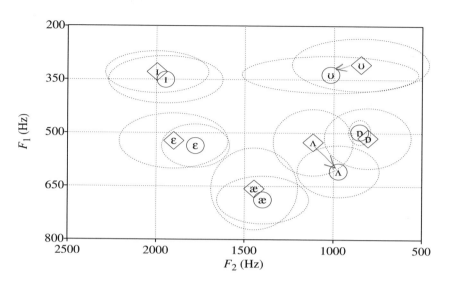

Figure 3: *F1-F2 plot showing Reading elderly (diamonds) and young (circles) normalised vowel data*

As with Ashford, there are relatively small changes in the three front vowels, involving a downward path at least for DRESS and TRAP. However, STRUT is lowered among the young speakers in Reading; in Ashford the young speakers showed a raised STRUT. This suggests that, in Reading, the movement of STRUT is not part of a putative chain shift involving LOT and FOOT. In both Reading and Ashford, FOOT fronting seems to be a development which involves the fronting of back vowels in line with Labov's Principle III (the GOOSE and GOAT vowels are also being fronted in these varieties). According to Labov, these movements in the back area of the vowel space may be caused by the raising of the LOT vowel, a chain-shift process which is not inconsistent with the Reading and Ashford data. However, unexpectedly, Reading STRUT and LOT are not moving in the same direction with F1 increasing for STRUT and decreasing for LOT. Our interpretation of this is that the different Ashford and Reading shifts represent movements towards a set of vowel targets 'set' by London. In Ashford, this results in a chain shift mirroring that in London; in Reading, we find STRUT moving towards a fully open position, against the direction of any chain shift. Figures 2 and 3 show that STRUT has moved to similar (though not identical) positions in the two towns. In Reading, the new quality is now peripheral, not mid-central, this peripherality being in line with south-eastern qualities generally. Ashford STRUT seems to have moved up from an open position.

In Torgersen & Kerswill (2004), we interpreted this as the outcome of dialect contact, in this case resulting from diffusion from London. However, this assertion was inevitably the result of speculation, since there were no available analyses from London which could support that argument. The remainder of this paper presents such analyses. Is the anti-clockwise short vowel shift more advanced in London?

2. The London localities and recordings

We have used three existing London datasets. The IViE (Intonation Variation in English) project (Grabe, Post & Nolan 2001) was set up to investigate intonation variation in the British Isles (United Kingdom and Ireland). From their nine localities, we selected the London speakers, who comprised teenagers of Afro-Caribbean, mainly Jamaican, descent. We also had access to the original recordings which form the COLT corpus (Corpus of London Teenage Language) (Stenström, Andersen & Hasund 2002). Localities represented in COLT are Tower Hamlets and Hackney (in east London) and Camden and Barnet (in north London). The speakers from Tower Hamlets and Hackney are working class while the speakers from Camden and Barnet can be classified as middle class. Some recordings made by William Labov in London in 1968 were also analysed. His speakers came from south and west London and are all broadly working class. Finally, we present data collected as part of an ongoing large project on language change in London (*Linguistic innovators: The English of adolescents in London*, ESRC ref. RES 000 23 0680) with informants from Hackney (inner London) and Havering (outer London). The localities were selected on the basis of demographic and social differences: Hackney is ethnically very diverse and economically relatively deprived, while Havering is an area with higher mobility and higher levels of prosperity.

3. Method of analysis

3.1   The speakers

The young speakers in the IViE, COLT and Labov data were about 14-16 years old at the time of the recording. The young speakers in Hackney and Havering are aged 16-19. The elderly speakers are in their 70s and 80s. Table 1 shows a breakdown of all informants. All are broadly working class.

In Hackney, half of our informants have a 'white London' background; that is, their families have relatively local roots. Henceforth we refer to this group as 'Anglo'. The other half are the children or grandchildren of immigrants mainly from developing countries. With the exception of the IViE speakers and an unspecified number of the COLT informants, all the remaining speakers are of Anglo descent.

Table 1: *Informants analysed in this paper*

	Year of recording	Borough(s)	Ethnic group(s)	Girls	Boys	Women	Men
IViE	1999	not specified	Afro-Caribbean (Jamaican)	6	6	-	-
COLT	1993	Tower Hamlets, Barnet, Camden	not specified	2	6	-	-
Labov	1968	not specified (south and west London)	Anglo	-	3	-	-
Hackney	2005	Hackney	Anglo and non-Anglo	9	15	3	4
Havering	2005	Havering	Anglo	5	20	5	2

3.2   The measurements

All soundfiles were downsampled to 11,025 Hz. F1 measurements, representing vowel height, and F2 measurements, representing vowel front/backness, were taken in the middle of the steady state portion of each vowel using the PRAAT program and the Akustyk phonetic analysis database. A control measurement was taken by LPC analysis, using the filter prediction order that best reflected the visible formants on the spectrogram and also formant measurements reported in earlier work. This is because the locations of the formants are calculated using an algorithm with set parameters, but as the filter prediction order parameter is the most important one, it must be adjusted to account for speaker and vowel variation (Vallabha & Tuller 2002). Around 4800 vowel tokens were analysed.

4. Results

4.1   London: IViE

Figure 4 shows the IViE short vowel system. The front vowels are similar to the ones in Reading and also to those reported by Hurford (1967) in London for most of his speakers; they are slightly more open than the ones found in Ashford. STRUT is raised in relation to TRAP. LOT is a high back and FOOT is a high back centralised vowel.

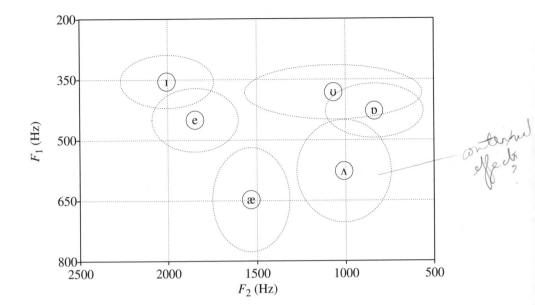

Figure 4: *F1-F2 plot for the short monophthongs in the IViE material*

In London, Labov (1994) describes an upward movement of LOT, forming part of a chain shift with GOAT and GOOSE, which are being fronted. In the IViE data, LOT is clearly a half-close vowel (so this is clearly different from Wells's [ɒ], though he describes it as less open than the corresponding vowel in RP). Its position seems crammed between STRUT and FOOT: one would expect a lowering of STRUT and fronting of FOOT (as in Reading), though this seems not to have taken place here. Does the IViE data perhaps reflect a more conservative vowel system or something completely different? The qualities of STRUT, TRAP and FOOT (but not LOT) seen here show certain resemblances to Creole features. Wells (1982: 576) describes Jamaican English STRUT as back and rounded between [ɔ] and [ɵ], which is clearly different from the quality for this vowel given for London. Acoustic measurements by Thomas (2001: 162-163) confirm this: STRUT is a back centralised mid vowel. TRAP is described as having an open, front or central [a] ~ [a+] (Wells 1982: 571) (though see below). Again, measurements by Thomas confirm this: TRAP is very open and front with an [a] quality. FOOT is described as having a pronunciation [ʊ], which is similar to British English varieties. Thomas's acoustic measurements similarly show FOOT as a back close vowel. According to Wells, LOT has an [ɒ] quality in the acrolectal variety in Jamaica, with a possible merger between LOT and TRAP in the basilect: they may both be realised as [a]; this is the case with Thomas's Jamaican mesolectal speaker as well. The speakers in our sample, however, have a quality for LOT which is more close and more back, and clearly distinct from

TRAP, which also is more central than front (which matches the description by Wells but not the measurements by Thomas, whose speaker was born in 1944 and is thus much older than the speakers in the IViE corpus). The distinct TRAP and LOT vowels represent perhaps an adaptation to a London vowel system, or else the IViE speakers are representative of the acrolectal Jamaican variety.

The speakers in the sample therefore either have qualities for the back vowels which, at least in part, resemble qualities described for Jamaican English, especially for STRUT, or else they represent different stages in the current development of the vowels in London, with the backing and raising of STRUT, but *not* the fronting of FOOT. While it is difficult to treat these qualities simply as a transfer from Jamaican English (these are after all speakers raised in England, with many London features such as th-fronting, t-glottalling and l-vocalisation), we should note that the IViE speakers also display other Jamaican features such as an auditory impression of syllable timing, stopping of /ð/ to [d], a monophthong [oː] in GOAT words and a very close-onset near-monophthong for FACE (at least for the male speakers).

4.2   London: COLT

Figure 5 shows the F1 versus F2 plot for the speakers in the COLT data.

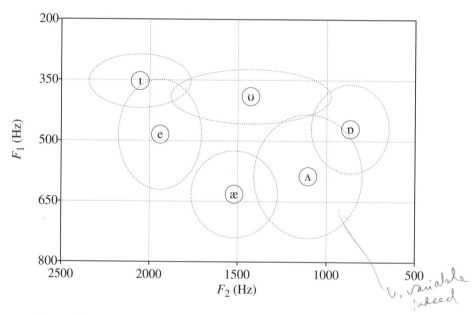

Figure 5: *F1-F2 plot for the short monophthongs in the COLT material*

There is little difference for KIT and DRESS compared to IViE. TRAP is, however, more centralised and STRUT is less backed than for the IViE speakers (recall that the IViE speakers had a fairly front/open TRAP, a feature typical of West Indian English and also a back STRUT vowel characteristic of Jamaican English). There is also much similarity with the young speakers in Ashford and Reading. For example, FOOT, which is more fronted in COLT than in the IViE data, is also fronted among the young speakers in Ashford and Reading. This suggests that young speakers in the whole south-east area have very similar short vowel systems, though with some significant differences related to ethnicity.

4.3   London: Labov's data

Figure 6 shows an F1-F2 plot for the vowels in the Labov recordings.

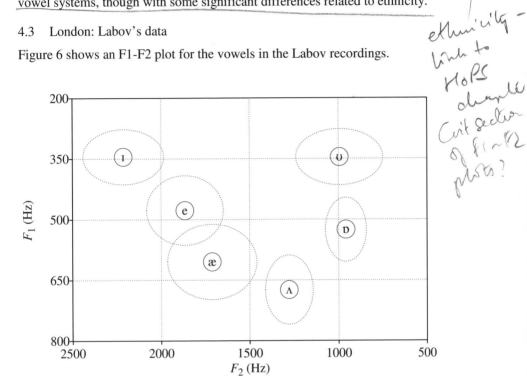

Figure 6: *F1-F2 plot for the short monophthongs in the Labov recordings*

KIT is slightly more front than in the COLT and IViE recordings. TRAP is also quite front, at least in relation to the IViE and COLT speakers. STRUT is fully open and centralised. LOT is not very close, nor is FOOT fronted. There is thus support for Labov's claim for peripherality for the front vowels, at least for KIT and TRAP. However, the support is only for the high F2 (fronting), not for low F1 (raising). With F1 values not differing appreciably from the newer IViE and COLT data, there is thus no support for his claim that the front vowels are currently rising (pattern 4; see Labov 1994). The high F2 gives a very front TRAP, more so than in the younger data as we have seen, and with the open and centralised STRUT as the lowest vowel in the system we get a snapshot of what could be called the 'traditional' working-class London system as described by Sivertsen (1960) and Hurford (1967).

4.4   London: Hackney

Figure 7 shows the short vowels in Hackney.

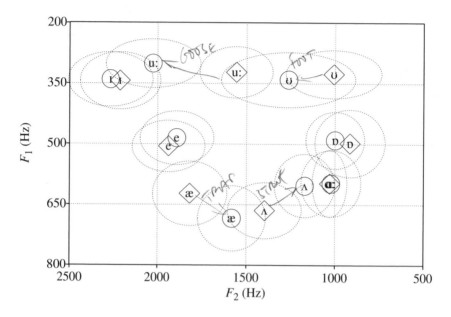

Figure 7: *F1-F2 plot for the short monophthongs in the Hackney recordings, elderly speakers (diamonds) and young speakers (circles)*

The elderly speakers have a system that very closely matches the Labov data and also earlier descriptions: DRESS and TRAP are fully front vowels and STRUT is relatively front and open — and lower than TRAP. Among the young speakers, KIT is slightly more front and DRESS is more central (but not more open) compared to the elderly speakers. The largest changes are for TRAP and STRUT, which clearly are a great deal backer for the younger speakers. STRUT is also raised. LOT is more close, and there is some fronting of FOOT. The long vowels START and GOOSE are also shown: START is raised and almost fully back with no change indicated, while GOOSE is now almost fully fronted from a central position. The Hackney data show the south-eastern vowel shift, though there is less FOOT fronting than in COLT but slightly more than in IViE. Additionally, FOOT occupies a quite wide area on the plot for the young speakers showing considerable variation within the data. In order to examine possible effects of ethnicity, we have included a plot for Anglos and non-Anglos. Figure 8 shows the vowels for four Anglo and four non-Anglo boys in Hackney (the non-Anglos are of West-Indian, Columbian, Bangladeshi and Kuwaiti descent) with each data point representing the mean formant value for each vowel for each speaker. The FOOT vowels for four of the non-Anglo boys (shown on the figure as triangles) are clearly more back than the ones for the Anglos (circles). We conclude that a back FOOT vowel seems to be a feature of the non-Anglo vowel system in Hackney regardless of ethnic heritage.

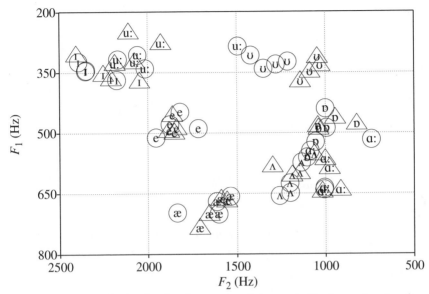

Figure 8: *F1-F2 plot for the short monophthongs in Hackney showing four Anglo (circles) and four non-Anglo (triangles) boys*

Taken as a whole, the Hackney younger speakers' data, which combines data from speakers of both Anglos and non-Anglo descent, is more similar to the IViE young Afro-Caribbean short vowel system than it is to the COLT system.

4.5   London: Havering

Figure 9 shows the vowel system for the Havering speakers. The elderly speakers show some differences from the Hackney speakers: they have less front (and arguably less conservative) TRAP and STRUT vowels, and STRUT is on a level with TRAP, rather than being lower. There are small differences for the other vowels. Among the younger speakers KIT is slightly more close and DRESS more central. TRAP and STRUT are much more back, and there is also raising of the STRUT vowel. START is also backed. LOT is backed and raised. The Havering data show some FOOT fronting (and GOOSE, surprisingly, is less fronted than in Hackney). All this means that the system follows the south-eastern vowel shift, as in the Hackney data, but Havering in addition has (some) FOOT fronting, more than both the Anglo and non-Anglo boys shown in Figure 8. The fronting of FOOT fits well with the young speakers in Ashford and Reading and also the COLT data, but serves to distinguish Havering from Hackney and IViE.

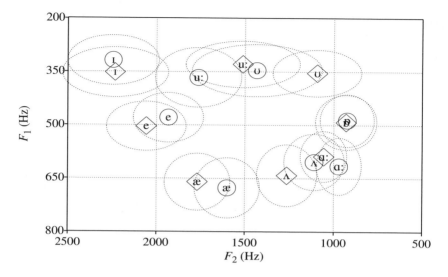

Figure 9: *F1-F2 plot for the short monophthongs in the Havering recordings, elderly speakers (diamonds) and young speakers (circles)*

4.6   Summary of the findings

Table 2 shows summary information of the vowel changes in all localities where we have apparent-time data. Table 3 separates data for Anglo and non-Anglo groups in Hackney — changes in both groups are in relation to the elderly Anglo speakers.

Table 2: *Summary information for vowel changes*

Locality	Ethnic group	KIT	DRESS	TRAP	STRUT	LOT	FOOT
Ashford	Anglo	Fronting	Stable	Backing	Backing/ Raising	Raising	Fronting
Reading	Anglo	Stable	Stable	Lowering	Backing/ Lowering	Stable	Fronting
Havering	Anglo	Raising	Centralisation	Backing	Backing/ Raising	Stable	Fronting
Hackney	Anglo (old and young), non-Anglo (young)	Fronting	Centralisation	Backing/ Lowering	Backing/ Raising	Stable	Fronting

Table 3: *Ethnic differentiation in Hackney*

Locality	Ethnic group	KIT	DRESS	TRAP	STRUT	LOT	FOOT
Hackney	Anglo	Fronting	Centralisation	Backing/ Lowering	Backing/ Raising	Stable	Fronting
Hackney	Non-Anglo	Fronting	Centralisation	Backing/ Lowering	Backing/ Raising	Stable	Stable

5. Discussion

The short vowel shift that was observed in Ashford is now confirmed for London. Our findings support Trudgill's (2004) argument for a vowel shift in south-east England: TRAP is becoming less front. In London, older data for boys (Labov) and recent data for older speakers (Hackney) have the conservative front TRAP vowel. Both groups have the same demographic background and represent traditional (white) London families. On the other hand, the young speakers in all localities (Reading, Ashford, Hackney and Havering) have an open, not fully front TRAP vowel. A similar change is observed in STRUT as well: compared to younger speakers, STRUT is very much more front among the older speakers in Hackney, and in general more front among the older speakers in Havering and Ashford (STRUT for the older speakers in Reading is more centralised), while the young speakers in Ashford, Hackney and Havering have almost identical back and raised STRUT vowels. The changes for TRAP and STRUT demonstrate convergence in these vowels in south-east England, but the changes are more dramatic in inner-London (Hackney) since the differences there are greater between the young speakers with backed vowels and the old speakers who have fronted TRAP and STRUT. TRAP and STRUT were traditionally less fronted in the areas outside of London. Because of the convergence in vowel quality, it is difficult to say if the backing process is caused by diffusion from inner-London or by levelling.

Meanwhile, Trudgill's *fronting and lowering* data for STRUT in East Anglia, a region which is at a further remove from London than the towns discussed so far, is in fact not inconsistent with a model of geographical diffusion of STRUT backing and raising starting in London. The process has simply not reached East Anglia, which is still accommodating to the older front qualities of STRUT in London. In the longer term, one could predict that differences in qualities for STRUT in the whole of the south and east of England (including East Anglia) will be reduced.

While the FOOT fronting observed in both Ashford and Reading is in line with the vowel shift, FOOT is a more back vowel in Hackney, and it suggests a *less* advanced stage there. This is a surprising result, the more so since GOOSE fronting is extreme in Hackney (see Figures 7 and 8). The failure of FOOT to front in Hackney may in fact be externally motivated. West Indian English is a possible model, as it also has a non-fronted FOOT. Recall the back FOOT vowel also in the IViE data. The FOOT quality in Hackney, which has a high density of people of immigrant descent including Afro-Caribbeans, may then be due to dialect contact with West Indian (particularly Jamaican) varieties. Havering is however in line with Ashford and Reading, and suggests that FOOT fronting is an element of levelled speech in the London suburban and peripheral areas (Torgersen 2002).

We therefore have conflicting evidence with respect to the diffusion of features from London to the south-east periphery. Some features found in London are found in both Reading and Ashford, suggesting shared participation in levelling and a situation where the origins of the changes are unclear. These are FOOT fronting, the backing and lowering of TRAP and the backing and raising of STRUT. However, a back FOOT vowel is observed in the IViE data and in Hackney. This means that there is variation between ethnic groups: speakers of Afro-Caribbean and other non-Anglo origins have a more conservative FOOT vowel than Anglo teenagers. The STRUT vowel, however, is a back half-close vowel for this group. This can be seen as conserving the Creole/Jamaican English quality of this vowel, but also as a model for the backing of the vowel in young Anglo speakers. Thus, it appears that Hackney FOOT *restrains* the fronting of this vowel, while Hackney STRUT arguably *promotes* the backing noted throughout the region. The relationships between the Anglo and non-Anglo vowel systems are complex, and they point to inter-ethnic relations as a source of innovation in London English.

We conclude that the progress of language change in inner London is influenced by contact with non-native varieties of English and a number of ethnicity-specific varieties ('ethnolects'), as well as social networks, social mobility and identity (factors to be looked at in later research on this dataset). This leads to innovation, much of which does not feed into south-eastern dialect levelling. For example, Cheshire, Fox, Kerswill & Torgersen (2005) discuss innovations in the diphthong system, which are not found outside inner London.[4] We are currently developing a model of dialect change which can take account of both dialect supralocalisation, motivated by high mobility, high contact and open networks, and dialect divergence, which emerges from contexts of low mobility, circumscribed networks, contact with non-British varieties of English, and youth subcultures.

References

Bauer, L. 1985. "Tracing change in the received pronunciation of British English". Journal of Phonetics 13. 61-81.
Bauer, L. 1994. Watching English change. London: Longman.
Beaken, M. 1971. A study of phonological development in a primary school population of East London. Unpublished PhD diss., University College London.

---

[4] See also Kerswill (2003) for a discussion of regional dialect levelling/supralocalisation in the south-east.

Cheshire, J., S. Fox, P. Kerswill & E. Torgersen. 2005. "Reversing 'drift': Changes in the London diphthong system". Paper presented at UKLVC5, University of Aberdeen.

Fabricius, A. 2002. "Weak vowels in modern RP: An acoustic study of happY-tensing and KIT/schwa shift". Language Variation and Change 14. 211-237.

Grabe, E., B. Post & F. Nolan. 2001. The IViE corpus. University of Cambridge: Department of Linguistics.

Hughes, A. & P. Trudgill. 1996. English accents and dialects: An introduction to social and regional varieties of English. London: Arnold.

Hurford, J. 1967. The speech of one family: A phonetic comparison of the speech of three generations in a family in East London. Unpublished PhD diss., University College London.

Kerswill, P. & A. Williams. 2000. "Creating a new town koine: Children and language change in Milton Keynes". Language in Society 29. 65-115.

Kerswill, P. 2003. "Dialect levelling and geographical diffusion in British English". Social Dialectology. In Honour of Peter Trudgill ed. by D. Britain & J. Cheshire, 223-243. Amsterdam: Benjamins.

Labov, W. 1994. Principles of linguistic change, Volume 1: Internal factors. Oxford: Blackwell.

Lobanov, B. M. 1971. "Classification of Russian vowels spoken by different speakers". Journal of the Acoustical Society of America 49. 606-608.

Plichta, B. 2004. Akustyk for Praat. User manual. Department of Linguistics, Germanic, Slavic, Asian and African Languages: Michigan State University.

Sivertsen, E. 1960. Cockney phonology. Oslo: Oslo University Press.

Stenström, A.-B., G. Andersen & K. Hasund. 2002. Trends in teenage talk. Amsterdam: Benjamins.

Thomas, E.R. 2001. An acoustic analysis of vowel variation in new world English. Durham, NC: Duke University Press.

Tollfree, L. 1999. "South East London English: Discrete versus continuous modelling of consonantal reduction". Urban voices. Accent studies in the British isles ed. by P. Foulkes & G. Docherty, 163-184. London: Arnold.

Torgersen, E. 2002. "Phonological distribution of the FOOT vowel, /u/, in young people's speech in south-eastern British English". Reading Working Papers in Linguistics 6. 25-38.

Torgersen, E. & P. Kerswill. 2004. "Internal and external motivation in phonetic change: Dialect levelling outcomes for an English vowel shift". Journal of Sociolinguistics 8. 23-53.

Trudgill, P. 1986. Dialects in Contact. Oxford: Blackwell.

Trudgill, P. 2004. New-dialect formation: The inevitability of colonial Englishes. Oxford: Oxford University Press.

Vallabha, G. & B. Tuller. 2002. "Systematic errors in the formant analysis of steady-state vowels". Speech Communication 38. 141-160.

Watt, D. & J. Tillotson. 2001. "A spectrographic analysis of vowel fronting in Bradford English". English World-Wide 22. 269-303.

Wells, J.C. 1982. Accents of English. Cambridge: CUP.

Levelling, koineization and their implications for bidialectism

Stavroula Tsiplakou, Andreas Papapavlou,
Pavlos Pavlou & Marianna Katsoyannou
University of Cyprus

Abstract: The purpose of this paper is to explore some aspects of the present-day Greek Cypriot dialect which suggest that levelling and koineization are taking place. These processes affect the stability of the diglossic situation between Standard Modern Greek and Cypriot Greek, in that the more formal registers of the dialect display code-mixing and code-switching between Standard and Cypriot Greek as well as novel, hybrid forms and structures. Native speakers of Cypriot Greek are able to identify various registers of the dialect, which are taken to be distinct both from formal or 'urban' Cypriot Greek and from regional idioms. The above observations raise two interesting theoretical questions. Firstly, which are the linguistic and/or sociolinguistic criteria which allow for the delineation of various registers within a language or a dialect? Secondly, in cases of (receding) diglossia, is it theoretically plausible to think of (a subset of) the speech community as bidialectal? If so, is natural acquisition of both varieties the criterion for bidialectism, or is the extent of the use of each variety a more relevant criterion? This paper outlines the problems associated with the first question, and demonstrates their relevance for the construction of a theoretically plausible answer to the second.

1. Introduction[*]

The functional convergence of the 'High' and 'Low' varieties (henceforth H and L varieties, *katharevousa* and *dhimotiki* in the case of Modern Greek), as correctly predicted by Ferguson (1959), has led to the resolution of Modern Greek diglossia. This, in turn, has led to further interesting developments with regard to the function of the variety called Standard Modern Greek (henceforth SMG) or *logia* "erudite" or, alternatively, *astiki dhimotiki* "urban demotic" (Triantafyllidis 1938, Horrocks 1997) vis-à-vis other varieties of Greek. Although there is not much relevant literature, it has been argued that the role of SMG in relation to regional Greek dialects is effectively that of the new H variety of Greek (Setatos 1973, Moschonas 2002). The pervasiveness of SMG in education and the media has arguably been operative in the levelling (see Kerswill & Williams 2000, Kerswill 2003) of other Modern Greek varieties. This new diglossic model, with

[*] The authors are grateful to Marilena Karyolemou, Anna Panayotou, Marina Terkourafi and to the reviewers for a number of valuable comments and suggestions. Matthias Kappler provided some very useful pointers on developments within Turkish Cypriot similar to those discussed here. Special thanks are due to Xenia Hadjioannou for her endless patience in discussing the data with us and for countless helpful insights. The authors also wish to thank the numerous informants without whose contributions this paper would not have been possible.

SMG as the H variety, is usually taken for granted in the case of the Greek-speaking community of Cyprus.

However, the description of the sociolinguistic situation in Cyprus in terms of this classic diglossic model fails to do it full justice. Recall that the classic Fergusonian definition of diglossia entails the co-existence of two codes which are distinguished both formally, i.e. on the basis of linguistic criteria, and functionally, since they occur within different domains of use (typically 'public' vs. 'private' or 'formal' vs. 'informal' situations). This bipartite distinction has, however, been argued against, as it can only account for part of the possible types of functional differentiation of the two varieties (see Gumperz 1981); this is especially true given the question of the 'domain' of language use (Fishman 1980), in view of the intricate patterns of language use which result from the particular dynamics of localized communicative situations. For example, in the interaction between students and professors in seminars and lectures in tertiary education, where the use of SMG is not merely expected but more or less imposed as the sole vehicle of academic literacy, the L variety may surface unexpectedly in order to signal a range of discourse/conversational functions (Tsiplakou 2006a). Similarly, Pavlou (2004) and Pavlou & Papapavlou (2004) have shown that there are numerous instances of the use of Cypriot in the media, i.e. in a domain which is typically reserved for H varieties.

The purpose of this paper is to discuss whether levelling and koineization, which are at work in the present-day Greek Cypriot dialect as a result of demographic and social changes as well as extensive contact with SMG, are also operative in effecting a shift from a regional dialect continuum to a register continuum within the Greek Cypriot dialect. A first attempt will be made to define linguistic and/or sociolinguistic criteria on the basis of which such register variation can be described. The paper will also address the issue of whether the more formal register(s) of the Cypriot dialect display properties of a mixed system, with heavy influences from SMG at the phonetic, morphological and syntactic level. The detection of these properties may in turn be applied to the definition of the linguistic profile of the bidialectal speaker.

2. Levelling, koineization and register variation

In his seminal work on Cypriot Greek (henceforth CG), Newton (1972) describes the dialect as the sum total of several regional varieties,[1] distinguished on the basis of phonetic, morphological, syntactic and lexical isoglosses, with the idiom of the central plain of Mesaoria and the capital, Nicosia, being seen as more standard. Newton's approach effectively advocates the paradigm of a regional dialect continuum consisting of a set of basilects and a geographically defined acrolect, with a concession to the fact that the acrolect may also be determined on the basis of sociolinguistic criteria (cf. also Bickerton 1973, de Camp 1971, Chambers & Trudgill 1998). Newton's research is valuable as it provides not only a meticulous

---

[1] Contossopoulos (1969: 105) reports eighteen Cypriot regional 'idioms'.

linguistic description of spoken CG but also a wealth of data against which present-day CG can be compared, and recent changes tracked. Such a comparison reveals that (i) the regional idioms are on their way to becoming obsolete and (ii) a form of the Mesaoria/Nicosia dialect is the basis of the *koiné*. That contemporary CG meets the sociohistorical criteria for koineization and concomitant levelling as set out in, e.g., Tuten 2003, has been argued for convincingly by Terkourafi (2005), who shows that criteria such as small population size, rapid demographic and social changes, due to the Turkish invasion and the war of 1974, which led to the separation of the Greek- and Turkish-speaking populations, weak network ties due to the emergence of an urban middle class with resulting increased speaker interaction (Siegel 2001) and younger speakers receiving rich and variable linguistic input (cf. also Siegel 2001, Kerswill & Williams 2000, 2005) apply in the case of the Greek Cypriot speech community.[2] Crucially, contemporary CG meets a number of structural criteria for levelling and koineization, in that all contributing varieties, including that of Mesaoria, on which the *koiné* is arguably based, are losing infrequent variants, and structural changes are taking place within the *koiné*. Below we provide a few examples of both processes.

At the phonetic level, there is loss of regional variants such as [v] in [vɔ^{n}ʝa] "teeth" (a feature of both northern and western CG varieties; cf. Newton 1972: 105) in favor of the allophone [ð], hence the preferred *koiné* form [ðɔ^{n}ʝa] (as opposed to SMG [ðɔ^{n}dja]); similarly, the variant [ç] in [çɛlɔ]"want.1S" is not a feature of the *koiné*, which favors [θ], hence [θɛlɔ] (cf. SMG [θɛlɔ]). Obviously, *koiné* forms may also diverge from those of SMG; thus, the regional (Larnaka/Famagusta) [ç] in e.g. [ɛçi] "have.3S", which is identical to SMG [ɛçi], surfaces with the more widespread variant [ʃ] in the GC *koiné* (for similar developments in a group of dialects of Dutch, see Hinskens 1998). The Mesaoria idiom has also undergone levelling, as is evidenced by the obsolescence of variants such as [tt] in, e.g. [pɛttɛrɔs] "father-in-law"; the *koiné* favors the more widespread [pɛθθɛrɔs] (but not the SMG [pɛθɛrɔs]; cf. Menardos 1969: 99, Newton 1983: 62, Terkourafi 2005: 327). Similarly, morphemes with a regional flavor are replaced by more widespread ones, e.g. the PAST 3P ending *-undasin* is now obsolete, having been replaced by the more common *-undan*; the Mesaoria copula form *enun* "are.3P" is felt to be distinctively 'Nicosian' and is thus not part of the *koiné*, which favors the more widespread *en(i)*. Similar phenomena abound in the lexicon, e.g. the regional (Famagusta) *vunno* "throw.1S" is *sirno* or *petasso* in the *koiné*, and the regional (Mesaoria) *sirko* "loathe.1S" is *anakatʃo* in the *koiné* (Terkourafi 2005: 328).

Structural changes as a result of levelling and koineization are also operational, and a number of them can be explained as influences from SMG. For instance, the *koiné* irrealis verb form *enna 'rkumun* "I would have come" is morphologically

---

[2] A full discussion of these criteria and their applicability in the case at hand is beyond the scope of this paper; the reader is referred to Terkourafi (2005) for extensive discussion, as well as for evidence that early koineization took place in medieval Cypriot Greek.

(as well as phonetically) Cypriot, consisting as it does of the Cypriot future morpheme *enna* plus the Cypriot past imperfective *(e)rkumun*, but syntactically it is modelled on the SMG structure *θa erxomun*, which consists of the SMG future marker *θa* plus the SMG past imperfective *erxomun*; the 'older', *bona fide* Cypriot, irrealis forms are *itan na'rto* "was.3S + SUBJUNCTIVE MARKER + come.PERFECTIVE.1s" or even *iʃen na 'rto* "had.3S + SUBJUNCTIVE MARKER + come.PERFECTIVE.1s" (Tsiplakou 2006b). At the phonetic level, inherited dialectal forms such as [aɛrca] "siblings" become [aðɛrfca] in the *koiné*, following a process that appears to be derivationally more 'transparent' in that the underlying fricative [f] in the consonant cluster (cf. singular [aðɛrfos]) is not elided (Malikouti-Drachman 2000). The *koiné* form [aðɛrfca] thus both parallels and diverges from the SMG form [aðɛrfça].

Not all structural changes within the *koiné* can be attributed to such direct influence from SMG, however; for example, CG displays clitic-second phenomena (Tobler-Mussafia effects — cf. Wackernagel's Law), while SMG displays proclisis (unless the verb is in the imperative):

(1) a. iða   ton   b. en   don   iða
        saw.1s   him.CL.ACC   NEG him.CL.ACC saw.1s
        "I saw him"   "I didn't see him" (**CG**)
(2) a. ton   iða   b. ðen don   iða
        him.CL.ACC saw.1s   NEG him.CL.ACC saw.1s
        "I saw him"   "I didn't see him" (**SMG**)
     (cf. Terzi 1999)

However, at least a subset of young *koiné* speakers prefer enclisis with *wh*-words such as *indalos* "how", especially so in clitic-doubling structures, as in:

(3) indalos lalun   do   to scillaci?
     how   call.3S it.CL.ACC   the doggie.ACC?
     "What do they call it, the doggie?"
     (Tsiplakou 2004)

Assuming that a structural change with regard to clitic placement in Cypriot Greek is at work, it is clear that this is not a change modelled on SMG, which requires proclisis in these syntactic environments, but rather a change that is internal to the *koiné*.[3]

The above brief excursus on levelling and koineization raises the question of whether variation in CG might best be described in terms of a register continuum rather than a geographically defined dialect continuum, at least for a substantial subset of speakers, especially younger educated ones. There are several arguments in favor of the former option. First, while speakers seem to be aware of the fact

---

[3] For similar developments in other south-eastern Greek dialects, see Drachman 1994.

that CG used to have a number of regional idioms, they are generally unable to identify them or mention any of their salient features; this is especially true of speakers born post-1974 (Pastella 2005). Speakers usually claim that they can identify a regional idiom, but on closer examination it turns out that the sole impressionistic criterion is intonation (*stin Pafon sirnun tin fonin allos pos* "In Paphos they have a different kind of lilt" is a typical speaker comment in this regard; cf. Katsoyannou, Papapavlou, Pavlou & Tsiplakou forthcoming). Second, the term *xorkatika* "peasanty" seems to have lost its original generic meaning of 'Cypriot dialect' (as opposed to SMG) (Newton 1972: 51) and is now used to denote a register containing features perceived as generically 'regional', in practice a non-formal register of the *koiné* shared by speakers irrespective of geographical provenance (Katsoyannou, Papapavlou, Pavlou & Tsiplakou forthcoming). A further piece of evidence in favor of idiom levelling and concomitant register variation comes from the hyperdialectism attested in young urban slang; Tsiplakou (forthcoming) has shown that, in informal communication with their peers, younger educated speakers may use either obsolete regional forms, about whose meaning they are often unclear (e.g. *vorʰos* "mule", which younger speakers use as a pejorative term for 'fat' and/or 'insensitive', usually without knowing its original meaning) or produce constructed pseudo-regional forms in terms of phonetics and morphosyntax (e.g. *tʃi pu to tʃi* "far out"). Leaving aside the social-performative dimensions of this type of linguistic production within the context of youth subcultures, hyperdialectisms can be treated as indirect yet strong evidence both for levelling and for a shift from geographical to social/stylistic variation.

3. Levels of language use

3.1   Problems with establishing criteria for the delimitation of registers

Having made the claim for treating contemporary CG in terms of a register continuum, we next turn to the establishment of linguistic criteria on the basis of which registers can be formally distinguished. This is a particularly challenging theoretical and methodological issue for monolingual and bilingual/diglossic situations alike, since boundaries between different varieties and different registers are usually fuzzy, particularly in the case of unplanned, informal face-to-face interaction. This is, in part, a reflection of the fuzziness of the boundaries between different communicative situations and events.

Speaker intuitions may provide some indication that there are varying 'levels' or 'forms' of CG, which they name and comment on in various ways. This distinction among levels is based on the degree of convergence to (or divergence from) SMG. The names used for these different forms of the dialect reveal both the criteria for the distinction and speaker intuitions on the number of levels. At one end of the continuum lies the *vareta kipriaka* "heavy Cypriot", which is also termed (*polla, telia) xorkatika* "(very, totally) peasanty", i.e. it is sociolinguistically marked, though *xorkatika* is not identified with any particular regional idiom, as shown in Section 2 above. In addition, speakers acknowledge the existence of *sosta, sistarismena kipriaka* "correct", "tidied-up Cypriot", which they further distinguish from *evgenika* "polite" Cypriot, based on the relative degree of convergence to SMG, Finally, the term *kalamaristika* "pen-pusher speak" is the (frequently pejorative) term for SMG, i.e. it denotes a variety which is perceived as lying outside the continuum.

Leaving speaker intuitions aside, we will next attempt to put together a set of linguistic criteria on the basis of which registers can be delimited; this preliminary attempt is based on data from a small number of previous studies (Karyolemou & Pavlou 2001, Papapavlou 2004, Tsiplakou 2006a) and at this stage it should only be seen as a working hypothesis to be empirically tested against much larger sets of data. Our approach is based on the assumption that speakers have at their disposal phonetically, syntactically and/or semantically equivalent — or almost equivalent — forms, and the choice of a particular form can thus indicate a particular register or level of use. The equivalent forms or structures can then be treated as sociolinguistic variables (cf. Labov 1980, *modulo* the problem that not all speakers have all the possible variants in their active repertoire). We will attempt to tackle a series of methodological problems relating to the identification of the variables and also to the detection of elements that cannot be variables and should thus be excluded. In the following discussion it will be shown that the latter distinction becomes particularly problematic, especially with respect to the more formal registers of CG, where diglossia often renders the situation unclear (see Section 4 below).

3.2   Towards the identification of variables and registers

With regard to the lexicon, it should be noted that CG contains a large number of words which come from SMG and can be treated as language-internal loans. Words like *prosfiyas* "refugee", *ðiicisi* "administration", *nomarxia* " prefecture", do not mark the register as 'high' or formal, nor do they signal a move outside the boundaries of the CG dialect continuum, given that there is no choice involved; in such cases the Cypriot speaker obligatorily uses elements from SMG, and, the use of these elements is moreover perceived as register-neutral. A further interesting dimension is the fact that in CG there are scholarly words such as *afipireto* "I retire" *pronia* "provision", which have SMG phonetics and morphology but do not exist in SMG. These Cypriot-specific developments are another aspect of koineization and register variation, namely the development of a (limited) Cyprus-specific formal vocabulary. Cases where there is choice among semantically equivalent forms (e.g. *oksino* (CG): *lemoni* (SMG) "lemon", *arfoteknos* (CG) : *anipsios* (SMG) "nephew", *c^hel:e* (CG) : *tʃefali* (CG) : *cefali* (SMG) "head", *vunno* (CG): *sirno* (CG): *petasso* (CG): *petao* (SMG) "I throw") are prime candidates for testing register variation. Two caveats are in order, however: first, we may anticipate cases where the use of the SMG form signals a move outside the Cypriot continuum; second, levelling and koineization may well entail that words from CG regional basilects are in practice no longer part of the active repertoire of large numbers of speakers. Such complications can only be teased apart through rigorous empirical testing.

The detection of phonetic variables appears to be an easier task, as there do seem to exist *bona fide* variables, that is to say elements with multiple realizations, the choice among which is free in the sense that it is not dictated by constraints imposed by the phonetic system.[4] In these cases, the selection of one variant over the other is arguably regulated by register considerations. For example, further fronting of SMG palatals [c] and [ç] is a typical CG, or, more generally, a southern/south eastern dialect trait; thus CG has a palatal affricate [tʃ] or an alveopalatal [ʃ] before the front vowels [i] and [ε], where SMG has [c] and [ç] respectively. However, CG also allows the variants [c] and [ç] in this environment, at least for a large part of the vocabulary (e.g. [tʃε] or [cε] "and", [çεri] or [ʃεri] "hand"), and the choice of the variant identical to that of SMG does not signal a move outside the Cypriot continuum. In other cases, however, the choice of allophone is subject to systemic restrictions. Thus, [ʃ] surfaces when the syllabic structure is /siV/, i.e. /s/ + unstressed /i/ + vowel. In this case the sequence /si/ is obligatorily realised as [ʃ], e.g. [tɛtrakoʃa] "four hundred", from underlying /tɛtrakosia/ (cf. Newton 1972: 113). In this case the use of the SMG variant /tɛtrakosia/ > [tɛtrakosça] normally signals a transition beyond the boundaries of the Cypriot continuum, and hence it can be treated as an instance of code-switching rather than continuum-internal variation. (Katsoyannou, Papapavlou, Pavlou & Tsiplakou forthcoming). This is also evidenced by the fact that in more formal registers of Cypriot the preference is neither for [tɛtrakoʃa] nor for [tɛtrakosça] but for the alternative form [tɛtrakosa]. Such complications need to be teased apart when attempting to demarcate phonetic variables in relation to register.

In morphology and syntax, there is an equal gradation in choices which can be associated with register shifts, and there are also problematic cases where testing against large sets of data is required for the purpose of distinguishing *bona fide* variants from elements whose use signals a move beyond the continuum. The data from the corpus in Tsiplakou (2006a) provide a first indication that the variants of the negative particles *en* and *men*, namely *ðen* and *min*, respectively, are both part of the Cypriot continuum despite the fact that the latter two are identical to the SMG ones, and the choice of one over the other is determined by register/stylistic considerations. The third plural present tense morphemes *-usin* and *-un* stand in a similar free allomorphic relation, although *-un* is also found in SMG, while the SMG variant *-ane* signals a move beyond the continuum, as evidenced by its relative sparseness and its non-collocability with CG variants. Similarly, the absence of the 'augment' *e-*, which used to be obligatory in CG past tenses, arguably no longer signals a crossing of the continuum boundary.

Syntactic variables can be identified in a similar manner. A typical example of a syntactic equivalence involves the twin strategies for forming *wh*-questions, i.e.

---

[4] Morpho-syntactically constrained variation will be discussed below.

either by clefting, which is the 'dialect' strategy, or by *wh*-movement,[5] the latter being the sole strategy available in SMG:

(4) a. pcos   embu   irten?
         who.NOM is-that came.3S
         "Who is it that came?"   **(CG)**

     b. pcos   irten?
         who.NOM came.3S
         "Who came?"   **(CG)**

     c. pços   irθe?
         who.NOM came.3S
         "Who came?"   **(SMG)**

(Tsiplakou, Panagiotidis & Grohmann 2006)

On the basis of the above considerations we can determine groups of equivalent forms and then examine whether each such group is internally structured according to a certain hierarchy in a way that points to a different, distinct level of language use. Following the proposal in Papapavlou (2004), we may suggest at least four levels, which we present by means of the following examples:

(5) a. en   dʒe   ia   ton
         not   FOC   saw.1S him.ACC

     b. en   dʒe   iða   ton
         not   FOC   saw.1S him.ACC

     c. en   don   iða
         not   him.ACC saw.1S

     d. ðen   don   iða
         not   him.ACC saw.1S

     e. ðen   don   exo   ði
         not   him.ACC have.1S seen
         "I have not seen him"

These are radically different

(6) a. pu   embu   epies?
         where is-it-that went.2S

     b. pu   embu   epijes?
         where is-it-that went.2S

     c. pu   epijes?
         where went.2S

     d. pu   pijes?
         where went.2S

---

[5] The two strategies are equivalent in the sense that, although clefting is usually associated with a contrastive or Discourse-linked interpretation for the *wh-* expression, this interpretation can also be achieved by intonation in the non-clefted structures (see Tsiplakou, Panagiotidis & Grohmann 2006).

e. pu   eçis   pai?
   where   have.2s   gone
   "Where have you gone?"

Preliminary testing with approximately 200 native speakers confirms that there is a hierarchy of registers ranging from *vareta xorkatika* "heavily peasanty" (examples (5a) & (6a)) to *evgenika* "polite", (examples (5d) & (6d)), (5b)/(6b) and (5c)/(6c) being *xorkatika* "peasanty" and *sistarismena* "tidied-up", respectively. The examples in (5e) and (6e) are characterized as *kalamaristika* "pen-pusher speak", i.e. SMG. In the examples there are sets of variants which allow for register hierarchization, namely intervocalic fricative elision (*ia* and *epies* in (5a) & (6a)), the presence of the exclusively Cypriot focalizer *dʒe* "and" ((5a) & (5b)), *wh*-clefts ((6a) & (6b)) and the past tense augment *e-* ((6a)-(6c)). Structures such as those in (5e) & (6e) are perceived as external to the continuum, due to the presence of the SMG present perfect tense, which is typically absent from Cypriot Greek. However, a substantial subset (around 30%) of the speakers involved in preliminary testing reported that such structures are Cypriot, albeit of a high or formal register. We return to this issue in Section 4 below.

    The division into different levels of use is clearly not an easy task. In practice, it is rare to find cases where the variants of a particular form display a one-to-one correspondence with the various registers. More importantly, the distinctions may well be quantitative, since what changes is the frequency of appearance of each feature or even the statistical correlation of the appearance of one feature with that of another. At this stage, the main question is if, and to what extent, the quantitative relationship between the variants (which can be analysed statistically in order to clearly differentiate the language levels) corresponds to the (socio-) linguistic intuitions of the speakers. It is not known if, and to what extent, the speakers distinguish among the various levels of the dialect/register continuum based on statistical relations (which could be interpreted on the basis of the hypothesis that speakers keep mental records of quantitative differences, a hypothesis which would be extremely hard to argue for, however; cf. Bickerton 1973), or whether the criteria are qualitative (for example an 'emblematic' use of a marked variant might be enough to characterize a level as 'peasanty' despite frequent use of this variant in other registers). Moreover, there are problematic and unacceptable combinations of variants (cf. Auer 1997), an issue which we must necessarily leave aside pending further research.

4. On diglossia and bidialectism

Participant observation confirms the intuition that speakers shift relatively smoothly from one choice to the other, especially in informal familiar communicative situations; this switching among levels may indicate increased or decreased familiarity or solidarity between speakers and may depend on the topic of the conversation, on social alignments among speakers or on conversational strategies such as hedging, etc. Our proposal for the redefinition of the dialect continuum as stylistic is directly related to this kind of ethnographic approach to switching among potential choices. As was mentioned in Section 1, however, the use of the SMG variety is also attested in domains of use typically requiring the use of CG. This relates to the fact that, at least for some speakers, the SMG forms in (5e) and (6e) above were perceived as belonging to the GC continuum, i.e. as forming part of its acrolect.

The theoretical question which arises may then be stated as follows: are such instances cases of interchangeable use of forms that are part of the natural repertoire of the speaker, i.e. of variation, or are they cases of constant code-switching and a transition from a naturally acquired system, that of CG, to a non-naturally acquired one, that of SMG?

If we take the first approach, then we effectively place SMG on the acrolectal pole of the continuum or posit that the continuum includes a large part of SMG morphology and syntax. The second approach entails that a large part of SMG can be used quite effortlessly, and generally correctly, to signal particular communicative or stylistic functions, despite the fact that SMG does not belong to the continuum and is not a naturally acquired variety.

A provisional answer at this stage is that the effortless use of morphosyntactic elements of SMG in everyday informal interaction may signify a re-structuring of the Fergusonian model of diglossia without necessarily implying the natural acquisition of the H variety. Research on code-switching and code-mixing has demonstrated that these are not necessarily directly linked to bilingualism in the narrow sense of the term. What is important in such cases is that increased language competence in two different systems is associated with quantitatively extensive and qualitatively different types of code-switching and code-mixing (Fishman 1980, Poplack 1980), an issue which requires extensive further research in the case of Cypriot Greek.

5. Conclusion

In this paper we have worked towards the hypothesis that the present-day Greek Cypriot dialect provides evidence in favor of a restructuring of Ferguson's classic diglossic model and of a move from a regional dialect continuum to a register continuum. We proposed a preliminary division into registers within the continuum and identified a series of theoretical and methodological issues which face any kind of experimental or longitudinal research aiming at identifying the criteria for differentiation of levels in this given speech community. Finally, we raised the issue of the natural acquisition of part of the H variety as a criterion for the precise delineation of the dialect continuum, as well as for the description of the language profile of the bidialectal speaker.

References

Auer, P. 1997. "Co-occurrence restrictions between variables: a case for social dialectology, phonological theory and variation studies". Variation, change and phonological theory ed. by F. Hinskens, R. van Hout & L. Wetzels, 71-102. Amsterdam: John Benjamins.

Bickerton, D. 1973. "Quantitative versus dynamic paradigms: the case of Montreal que". New ways of analyzing variation in English ed. by C. J. Bailey & R. Shuy, 23-43. Washington, DC: Georgetown University Press.

Chambers, J.K. & P. Trudgill. 1998. Dialectology. Cambridge: CUP.

Contossopoulos. N. 1969. "Simvoli is tin meletin tis Kipriakis dialektou [A contribution to the study of the Cypriot dialect]". Epetiris tu Kentru Epistimonikon Erevnon [Yearbook of the Cyprus Research Center] 3. 87-109.

de Camp, D. 1971. "Toward a generative analysis of a post-creole speech continuum". Pidginization and creolization of languages ed. by D. Hymes, 349-370. Cambridge/New York: CUP.

Drachman, G. 1994. "Verb movement and minimal clauses". Themes in Greek linguistics. Papers from the 1st International Conference on Greek Linguistics ed. by I. Philippaki-Warburton, K. Nicolaidis & M. Sifianou, 45-52. Amsterdam: John Benjamins.

Ferguson, C. 1959. "Diglossia". Word 15. 325-340.

Fishman, J. 1980. "Bilingualism and biculturism as individual and as societal phenomena". Journal of Multilingual and Multicultural Development 1. 3-15.

Gumperz, J. (ed.) 1981. Language and social identity. Cambridge: CUP.

Hinskens, F. 1998. "Dialect levelling: a two-dimensional process". Folia Linguistica XXII:1-2. 35-51.

Horrocks, G. 1997. Greek: A history of the language and its speakers. London & New York: Longman.

Katsoyannou, M., A. Papapavlou, P. Pavlou & S. Tsiplakou (forthcoming). "Didialektikes kinotites ke glossiko sinexes: I periptosi tis kipriakis. [Bidialectal speech communities and the notion of linguistic continuum. The case of Cypriot Greek]". Proceedings of the Second International Conference on Modern Greek Dialects and Linguistic Theory ed. by M. Janse, B. Joseph & A. Ralli.

Karyolemou, M. & P. Pavlou. 2001. "Language attitudes and assessment of salient variables in a bi-dialectal speech community". Proceedings of the 1st International Conference on Language Variation in Europe, 110-120. Barcelona, Universitat Pompey Fabra.

Kerswill, P. 2003. "Dialect levelling and geographical diffusion in British English". Social dialectology. In honour of Peter Trudgill ed. by D. Britain & J. Cheshire, 223-243. Amsterdam: Benjamins.

Kerswill, P. & A. Williams. 2000. "Creating a new town koiné: children and language change in Milton Keynes". Language in Society 29. 65-115.

Kerswill, P. & A. Williams. 2005. "New towns and koinéisation: linguistic and social correlates". Linguistics 43. 1023-2048.

Labov, W. 1980. Locating language in time and space. New York: Academic Press.

Malikouti-Drachman, A. 2000. "Paratirisis se dialektikes ipoxorisis tis kipriakis [Remarks on the recession of the Cypriot dialect]". Studies in Greek Linguistics 20. 292-302. Thessaloniki: Kyriakidis.

Menardos, S. 1963. Glossikai Meletai [Language Studies]. Nicosia: Cyprus Research Centre.

Moschonas, S. 2002. "Kini glossa ke dialektos: to zitima tis «glossikis dimorfias» stin Kipro [Koiné and dialect: the question of "diglossia" in Cyprus]". Nea Hestia 151. 898-928.

Newton, B. 1972. Cypriot Greek: its phonology and inflections. The Hague: Mouton.

Newton, B. 1983. "Stylistic levels in Cypriot Greek". Mediterranean Language Review 1.   55-63.

Papapavlou, A. 2004. "Verbal fluency of bidialectal speakers of SMG and the role of language-in-education practices in Cyprus". International Journal of the Sociology of Language 168. 91-100.

Pastella, S. 2005. Apolia leksilogiu stin kipriaki [Vocabulary loss in Cypriot Greek]. Ms., University of Cyprus.

Pavlou, P. 2004. "Greek dialect use in the mass media in Cyprus". International Journal of the Sociology of Language 168. 101-118.

Poplack, S. 1980. "Sometimes I'll start a sentence in Spanish y termino en español: toward a typology of code-switching". Linguistics 18. 581-618.

Setatos, M. 1973. "Fenomenologia tis katharevousas [The phenomenology of katharevousa]". Yearbook of the School of Philosophy of the Aristotle University of Thessaloniki 12. 71-95.

Siegel, J. 2001. "Koine formation and creole genesis". Creolization and contact ed. by N. Smith & T. Veenstra, 175-197. Amsterdam: John Benjamins.

Terkourafi, M. 2005. "Understanding the present through the past. Processes of koineisation in Cyprus". Diachronica 22. 309-372.

Triandafyllidis, M. 1938. Neoelliniki Grammatiki [Modern Greek Grammar]. Thessaloniki: Institute for Modern Greek Studies.

Tsiplakou, S. 2004. "Stasis apenanti sti glossa ke glossiki allagi: mia amfidromi sxesi? [Attitudes towards language and language change: a two-way relation?]". Proceedings of the Sixth International Conference of Greek Linguistics ed. by G. Catsimali, A. Kalokairinos, E. Anagnostopoulou & I. Kappa. Rethymno: Linguistics Lab. CD-Rom.

Tsiplakou, S. 2006a. "The emperor's old clothes. Linguistic diversity and the redefinition of literacy". International Journal of Humanities 2. 2345-2352.

Tsiplakou, S. 2006b. "Cyprus: language situation". Encyclopedia of Linguistics, 2nd edition ed. by K. Brown. Oxford: Elsevier.

Tsiplakou, S. (forthcoming). "Linguistic attitudes and emerging hyperdialectism in a diglossic setting: young Cypriot Greeks on their language". Berkeley Linguistic Society 29. Minority and diasporic languages of Europe ed. by C. Yoquelet. University of California at Berkeley.

Tsiplakou, S., P. Panagiotidis & K. Grohmann (forthcoming). "Properties of Cypriot Greek Wh-question formation". Proceedings of the 7th International Conference on Greek Linguistics ed. by G. Tsoulas.

Tuten, D. 2003. "Koineization in Medieval Spanish". Contributions to the Sociology of Language 88. Berlin: Mouton de Gruyter.

Subject index

not v. useful only index would be fuller, e.g. only 2 entries for T.